The American Quest for the City of God

The American Quest for the City of God

by
Leland D. Baldwin

Mercer University Press
Macon, Ga. 31207

All books published by Mercer University Press are produced
on acid-free paper which exceeds the minimum standards set by the
National Historical Publications and Records Commission.

Library of Congress Cataloging in Publication Data

Baldwin, Leland Dewitt, 1897-1981.
  The American quest for the City of God.

  Includes bibliographical references and index.
  1. United States—Civilization.   I. Title.
E169.1.B214   973   81-14125
ISBN 0-86554-016-0   AACR2

Foreword

One of the most magnificent and yet least publicized wonders of the modern world can be seen on any clear night by the traveler on a plane flying between Boston and Washington. For a distance of four hundred air miles the observer is never out of sight of the myriad, multicolored lights that give the veritable impression of a vast celestial city, though the impression will be lost if one tries to breast the traffic next day. It is this urban conglomerate, centered on New York City, that has become the financial and to a considerable extent the commercial, industrial, cultural, and political heart of the world.

And yet less than four hundred years ago there was nothing in this region but forests and the cornfields of the scattered Indian nations. The purpose of this book is to tell something of how the wilderness of North America gave way to civilization. I shall not attempt to find some exotic symbolism in American history such as a return to the primitive innocence of the Garden. Rather I shall attempt to trace the evolution— or perhaps devolution—of one of the oldest concepts in Christendom, the City of God, through its many transformations in America, so the process has to be presented with a historical framework. Unfortunately lack of space prevents giving detailed attention to the numerous millenial sects and utopian experiments which in the last century were aspects of the quest for the City of God.

Of course the vision of the City of God is not an American monopoly, for nearly every nation has its own version of this goal. Moreover almost all of them have evolved from a religious view of God's unfolding purpose to some form of secularity. For example, the Russian historic idea of "world mission" was thoroughly religious and Messianic: it should, perhaps, be a warning to us as we observe how the communists not only secularized it but emptied it of its spiritual content and filled it with materialism.

It may be that at the end the reader will be tempted to say that the title should have been *The American Quest for the City of God—and Why It May Fail*. I can only say that a thorough diagnosis of a disease and an examination of its history must come before any attempt to cure it. Such cures as I propose are obviously tentative, and I trust that there are better ones. In any case I can only hope for ameliorations, because democracy by its very nature cannot lay claim to perfection. That may be small comfort, but it is more realistic than a dependence on sentimentalities and moral clichés; at the end of that road lies the Orwellian state with "Big Brother Is Watching" inscribed over its gates.

Leland D. Baldwin
Santa Barbara, California

Contents

Prologue

The walls of Rome had not been breached for eight hundred years by a foreign conqueror, and in the midst of a decaying empire its citizens still spoke of it as the Eternal City, the inviolate center of civilization and world power. It is difficult for us to imagine the shock to the Mediterranean world when in the year 410 Alaric's Goths burst into the city and subjected it to sack. To pagan Romans the fall of the city was a just punishment by the old gods because they had been displaced by Christianity, and the belief seems to have found some credence among a populace not yet generally confirmed in the new religion.

It was to combat this belief that in 413 St. Augustine, Bishop of Hippo in what is now Algeria, began to write his *City of God* which was to become the guiding light of the Middle Ages. Rome, he assured Christians, was temporal, the City of this World. Their eyes should be fixed on the truly eternal city, the City of God. He opened his great work with these words:

> Most glorious is and will be the City of God. That city belongs to two spheres. The one on this earth lies by faith, a stranger among unbelievers, but when justice issues in

judgment she shall be established in her eternal heavenly home.

In his long disquisition on this theme St. Augustine introduced for the first time an evolutionary philosophy of history—that God is working out His divine purpose in human society. In the light of the final judgment all things will be made clear; human sufferings and the rise and fall of earthly kingdoms will be seen as divine instruments in preparing the way for the coming City of God. But meanwhile we need not despair; the City of God endures on earth in the form of the Church; moreover it is within us, in the love and trust of the pure in heart.

The medieval papacy followed St. Augustine in holding that the Catholic Church was the visible City of God on earth, the imperfect Platonic shadow of the invisible heavenly city. Its imperfection, if it needed proof, was shown by the numerous efforts at purification made by reformers. Nevertheless it was the organization to which all men owed fealty and which never for long lost sight of its mission to build the holy city both seen and unseen. The spirit of the Middle Ages was that though Church and State each had their functions they were still a unit in promoting the building of the City of God on earth; of course popes and kings battled over the problem of which should rule on mooted points but there was little contention over the basic thesis.

The quest, therefore, became the preoccupation of what we now call Western Civilization. The goal of the quest appeared under many names—the city on a Hill, the New Jerusalem, the Earthly Paradise—and of course did not refer to a city as such but to a heavenly realm. The quest still goes on, perhaps even more intensively, amidst the tumults of the modern age; indeed the tumults arise in no small part from rival idealogies which, however, seek somewhat the same end—a perfect order of society, a secular form of the City of God. The quest has, of course, been most evident over the longest time in the Roman Catholic Church, but it was bequeathed to the Protestant nations—indeed, the Reformation arose from new concepts of the directions the quest should take.

The quest, as we shall see, has from the beginning run like a golden thread through the web of American history. It has appeared in every generation under one name or another—the American Mission, the New Freedom, the New Deal, the New Frontier, the Great Society. The crusades that we shall examine, even when mistaken, even downright destructive, were aspects of the quest for the City of God—such crusades as Manifest Destiny, Inevitable Destiny, making the world safe for democracy, and Containment. Even our Civil War rose from antagonistic interpretations of the quest.

The thread was first spun by St. Augustine from the gold of faith, and then carried through the ages by other men of faith. Faith and conscience, as we shall see, are not invariably reliable litmus tests of truth and social welfare. Because we are a part of Western Civilization the quest has with some differences been carried on in terms of our European origins, and especially in terms of our English origins. Many Americans have been reluctant to concede this, and have sought to find the derivation of such virtues as we have in our peculiar circumstances.

During the nineteenth century when the United States was still in the formative stage and England, after two wars, was regarded as the hereditary enemy, it was popular among Americans to minimize the role that English culture and institutions had played—and still were playing—in American development. They were particularly sensitive to the way in which British travelers denigrated the raw young country and prophesied that it would collapse, or at least break apart, because of its heedless democracy and its contradictions between ideals and practices.

American peevishness proved irksome to an anonymous contributor to the February 1821 issue of London's *New Monthly Magazine and Literary Journal*, and he ventured to criticize American unwillingness to give credit where credit was due. What he wrote is so appropriate to our own time that it is worth quoting at some length.

> The American propensity to look forward with confidence to the future greatness of their country may be natural and laudable. But when they go further and refer to the wished-for period as one in which the glory of England shall be extinguished forever, their hopes become absurdities. Let us suppose the day is come when their proudest predictions are accomplished, when the continent shall be theirs from sea to sea; when it shall be covered by contiguous circles of independent states, each a kingdom in itself, with the great Federal Constitution like a vast circumference binding them together in strength and union, and when it shall be the home of countless millions of free and enlightened Americans. Let us suppose the time arrived when American fleets shall cover

every sea and ride in every harbor for purposes of commerce, of chastisement, or protection; when the land shall be the seat of freedom, learning, taste, morals, all that is most admirable in the eyes of man, and when England, sinking under the weight of years and the manifold casualties by which the pride of empires is levelled in the dust, shall have fallen from her high estate.

In that day of her extremity, what language might an Englishman hold to an American boasting of the superior grandeurs of his country? Might he not truly say: America has reason to be proud; but let her not forget whence came the original stock of glory she has laid out to such good account.... From what code did you catch the first spirit of freedom which won and has so happily maintained your independence? From the laws and institutions of England. Where did your infant science and literature find their models of deep thought, of exquisite composition, of sublime conception? In the writings of immortal Englishmen, your ancestors and instructors. No, *America can achieve no glory in which England has not a share.* Let the name of England fade from the list of nations, let her long line of statesmen, heroes, scholars, be buried in oblivion; yet so long as an empire of Americans survives, speaking her language, cherishing her institutions, and imitating her example, her name shall be pronounced with veneration throughout the world, and her memory be celebrated by a glorious monument.

The time foretold by impatient Americans has now arrived, but no thoughtful person can rejoice in it. What Americans of a century ago failed to realize was that great power entails great burdens, and that when Americans attained the preeminence toward which they were panting, their position would force them to shoulder the responsibilities which they reviled England for assuming. Greatness is always accompanied by loneliness; England adjusted to it eventually: we have not.

Along with our dawning recognition that power brings more worries than joys, we can now put aside some of our peevishness and acknowledge the justice of the London observer's claim that "America can achieve no glory in which England has not a share." When all is said and done, when due credit is given to the rich cultural contributions of numerous peoples from Europe and Africa, and all the convolutions, digressions, and new directions in our history are taken into account, the fact remains that the United States in language, institutions, and culture is fundamentally English.

This, then, is the reason why the first chapter of this work is devoted to an examination of the English background—to the practical bases of English evolution and to the theories of how society should be organized.

Chapter 1
The English Roots

Proem

What is Democracy? The simplest definition of democracy is "rule by the people"—as Lincoln said, "government of the people, by the people, for the people." Winston Churchill once said that democracy is the worst form of government known to man—except for all the others that have been tried from time to time.

It emphasizes not perfection but flexibility, a reasonable degree of willingness to listen to new ideas and to use them. It has three readily recognizable standards. (1) It is *government by law,* not by the whims of rulers; this includes the right of the accused to have recourse to the courts, and the duty of the courts to judge whether the laws are just in the light of a code of principles expressed in a constitution or a bill of rights. (2) It is based on *progressive compromises* that affect everything except the basic integrity of civil liberties. (3) It is a *process,* not a set structure, and so can never lay claim to perfection.

The test of democracy does not lie in the form of the constitution or the executive but in whether it is open-ended: whether the people can and sometimes do put out the executive and the lawmakers and put in others more nearly to their liking. At any given moment there may be shortcomings in its practices, and only a part of the people may share in the government, but so long as it is open-ended, with the way left open for improvement, it is democracy. By this definition the Thirteen Colonies were democracies even before the Revolution, and if England was not democratic, it was certainly in process of becoming so.

Democracy thus seeks to put the will of the people into effect by means of a changing balance of political conflict—that is, by a never-ending regrouping of political forces in temporary alliances to promote their own interests. This means that the two opposing forces must agree (1) on fundamental values, and (2) on the rules of the formalized political conflict. They will pretty generally agree on eventual goals but will differ on how to reach them and on the speed with which they should be approached. If they do not have this fundamental agreement, the chances are that the democratic process will break down and there will be civil war—as happened in 1861.

The result is that in democracies, political attitudes tend to divide between liberalism and conservatism or, as it is often expressed, between left and right. They are the two necessary faces of democracy, and there is constant tension between them. But in the end they compromise according to formal rules in order to advance toward common goals.

The meanings of liberal and conservative thus become important to an understanding of democracy. The *Oxford English Dictionary* gives the meaning of the word liberal as "free from . . . unreasonable prejudice in favour of traditional opinions or established institutions; open to the reception of new ideas." Conservative it defines as "characterized by a tendency to keep intact or unchanged." These refer to attitudes of mind, and most of us are influenced by one of these attitudes in our whole approach to life, not merely to political problems.

The Moral Basis of English Democracy

In the fifteenth century, England, a little nation of perhaps two-and-a-half million people on part of an unimportant island on the fringe of the known world, was apparently doomed to a perpetual role as a semibarbarian state. Then suddenly it cut loose spiritually from the continent, and at the same time the discovery of the New World made it apparent that England lay at the center rather than at the edge of the world. No people since the days of the Roman republic had showed such vigor and enterprise. The coal in the English ground became the foundation of unprecedented industries, and the oaks of the English forests were hewn into mighty fleets whose mission it was to protect and extend the empire built on those industries. Yet the success of England depended less on industry and naval might than on the fact that, despite all her faults, she rode upon the crest of the wave of the future. And she rode this wave because the inscrutable process of evolution had bred in the English people the early stages of the way of life that we know as democracy.

Democracy did not, even in its modern form, develop solely in England nor among the English-speaking peoples. But though there were forms of democracy rising in the Middle Ages in most of the countries of Western Europe, it may be doubted if they would have survived, or at least triumphed, without the example and encouragement (often unconscious) of England. Certainly the evolution of the democratic process can be traced most clearly in England, and its mechanics can be best observed in the English-speaking countries.

Because laws and institutions are the creations of the circumstances and the psychology of a people, we must first look into the background and the mind of the Englishman. The first fact to be noted is that England is an island. The Englishman never loses his consciousness that he is an islander, for at no point is he more than about seventy miles from tide water. He and his fellow islanders have a sense of being shipmates voyaging together into the sun of destiny. Out of this physical and psychological insularity arises the fact that the Englishman can be and is selective in what he accepts from the outside world. Second, the English weather and the English landscape possess few sharp contrasts.

To these fundamentals the centuries added men with characters already formed; the imaginative, style-conscious, and charmingly impulsive Celt; the brooding, individualistic Saxon, whose caution bred tolerance and hesitancy to the extent of sluggishness; the Dane, half merchant and half pirate, a master realist, shrewd, practical, concise; and the parvenu Norman, intellectually subtle but bound to earth by an unparalleled administrative genius, a worshiper of good form in law, religion, and the arts, and who never moved without legal excuses, sound if possible, but at least plausible. To the Englishman who was being formed the Celt furnished the soul, the Saxon the body, the Dane the mind, and the Norman, ably assisted by the medieval Church, breathed into him the life of discipline, order, and good form.

The Englishman has been a persistent peasant, with a peasant's consciousness of the vagaries of nature and suspicions of new-fangled methods. Judgment becomes utilitarian and policies are weighed by their results. Six centuries ago William of Occam slashed the throat of medieval utopianism with his well-known "razor." There is no such thing as a universal, he asserted, no perfect scheme of things, no absolute. We take from the particular objects that we know such qualities as seem common to them and create the universals—and into what absurdities this leads us! Here we see both the virtues and vices so dear to the English-speaking peoples—understatement, muddling through, compromise, tolerance, and reverance for the old and well-tried.

But this is only half the story, for the Englishman even more than the rest of humanity is dualistic. Action forces a comparison and choice of modes of action, and out of this conflict arises conscience—the individual's view of what the group would have him do. The peasant Englishman tried to follow Nature, which judged by the results (reality); pure Christianity judged by the means (morality), and put others above self in a completely idealistic sense. The dilemma has always puzzled the world. We call the Golden Rule our ideal, but note how any attempt to force it on others results in oppression and intolerance and destroys its idealism. It is the same way with most naked ideals; they are quite impractical in a workaday world, and will remain so until humanity is perfected.

This dualism makes the Englishman a dreamer and a man of action, a poet and a merchant, a missionary and a grinder of the poor, a worshiper—and a successful one—of both god and Mammon. At least up until the Enlightenment the highest stated interests were those of religion, so economic and national aims had to be justified as advancing the kingdom of God. Hence a rationale that seems to us to be warped and hypocritical, as for example that given for the colonization of America. This rationale can be called the mythus, and whether true or false (it can be either) it explains the origins of our beliefs and furnishes a standard around which we can rally for action; it becomes, in many cases, an article of conscience by which men live or die.

David Hume pointed out that moralists begin rationally with *is* and *is not*, then suddenly jump to *ought* and *ought not*. The natural tendency of man is to reorient the world into harmony with himself. Thus conscience is ambivalent; it has both a will to dominate others and a will to dominate one's self. This double and contradictory motivation emerges as a desire for domination and a desire for equality—in other words selfishness and altruism, aggression and repression, hostility and good will, hate and love. Both functions are normal and have a proper place in the struggle for existence, but it may not be far amiss to say that it is an imbalance between them that causes war, oppression, and well-meant but impractical social crusades. The unhealthy conscience is the parent of bigotry and oppression. When conscience ceases to look upon a certain course as important it ceases to choose, or at least to attempt to make its choice dominant; this is tolerance in the pure sense, though not always in the sense understood in English-speaking countries. At any rate the two aspects of conscience are incompatible and the man who lives by conscience will always be troubled.

Out of the equalitarianism of conscience rises our concept of right and duty. Right we may define as our own view of equality, and duty as the necessity of defending the other fellow's rights. It is becoming increasingly apparent that the two are inextricably joined; we must defend the rights of others or we shall have none of our own. There is a sense in which feudalism can be spoken of as the medieval phase of the concept of right and duty—the attempt of the barbarian to defend his individualism by defining right and duty in feudal contracts.

But eventually Roman law with its emphasis on society won out on the Continent. Conscience became a social possession; we see the result today in a breakdown of international morality, promoted by nothing so much as the eclipse of the individual phase of conscience with its power to hinder or direct social action. The equalitarian instinct has been drugged by false doctrines, and the will to power suborned to serve the state. We are witnessing the growth of a foul tumor on the body of conscience, a morbid excrescence which may well destroy its host.

But the subornation of conscience has not yet broken down all the barriers in English-speaking and certain other like-minded countries. Moralists are inevitably concerned because though conscience makes the equality of men its great object, yet Nature itself has made them unequal in physical and intellectual powers. There may be no escape from the dilemma; the best we can hope for now is to have men "equally considered"—not considered equal. "Live and let live" is our motto. We have come to pay such respect to justice—that is, to conscience—that it has become commonplace for the stronger party in a physical sense to bow before it. It is this practical compromise, imperfect as it may be in operation, that constitutes the great contribution of England to the world. This is the Anglo-Saxon spirit, and we in America have had a share in its development.

There are three possible attitudes toward virtue. The cynic tries to deny its existence and to judge honor and justice frankly by whether or not they are to his own advantage. The idealist accepts it as the sole standard and his conscience makes him a saint or a bigot intent on converting the world to perfection either by example or by force. The third man is impressed by virtue, but he is drawn by the solid advantages of discreet sin. He cannot, like the cynic or the bigot, blind himself to one or the other. So he ends by becoming a hypocrite; he makes sin pay tribute to virtue. There may be no philosophical way station between right and wrong, but there certainly is a practical one. That is why the perfectionist Frenchman is a cynic and the opportunistic Englishman is a hypocrite.

Look at the problem in other terms. As Hume pointed out, our regard for moral standards prompts us to jump from what *is* to what *ought* to be. The moral judgment may agree with what *ought to be*, but if that goal is not realistic our leap will fall short and we will light on what *can be*; any refusal to accept that results in breaking down social order and ushers in a new era which may well be worse than the old. The hypocrite chooses what *can be* but he is not content: he endeavors to obtain credit for having chosen what *ought to be*.

There is reason in the dictum that hypocrisy is the first station on the line that goes from vice to virtue. The hypocrite has not lost his sense of right; he has only compromised with it. But he has acknowledged the superiority of virtue and has sentenced himself to a life of attempting to make his actions and his conscience agree; henceforth he becomes absorbed in the problem of good and evil—ethics. His conscience must accommodate itself to facts and submit to serve as an apologist in exchange for being permitted to guide him toward eventual good. His standards become moral, even if he does not live up to them. His heroes must be endowed with moral grandeur, real or legendary. Robin Hood may rob, but it must be in order to help the poor; Robert E. Lee can be mistaken but he must be deadly sincere. The danger in the attempt to reconcile good and evil is that those who do not have a conscience to guide them merely find a cynical excuse for self-interest; that is why most philosophers and theologians have opposed compromise. The Englishman does evil that good may come, but he pays the penalty; thenceforth he is neither a convinced saint nor a hearty sinner. Other nations comment upon the lack of joy among English-speaking peoples.

The role of the Bible in molding Anglo-Saxon culture has not always been recognized by historians beyond references to its service as a light unto the feet of the Puritan fathers. During the centuries, it has become an English book, the fullest expression of the genius, the conscience, and the outlook of the English-speaking peoples. Its words are no longer words from the kings, prophets, and teachers of Palestine; they fall from the lips of Lollardy's "poor priests," working in hidden places to render the Scriptures they love; from panoplied bishops and doctors proudly seated in a king's hall; from sailors burying their dead at sea; from worn ascetics in jungle and desert thirsting for a glimpse of England; from men in search of El Dorado, or markets for opium, or land to farm.

Written for a race of shepherds and vintners they became the comfort, the admonition, and the marching orders of another race that carried its power to every part of the earth. Consider with what clarity and certainty our ancestors read their high destiny in Holy Writ. Thus, the chosen people: "Ye are the salt of the earth"; superiority: "Thou has made me wiser than mine enemies"; comfort: "He that keepeth Israel shall neither slumber nor sleep"; triumph: "Thy foot shall be dipped in the blood of thine enemies"; dominion: "I have this day set thee over the nations, to root out, and to pull down, to build and to plant"; marching orders: "Get thee out of thy country into a land that I will show thee"; promise: "And all nations shall call you blessed."

The Bible has been like a great quarry from which every builder may draw. Scarcely a book is written in English that does not somewhere show treasures drawn from Holy Writ. Our major poets have almost without exception found theme or inspiration in the book. Not only has it— especially the King James Version—given our language texture and cadence but it has served to anchor it from too much drifting. Statesmen and orators, it must be confessed, have found there a model for the stately turgidity and sonority which they sought and which was as much the stock-in-trade of the American after-dinner speaker or the political pontifico as it was of the Hebrew prophet and psalmist.

The Role of Concrete Liberties

Upon the balance between sordid facts and idealistic aspirations the Englishman has based his laws and his institutions. What exists is right, and if any person or interest perceives that facts have changed, it is his or its responsibility to bring the condition to public attention—otherwise nothing will be altered. Changes thus come by conflict between force and a rising counterforce. Democracy operates only to the extent that we take a personal interest in making it work. English law was (like our own Bill of Rights) devoted to the protection of the privileges of the citizen. Duties and responsibilities were not legal positives, but social and moral. In a way this is only realistic: what law can prevent the coal miner from striking if he chooses? The social or moral sense is the only restraint that free men can afford to acknowledge.

To the medieval Englishman the word liberty meant franchise or privilege and hence its pluralization. The liberties of the woodcutter, the abbey, the town, or the baron were the privileges that had been granted to them as individuals, institutions, or classes, or what was even better, had come down to them out of the past. They were in effect the constitution, written or traditional, of the individual or institution.

Medieval Englishmen (aside from the more rarefied philosophers) held a concept of liberties quite unconnected with such idealistic universals as the natural rights of mankind. Each individual struggled for concrete liberties, liberties not drawn from inspired essayists but which he could count off on his thick Saxon fingers. Note the liberties that Thomas Jefferson ticked off in the Declaration of Independence as having been denied by King George. The historical sense of medieval men was very weak, so liberties were frequently based on traditions or misinterpretation of charters. Among these was the Magna Charta, which was forced from the king by the barons, in 1213, in an attempt to limit the royal power in their favor. Revolution was looked upon not as change, but as a restoration of the good old way of doing things—a view closely allied to the ancient hope of restoring the Golden Age. The attitude became habitual and was transferred to the United States. The American revolutionists fought to *restore* the "rights of Englishmen," and the Confederate States fought to restore the original meaning of the Constitution of the United States.

Now your liberties and mine have a habit of clashing. Hence the English Common Law. Here we see a curious illustration of the Englishman's opposition to change even when he was taking full advantage of it. New things arose constantly, but they had to be identified as something old, or at least concealed in its clothes. The Common Law was an organic growth. It did not spring into being as the champion of the liberties of the individual; indeed, it was for a long time an instrument for imposing the royal will and then for imposing conformity to the will of the community. But it grew and it changed, and in so doing gradually assumed the role of protector of the individual. As a matter of fact, the evolution (at least of constitutional interpretation) is still in process, as is proved by the United States Supreme Court's rulings in favor of individual rights.

There is an amusing incident in *Huckleberry Finn* which Roscoe

Pound cites as an illustration of the Anglo-Saxon insistence upon abiding by tradition and yet meeting practical exigencies as they arise. When Tom Sawyer and Huck Finn undertook to rescue their friend, the runaway Negro, Jim, from the cabin in which he was being held, Huck maintained that prying off a board from the window would be the easiest way. But Tom with a fine romantic scorn asserted that according to all the precedents a prisoner must be dug out. Thereupon Huck produced some picks, but Tom insisted that the rules specified that the digging must be done with case-knives.

The boys plied their case-knives industriously until midnight. By then they were dog-tired, their hands were blistered, and it was evident that the task would take many nights. Tom stopped to rest and think.

"Well," he said finally, "right is right, and wrong is wrong, and a body ain't got no business doing wrong when he ain't ignorant and knows better. It ain't right, and it ain't moral, and I wouldn't like it to get out; but there ain't only just the one way: we got to dig him out with the picks, and *let on* it's case-knives. Gimme a case-knife."

Tom had a case-knife in his hand, but the obliging Huck handed him another. Tom threw it down.

"Gimme a *case-knife*."

Then the light broke in pragmatic Huck's mind. He scratched around among the old tools for a pickaxe and handed it to Tom. Tom took it without a word and went to work. "He was always just that particular," commented Huck. "Full of principle."

Says Dean Pound: "The law has always managed to get a pickaxe in its hands, though it steadfastly demanded a case-knife and to wield it in the virtuous belief that it was using the approved instrument." Two fundamentals marked its history: the doctrine that the law is supreme, and the doctrine that law is based on precedent. By the first the Common Law was superior to all men, even the king. "The King," said Bracton, "is not subject to man, but is under God and the law."

Even by the year 1300 the practice of law had become a professional mystery, the peculiar preserve of the lawyer. Royal judges were drawn from the ranks of the lawyers and whenever a new problem arose they settled it as nearly as they could in the spirit of the law. Thereafter that decision furnished a precedent that was followed when the same problem arose. The Common Law was thus a living organism that grew from generation to generation by cellular multiplication, and as it grew it added more protections for the individual. The law was complicated, but it was indestructible. Even when the people lagged in their zeal for their liberties the vested interests of the "sergeants-at-law" prevented king or people from straying far from the path they had entered.

Out of this tangle there arose certain clearly defined rules to protect the individual. Warrants were necessary for arrests or for search and seizure; freedom of speech, though not absolute, was in process of development; convictions for important crimes could be only by jury and then by increasingly strict rules governing procedure and evidence; even in religion, Christendom probably had no freer country than England, and no doubt this afforded scope for the flowering of conscience. By 1300 Parliament had begun to take on recognizable shape. As a matter of fact Parliament was regarded as fundamentally a court, so that its enactments were in a sense judicial precedents. At first the membership was composed of all nobles, clergy, and judges summoned to attendance by the king, plus representatives of the county gentry and the well-to-do townsmen; the working classes had not yet developed political consciousness. Gradually this "Great Council" split into two houses— Lords and Commons. The Commons, which was one day to rule a quarter of the earth, literally entered history on its knees. Old pictures show the king on his throne, with his councilors seated before him on woolsacks and the lords spiritual and temporal at each side. At the end of the hall and outside of a wooden bar knelt the Commons. They were not permitted to address the throne but could be heard only through the "Speaker," their presiding officer.

Every opportunity was taken by the Commons to levy on the king what has aptly been termed "constitutional blackmail." The Commons thus strengthened their right to initiate taxes and money appropriations; they specified the manner in which money should be spent; they sometimes managed to force the king to abandon the slick and "unconstitutional" methods by which he supplemented his income. Perhaps some of this boldness rose from the growing conflict between king and great nobles: really two great alliances of nobles, each of which strove to put its own man on the throne and control elections by force or fraud and thus pack the Commons. One worthy result was that Parliament established its right to elect or depose the king. Eventually the struggle degenerated into a civil conflict known as the Wars of Roses (1455-1485) in which the nobles were so obliging as to weaken themselves in senseless massacres, and thus clear the way for the initiation of a truly national policy.

It was the gifted royal House of Tudor that saw England through the difficult national adolescence of the sixteenth century. The Tudors reigned with a semblance of despotism, but their policy succeeded only because they shrewdly anticipated and expressed the will of the nation. In effect the English had gained more liberties than they knew how to reconcile with each other, and the result had been chaos. The mission of the Tudors was to pare away the conflicting edges of inconsistent liberties, develop a sense of common interest among Englishmen, and clear the way for a truly national policy. When Henry VIII led England out of the Roman Catholic Church, the alacrity with which Parliament consented to sever the ties with Rome was indicative of a will which, if it was not unanimous, was at least effectively national. By 1558 when Elizabeth ascended the throne, foreign events had forced the English Church more and more to the Protestant side.

Elizabeth reigned in the midst of what has been called the Commerical Revolution, when Europe was making contact with the outside world, stepping up trade at a remarkable rate, and creating a parallel growth of prosperity and poverty, a spectacle that has too often accompanied the great ages of history. At the time the prevailing theory of economics was mercantilism, which sought prosperity and security by making the nation economically self-sufficient. This meant that each nation set up what today we would call a planned economy with strict controls over trade and industry at the expense of agriculture, with the object of insuring an excess of exports over imports. The passing of barter and the rise of the wage system (in place of feudal dues) had given a new significance to money, and this was now vastly enhanced by the gold and silver poured into Europe from Spain's American colonies. It soon became easy for many people to accept the bullionist theory that a nation's wealth depended on amassing gold and silver.

It was Sir Walter Raleigh who saw that the central idea of mercantilism was unsound and that gold was only an instrument of commerce. As one of his followers wrote, "That is the richest land that feeds the most men." Moreover, "he that rules the sea, rules the commerce of the world and to him that rules the commerce of the world belongs the treasure of the world and indeed the world itself." Raleigh hoped to gain this rule for England by adding her surplus population to the vast strategic and natural resources of North America.

English merchants were now developing that penchant for "calculated risk" without which no commercial empires are built. Along with this went the development of the joint-stock company, in which each member received a share proportionate to his contribution of capital. The stockholders chose a "court" to run the affairs of the company, usually with a "governor" presiding over it. It was natural that joint-stock companies should seek royal charters which set up their rules of governance and forbade other subjects to trespass on their monopoly—a technical process, the right to deal in certain articles, or the right to trade in a certain area. The chartered joint-stock company was so useful that it was to become the typical European instrument of overseas enterprise. Englishmen were to be notably successful in its use, and several of the English colonies in America were to be founded by such enterprises.

When in 1603 the shambling, slobbering little Scotsman, James Stuart, ascended the English throne by virtue of his descent from Henry VII, he was gratified to exchange the halter of Scotia's long-faced moral dictators for the divinity that hedged English kings as the result of a century of Tudor rule. As a matter of fact Stuart rule was milder than that of the Tudors, but the Stuarts were not ruling over the same people as had their predecessors. The nobility and the middle class of bourgeois—the common people scarcely counted yet—were each richer, stronger, and more united, and therefore harder to manage. It was only by heroic restraint in asking Parliament for special money grants to run the government that James I and then his son Charles I managed to avoid disaster. Not satisfied with what the Tudors called the "royal prerogative," they sought to enforce their "divine right." James called it the "law of free monarchy" and Charles spoke of government as his "liberty."

In those days the line between religion and politics was so thin as to be invisible; that is, it was just as much treason to deny the king's religious authority as to deny his civil authority. James and Charles sought to force everyone to conform to the established Church of England and harried Nonconformists; Archbishop Laud of Canterbury was Charles's chief instrument in this activity. The result of the religious and civil oppressions of the Stuarts was that party lines were gradually drawn. There were three: (1) the king's party, which upheld divine right; (2) that of the great nobles, which wished to make a puppet of the king; and (3) that of the Puritans, including the gentry and the wealthy bourgeois (the middle class of that day), who did not propose to let either of the other parties interfere with their liberties or with what was much the same thing, business.

It was with the last party that the Puritans found their niche, and indeed they gave it its name. The Puritans were those zealous Protestants who desired to "purify" the Church of England of "Romish" practices. In general, there were three kinds. The "Low Churchmen" wished to remain in the Church of England, but to purify it. The Presbyterians wished to adopt John Calvin's system of church organization by which each congregation should elect representatives to a central body, thus changing the Church of England from a monarchy to a republic. The Brownists wished each congregation to settle its own organization and doctrines; hence they were also known as Separatists, Independents, and Congregationalists; such differences as there were among them were too complex to concern us here. Despite Archbishop Laud's vigorous efforts to stamp them out, the Puritans now almost controlled the eastern counties of the kingdom and included in their ranks or among their sympathizers a majority of the wealthy merchants and manufacturers of the cities.

The Puritan adopted Calvinism not from any naive admiration for John Calvin, but because his study of the Bible convinced him that John Calvin had come closest to truth. It was the typical independence of the Englishman transferred to the religious sphere. Moreover, like English customs, Calvinism concealed the seeds of both aristocracy and democracy and thus furnished another reason for being welcomed. All men were equal at the judgment bar of God, and that God saved whom he would had nothing to do with the case; every man, elect or damned, had an equal duty toward God. No man had a priestly right to mediate between God and man, hence the democratic form of Presbyterianism by which the laity controlled the Church and that often formed a sounding board for discontent.

Yet this form of democratic control was, with true English inconsistency, often vitiated in fact, for vigorous and disputatious clergymen could and did control their congregations. This was quite in line with the aristocratic principle in Calvinism. The elect could scarcely avoid forming an aristocracy among themselves, for they would be saved and the damned would not be. There was, moreover, a deep distrust of human nature, and it was the duty of the clergy and gentry to restrain their less well-instructed and more impulsive brethren—that was a duty for which they were responsible to God. Ergo, how could they be responsible to men? This is a beautiful example of the Anglo-Saxon ability to reconcile altruism with self-interest and call it duty; a long string of words can be substituted, such as idealism and realism, the desirable and the attainable, fancy and fact, justice and injustice, right and expediency, truth and falsehood, virtue and necessity, tradition and progress, and even, by the cynic or the saint, good and evil.

For that Puritan who was not a hypochondriac it was only a matter of simple deduction and self-persuasion to arrive at the conclusion that he was one of the elect. He was good, he was pious, he was holy in life and conversation. God enjoined the necessity of work, so he lived soberly and worked long hours. God prospered the righteous, so if he was rich he was righteous. The concept was a valuable urge to industry and frugality—and, in the end, legalized chicanery and oppression, for the doctrine that righteousness breeds prosperity is dangerously akin to the statement that might makes right. But what if he were not prosperous and successful? Cromwell learned the answer when he invited his Puritan Parliament to consider the party's reverses as proofs that it was not in the will of God. "No," answered those casuists, "God is only testing our faith."

It was a system that could not be beaten. It had the toughness of realism but the advantages of idealism, for it came close to letting one enjoy the fruits of evil deeds with a good conscience. The Puritan was a visionary who set about attaining his dreams by practical means, but if he failed he was not disappointed; he had been prepared for the worst and really expected nothing else in the light of his own and others' fallibility. No spirit of meekness made him suffer the buffets of the wicked a moment longer than it took to collect his might against them. He was a radical but not a destroyer, a revolutionary but not an enemy of government. His feet were always on the ground and his head was never above the clouds, save when his Bible was open before him. His life was a strange mixture of zest and frigidity, of inner light and outer restraint, of soul-searchings and worldly pursuits.

It is all but impossible to express in terms of our century that queer bundle of zeal and casuistry—or rather those queer bundles, for the Puritans were very much divided among themselves. Such Puritans as Milton sought to preserve the traditional medieval unity and at the same time be hospitable to the new classical learning and to dawning science. And yet Hellenism and Christianity were natural enemies, and the fact was recognized all the more promptly because the struggle between the two outlooks had been going on in the Englishman's soul for centuries. Therefore the Puritans sought to straddle; they proposed to use the new learning as an instrument in expounding the Scriptures—for truth and reason must agree—but they wished to keep the unlearned from simplifying doctrine and going off on erroneous tangents. The result was a marked emphasis upon a learned clergy.

This emphasis was all the more important because the Puritan found in the Bible the complete guide for life and eternity, the mentor of morals and manners, the form of church organization and ritual, and even a political constitution. He appealed from the tyranny of king and Church to the tyranny of a Book. Intolerance rises when one feels that he has found *absolute* truth, and the Puritan was in this position. Yet the man who is lukewarm or indifferent in religion may support a certain view for economic or social reasons; the Anglican was in this position. The Puritan espoused John Calvin's doctrine that God had doomed the entire human race to destruction but that for reasons best known to Himself He had decided to lift certain ones to salvation; the ones elected to be saved had done nothing to deserve it—they were merely resoundingly fortunate.

The Anglican on the other hand adopted the convenient doctrine that the Bible only laid down general principles and that man was entitled to use his reason in working out the details—or at least the archbishop of Canterbury could use his reason. The Anglican moreover taught that men were not doomed to damnation but that each one had the power of choosing salvation.

Centuries before this an English bishop had proclaimed that "Manners makyth man." The proof was seen now. The points on which Anglican and Puritan clashed were those of conduct, for beyond the question of predestination and free grace they differed little in theology. The Puritans approved the separation of the Church of England from Rome, but why, they asked, should it keep the vestments and so much of the ritual when the plain intent of the Bible was to dispense with them? The Anglican encouraged a reasonable degree of gaiety and spontaneity and admired beauty whether in the moods of Nature or the stained glass of churches. Not all Puritans disagreed—remember Cromwell dancing on the green and Milton's inspired poem, *L'Allegro*—but as the lines between the two parties became more distinct many of the Puritans adopted the harsh and narrow views and the vinegary countenances that are now supposed to have characterized them.

But save in these matters of conduct the Puritan was not far from the norm of his time in England. He was, generally, far from being a democrat, in fact he was insistent that the common people must submit to their spiritual and temporal rulers. He abhorred religious liberty because it would break down his concept of the divine system. He was not a sentimentalist or humanitarian. He rejected liberty of thought lest it lead to error. He discouraged, even to the extent of persecution, those who thought they had received divine revelations or who were "enthusiasts"—that is, boisterous or uncouth or unusual in their piety. But the Puritan himself was an enthusiast in the sense that he was immoderate in his determination to squeeze Church, State, and society into his mold.

With an inscrutable Providence always busily guiding, testing, and punishing His elect, the Puritan did not always demand to see a clear course before him. Yet he believed that right would prevail; at least he would get a gold star in the Book of Life if he strove mightily—so his belief in predestination never abated his determination. Like Cromwell's Ironsides the Puritan's motto was, "Fear God and keep your powder dry." Or better yet was John Cotton's brace of Christian virtues: "Diligence in worldly business, and yet deadness to the world." It might have been for our benefit that he added these words: "Such a mystery as none can read, but they that know it."

James I had clashed with Parliament over the concept that the king was under the law. When Charles I sought to collect illegal taxes Parliament wrested from him the "Petition of Right" by which he consented to limitations on his authority. Years of bickering followed until finally in 1642 Charles found himself in civil war with Parliament and the Puritans of town and country. After some years of indecisive conflict Oliver Cromwell came to the fore with his brigade of Ironsides raised in the eastern counties among "honest sober Christians" who "made some conscience of what they did." The result was to stiffen the Parliamentary army and put it under the control of Cromwell and the Puritans. Many of the great nobles had sided with Parliament in the hope that they could make the king their puppet. Now they retired to their estates or went over to the king. The war thus became a straight issue between Cavaliers and Roundheads, as the two sides were called. In the end Charles was captured, tried for treason, convicted, and beheaded (1649). The law had vindicated its supremacy over the king.

The republic—called Commonwealth—set up by the Puritans was

held together only by making Cromwell a virtual dictator under the title of Lord Protector. By now it was apparent not only that rigid Puritanism had no attraction for self-indulgent nobles and earthy peasants, but that the wealthy bourgeois supporters of Parliament would not abide a Puritan theocracy any more quietly than the old church-state censorship. They wanted freedom from both political and religious trammels. With the death of Cromwell they got their way. Charles II, another Stuart, came to the throne in 1660. Technically the Church of England resumed its sway, but it was never again to be its old self. Secularization was by no means complete, but it was on the way. The Puritans passed under a cloud, and were now ridiculed as hypocrites. In his *Hudibras* Samuel Butler jeered at them as

> A sect, whose chief devotion lies
> In odd perverse antipathies . . .
> That with more care keep holy-day
> The wrong, than others the right way;
> Compound for sins they are inclin'd to,
> By damning those they have no mind to:
> Still so perverse and opposite,
> As if they worshipp'd God for spite.

The civil war had given England one of the severest lessons in its history. It renewed the English horror of civil war and standing armies; it inculcated a new respect for gradualism as an instrument of change; it bred a new sense of discipline, the belated bequest of rigorous Puritan training, and convinced the nation that it must act as a unit. Strongest of all, perhaps, was a healthy distrust of "popular" government which kept the nation from advancing faster along the road to democracy than the preparation of the people warranted.

Charles II aimed at absolutism, but such progress as he made was destroyed by his brother and successor, James II, who moved too fast toward his objective of restoring divine right and Catholicism. Politicans had fallen into the Country and Court parties, soon known respectively as Whig and Tory. In 1688 the Whig and some Tory lords united in offering the throne to Mary, James's Protestant daughter, and her husband, William of Orange. The throne had become something of a hot seat, and William accepted it only because as stadtholder of Holland he was the Protestant champion of Europe against the overwhelming might of Louis XIV, and he needed England's help. William readily paid for

English support by assent to the Bill of Rights, the third great document (after Magna Charta and the Petition of Right) in the English constitution. By it the king as executive of the realm was forbidden among other things to suspend the laws, to levy taxes, or to require excessive bail, lay excessive fines, or impose cruel or unusual punishments; and the freedom of members of Parliament from royal interferences or arrest was confirmed.

This so-called Glorious Revolution of 1688 fastened a Whig oligarchy on England. The significant thing was that Parliament (really the House of Commons), not the oligarchy as such, had assumed control over English purse strings and policies. This was made clearer in the next century, when a committee of Parliament known as the Cabinet began to take over the executive functions of the king. For centuries kings and nobility had striven to control the Commons by packing; but packed they ever so well, the old spirit of truculent independence flared forth in every generation. As long as the Commons continued to be drawn from any large section of the nation it was impossible for one party to control it. A sufficiently aroused people could always make itself heard through this hereditary trumpet of popular liberties. The final decision was made in 1688. Once and for all the power of the people as expressed in Parliament superseded that of the king.

The essential characteristics of English law and politics were now complete. It was, however, the molding of a process, of methods and attitudes, rather than of a clear-cut goal or even of a program. There were still a host of political and social details to be worked out, but the process was set. Religious toleration was to make its entry, and religion was confirmed in its historic English role as social rather than spiritual. The House of Commons was to triumph over the Lords. The king was to lose his executive functions, and the middle class was now in a position where it could eventually take over. Parliament was to be the instrument of change. Thereafter amendments were to be the results of slow pressure upon Parliament, pressure exerted by public opinion and formed by merchants, journalists, economists, philanthropists, and the rising voice of the laboring man as he shouldered his way to the front and demanded that he be given a share in the good things of life.

The Doctrine of Natural Rights

There was yet one more factor to be added, a purely theoretical one, but one that nevertheless was to affect the world profoundly. Rebellion against kings had long been regarded as a sin against God, but Puritan apologists excused it by asserting that among God's natural laws for the universe was the right of men to govern themselves. It was thus a duty to resist tyranny.

The doctrine of natural law, by which men are entitled to certain natural rights simply because they are men, rose in ancient Greece, was transmitted to Rome, and was accepted by medieval philosophers. Richard Hooker, the Elizabethan divine who sought to reconcile medieval tradition with the new learning, relied on natural law. In his *Laws of Ecclesiastical Polity* Hooker undertook to argue against the Puritan insistence on the Bible as the fount of all belief and conduct by (1) asserting that God revealed Himself in many ways, and (2) by upholding tradition, authority, social convenience, law, and good order. Reason supplements revelation, and natural law, discovered by reason, supplements the divine law of the Bible. He distinguished between society and government but posited that both were under law. Church and State were different aspects of the same body, not separate societies as the Puritan taught, and which he accused them of using as an excuse to make the Church supreme over the State.

The law that Hooker set forth was not rigid, but unfolded with man's understanding as formed and evolved by society. Since men were imperfect— and always would be—they had set up civil societies; if this was not done by deliberate contract at least government must act as if it ruled by contract, and its laws could be changed only by the people. The notable exceptions were that laws on "things indifferent" could be disobeyed when they were contrary to divine or natural law. Among "things indifferent" he numbered the vestments and ceremonials attacked by the Puritans. On things not "indifferent" there could be no disobedience. (Perhaps he would have permitted disobedience to laws prohibiting alcoholic liquors because they violated right reason as portrayed in divine and natural laws.)

As Hooker saw it, the state must have undivided authority, though he was not prepared as yet to accept popular sovereignty—indeed he placed authority above liberty. On the other hand his view of a unified society prepared the way taken by Britain when the House of Commons became supreme. The road of divided sovereignty taken by the United Staes has posed the problem of tensions between liberty and order foreseen by Hooker. As he put it:

> Suppose to-morrow the power which hath dominion in justice require thee at the court; that which in war, at the field; that which in religion, at the temple; all have equal authority over thee, and impossible it is that thou shouldst be in such case obedient to all; by choosing any one whom thou wilt obey, certain thou art for thy disobedience to incur the displeasure of the other two.

Hooker realized that valuable as liberty was it could not be attained at the sacrifice of order; failing any other solution the best that could be hoped for wa a continual and precarious state of tension. We have never managed to resolve the problem, and therein lies our present peril. Wherein does our duty lie between liberty and order, between conscience and obedience, among legislature, executive and judiciary?

Hooker had sought with astonishing success to reconcile English and European medieval traditions with the rising belief in natural rights, and in so doing he sought to weld Church and State together as one body under law. Hooker died in 1600 with his great work uncompleted. Half a century later he was attacked by two Englishmen, Thomas Hobbes and Robert Filmer, both concerned with justifying the divine right of kings.

Hooker had assumed the social reality of the community. In his *Leviathan* (1651) Hobbes tried to show that the community as portrayed by Hooker was pure fiction. Such cooperation as existed rose from the members' desire to enjoy selfish advantages (quite consistent with the prevalent belief in the natural depravity of men) and even then it could work only because a powerful individual imposed his sovereignty.

Filmer in a number of publications issued around 1650 and in his posthumous *Patriarcha* (1680) set forth the medieval portrait of society—indeed the universe—as patriarchally governed: the father over his family, the bishops over the Church, the king over his subjects, and God over all. Filmer and others of his opinion were in considerable part only expressing the concept of society held by the commonalty, and the concept was carried to America. There it survived most strongly in the South—perhaps because of slavery, perhaps because Southerners were less conscious of the arguments raised against Filmer by such philosophers as John Locke, who devoted a *Treatise on Government* to refuting the patriarchal theory.

Hooker had enjoined the common good of society. John Locke undertook to refute Hobbes' defense of divine right, and proclaimed that the "judicious Hooker" was his master. Perhaps without realizing it he, in the words of George Sabine, "set up a body of innate indefeasible individual rights which limit the competence of the community and stand as bars to prevent interference with the liberty and property of private persons." As he saw it the common good was synonymous with the protection of private rights.

Locke wrote soon after the Glorious Revolution and was intent on justifying it, by his *Second Treatise on Government* (1690) which appealed to natural law. All liberties, said Locke, had originally been vested in men, but conflicts among them had led to the setting up of a government by a *social compact* among the people which was intended to reconcile and protect natural rights. The king was merely the agent of the people, appointed to administer the laws. Thus, men are not antisocial creatures to be kept in order by the stern hand of a king but are rational beings who preserve good order by the checks of common sense and the balancing of powers between executive and legislature. Englishmen had rebelled against a king who had attempted to upset this balance.

Locke continued. The business of government is not to regulate every move of the individual but to preserve order and protect private property. The protection of property, in fact, is the tie that binds sensible men together in the common interest and forestalls useless revolutions. With an agreement on property as the center of life, it will be possible to permit majority rule, religious tolerance, and freedom of thought and speech. Government must be by laws that act on all alike; such laws are based on the public good and can be passed only by the legislature; and taxes can be levied only by the consent of the people through their legislators.

The doctrine of natural rights was a fateful one for Englishmen. Hitherto they had fought for limited and concrete liberties, one or a few at a time, without deep thought of any goal. Now they were told that a whole galaxy of liberties was theirs by natural right; all they needed to do was to ensure good order by protecting private property. Vested interests, obviously including the great nobles and the merchants and industrialists, saw the point at once. It was their moral *duty* to ensure good order by upholding natural rights, among which the central one just happened to be the amassing and holding of property. Lawyers leaped at the chance to proclaim that the common law was the perfect and completed expression of the eternal principles of natural rights. For a hundred years the common law almost ceased to evolve, except that it carefully trained around property a thorny hedge warranted to be proof against the attacks of a hungry populace.

With the modern entry of natural rights the evolution of democracy was split into two streams. Inherent in the theory was the claim that all men not only possessed liberty but were equal—and here lay a dilemma. If liberty were complete, the more intelligent or unscrupulous would be able to subject their fellows, and thus destroy not only liberty but also equality. The only way to avoid this is to preserve a tension between the two, and that dooms democracy to continual crisis. The history of democracy has thus become the record of its attempts to escape this dilemma—to find an automatic way of preserving the tension.

Inevitably, democrats have had to choose which way they would prefer to have the balance tip. Locke had profited by the lesson of the Puritan Revolution and did not expect society to reach a state of equality very soon—if ever—and was content to place its guidance in the hands of its responsible members, retaining as much liberty as possible for all. Rousseau, writing for the coming French Revolution, welcomed Locke's defense of natural rights. But, alarmed by the way in which France suffered from the survivals of feudalism, he proposed with admirable French logic (though he was a Genevan) to bring in absolute equality at one swoop. In contrast, England had never surrendered itself wholly to feudalism and, as we have seen, its people had always preserved a modicum of liberties.

At any rate, Rousseau took issue with his master on three points. He denied that men are reasonable creatures, and insisted that they are driven by irrational impulses. Only when he becomes a citizen, when "the voice of duty takes the place of physical impulses and the right of appetite," does man become a social and moral being. This being true, the salvation offered by the state cannot be limited by any reserved liberties; the General Will of society comprehends all right and all morality, leaving nothing to the individual. Finally the citizen cannot join in political parties or other private associations because they divide his loyalties; in the showdown he cannot even have religious freedom, for a good Christian or a good Mohammedan would be a bad citizen.

After the first Napoleon the Rousseauvian stream can be traced through Hegel—and others—until it divided into two currents: one through Marx and Lenin to modern communism; the other through Treitschke and Houston Chamberlain to Mussolini's and Hitler's fascism. What they had in common was totalitarianism. France, proud of its logic, has long been torn between the two logical extremes of individualism and the General Will. As a result it vacillates between centrifugal and centripetal political forces, experimenting more or less in turn with near-anarchy and authoritarianism.

Locke had accepted the reasonableness of man, but the rise of Rousseau's General Will and the triumph of romanticism's irrational mystique undercut him sadly. Edmund Burke, Irish orator and moving force behind the English Whig Party, attacked the French Revolution. To him it seemed utterly irrational, and so he felt that he had to accept the irrational as the great human motivator; the only counter was a wise adherence to tradition. From Burke there sprang (aided by Adam Smith and Jeremy Bentham) the economic liberals of the nineteenth century and the once-powerful Liberal Party, the party of business enterprise. But also from Burke through Disraeli there sprang the Conservative Party—not a party of business nor, for that matter, of any class. It is not dogmatic (as Liberals and Labour long were) but in the Hooker tradition sees society as a seamless web and is ready to fuzz the line among theories to promote social good.

It is not necessary to trace the influence of hard-souled natural rights in the victory of laissez faire over mercantilism and in the rise of Utilitarianism. These callous views of economics bore down on the laboring class and, along with the decline of religious checks on human conduct, made the century of the Industrial Revolution (roughly 1750 to 1850) a time of pitiful oppression. Yet England being what it was, it was impossible that such a state of affairs should endure. Just when men were sinking under the weight of social, economic, and political exploitation the Wesleyan movement brought them word of a salvation that was free to all, of a God before whom laborer and noble stood naked and indistinguishable.

It was Wesley who rescued the Anglo-Saxon ideal from dry rot, breathed new life into the soul and re-created the conscience of England, armed the land against internal revolt, revived the old zeal for social service, shook together the dry bones of empire and clothed them with the flesh of industry, integrity, and honest good will. The work of Wesley, says Lecky, was "of greater importance than all the splendid victories by land and sea won under Pitt." More than that, Wesley's true memorial is the world of today just so far as it has been shaped by English ideals.

Smith's doctrine that the automatic controls of the market place ("the invisible hand") would bring about universal peace and prosperity may have been sound, but industry and finance have never given it a chance to prove itself. Smith's argument for social cooperation and restraint was flouted. Cutthroat tactics to monopolize business were used from the first, and in the struggle the laboring man suffered and the weaker manufacturers were ruined. England's bankers had financed the Industrial Revolution with profits gained in trade, squeezed from the hides of subject peoples, or from the hoards of Indian rajahs. In a mushrooming economy there was a continual demand by industrialists for loans on the security of mortgages, and the bankers learned to take shrewd advantage of this. Since money was scarce (and made scarcer by carefully loaded currency laws) interest rates were high, and frequent depressions afforded opportunities to foreclose mortgages on industrial properties. Financiers thus gained control of industry and piled up vast monopolies and cartels to institute the reign of finance-capitalism. They were, in effect, masters of the market and of the national life, and their tentacles literally clutched the resources of the earth. So much for the perfectionist dream of Adam Smith.

And yet there was progress. The rich became richer, but the poor also became less poor. Now the common people had leisure for education during childhood days and adult evenings and were able to catch a glimpse of an even better future. Such confidence had the vested interests in their hedge that they believed it impenetrable to political attack, and so they yielded step by step to the popular demand for the extension of the franchise until at last manhood suffrage was the rule throughout the English-speaking world. Their confidence was misplaced. Political democracry breached the hedge of property rights in the democratic nations by seizing one concrete liberty after another—the right to strike, accident compensation, minimum-wage laws, social security, laws against labor injunctions, graduated income taxes, and others too numerous to mention. But it was an uphill fight. Locke had not balanced natural rights with natural responsibilities, and the right to amass property led inevitably to a clash between the economic power of the few and the liberties of the many. Finally society came to see that it was possible to let the individualistic basis of law prevail to the point where the predatory individual could legally injure society itself; the result was the revival of Hooker's traditional view of the unity of society and the supremacy of its claims.

Natural rights have been used chiefly as an excuse for some action whose legality is troublesome to defend or doubtful. When it has come to an acutal defense of their rights, the English-speaking peoples have used their traditional method of evolution by conflict between the new and the old and the seizure of concrete liberties. Natural rights passed long ago as a philosophically tenable doctrine, but English-speaking people still cling to them as a rather vague goal, a sort of expression—a hypostasis—of desire. At that they have their uses, because in theory they bring us closer to the goal of respect for human dignity. A race wedded only to concrete liberties will have difficulty in acknowledging the right to respect of anyone who has not yet "earned" it, the Negro, for example; but if it believes in natural rights, such acknowledgment is a powerful psychological reinforcement to the Negro's own struggle to attain equality.

Chapter 2
Errand into the Wilderness

Proem

When the English undertook to plant colonies in America, they commenced—
whatever they ended with—not with propositions about the rights of man or with the
gospel of wealth, but with absolute certainties concerning the providence of God.

(Perry Miller)[1]

*   *   *

There was a wind over England, and it blew,
(Have you heard the news of Virginia?)
A west wind blowing, the wind of a western star,
To gather men's lives like pollen and cast them forth,
Blowing in hedge and highway and seaport town,
Whirling dead leaf and living, but always blowing,
A salt wind, a sea wind, a wind from the world's end,
From the coasts that have new, wild names, from the huge unknown.

(Stephen Vincent Benét)[2]

---

[1]Perry Miller, *Errand into the Wilderness* (Cambridge, Mass.: Harvard University Press, 1956), p. 115.

[2]Stephen Vincent Benét, *Western Star* (New York: Farrar and Rinehart, 1943), p. 17.

Considering so good a Countrey, so bad people, having little of Humanitie but shape, ignorant of Civilitie, of Arts, of Religion; more brutish then the beasts they hunt, more wild and unmanly then that unmanned wild Countrey, which they range rather then inhabite; captivated also to Satans tyranny in foolish pieties, mad impieties, wicked idlenesse, busie and bloudy wickednesse: hence have wee fit objects of zeale and pitie, to deliver from the power of darknesse. . . . And let men know that hee which converteth a sinner from the error of his way, shall save a soule from death, and shall hide a multitude of sinnes. . . . Thus shall wee at once overcome both Men and Devills, and espouse Virginia to one husband, presenting her as a chast Virgin to Christ. If the eye of Adventurers were thus single, how soone and all the body should be light? But the loving our selves more then God, hath detained so great blessings from us to Virginia, and from Virginia to us. Godlinesse hath the promises of this life, and that which is to come. And if wee be carefull to doe Gods will, he will be ready to doe ours.

All the rich endowments of Virginia, her Virgin-portion from the creation nothing lessened, are wages for all this worke: God in wisedome having enriched the Savage Countries, that those riches might be attractives for Christian suters, which there may sowe spirituals and reape temporals.

(Purchas His Pilgrims)[3]

*   *   *

The whole earth is the Lord's garden, and he hath given it to the sons of Adam to be tilled and improved by them. Why then should we stand starving here for the places of habitation, (many men spending as much labor and cost to recover or keep sometimes an acre or two of lands as would procure him many hundreds of acres, as good or better, in another place,) and in the mean time suffer whole countries, as profitable for the use of man, to lie waste without any improvement.

(John Winthrop, 1629)[4]

---

[3]*Purchas His Pilgrims*, 20 volumes (1906), 19:231-32.

[4]From R. C. Winthrop, *Life and Letters of John Winthrop*, two volumes (Boston: Little, Brown, 1869).

"Virginea Britannia"

Though the phrase "errand into the wilderness" was first used about 1670, probably by the Reverend Samuel Danforth, the concept that the Puritan immigrants were founding a holy city was imbedded in their consciousness. That is not all: Catholic Maryland, utopian Pennsylvania, philanthropic Georgia, and Episcopalian Virginia all were based on some form of a holy errand into the wilderness.

To understand this one must understand the times. The first settlers of America, as Perry Miller points out, inhabited "a mental universe in which religion was the main ingredient in human motive." Politics and religion, state and church, were one in seeking first the glory of God and the salvation of humanity. God's will was looked upon as the "first cause" and the "second cause" lay in the natural phenomena and human actions through which God worked, as also the machinations of a devil who was as real to Englishmen as he was to Job and who was permitted by God to test the faith and endurance of Christians. Thus wars, pestilences, and earthquakes were divine retributions for human wickedness. Actually Anglicans and Puritans agreed on so many points of theology that the modern reader may wonder why they quarreled. The answer, of course, is that they differed on special points which to them seemed so vital that they were worth fighting for.

Europeans believed with all their hearts in the dogmas of natural depravity and in Christ's atonement. Indeed, despite the warnings of the clergy that true repentance must be followed by changed conduct there was an all too frequent pattern of accepting faith in the dogmas as sufficient to assure salvation; the sinner was therefore free to go on sinning. This separation of faith from works was the core of the heresy called Antinomianism, and it must be acknowledged that it is still rampant in the Christian world, especially among unthinking fundamentalists. Whether this separation of faith and works is hypocritical or sincere is best left until the Day of Judgment.

It cannot be denied that among the reasons given for the settlement of America there were frequent echoes of assurance that there was cent percent to be gained on the investment. Still, it would be unfair to assert that the settlers and investors were always hypocritical in expressing their desire to glorify God by converting the heathen and expanding His kingdom. In a very real sense Christians believed that, since God moved in many mysterious ways, whatever came to pass inevitably was for the best. No doubt many repined when hardship overtook them, when they lost their investments, or saw their homes go up in flames and their families fall beneath the tomahawks of the savages. To grieve was only natural, but to "curse God and die" was a sin in a world in which worldly ties and worldly goods ran second to the inscrutable will of Providence.

Take Virginia as the first example of the belief that settlers in America were engaged in carrying out the will of God—an errand into the wilderness intended to fulfill God's grand design for humanity. From the outset the province was proclaimed to be a holy experiment. The literature about Virginia, whether written by Virginians or English stay-at-homes, breathes the same piety and advocates much the same standards of conduct as we find in New England. Over and over we find Englishmen appropriating to themselves the promises made to Abraham by God. An example is seen in the sermon titled "Virginea Britannia" preached in 1609 by William Symonds before a company of "Adventurers and Planters" about to set sail for Virginia. There was also the intimation that the natives could easily be subdued.

> For the Lord has said unto Abram, get thee out of thy Countrey, and from thy Kindred, and from thy father's house, unto the land that I will shew thee. And I will make thee a great nation, and will blesse thee, and make thy name great, and thou shalt be a blessing. I will blesse them also that blesse thee, and curse them that curse thee, and in thee shall all the families of the earth be blessed. . . .
>
> The land, by the constant report of all that have seene it, is a good land, with the fruitfulnesse whereof, and pleasure of the Climate, the plentie of Fish and Fowle, England, Our Mistresse, cannot compare, no not when she is in her greatest pride. . . . As for the opportunitie of the place, I leave it to the grave Polititian: and for the Commodities, let the industrious Merchant speake: but for food and raiment, here is inough to be had for the labour of mastring and subduing the soile.
>
> The natives were not like "the sonnes of Anak." There are but poore Arbors for Castles, base and homely sheds for walled townes. A Mat is their strongest Port cullis [door], a naked breast their Target [shield] of best proofe: an arrow of reede, on which is no iron, their most fearfull weapon of offense, heere is no feare of nine hundred iron charets [chariots]. Their

God is [the devil] the enemie of mankind that seeketh whom
he may devoure.

Let us be cheerfull to goe to the place that God will shew us
to possesse in peace and plentie, a Land more like the garden
of Eden: which the Lord planted, than any part else of all the
earth.[5]

In 1625, five years before John Winthrop came to Massachusetts Bay,
Samuel Purchas was explaining God's design in opening up the New
World to Christians. In doing this he gave a quick sketch of world history,
unfolding God's grand plan by which mankind could regain the grace and
dignity lost by Adam's fall. The Christian's task was to convert the
savages and subdue the wilderness and in doing this there would ensue a
material reward. But let the Christian beware. If the savages were abused
and profits were set ahead of the divine mission then the settlers would
suffer from God's wrath; the late Indian massacres in Virginia were but a
foretaste of more that could come—and did.

On the day of the first landing the founders of Jamestown set up an
old sail as an awning, nailed a board between two trees for an altar, and
sat upon fallen logs while the chaplain conducted services. Granted that
the settlers were a lazy and vicious crew, drawn from the scum of London,
yet religion must have been something more than the outward
observance of ritual when in the midst of the "starving time" the gaunt
inhabitants of Jamestown turned out on Sundays to hear sermons. Every
governor initiated his term by attending divine service. When the House
of Burgesses first convened in 1619 it opened its proceedings with prayer
and then passed laws providing for compulsory church attendance;
punishing idleness, gaming, drunkenness, and whoring; and fining those
wearing apparel beyond their stations. Eventually the laws provided for
Sabbath observances even more rigid than those of New England, and
everyone was taxed for the support of religion. Violators of moral law
who did not reform were excommunicated and their goods confiscated.

It is all very well to point out that the imposition of good morals in
Virginia was, at least in part, designed to curry public favor and attract
investors and settlers. Yet the fact remains that the policy only

---

[5]From the excerpt in Alexander Brown, *Genesis of the United States*, two volumes
(1890), 2:289.

exemplified the spirit of the times—hence the almost startling resemblance between the moral codes of Virginia and New England. Says Perry Miller:

> No nation of Europe had yet divided the state from the church; no government had yet imagined that religion could be left to the individual conscience. Society, economics, and the will of God were one and the same, and the ultimate authority in human relations was the ethic of Christendom. All the transactions of this world held their rank in the hierarchical structure, with salvation, to which all other activities ministered, at the apex.[6]

When King James granted the Charter of 1606 to the Virginia Company he inserted in it a statement of his own to propagate the "Christian religion to such people as yet live in darkness and miserable ignorance of the true knowledge and worship of God." When Captain John Smith's account of the founding of Jamestown reached London in 1608 it was printed with a preface asserting that the worst was over: there remained only the honorable end of glorifying God "to the erecting of true religion among Infidels, to the overthrow of superstition and idolatry, to the winning of many thousands of wandering sheep into Christ's fold, who now, and till now, have strayed in the unknown paths of paganism, idolatry, and superstition."

True, the Spanish ambassador observed sourly that the Virginia merchants "have actually made the ministers in their sermons dwell upon the importance of filling the world with their religion"— presumably as a cover for their economic enterprise. John Smith made the same point when he jeered at the absurd instructions issued to the settlers by the Company. "We did admire," he wrote, "how it was possible such wise men could so torment themselves and us with such strange absurdities and impossibilities: making religion their color, when all their aim was nothing but present profit."

The Virginia Company's directors had made grandiose plans and their clerical propagandists had prated about colonization as a means of carrying out God's great design for the salvation of the New World.

---

[6]Miller, *Errand into the Wilderness*, p. 105.

Nevertheless, by 1622 the quarrels among the directors, the viciousness of the settlers, the Indian massacres, and perhaps above all the profits to be made by growing tobacco had resulted in the collapse of the Company. Francis Bacon, looking at the whole enterprise objectively, brushed aside the high-sounding claims about God's designs and suggested that greater care be taken in suiting plans to the actual products of the soil.

The Virginia Company failed at least partly because it did not take the advice of the clear-minded Francis Bacon. The result was that the aristocratic leaders of Virginia were eventually displaced by a group of men who by birth had no claim to leadership but were tough-minded and unscrupulous enough to survive under American conditions. Their rise was signalized in the plantation colonies by armed revolts against the old regimes and by other forms of revolutions in the North.

These experiences seemed to contradict the current beliefs about God's providence working through men. But, as we shall see, the Puritans were to base yet another essay on the concept when they settled Massachusetts Bay. Meanwhile the London preachers omitted Virginia from their prayers "finding the action to grow either odious or contemptible in men's minds." In Virginia itself men may or may not have continued in the old faith, but at least by their actions they showed— as Perry Miller puts it—that Virginia was changed from a holy experiment to a commercial plantation. "Even before Massachusetts Bay was settled... Virginia had already gone through the cycle of exploration, religious dedication, disillusionment, and then reconciliation to a world in which making a living was the ultimate reality."[7]

The fate of Virginia foreshadowed the English Civil War of the 1640's in which two absolutes fought each other to a standstill in defence of differing interpretation of the role of Church and State, with a result that was basically abhorrent to both—Church and State separated for all practical purposes, and a religious tolerance based in the last analysis on indifference.

In the long run so little was done in Virginia to convert the Indians that it was lost sight of in the press of other matters, especially the craze for tobacco culture. Moreover Virginia's piety faded after the first few decades, and attempts to foster the religious life of the settlers received

---

[7]Miller, *Errand into the Wilderness*, p. 139.

little encouragement even in England until the Society for the Propagation of the Gospel in Foreign Parts, founded in 1701, undertook to missionize among Indians, Negroes, and backwoodsmen on behalf of the Church of England.

About 1690 James Blair, head of the Anglican commission in Virginia, got a royal charter to found William and Mary College, and the sovereigns ordered Attorney-General Seymour to see to the financing. That official protested. England was engaged in war, and the money was needed for other and better purposes than training students of divinity.

"The people of Virginia," retorted Mr. Blair, "have souls to be saved as well as the people of England!"

"Souls!" exclaimed Seymour, "damn your souls! Make tobacco!"

Though the Church of England was established in the Southern colonies it did not flourish in any spiritual sense, and the back country was given over to a welter of sects. And yet it would be wrong to hold that Virginia and its neighbors consciously violated what they took to be the will of God. The modification that took the place of the pristine sense of mission was the concept of a divinely structured patriarchal society, handed down from the Middle Ages and interpreted by Sir Robert Filmer in his *Patriarcha*. This patriarchal concept was suited both to a plantation system based on slavery and to white, non-slaveholding, rural dwellers, and was in time to spread across the South and become one of the standards around which the Confederacy rallied its forces.

New England's Polity

While the sense of mission was faltering in Virginia it was also weakening—or at least changing form—in New England. That area had been peopled by representatives of several parts of English society. Plymouth was dominated by Separatists who had left England because they did not choose to adhere to the Anglican communion. On the other hand, the chief impetus for the founding of Massachusetts and Connecticut came from Puritans who were quite willing to remain in the Church of England but regarded it as their duty to reform it.

In time as England became more tolerant of disparate religious opinions the Bay Puritans divided between those advocating the Presbyterian form of church government and those who preferred to become Separatists. Meanwhile there had been an influx of Quakers, Baptists, Antinomians, and other more or less Puritanical sects. They were not welcome, and when they persisted in proselyting they were persecuted so severely that they were forced to seek refuge in Rhode Island, the province of the "otherwise-minded." This discloses that in our enchantment with the ideal of democracy we have seized on wisps of fact and fancy and odd sayings taken out of context to assert the myth that the American colonies were settled to ensure political and religious liberty. Doubtless some of the colonizers did have this aim, but in by far the most cases they refused liberty to others. The shining exceptions were the Quaker colonies; there were flaws even in the liberties of both Rhode Island and Maryland.

Among strict Puritans admission to the church followed only on the definite personal experience of regeneration which was the witness that the person was accepted by God into salvation—that is, had become a "visible saint." Even before the migration to America Puritan divines (perhaps following various Reformed writers) had eroded Calvin's doctrine that God in his inscrutable wisdom had predestined every man to salvation or damnation regardless of what might seem to be his merits. By the so-called "federal theory" the Puritans held that Adam had lived under a "covenant of works" that blessed him so long as he was obedient. "With Adam's fall, we sinned all"—as the Puritan doggerel had it—but now men lived under a "covenant of grace" that gave the same blessings to all who believed in Christ, the "federal" head of the Church.

God worked through "second causes" (mentioned above) but He used men's motives—the profit motive, for example—in carrying the gospel to America. He also drew men to His will and persuaded them to seek salvation by "means"—prayers, sermons, the reading of the Bible. "Means" thus, among some Protestants, took the place of the Catholic sacraments except for baptism and communion. Neither Puritans nor Episcopalians hesitated to set in motion the "second causes" that would favor themselves. Thus Roundheads and Cavaliers could fight in the full conviction that they were carrying out God's intentions. Defeat was no disproof; God was merely testing their faith and endurance.

John Winthrop, a learned and pious London lawyer, was chosen by the Massachusetts Bay Company as their governor, and in 1630 he led a thousand immigrants to the new colony. In a lay sermon delivered aboard the flagship *Arbella* he set forth the reasons for the venture. There were the usual ones offered: to relieve England's over-population, to afford a refuge for the oppressed, and to expand the kingdom of Christ. He then went on to define some of the tenets to which the colony must adhere.

God, he asserted, had organized men in a social hierarchy so that "some must be rich, some poor, some high and eminent in power and dignity, others mean and in subjection." The settlers had entered into a covenant with the Almighty and been assured of His blessing in seeking out a place of cohabitation under a "due form of government both civil and ecclesiastical." It was likely, he reminded his hearers, that God had some great work in hand for them.

> We shall be as a city set upon a hill; the eyes of all people are upon us, so that if we shall deal falsely with our God in this work we have undertaken and so cause Him to withdraw His present help from us, we shall be made a story and a by-word through the world. We shall open the mouths of enemies to speak evil of the ways of God and all professors for God's sake. We shall shame the faces of many of God's worthy servants and cause their prayers to be turned into curses upon us till we be consumed out of the good land whither we are going.[8]

Winthrop was so far from being a lone voice crying in the wilderness that the civil and religious establishments of Massachusetts Bay agreed with him. State and Church were separate in the Bay Colony, but the State could and did join in persecuting heresy. Baptists were scourged and Quakers hanged. Even the eminent Roger Williams escaped arrest only by flight. John Cotton, the Puritan pope of Massachusetts Bay, aligned himself with Torquemada and Lenin when he declared that "It is wicked for falsehood to persecute truth, but it is the sacred duty of truth to persecute falsehood."

New England's divines were in no doubt as to the nature of the great work set before them. They were not fleeing in cowardly fashion from their duties at home. Quite the contrary. The vision of St. Augustine was a continual inspiration to them. If the City of God could be erected in New England the time would surely come when Old England would rouse from its spiritual slumber and seek to follow the holy example; and then would follow Europe. The concept was incredibly arrogant; yet in secularized form it was to become the vaunt of the United States.

When Charles I granted the charter of Massachusetts Bay Company giving absolute powers to the Company, he provided only that its actions

---

[8]*Life and Letters of John Winthrop*, 1:309-11.

be consistent with the laws of England. Charles probably did not look on the charter as a covenant among the grantees. When the colonizers led by Winthrop took the charter to Massachusetts to get it out of the king's reach they fully intended to set up a Bible commonwealth; the charter was simply the symbol—perhaps not even the vehicle—of the covenant among them. Government by terms of the charter was in the hands of the General Court composed of the dozen or so stockholders of the Company called "freemen." The Court elected the governor and deputy-governor, and eighteen assistants. Over a hundred freemen were soon admitted to the Company.

When Winthrop and his colleagues found that the charter did not meet their ideals of government for a City of God they quietly performed some actions at their own discretion, for obviously the law of God did not always agree with the law of England. The freemen resented these actions, and upon demanding a view of the charter found that they were entitled to share in the making of laws. Presently they compromised by sending deputies from each town to perform that function and eventually these deputies sat apart from the assistants. Even then the magistrates (the assistants) were able to interpret the laws to suit themselves until in 1641 they were dragooned into approving a Body of Liberties.

It has been denied that Massachusetts Bay was a theocracy, and in the strictest sense that is correct. Clergymen could not hold public office, but their synods were sometimes convened at the same time as the General Court and could be consulted on knotty problems. When the deputies and the magistrates disagreed the two sides courted the ministry and thus added to their weight in provincial affairs. As it was the ministers agreed with the deputies in wishing to limit the authority of the magistrates.

The Body of Liberties of 1641 confirmed the moral laws as understood by Puritans but went further and confirmed many of the traditional rights of Englishmen such as trial by jury, freehold tenure of land, and freedom from monopolies and capricious fines and taxes. Just as important the Body of Liberties confirmed the emerging system of local government by towns (townships) with decisions made and ordinances passed in town meetings. The next year Massachusetts adopted the first system of compulsory public education.

It may be that previous descriptions of the beliefs and church polities held by the various categories of Puritans have given an impression of rigidity. Actually there was considerable fluidity and change among them.

Thus John Cotton was attracted by the teachings of Anne Hutchinson when she appeared in Boston in 1634. In explaining the Covenant of Grace she emphasized the soul's direct communion with the Holy Spirit; with the Holy Spirit directing the individual's life the person became helpless, and so was not really responsible for his conduct.

This was a direct contradiction of the official dogma that all truth came from the Bible and laid her open to the charge that learning could be spurned and reason be swayed by emotion. Even worse was her accusation that the colony's clergy were living under a "covenant of works"— that is depending on their works for salvation. Moreover her teachings were close to the heresy of Antinomianism—that is, once saved by faith, conduct was no clue to the person's state of grace. As a consequence she was expelled from Massachusetts Bay and went eventually to New Netherland where in 1643 she perished in an Indian massacre. John Cotton saved himself from exile by hedging sufficiently to satisfy the authorities. In the end the Hutchinson controversy seems to have furnished the wedge for opening New England to the Arminian doctrine that salvation is open to all—not merely to those selected by divine favor.

Another case of opposition to official doctrines is offered by Roger Williams, a clergyman who was an avowed Separatist, and who appeared in Boston in 1631. Williams was so charismatic and sweet-tempered that he was loved even by his doctrinal enemies, including Winthrop. So great was his God-intoxication that he carried his beliefs to the extreme of fanaticism. For example he not only refused to regard the Church of England as a church because it admitted unregenerate persons to communion; even worse, he refused to worship with the New Englanders because they did not separate themselves from the Church of England. Moreover he asserted that civil magistrates had no authority over religious affairs; they could not even enforce Sabbath observance. Then to make it worse he denounced the charter of the Massachusetts Bay Company on the ground that the king had no right to give away the land of the Indians.

Williams failed to find a comfortable niche in either Separatist Plymouth or in Massachusetts though he did become minister of the church in Salem in the latter colony. Finally his criticisms had so multiplied that he was arraigned before the General Court in Boston and lost the support of the Salem church. In the end he escaped arrest and deportation to England only by fleeing to Narragansett Bay (1636) where he settled at Providence and became one of the founders of Rhode Island.

There has been controversy over the degree of influence that Williams has exercised in the growth of American institutions. To his contemporaries he seemed to be both feckless and reckless in his foolish absurdities and disregard for realities; at the most charitable estimate he was an eccentric torn between intransigence and magnanimity. The charges were certainly valid, and Cotton Mather had some justification for comparing him to a Dutch windmill. During a long life Williams veered from time to time. From the Separatists he turned to the Baptists and then became simply a "seeker" after truth. His fault was that he demanded perfection; the City of God on earth—that or nothing. His glory was that he objected to civil control of religion and would have put power into the hands of the people—hence his efforts to implant religious freedom in Rhode Island.

Actually he was a Calvinist, finding his guide in the Scriptures, and denying the inner light of Anne Hutchinson and the Quakers. If he can in any way be called the father of American democracy it was only in a back-handed way and because of a reputation that was at least in part ill-founded. As it was, he regarded freedom as unimportant in itself save as it opened the way to Christian perfection. Even this idea he seemingly vitiated when he proclaimed that the Church itself must be subject to the changeable pleasure of the people even in matters of heavenly and spiritual nature.

In 1636 the Reverend Thomas Hooker led his congregation from Newtown (Cambridge) near Boston, to the wilds of Connecticut. He probably was quite unaware that the movement would later be regarded as a democratic secession from theocratic Massachusetts. Actually, it seems to have been prompted by personal rivalries, desire for more land, and perhaps adherence to a looser interpretation of the right of a congregation to self government than Massachusetts permitted. At any rate, both before and after his removal Hooker frequently took the side of Bay Colony orthodoxy in its various disputes with dissenters, and seems to have repudiated notions of religious tolerance.

On the other hand the people of Connecticut elected the magistrates and defined their powers "according to the blessed will and law of God." The frame of government was set forth in the Fundamental Orders of Connecticut (1639), the first popularly written constitution; it was essentially a confirmation of existing customs and a covenant among the people. The privilege of the vote was not confined to church members as in Massachusetts. The notes of Hooker's famous election sermon preached in 1638 certainly appear to champion democracy, but it should be noted that Connecticut did not have to deal (at the time) with dissenters and ungodly characters. Later on those convicted of crimes and scandalous offenses were deprived of the vote. As a matter of fact penalties for scandals and crimes were more severe than in Massachusetts.

God's Controversy with New England

There is no intention here to delve more deeply into New England's theology or the details of ecclesiastical polity. The Puritan leaders were humanists after the fashion of Petrus Ramus, and so denied that God was entirely capricious and unpredictable. Man could use his reason to get some view of the "serene order" of the universe behind the harshness of Calvin's *Institutes*. They abhorred anti-intellectualism, and deplored an unlearned clergy as likely to lead the commonalty on emotional binges. They did not believe in freedom of enterprise; they regulated business by prohibiting monopolies, setting just prices, and limiting profits. Psychologically they partook of the sane tense earnestness and tough-mindedness as the English Puritans described in the previous chapter, but also of a certain joyousness; recall again Cromwell dancing on the green.

The traditional view of the Puritan as invariably narrow and harsh was controverted by Perry Miller over the decades from 1930 to 1960, and his is largely the view taken here. Recently there has arisen a school that attacks his conclusions on the ground that he relied almost altogether on the provincial records and the writings of the Puritan leaders, chiefly clergymen. One critic goes so far as to say that the Puritan is a stereotype created by Perry Miller.

More temperate critics point out that the system of established churches never took deep root in Massachusetts; that ministerial synods had no control; that conformity was enforced by the state, not the church; that there was no agreement among the congregations on dogma; that the authority of the local clergymen was flouted; that the congregations in general went their own way; and that the churches, far from imposing conformity; went so far as to admit Baptists, Quakers, and Antinomians to the communion table. In effect, the local congregations had become Separatist long before William and Mary's Charter of 1691 ended the tenuous connection between the New England churches and the Church of England. These conclusions are drawn in large part from town records and undoubtedly have considerable validity. Anyhow it was probably these conditions that led to the formulation in 1648 by the clerical synod of the Cambridge Platform which adopted the Westminster Confession and set forth rules for the organization and procedure of the churches and their relations with the state.

Did the majority of the commonalty ever agree with the strict Puritanism of the two Johns—Winthrop and Cotton—the Moses and Aaron of the New England City of God? It is not at all likely. The Puritan movement itself was shot through with dissent—not merely Levellers, Fifth Monarchy men, Diggers, Seekers, Separatists, and Presbyterians, but also the allied Baptists and Quakers; doubtless also there came many Episcopalians and Arminians. Other thousands came solely to acquire land or to ply their crafts—as the fishermen of the Marblehead frankly admitted that they had come not to save souls but to catch fish.

New England's towns were on the frontier and they often showed the typical characteristics of frontier individualism; and that was certainly also a manifestation of English individualism. From the very first there was complaint of the way that "lawless" elements ran off to "the woods," and it is probable that by the time of King Philip's War (1676) the frontier type was well developed. Such men were doubtless little concerned with what Edmund S. Morgan has called the Puritan dilemma—how to live in the world and still remain pure.

At the first when there was probably a preponderance of church members there was doubtless agreement on the nature and aims of the errand into the wilderness. Groups met regularly to discuss points of theology, as was shown by the widespread acceptance of Anne Hutchinson's Antinomianism which came close to displacing the official Calvinism. The ministers usually found ready ears for their assertions that calamities had befallen the colonists as punishments for their sins, and the people joined in days of humiliation, fasting, and prayer in an effort to regain divine favor.

In later years the procedure was reversed as the ministers began to demand that the people repent of their sins before the calamities were visited upon them. With the growth of prosperity there had sprung up— said the accusers— a spirit of apathy, marked by a lessening of spiritual strivings, a reliance on morality rather than saving grace, and a careless and easeful contentment. There was a rising tendency to buy cheap and sell dear and to grind the faces of the poor, and in their search for riches the people were demanding more land on the excuse that they needed elbow room. Allied (it was said) to all this because it was one cause, was the low state of learning—indeed, its neglect.

If the jeremiads portrayed the true state of society then New England was in a bad way. The Puritan dilemma seemed unresolvable. To live in the world meant to follow its pursuits, to amass wealth through thrift, industry, and shrewd trading. On the other hand these pursuits inevitably bred the sins of which the ministers complained. Puritanism—at least that of the clergy—took on a gloominess quite foreign to the earlier generations, while an attempt was made to tighten the loose Congregational organization of the churches by the Presbyterian form of government.

Leaders in this endeavor were Richard Mather and his son, Cotton Mather, and the latter became the high priest of the new ascendance of doom and gloom. Unfortunately historians of the 1890's confused the two generations and presented the latter as typical of all Puritans and so undermined the respect hitherto held for the founders of New England. It remained for Perry Miller and Samuel Eliot Morison and their successors to set the record straight.

In the end the ministry had to yield to facts. Their adoption of the Halfway Covenant in 1662 accepted into church membership the children of church members even though they gave no evidence of the deep emotional experience of regeneration that marked them as "visible saints." There were other discouragements. Winthrop and his colleagues had high hopes of the Parliamentary Revolution of the 1640's, so what must have been their despair when they saw Cromwell ignoring their holy example and welcoming religious toleration and edging toward a complete separation of Church and State not merely in name but in fact. More than this a committee of English Independent clergymen wrote to Massachusetts censuring it for its religious persecutions. No wonder that Massachusetts Bay refused to obey Cromwell's Parliament!

There now followed a half century or more of agonizing over the failure of the errand into the wilderness and over the problem of whether or not to catch up with the times. William Stoughton consoled himself in 1668 by proclaiming that "God had sifted a whole nation, that He might send choice grain into the wilderness." Nevertheless he was whistling in the dark. The stalwart founders had died or become senile, and their successors were, he complained, given to frustrating and deceiving the Lord's expectations; perhaps he saw himself as carrying on with the errand when he presided with such severity over the Salem witchcraft trials. Certainly he saw crop failures, epidemics, and King Philip's War as just punishments for causing the "workings of God's salvation to cease." This was the period of what Michael Wigglesworth called "God's controversy with New England" (1662) because it had broken the covenant the founders had made with God to erect a holy commonwealth ruled by "visible saints." This was the time when Samuel Danforth preached his sermon entitled *A Brief Recognition of New England's Errand into the Wilderness* (1670) in which he accused the people not only of failing themselves but the God who had sent them on the errand.

The truth was that the Jeremiahs of New England had been left behind by history. Nevertheless the Puritans of Old and New England had made their contributions to modern history. The American evolution toward democracy was an apt illustration of St. Augustine's philosophy of history, though the good saint might have doubted that it was the unfolding of God's purpose. Alan Simpson lists a number of ways in which the Puritan movement influenced the future. Stripped of detail, the Puritans' distrust of arbitrary power helped promote our allegiance to limited government; their self-reliance contributed to self-government; their elite of "visible saints" cut across class boundaries; they contributed profoundly to education—Massachusetts Bay was the first English-speaking government to make elementary education the business of the state; and they inculcated morality with its "habits of honesty, sobriety, responsibility, and hard work."[9]

Finally the imprint left on the religious ideals of the English-speaking nations was profound, though hardly what John Winthrop would have favored. This refers to the Puritan's insistence on searching the Scriptures for himself, with the result that sects multiplied to the extent that no one of them could dominate, thus leading to the discovery that they could enjoy liberty only if they tolerated others. To paraphrase

---

[9]Alan Simpson, *Puritanism in Old and New England* (Chicago: University of Chicago Press, 1955), pp. 99-114.

Voltaire's famous quip: one religion, despotism; two religions, civil war; thirty religions, toleration, peace and happiness. Of course Voltaire exaggerated a little, for the narrow conservatism and religious bigotry of the Bible Belt are the creation of forces that emerged from the decaying corpse of Puritanism.

Chapter 3
Colonial Growing Pains

Proem

Toward the end of the seventeenth century, Isaac Newton destroyed the medieval view of natural phenomena as divinely inspired when he showed the connection between cause and effect. Thus he prepared the way for the Enlightenment with its belief in a transcendent God, creator of the world and final judge of men, who had implemented a divine plan as revealed in nature. But while this plan unfolded the deity had left the universe to run itself like a perpetual motion clock. The way was now cleared for the defense of the American Revolution as an assertion of natural rights against a tyrannical king. Moreover it was now possible to shear the religious meaning from the errand into the wilderness to build a holy city, and reinterpret it in secular and political terms. Winthrop's City of God could now become the City of Man. It did not deny God: it merely engraved over its portals Benjamin Franklin's motto: "What is serving God? 'Tis doing good to man."

* * *

What is an American? The American is a new man, who acts upon new principles; he must therefore entertain new ideas, and form new opinions. . . . Here individuals of all nations are melted into a new race of men, whose labours and posterity will one day cause great changes in the world. . . . An American when he first arrives . . . no sooner breathes our air than he forms new schemes, and embarks in designs he never would have thought of in his own country. . . . He begins to feel the effects of a sort of resurrection; hitherto he had not lived, but simply vegetated; he now feels himself a man, because he is treated as such; the laws of his own country had overlooked him in his insignificancy; the laws of this cover him with their mantle. Judge what an alteration there must arise in the mind and thoughts of this man; he begins to forget his former servitude and dependence, his heart involuntarily swells and glows; this first swell inspires him with those new thoughts which constitute an American.

(Hector St. John de Crévecouer)[1]

* * *

To America, one schoolmaster is worth a dozen poets, and the invention of a machine or the improvement of an implement is of more importance than a masterpiece of Raphael. . . . Nothing is good or beautiful but in the measure that it is useful: yet all things have a utility under particular circumstances. Thus poetry, painting, music (and the stage as their embodiment) are all necessary and proper gratifications of a refined state of society but objectionable at an earlier period, since their cultivation would make a taste for their enjoyment precede its means.

(Benjamin Franklin)

The Racial Complex

Between 1650 and 1750 American society evolved into something quite different from what had been envisioned by the founders. Not only had it become secularized to a large extent but it was developing a merchant economy devoted to trade, especially in timber and agricultural products and in semi-finished articles such as bar iron, and so was adopting the ideology of capitalism.

Democracy did not spring up suddenly; even when it appeared under Quaker auspices in Pennsylvania and West New Jersey the vote was confined mostly to freeholders. It is difficult to see how democracy as we understand it could have developed without the existence of the vast tracts of land and the enormous natural resources that lay ready to the axes and plows of the colonists. For the first time in history democracy had a fighting chance to win in the age-old battle with authoritarianism.

---

[1]Hector St. John de Crèvecoeur, *Letters from an American Farmer* (1782).

The riches of North America were breeding a society in which abundance took the place of scarcity; for the first time privilege could not snatch all the economic power for itself and tread down the common man. The end of government and industry, Americans were learning to insist, was to serve the whole community, not merely the elite. They were demanding that cultural and material resources should no longer be the exclusive property of a chosen few but must become of service to all.

Another factor in the evolution of American society was mentioned in the preceding chapter. The founding gentry believed that they combined in themselves a natural right to political, social, and economic leadership. As it was, those who could not adapt to American conditions, were displaced by a group of men who had no claim to rule by birth but who were tough-minded and unscrupulous enough to survive and seize wealth and authority. Unlike their predecessors they trusted not in God but in their own power and shrewdness. In time their sons were to seek with some success to combine political, social, and economic leadership, but they no longer held it by divine right. Not only were their controls vitiated by the new skepticism brought in by deism and the collapse of religious unity, but a newer immigration had drastically altered whatever homogeneity there had been among the first comers.

Until almost 1700 the English colonies were overwhelmingly English (and to a certain extent Welsh) despite some disparate elements. The colonies were settled in the first instance by men and women who sought economic betterment, adventure, and refuge from oppression. But they did not regard themselves solely as settlers and planters in the New World; they were Englishmen who proposed to retain all the concrete liberties of Englishmen in the new realm which some of them regarded as a prospective City of God. During the seventeenth century England was torn by civil tumult and during the succeeding decades the British Government, in its endeavor to let nature take its course, deliberately "let sleeping principles lie." The result was that a century and a half of what has been happily termed "salutary neglect" enabled the colonists to succeed in their object, so that long before the American Revolution the English view of man and his place in the universe was as firmly planted in America as it was in England.

The purely English contributions to the American background are evident from the examination we have made of the history of English thought and institutions. One side of this, the Merrie England side if we may call it that, was most evident in the Southern colonies where aristocratic and patriarchal institutions and the Anglican Church united to free life of the worst of the Puritan inhibitions and even to a certain extent spread worldly attitudes down through the poor-white class. The stronghold of Puritanism, of course, was New England, but Puritanism, under the guise of numerous dissenting sects, notably Presbyterians, Quakers, Baptists, and pietists, was strong in the middle colonies, and ran down the frontier line to the German and Scotch-Irish of the Carolinas and Georgia. Thus, though New England was the only region that could boast of strictly Puritan commonwealths, Puritanism entered more or less into the background of all the colonies.

The United States has been called an Anglo-Saxon nation, and also, because of its mixture of European bloods, the first truly European nation. Both claims are true, and yet they do not contain all the truth. For one thing, perhaps a fifth of the American population is largely non-European in blood—Negro, Indian, Mexican, Semitic, and Oriental. Still, in this curious mixture there has grown up a spirit which is probably best called Neo-Anglo-Saxon. The spirit, brought over by the early English settlers, has been altered by environmental and historical forces, not the least of which has been furnished by interplay among the peoples and races who contributed to the American populace.

The national and racial composition of the population of all the colonies underwent a profound change during the eighteenth century. The Swedes of the Delaware seem to have had little influence beyond their introduction of log architecture. The Dutch, also, after their heyday were readily assimilated and today are remembered chiefly by a faint historical and architectural aroma, by the popularity of Santa Claus, and by a succession of "vans" in New York's social register. French Huguenots came to all the colonies after Louis XIV revoked the Edict of Nantes, which had protected Calvinism in France. They brought with them a great variety of manufacturing and mercantile skills, an aura of much-needed culture, and an undying hatred of France. Fewer in number were Spanish and Portuguese Jews, but from the very first they were prominent in the mercantile pursuits and in the benevolences for which Jews are noted. They were not numerous enough to rouse more than a modicum of jealousy. Their principal center was Newport.

The only early immigrants from the European continent who have managed to avoid being absorbed into the mass of the American people have been the so-called Pennsylvania Dutch. These people are descended largely from Rhineland and other Germans whom William Penn had induced to come to his province by liberal offers of land, and who by the time of the Revolution occupied a broad arc of territory between Philadelphia and the mountains. The Pennsylvania Dutch fled not only from religious persecution, but from economic oppression and the ravages of armies. But what has given some of them the will to preserve their identity even into our own century has been their insistence on remaining separate from the world.

The dominance of the Roman Catholic Church in medieval Europe had from time to time been challenged by heretical streams that had existed more or less underground from earliest Christian times; in examining them it is often difficult to know whether their adherents were Manichaeans, mystics, or merely anti-clericals. At any rate there was a striking external similarity among many of those streams that reached the surface, for they taught that the Bible was the source of all belief, preached simplicity of worship and purity of life, practiced few rituals, and rejected church hierarchies, above all that of the Roman Church. These sects, transferred in one form or another to America, are represented today by numerous fundamentalist denominations, by the Quakers, and by certain pietist sects among the Pennsylvania Dutch. The majority of the Germans, however, belonged to the Lutheran Church and the Reformed Church, the latter being Calvinist.

Germans have constituted one of the most valuable elements in the American heritage. The German colonial immigrant sought no shortcut to affluence. In those days German farmers were renowned for their thoroughness and intelligent application of scientific methods, qualities which it must be admitted did not distinguish their British, Irish, and Scotch-Irish neighbors. Fully as evident were the manual dexterity and the mechanical inventiveness which, together with German agriculture, made the Pennsylvania-German counties the most prosperous and progressive region in the English colonies. Germans were the finest iron workers of the colonies, to mention only one of their products, and the Revolution and the frontier wars were fought in considerable part with the rifles they developed in the shops of Lancaster, Pennsylvania. The Yankee is justly renowned for his ingenuity and ability to improvise, but it is only fair to attribute the engineering genius of Americans fully as much to the German mental habits of patient thoroughness and mechanical insight.

It would be difficult to lay one's finger on any important cultural contribution that the Celtic Irish brought to America, yet nothing can be more certain than that they have done more to alter the Anglo-Saxon temperament than has any other race. The Irishman gave a romantic dash and color to American political and military life. His lovableness was transmuted into that American friendliness that seems so brash to the Englishman. Celtic hyperbole reappeared as giantism in American story and American ideals. Not English patter, but the crackle of Irish humor was adopted by the American—though along with it also came Scotch dryness and the English sense of incongruity. Then Celtic flexibility found a place in the too-common attitude that an action is justifiable if one can "get away with it." Even more reprehensible was a certain volatility—however, doubtless found in most democracies—which has laid the American nation open to social nostrums, political slogans, and frequent changes in the winds of public opinion.

The backbone of American Presbyterianism was composed of Scottish and Scotch-Irish settlers (called Scotch-Irish in Ulster). Attempts have been made to show that the Scotch-Irish were nothing but Presbyterian Irishmen and it is certainly true that the original immigrants were born in Ulster and in fact were known contemporaneously as Irishmen. Yet there is some justification for the invention of the double name. They were descendants of Scottish settlers in Ulster, with some admixture of English and Irish. James I had tried to solve the Irish "problem" by driving out the Irish Catholics and planting Scots and English Protestants in their place, but the "plantations" got no farther than Ulster. Unfortunately the English Parliament discriminated against their woolen industry, then when they turned to linen hampered that by subsidizing English and Scottish linens. The result was ruin, and this was compounded by a succession of penalties laid on dissenters.

It so happened that around 1717 thousands of farm leases expired, and landlords demanded two or three times the old rental to renew them. The Catholic Irish, accustomed to dire poverty, often could outbid the Ulster Scots. The result of this and other conditions was that from 1700 thousands of Ulster Scotch-Irish left for America, and the flood ran strong until the eve of the Revolution and set in again after the war. Unlike the rest of Ireland, Ulster tenants had the right to sell any improvements they may have made, so many of them had the means to pay their way to America and perhaps make a payment on a farm.

There was much of Irish violence and restlessness in the Scotch-Irish, though little of Irish charm and imaginativeness. In fact they were psychologically more akin to the Lowland Scots. Their old home in Ulster had been a frontier between Protestantism and Catholicism, subject like the new home to massacre and counter-massacre—at least, so Scotch-Irish writers have said. As a result, they had developed frontier characteristics before they emigrated. Contentious, individualistic, restless, proud, mentally rigid, and impatient of restraint, they were natural-born pioneers. Essentially unimaginative and unaesthetic, yet always dreaming of better land farther on, they only scratched the soil where they were because they knew their stay would be brief. In them the democracy inherent in one side of Calvinism found complete expression; the Presbyterian kirk was as important a school for self-government as the provincial assemblies—a rough and ready school for men who believed in self-reliance and direct action. Not least, their experiences in Ulster meant that they brought with them a vigorous distrust of English government—not to say hatred—which in the American milieu was to make so many of them supporters of revolt against the Crown that the American Revolution was often dubbed the Presbyterian rebellion.

The Scots—that is, the Lowland Scots—have influenced America not only through the Scots-Irish but in their own right. Their frugality, caution, and shrewd business sense are proverbial and it is significant that Scotsmen and their descendants have always been prominent in the business life of the United States. The Englishman is imbued by the knightly tradition of good form, display, and generosity, but the Scotsman will have none of that. He is bumptiously independent and no false notions of what is or is not done will restrain him from making a fuss to get what he deems to be his rights. The American shows this same directness—though on occasion he is ambivalently capable of bowing down to the chivalric ideal.

The Scots are devoted to education, and they show a reverence for logic that is all but French in its intensity. Yet somehow they have managed to preserve individual liberty in spite of the blandishments of Roman law. At any rate Scotland has given the United States a quite un-English respect for logic and universal education—indeed the Scottish universities were the Meccas of many colonial American youths. The lawyers that it sent to the colonies were prominent as logicians of American revolutionary theory and cultivators of the Lockean ideal of natural rights. The peculiar homespun brand of American democracy is as much the child of Scotland as of the frontier, and so is the mythus which envelops it like a shining veil.

There is a leaven in Scottish democracy that is lacking in the democracy of hierarchical England, despite its many virtues. Robert Burns in *A Man's a Man for A' That* examined fine clothes and fare, and noble blood and high degree. It is difficult to imagine that the typical Englishman of the eighteenth century would, with Burns, "look and laugh at a' that" or would agree that

> The rank is but the guinea's stamp;
> The man's the gowd for a' that.

Yet these are the inherited beliefs of the average American—a heritage blended of the rocky soil of Scotland, the insistent pressure for English "liberties," the individualism of the frontier, and the rights of man.

Fully as important as any of the foregoing was the Negro. Most Negroes brought to the New World came from a strip perhaps two hundred miles deep along the coast of West Africa between the Senegal River and Angola, though slavers' wars farther inland no doubt contributed a share to the slave pens. The traditional view was that West Africa was without history or civilization, that organization, whether social or political, was rudimentary, and that religion was nothing more than an array of superstitions. These beliefs were long used to justify white exploitation of Negro slaves and were the foundation of the race prejudice that still plagues the world.

Recent scholarship has shown that the cultures and institutions of this area, though nonliterate, were sophisticated, complex, and highly organized. Moreover the languages and cultures were similar enough to enable the slaves of the various nations to find common denominators when they were thrown together in the New World. Negroes had different inhibitions than Europeans and perhaps were more volatile, and these things encouraged the white opinion that they were at best children, at worst savages. Actually, the fact that they had an advanced agricultural economy helped them to survive and even flourish under the system of plantation slavery. Moreover, though they accepted many aspects of the European technical and religious pattern, they retained a strong West African subcurrent that influenced the form their adopted customs and religion took. Even in the United States, where acculturation to the European pattern was most thorough, the West African influence is still occasionally found in Negro religious beliefs and practices, in music and perhaps in the dance, in social intercourse, and in family standards. Moreover, the persistent African influence has not only created an American subculture, but it has given American life a mood, color, and dramatic value quite foreign to Northwestern Europe.

It remains to say, however, that the American Negro subculture shows its Anglo-Saxon bias clearly when directly contrasted with West Africa. Many, if not most, American Negroes now have an admixture of white blood, and moreover their environment and education have given them—at least are giving them—American social, economic, and political ideals and are inculcating American standards of responsibility. The proof is seen in the way in which Negro leaders have adopted American democratic techniques of political pressure and civil disobedience in order to gain equality. It is all too often lost sight of by the American public that this is the very way in which classes rose to equality in Great Britain, and in which in the United States women, foreigners, and the unpropertied forced their way to a share in their own government.

The Settler and the Land

In addition to the influx of non-English immigrants there rose two influences that were to affect the country profoundly: the introduction of the European movement known as the Enlightenment and the westward march of settlement. We will turn first to the latter.

The English government had historically included only those who had a "stake in society" because of their ownership of land. Land was the open sesame to independence, wealth, power, and prestige. Naturally, then, the average man found America's chief attraction its cheap land. The proprietors in the proprietary colonies such as Pennsylvania and the Carolinas, and also the other great land owners in all the colonies, were land speculators on a grand scale. These men were quite ready to sell unlimited acreage cheaply or even to give it away to attract settlers.

The result was a growing pressure of population on the western outskirts of settlement. The fur traders normally led the van, and they were followed by cattlemen, or by farmer-hunters who were really no more than squatters. After them came the "equipped farmer" and finally the townsmen with their stores, schools, and industries. The last phase in the South saw the rise of plantations that, like industry, denoted the ascendance of capital.

The words *frontier* and *West* have been used so loosely that they have lost preciseness and, indeed, have come to be synonymous. We need to distinguish between them. The frontier was the advancing line—actually a broad, serrated belt or border—of contact between the wilderness and the forerunners of civilization. It was an area of open spaces and conflict, the domain in which the Indian contested for control with traders, trappers, pioneer hunter-farmers, cattlemen, miners, and the Seventh Cavalry. The West was the sparsely settled, definitely agricultural, and politically vociferous area behind that frontier, sometimes still menaced by Indians. It was differentiated from the old settled area by its interests; when the two became enough alike to be able to support much the same program for much the same reasons, the West ceased being identified as having a separate existence. Thus there were a number of "Wests," one after another disappearing. What we call the West today is a geographical description, not a designation of vitally different interests and therefore of a basically different way of life.

In 1893 a young historian named Frederick Jackson Turner proposed the famous Frontier Hypothesis: that abundant free lands (or at least cheap lands) at the edge of settlement not only caused the rapid advancement of the frontier to the Pacific but were instrumental in developing (from eastern and European seeds) American democracy and nationalism. It gave the people a host of characteristics, such as individualism, inventiveness, energy, equalitarianism, exuberance, and belief in freedom of opportunity.

For a generation after 1893, historians presented the West as the paramount molder of American institutions; indeed, Turner's followers were more dogmatic and sweeping in their claims than he ever was. Then the reaction set in as the contributions of other regions began to be stressed. The heritage of the English democratic process was re-emphasized, and the bitter struggle of the honest mechanics of Eastern cities for their democratic rights was shown to have been little influenced by the West. Probably the pendulum has gone too far to the opposite extreme, and the truth will eventually be found to lie somewhere between.

The term "Old West" has been used by historians to denote the "up country" or "back country" settlements in the eighteenth century. These comprised, in general, the area between the Fall Line and the mountains, with the addition of the Great Valley (Shenandoah) beyond. The area was more a unit than the East. This unity arose from like conditions and like problems—problems that were to follow the frontier west to the Pacific. First was the danger from the Indians, who resisted the forest-destroying whites. Next was the problem of how to get legal possession of land quickly, cheaply, and in large quantities. Then came transportation, for the pioneer's flour, ginseng, and lumber products were too heavy to be carried far over mud roads, even when no mountains intervened. Poor transportation meant chronic indebtedness, for exports were never sufficient to pay taxes and quitrents and leave enough to buy tools, gunpowder, salt, and the few other imported necessities. There was therefore no surplus to support schoolmasters and clergymen, and the West inevitably slipped down the cultural scale in the second generation. The only cure for these problems lay in self-government, but this the East refused to consider until after independence.

The Old West was the meeting place of the nations, and its mountain valleys, especially the Great Valley which ran almost unbroken from the Hudson River to Georgia, were the mixing bowls of the new nation. The restless, the adventurous, and the needy of every nation were there, helping to mold the characteristics of the Old West. The traveler in the hinterland saw what he chose to see. The aristocrat called it a "lubberland," and even the best-disposed admitted that dirt and laziness existed among the froth of outcasts who were thrust continually ahead of the settlements or who were left, like islands, in pockets of poor soil. But, as one observer recorded, the European who went West felt a "sort of resurrection . . . he now feels himself a man, because he is treated as such."

The Western European, long since removed from ancestral forests and lapped in the security of town and castle, was now breeding the pioneer once more. This was a free society and, like all free societies, it was democratic. The pioneers, like their surroundings, were insensitive, uncouth, and at times semibarbarous. But taste and refinement were not proper weapons to conquer savage and wilderness. The man of the Old West gloried in his freedom from restraint and bitterly fought any attempt to subject him to regulations. He had no regrets for the civilization of Europe or even of Tidewater. He was not English, Scotch-Irish, or German, nor even Pennsylvania or Virginian, but that new man, an American.

He looked about him at the vast wilderness owned by Indians and proprietors and held that "it was against the laws of God and Nature that so much land should lie idle while so many Christians wanted it to work on and to raise their bread." This was simply an eighteenth-century way of saying, "The earth belongs to him that gives it value"—to the cultivator, not the hunter, the speculator, or even the cattle-man. He had a clear idea of his "errand into the wilderness"—to clear the land and make it the fruitful abode of God-fearing people.

He therefore hated the Indians because they in their dependence on game sought to stop the whites from leveling the forests and killing off or driving out the game. He hated the speculator, who got hold of vast tracts of land and held them unoccupied for a rise in value or sought to make the land a source of permanent income in the form of quitrents. This attitude toward "engrossers" of land was fundamental and permanent and was used by the pioneers to justify all sorts of violence.

The man of the West was not a sensitive creature, and because of the anti-nomianism inherent on one side of his nature he found it possible to keep a relatively clear conscience while he defied proprietors and quitrents, squatted wherever he found a fertile valley, and massacred the Indians who protested at his high-handedness. His Calvinism made him look upon God as a business partner and a tribal deity who regarded with favor self-reliance and direct action. There is a story of a Western preacher—a Scotch-Irishman—who during the Revolution opened a recruiting meeting with this remarkable prayer: "Lord God, if Thou art unwilling by divine grace to assist us, *do stand aside and let us fight it out!*"

The Enlightenment

Many members of the educated classes rejected the high-handed deity of Calvin and the divinity of Christ and acquired faith in the self-sufficiency of man. Some professed to find no proof of the existence of sin and immortality. This new view of God, known as deism, did not come suddenly, of course—nor did it ever displace formal religions. But it was common among educated persons.

The Enlightenment regarded God as revealed in Nature rather than in Scripture. He was an engineer, and the universe was a completed machine. (In contrast Darwin and Marx regarded it as an unfinished process.) The typical savant presumed that the advance of knowledge and the perfection of reason would solve all problems, usher in the perfect society, and enable men to be good citizens—perhaps without hope of heaven or fear of hell. Indeed, some supposed that all the stimulus needed to do well was to earn the approval of posterity.

The belief that perfection could be built from the opportunities that lay around them prompted men to seek rose-colored interpretations of Oriental society and idealized portraits of the "noble savage" as he was thought to exist in the Americas. Thinkers in both Europe and America presently began to construct new social and political plans that emphasized the purifying effects of simplicity in manners or religion, liberal education, political democracy, or economic cooperation. The remarkable results are evident to even the most casual observer. The Constitution of the United States and the American system of public education are examples.

The Englishmen Locke and Newton had been two of the most vital influences in the inception of the French phase of the Enlightenment, though indeed Voltaire and Rousseau must have influenced English thought in turn. Montesquieu (died 1755) was widely read and commented on in the colonies, probably because his emphasis on the molding effect of environment was so plainly proved in America. Even the French Physiocrats, with their emphasis on agriculture as the basis of all wealth, had nothing to offer the agricultural Americans but a systematic, "scientific" explanation of the American economic scene. Indeed, the flow in the pre-Revolutionary era was the other way, and Rousseau drew his "noble savage" at least in part from America.

Despite their widespread deism the upper classes regarded the moral precepts and the terrors of religion as necessary to keep the masses in order. Even a natural meliorist and deist like Franklin could say, "talking against religion is unchaining a tiger; the beast let loose may worry his liberator." As a result the gentry in general clung to the old forms, fought for the right of the Church to associate itself in political control, and even upheld much of the old theology, though they might not believe it themselves.

Since American problems were practical, colonial thought reflected for the most part the utilitarian standards of a new and unstabilized society. Benjamin Franklin, whose contributions to physical research were invaluable, was one of the few major American scientists who lived before the twentieth century. John Winthrop IV, a Harvard professor, shocked the orthodox by showing that earthquakes and comets were natural phenomena, not vehicles of the wrath of God. Above all, Jonathan Edwards was one of the profoundest religious philosophers of the eighteenth century.

American intellectuals may not have been as profound as their European contemporaries, but it would be a mistake to suppose that they lagged behind in their grasp or appreciation of advanced ideas. They never lost contact with Europe, especially with the dissenting theologians and theorists who had always been in the forefront of European social and intellectual progress. The Enlightenment's deism was accepted by only some of the secular leaders, notably some of the men who were to become Founding Fathers of the new nation, but its secularism was widely welcomed, and its doctrine of improvement was almost universally accepted.

On the part of the masses, belief in improvement was not a philosophical acceptance, of course, but a practical one, drawn from the visible evidence that the wilderness was giving way to civilization. There is an implication here that is often overlooked. In practical political experience and maturity, Americans were ahead of Europe—possibly even of Great Britain. There is inherent in this fact a warning that though the principles of the Enlightenment were well known they should not be given all the credit for American political and social progress.

Rising secular interests led to the triumph of religious toleration as both a necessity and a conscious virtue. By the eighteenth century there were too many sects for them to be combated successfully. Moreover, toleration helped attract the immigrants vitally necessary to the economic growth of the colonies. Though state churches were established in the nine colonies, there were only occasional flurries of persecution, and these died out by the eighteenth century.

The decaying theocracy of New England, led by Increase Mather and his son, Cotton Mather, had fought to preserve its control by replacing the loose congregational system of church organization by a more tightly knit Presbyterianism. The greatest opponent of the Mathers was the Reverend John Wise of Ipswich, who in the early 1700's wrote two notable pamphlets ably (and with some satirical humor) defending democratic control by congregations on the ground of Natural Rights. "The end of all good Government," he wrote, "is to Cultivate Humanity, and Promote the happiness of all, and the good of every Man in his Rights, his life, Liberty, Estate, Honour, etc. without injury or abuse done to any." It was a significant argument, for in defending democracy's superiority in church government he also defended its superiority in political government. Wise had a demonstrable effect on the ideas of

Samuel Adams, one of the most democratic and influential of the Revolutionists.

It is of interest to observe that Wise seemed to regard Americans as a chosen people when he contrasted their natural felicity to the miseries of artificial Europe. Somewhat later Jonathan Edwards proclaimed that the New World had been chosen as the seat of redemption because the Old World had slain Christ and His martyrs. Even English divines spoke of the gospel fleeing westward and asked "Why may not that be the place of the New Jerusalem?" That learning was following the sun westward was already a familiar theme. Bishop Berkeley summed it up in his lines:

> Westward the course of empire takes its way;
> The first four acts already past,
> A fifth shall close the drama of the day,
> Time's noblest offspring is the last.

Though the Church of England was established in all the Southern colonies and counted most of the gentry among its members, the dissenting churches—chiefly Presbyterian, Baptist, and German sects—were strong west of the Fall Line and were to dominate in the settlements west of the mountains. Any influence the ministers of these sects had on their people was probably due more to personality than to any approval of theocratic ideals—that and the fear of hellfire.

It must not be supposed that the secularists had everything their own way. Indeed, there was a strong evangelical movement which, emphasizing piety and emotions, found a ready response among those who could not or did not accept the new importance accorded science and the intellect. The evangelical movement in America was parallel to one on the European continent and to the Wesleyan revival in England. Closely related was the Great Awakening (from 1726), the most remarkable manifestation of evangelicalism in colonial times.

The Great Awakening has been presented in two ways. One is as a facet of an evangelical movement that originated in the hunger of ordinary folk for the spiritual provender which the rationalism of the Enlightenment was withholding. The other view would have it that the movement rose from certain cultural developments within the colonies—notably the loosening of the bonds of authority and the rising emotional instability which was to become a continuing element in American history. Perhaps it is not too much to assert that both views have validity.

During the generation after 1726 the revival penetrated all parts of the country and all parts of Protestant society, though probably least among the Episcopalians. It found its most hospitable reception west of Tidewater and was to follow the settlements westward. It was accompanied by scary preachments of eternal torment in hell and by hysterical shouts, trances, and babbling in "tongues." Such manifestations were regarded by the more sober element as not only disgraceful but opposed to the true spirit of religion. As a result, the clergy lost much of its traditional influence—the "ranters" because conservative people despised them, and the sober ministers because emotional people distrusted them.

Out of the religious ferment of mid-eighteenth century there arose factors of immense significance to the future of the United States. Puritanism had divided into two streams: Evangelical and Rational. The first was to breed the modern fundamentalist sects; out of the latter came the Unitarians and also the relaxed theology of certain wings of present-day institutionalized churches.

Minor religious differences led to a further multiplication of sects and made control by state churches more hopeless than ever. Toleration was made necessary by diversity and was promoted by the growing power of secularism. The decline of social uniformity forced relaxation of the so-called Blue Laws, which regulated manners and morals. The revivalists' emphasis on individual responsibility for repentance and conversion was in line with growing democratic feeling, and so was the weakening of control by the state churches. The stimulation of religious activity also stimulated the interest of the denominations in higher education, and led to the establishment of—among other colleges—Princeton, Brown, Dartmouth, and Rutgers. The widespread nature of the Great Awakening greatly increased inter-colonial contact and so in a sense was a preparation for nationalism. The feeling of Christian brotherhood awakened by the revivals was also a powerful humanitarian influence.

There were curiously contradictory psychological results of the religious ferment. Emotionalism (almost to the extent of a neurosis) entered into American life, but at the same time, there were planted among the masses the seeds of respect for intellect and education. Individualism and social pressures grew side by side and were later to make possible the simultaneous flowering of "rugged individualism" and prohibition of alcoholic beverages!

These contradictions came in part from the contradictions of Calvinism but perhaps even more from the contradictions of human nature. Even while political democracy was maturing, its great enemy, concentrated and privileged economic power, was also maturing. Calvinism had followed historical precedent by setting up control of society by church and state—that is, ministry and gentry. When Calvinism and ministry decayed, the gentry retained the concept of leadership and responsibility (regardless of their church affiliation) and came to exercise control through economic power. The shift in approach was significant, for it foreshadowed one of the most powerful conservative influences in American development.

Edwards, Franklin, and the City of God

In order to understand the American society of 1776 let us turn for a moment to the two giants who bestrode the pre-revolutionary scene— Jonathan Edwards and Benjamin Franklin. Perhaps it is significant that they were both born New Englanders. Of the two, Edwards possessed by far the more profound intellect. He is remembered as the avatar of the evangelical movement—that is, the Great Awakening—who in his sermons preached that hell is paved with the skulls of unbaptized children, and of an angry God who shook sinners over the blazing pit of hell as one held a spider over the fire. Certainly Edwards was in many respects a Calvinist. He believed in predestination, original sin, the final judgment, and eternal damnation. Though he was profoundly influenced by the Enlightenment he combated the new current of deism by putting a certain amount of warmth and emotionalism into Calvinism, and with melting heart invited the sinner to repent and partake of the "surpassing sweetness" of the covenant of grace.

In preaching the accessibility of salvation to all he unconsciously opened the way for modern fundamentalism with the denigration of science and learning; for evangelical mysticism and anti-intellectualism; and even for Emersonian pantheism. Perhaps more to the point of our thesis, Edwards realized that the magistrates and the clergy no longer ruled by divine right but were now ruling by sufferance of the people. He looked about him in the Connecticut River Valley and saw the rich men he called "river gods" engaged in usurping the powers of government in order to promote and secure their ruthless business of gouging the people in trade and land sales.

In the end the "river gods" drove him out of his pulpit. In the sermon that might be called his Parthian shot at his enemies he denounced their get-rich-quick schemes less for their immortality than for their betrayal of the public welfare. He portrayed the magistrate not as a democrat—for Edwards was no democrat in our sense—but as a man of ability, learning, wisdom, and experience, who listened to his people and encouraged them to speak up. The business of the leader was to conform to human and social realities, to fight against those who "screwed upon" their neighbors, to seek the public welfare, and to fend off calamity. Only as an addendum did Edwards list piety, property, and good family as the qualifications of the leader. Quite apparently he rejected Winthrop's assertion that these qualifications were first and foremost the sine-qua-nonities of the magistrate.

Perry Miller, who studied Jonathan Edwards deeply, drew the conclusion that he was a child of the wilderness as well as of Puritanism, and marks the Great Awakening as the point at which the wilderness took over the task of defining the objectives of the Puritan "errand into the wilderness" of which Samuel Danforth had preached in 1670. Miller thus explains the real meaning of the Great Awakening and its role in freeing the American mind from a "European and scholastical conception of an authority put over men because men were incapable of recognizing their own welfare."

When we turn to Benjamin Franklin we find that he was an amalgam of much that Edwards rejected, for he was at once a deist, a democrat, and a land speculator, and in the long run, though some may deny it, he probably contributed more to the American spirit than did Edwards.

Franklin's roots, like those of Edwards, were in Calvinism or some reasonable facsimile thereof, and in Poor Richard's saws he blended it with conventional morality—but with something withheld, even as Shakespeare subtly ridiculed the folk wisdom that he placed in the mouth of Polonius. This was by no means understood by the nineteenth century which saw Franklin in the light of *Poor Richard's Almanac* and took him to its bosom as the exemplar of middle-class virtues. Poor Richard became the guidebook of the dawning bourgeois civilization not only in America but in Europe. It was translated into all the European languages, including the Scandinavian, and was published in innumerable editions by associations devoted to uplift, among them the Society for the Preservation of Property against Republicans.

It is true that there was a shrewd materialism included in Franklin's philosophy, a willingness to conform to society's demands in exchange for filthy lucre. But materialism is not the key to his character any more than it is the key to the character of the nation he helped to mold. Carl Becker has said that in all of Franklin's dealing with men one feels that he was nevertheless not wholly committed, that something remained unexpressed. Was this, perhaps, because of his ability to look at life from the outside, to see every matter in its due proportion? When the earnest young men in Philadelphia decided to draw up a Declaration of Independence they entrusted the task to the humorless Thomas Jefferson, not to Ben Franklin lest he conceal a joke in it.

Frankling recognized from the first that personal inclinations and practical necessities were frequently irreconcilable and that in such cases the latter must rule. For years he was disturbed by the irreconcilability of determinism and freedom of the will. Finally he decided that "freedom of the will" is a logical impossibility but a practical necessity"—which is one way of stating the pragmatists' decision to substitute ethics and common sense for conventional morality. The method is not infallible but it works reasonably well when it is based on facts and a knowledge of human nature, as Franklin sought to do.

At any rate, Franklin's aphorisms were primarily for others; himself, he worked from the practical to the theoretical, from experience to the generalization. This is not for a moment meant to imply that Franklin would not have agreed with Poor Richard in recommending hard work, frugality, thrift, and all other virtues in the Calvinist showcase. However, it seems apparent that he would have felt they were chiefly for the man on the make, and that the *arrivé* should let up, at least on hard work and frugality. One may doubt moreover that he would have recommended the virtues simply because they were virtues or because the community demanded conformity; rather, he would have pointed out their usefulness both to the individual and to society. If Franklin in his young manhood conformed to community sentiments it was a means to an end—a means of getting money in order to live the kind of life which was dictated by his insatiable curiosity and his love of doing good. When at forty-two he had attained sufficient wealth he retired from active control of his business and announced his intention of devoting the remainder of his life to science. As it turned out, his active life was only beginning; his careers as politician, propagandist, and statesman lay ahead of him.

It is also instructive to see how he broke away from conformity to community standards. True, he had already broken over and begotten an illegitimate son (though the mother may have been Deborah Read, whom Franklin presently married). But now, without abating his scientific activity, he gave up physical exercise and ate and drank generously with convivial companions, even to the extent of acquiring the bon vivant's disease of gout. He rejoiced that duty enabled him to spend twenty-five years of his mature life amid the fleshpots of London and Paris where he could attend on routs and assemblies and engage in flirtations with pretty and intelligent women. His way of life was thus a constant challenge to the Puritan axiom that "the greater the Self-Denial the greater the Virtue." If this gives the impression that Poor Richard furnished the ladder to a plateau of sybaritic pleasure for Dr. Franklin, that is exactly what it is intended to mean. But this plateau was paradoxically also a moral elevation. Franklin had decided to believe and practice what was socially useful and he continued to do so—most of the time.

The moral approach shines forth in Franklin's later and more easy-going phase even more brightly than in his earlier and conformist phase. Still, experience tempered his moralism—perhaps it would better be called ethics, a somewhat higher and more disinterested thing. It was a coin, a useful material piece of metal exchangeable in the marketplace; but a coin which bore on its obverse the rising sun of enlightened Self-interest and on its reverse the face of Altruism. Let us note a few of the ways in which this pragmatist from the City of Brotherly Love managed to serve both God and Mammon.

For one thing—and contrary to usual report—he did not share Jefferson's confidence in human nature; indeed, though he was fundamentally a meliorist, he was frequently pessimistic about it. He had no belief in the goodness and altruism of the aristocracy, and he had a Spencerian tendency to regard poverty as the divine punishment for a want of virtue and to oppose aiding the poor at the expense of the rich. Still he opposed class rule and denounced its concealment under the guise of a second legislative chamber, the Senate.

His democracy was simply a demand for equality *and* opportunity, for (*vide* Franklin himself) wisdom, virtue, and ability sprang up among the poor as well as the rich. Without belaboring the point here, it may be suggested that our social, economic, and political history has shown a strange interplay between optimism and pessimism. On one side we assert confidently that all problems have a solution and that God is on the side of America. On the other, everything will turn out wrong because human nature is depraved and the masses will be too strong for the enlightened few and eventually will bear them down in a vast Ragnarok. This may help to explain our violent political oscillations and our intense emotionalism, but through it all there has persisted the balance wheel of Franklin's cooler, more pragmatic approach.

The public's persistent worship of Poor Richard as a bourgeois saint has until recently obscured one of Franklin's most firmly held tenets about property. In this connection he asserted that:

> All the Property that is necessary to a Man . . . is his Natural Right. . . . But all Property superfluous to such purpose is the Property of the Publick, who, by their Laws, have created it, and who may therefore by other Laws dispose of it. . . . He that does not like Civil Society on these Terms, let him retire and live among Savages.

Now the interesting thing is that this is essentially what Richard Hooker meant when he upheld the rights of the community, as superior to those of the individual—though without violating reason and tradition. And, according to some recent interpreters, Locke did not mean to champion the right of property to override all other rights. When Jefferson wrote in the Declaration of Independence of the human right to life, liberty and property it seems to have been Franklin who amended it to the form we know—life, liberty and the pursuit of happiness.

This picture of Franklin as the prophet of the welfare state is no more out of keeping with the traditional view than his role in foreign relations. During most of his life Franklin was an active champion of imperial union as good for mankind, and during the ten years previous to the Revolution he strove desperately to prevent the suicide of the British Empire. This stress on cooperation did not weaken his Americanism, for he was convinced that the center of empire must presently come to rest in North America. The Revolution altered the form but not the substance of his dream, which now reappeared as the American mission to spread the gospel that in the democratic process we have found a universally applicable way of life. This sense of mission (however much we may now have our doubts about it) runs through our entire history and is found alike among isolationists and internationalists. Franklin, with his usual ability to eat his cake and have it, was both.

A Frenchman once said of Jefferson that despite his admiration for

France, Jefferson was still an enemy, for "an American is the born enemy of every European nation." This was no less true of Franklin, for his isolationism glints through all his expressions of gratitude to France. Yet nothing is more certain than his belief that nations must work toward some method of cooperation or else sink into chaos. Hence his lifelong opposition to protective tariffs. Hence his belief that justice was more important than peace. Hence his assertion that America in fighting for her own liberties was fighting for those of all mankind. Hence also his long search for the common bases of enlightened self-interest among nations.

Franklin perforce had to yield to certain American tendencies he did not approve, and which in fact are vigorously castigated in his writings—moralism, emotionalism, and sentimentality, and an intolerant conformity that was carried to the extent of a general approval of mediocrity. Franklin knew that he had to deal with human nature as it was and that he had to yield to popular imperfections. His rule as a politician was that he should be influenced by public expedience but under no circumstances by his own private interest. Reality had to come ahead of theory (even sometimes ahead of morals) and time after time he was forced to accept compromises, in politics, in constitution making, in diplomacy. Yet the public penchant for moralism meant that reality must sometimes be played down—that the power necessary to national security must be concealed by a moral cloak. He denied that power could create right or that power alone could solve human problems. Just as evident was his belief that morality, standing alone, was helpless. Power and morality might be antagonists, yet they also were necessary allies in the building of justice and human happiness. Inherent throughout Franklin's writings and actions was the realization that might gives to right the power to survive and right gives to might the moral reason to fight for survival.

Perhaps what we need as a nation is more of Franklin's serene ability to equilibrate uncertainties. It does not seem that he suffered much from a guilty conscience. He marked down his errata not to fret about them but to help himself mend them. When high living gave him the gout he took his punishment like a man and did not blame it on foreign subversive elements. We must, said he, "reflect how many of our duties Providence has ordained to be naturally pleasures; and it has had the goodness, besides, to give the name of sin to several of them so that we might enjoy them the more." And then he added a great truth which has thus far been our national motto—not stated with ringing trumpets, for that was not his way, but simply and modestly—"We only live once, and if we choose security and propriety—even to shield those we love—we lose something of what might have been."

Edwards and Franklin were men with differing tastes and outlooks but I have tried to show that they were not simple exemplars respectively of idealism and materialism. Each man was a bundle of complexities—as who is not? They differed in theology, but they had pretty much the same view of the qualifications of a ruler and of the people's right to promote their own welfare. Above all they agreed that the "errand into the wilderness" was to construct a better way of life, a more perfect society. And this has been the key to the American psyche, the touchstone by which we have tested every plan and policy. Together these two great contemporaries helped to mold the spirit which fought the war for independence and which has deepened and broadened during the two centuries which we are now celebrating. Certainly they played a part in assuring that the Revolution would not be fought in support of Winthrop's aristocratic and theocratic ideas.

Chapter 4
The Revolutionary Surge

Proem

The Revolution was one of the glories of British history. The colonies of no other nation in that age had progressed so far in the attainment and enjoyment of political liberty as to have "snuffed" the taint of tyranny in those acts of the British Government which precipitated the struggle. The freest of people were the first to rebel.

(Claude Van Tyne)[1]

*   *   *

In this character of the Americans, a love of freedom is the predominating feature which marks and distinguishes the whole; and as an ardent is always a jealous affection, your colonies become suspicious, restive, and untractable, whenever they see the least attempt to wrest from them by force, or shuffle from them by chicane, what they think the only advantage worth living for. This fierce spirit of liberty is stronger in the English colonies probably than in any other people of the earth. . . .

In other countries, the people, more simple and of a less mercurial cast, judge of an ill principle in government only by an actual grievance; here they anticipate the

---

[1]Claude Van Tyne, *Causes of the War of Independence* (Boston: Houghton Mifflin, 1922), p. 456.

evil, and judge of the pressure of the grievance by the badness of the principle. They augur misgovernment at a distance and snuff the approach of tyranny in every tainted breeze. . . .

To prove that the Americans ought not to be free, we are obliged to depreciate the value of freedom itself; and we never seem to gain a paltry advantage over them in debate without attacking some of those principles, or deriding some of those feelings, for which our ancestors have shed their blood. . . .

We cannot, I fear, falsify the pedigree of this fierce people, and persuade them that they are not sprung from a nation in whose veins the blood of freedom circulates. . . . An Englishman is the unfittest person on earth to argue another Englishman into slavery.

(Edmund Burke)

* * *

We hold these truths to be self-evident, that all men are created equal, that they are endowed by their Creator with certain unalienable Rights, that among these are Life, Liberty and the pursuit of Happiness. That to secure these rights, Governments are instituted among Men, deriving their just powers from the consent of the governed. That whenever any Form of Government becomes destructive of these ends, it is the Right of the People to alter or to abolish it, and to institute new Government, laying its foundation on such principles and organizing its powers in such form, as to them shall seem most likely to effect their Safety and Happiness.

(Declaration of Independence, 1776)

Why a Revolution?

The American Revolution grew out of a specific argument between the British government and the Thirteen Colonies: would the colonies submit to the idea that the London government could levy a tax upon them? The problem arose because the British government decided at the end of the French and Indian War in 1763 that its empire was badly in need of thorough overhauling. It was this fatal decision that lay at the root of all later difficulties. However haphazard and confused a political and economic arrangement may seem to be, it cannot be overhauled in important ways without causing major upheavals. But as in any great human conflict, it is superficial to seize upon any one aspect of the situation—even though the most important one—and ignore the rest. There was far more behind the conflict. There were so many different people and interests involved, indeed, that the motives for taking one side or the other became all entangled.

Overhauling the empire and strengthening central control also coincided with the ambitions of the young George III, who had come to the throne in 1760. George had resolved to "be king"—that is, he wished to restore the royal "prerogative" by which the king was the active leader of national policy rather than a figurehead. He strove consciously to fulfill his ideal of the "patriot king" and to bind the empire into an efficient, well-articulated, and centrally controlled unit. In so doing he was only advancing one step further the ideal of such statesmen as the great William Pitt (and Benjamin Franklin)—that the British Empire was a union of free peoples. It is quite clear that George III did not regard his exercise of the prerogative, nor his means of restoring it, as an infringement on liberty.

The reorganization involved tightening the enforcement of mercantilism, for several reasons. First, British manufacturers (not primarily the merchants) feared the growth of fabricating industries in America, asserting that English prosperity would decline as America gained. (They were wrong, but their argument was consistent with mercantilism.) Second, the West Indian sugar planters' lobby wanted to stop the mainland's trade with the French and Spanish sugar islands.

Finally, the French wars, fought partly for American defense, had left Britain with an enormous debt, and Parliament sought to ease the burden by taxing the American colonies to pay part of the current expenses of colonial administration. This was as though the king in cleaning the imperial cupboard had taken down and opened a Pandora's box in which had been imprisoned all the troubles that were to plague him. It is highly probable that the other causes of conflict which we will presently mention would not have been brought to bear without this decision. The colonies were extremely jealous of their control over their own taxation and were prepared to defend it by completely rejecting the mercantilist doctrine that the metropolis had full power over the colonies. As it was, George worked so quietly that it was not publicly known in America until 1776 that he was behind the new policies. The Thirteen Colonies supposed that the revival of mercantilism was the work of Parliament alone.

For a number of reasons the new policies were a threat to American prosperity, for it must not be thought that economics had no part in encouraging rebellion. Merchants resented imperial control of the exchange of products with Europe, and particularly with the French and

Spanish in the West Indies. Nascent manufacturers resented restrictions on their fabrications, particularly of finishing certain iron products. Debt-ridden planters resented the exactions of London factors. Land speculators and land-hungry pioneers resented the British attempt to close the trans-Allegheny West to settlement.

However, none of this is to say that the Revolution was primarily a protest against the theory of mercantilism. Rather, the colonists thought of the crisis as constitutional. Greater flexibility on the part of king and Parliament would have solved the colonists' economic problems and prevented—at least for a while—the solidification of the disparate Thirteen Colonies in defense of a constitutional issue.

Probably of far greater importance was the fact that the revival of mercantilism was a threat to their evolving concept of democracy. In their search for legal justification for their view, the Americans were dismayed to discover three things. (1) Their charters, even when interpreted literally, did not exempt them from royal regulations. (2) Those royal colonies which did not technically have charters but were governed according to the crown's instructions to their governors were theoretically subject to whatever demands the crown might make; normally they were protected by precedent and custom, but it was disheartening to find that the crown—that is, Parliament—claimed absolute sovereignty over them. (3) The "rights of Englishmen" in England and America were evolving toward somewhat different forms.

England and America were evolving differently and at different paces, but to much the same goal, as later history showed. Perhaps nothing the crown could have yielded would have prevented eventual separation. Americans awoke to the realization that they wanted, not someone else's institutions, however favorable to them, but their *own* institutions. No doubt peoples had been revolting from foreign rulers for thousands of years because they wished to live under their own institutions. The difference in this case was that Americans proclaimed this right to be universal, and they summoned the conscience of mankind to approve their actions. This was the trumpet call of that generation—a call that has echoed down the corridors of time and today, more than ever, rouses the peoples of the world to demand the right to live under their own institutions. The result was that, without abandoning their own view of the "rights of Englishmen," Americans added reliance on natural rights.

The doctrine of natural rights appealed to Americans for a number of reasons, and even the New England clergy preached that they were independent of and above the laws. Some of the colonies had actually set up governments by compact, so that this seemed to be a resasonable theory about the origin of government. Locke's emphasis on equality before the law and taxation by consent was quite in line with American experience. Taxation without the consent of their own legislatures they regarded as a violation of government's true business—the protection of property. Locke had justified Parliament's revolt against the Stuarts; as the Americans saw it, Parliament was now the oppressor. It was inevitable that Locke's arguments should be revived.

Possibly, though here opinions still differ, the Revolution was bred more in the psychology of the people than in their economic and political conditions. There was American resentment at British sneers and patronizing, at the opinion that an American was inferior simply because he was a colonial. There was resentment that the best government positions in the colonies went to English placemen. There was resentment that holders of the king's commission outranked colonial officers and at the open contempt with which British officers regarded American officers and soldiers. There was continually growing resentment that British investors, merchants, and manufacturers expected to pluck the American economy at will, demanding perquisites and privileges that were not so much impossible to bear as insulting. Despite the prominence of aristocrats in Tidewater affairs, the average American was very proud and self-reliant, and the farther inland one went, the more common this was. Americans saw no reason for continuing to yield. They were big enough to rebel, and they did.

It has been held that revolutions do not arise out of the desperation of misery but out of a vision of something better. British economic pressure was unwise and oppressive, but the Thirteen Colonies were even at the worst treated far more leniently than were the colonies of any other power in that century. Had George III realized his wildest dream of imperial centralization, the Thirteen Colonies would still have been the freest on earth. The American Revolution did not arise from the desperation of misery, whatever the protests made by its shrewd and highly articulate apologists. It arose from the belief that conditions could and should be better and that self-government was the only guarantee of this betterment. "The Revolution," says the historian Claude H. Van

Tyne, "was one of the glories of British history. . . . The colonies of no other nation in that age had progressed so far in the attainment and enjoyment of political liberty as to have 'snuffed' the taint of tyranny in those acts of the British Government which precipitated the struggle." Well did he conclude with the words: "The freest of peoples were the first to rebel."

If it was true—and it certainly seems true—that Americans enjoyed a degree of freedom and equality such as then existed nowhere else, it would seem that the Revolution was fought less for a definite program than to open up the road for continued evolution. Perhaps we can throw light on this problem by examining the nature of the colonial political struggle and of the weapons which Americans had developed in connection with it.

It is not necessary to cover in detail the long political struggle to limit the power of the governors, most of them sent out from England; to gain control of the courts; and to enlarge the franchise and confirm local control of local affairs. These struggles were carried on largely in terms of demanding concrete liberties.

Out of the colonial political melee several facts and trends became clear. For one thing, the Americans were highly satisfied with the British constitution: the quarrel was over its interpretation. The British tended to regard Parliament as the supreme expression of "the people"—a term with changing meanings—and thus able to change the constitution; this is still true. The British were slowly beginning to heed Richard Hooker's warning against divided sovereignty (see above, page 26). Americans, fearful of the authoritarian pretensions of the royal governors, the creatures of the king in Parliament, were desirous—or soon would be— of dividing sovereignty. Each branch of government should be a higher written law subject to change only by direct order of the people. The people thus should have two means of expression: a government frequently changed in personnel and a constitution amended only after long reflection.

In actual practice, the British Empire of the eighteenth century—that is, the English-speaking parts—was really a new kind of political state: a federation. The colonies handled local affairs through their own legislatures, but on matters of common interest the British Parliament took over—on such matters as foreign affairs, defense, international and intercolonial trade, the post office, coinage, Indian affairs, and the disposition of the public lands. This situation was in practice a division of sovereignty—the very thing against which Richard Hooker had warned. Nevertheless the system worked fairly well until London tried to levy a tax not for regulative purposes but to raise revenue.

The Americans pled for continuance of the system pretty much as it had evolved. English legalists, however, insisted that the provinces (such as Massachusetts and Virginia) were analogous to English counties, and the corporate colonies (Connecticut and Rhode Island) ranked with such English municipalities as Bristol and London, originally chartered by the king but now subject to Parliament. Since Americans had unwisely been permitted to govern themselves they had come to believe they were practically independent; it was high time that Parliament's supreme power be reasserted.

Two rival ideas of the structure of the empire were thus growing up. The British regarded the empire as an aggregation of states under the Parliament elected by the people of Great Britain. The American interpretation may have followed after the failure of every other recourse to avoid British taxation; certainly the specific recognition of the belief in a federation did not come until the eve of the Revolution. At any rate, Americans rejected the arguments of the English legalists and asserted that the empire was made up of equal states, each under its own parliament, with the king as the coordinator. The Parliament of Great Britain legislated for him in imperial matters, but only when they were distinctly and incontrovertibly of common imperial interest. Thus Americans denied that Parliament could levy taxes on them except for the incidental revenues collected under the customs duties, whose main purpose was to regulate trade.

They were accustomed to having taxes levied only by the consent of the people of the various localities as represented in their legislatures; they were not represented in Parliament, ergo, Parliament could not justly tax them. In England the electoral districts had not been altered since the time of Elizabeth, so the newly sprung up industrial cities were poorly represented, if at all. The House of Commons was made up to a large extent of representatives who bought their seats from the electors of "rotten boroughs" or were appointed by the owners of fields once the site of old towns. The privileged classes thus controlled the House of Commons. When Americans or Britons complained that they were not represented, the answer was made that every member of Commons represented the citizens of any area—including the colonies—where no vote was cast. This was called "virtual representation." To Americans and probably to most Britons this was absurd, and there was a swelling cry of "No taxation without representation!"

The assertion sometimes made that democracy did not exist in the Thirteen Colonies results from a failure to understand that democracy is a process, not a completed structure of popular government. As a process democracy was very much alive during the entire colonial period.

(1) There was a relatively widespread franchise, much closer to white manhood suffrage than was once supposed.

(2) Special legal privileges had practically disappeared, and there was essential equality before the law.

(3) There was a movement among the common people to widen their political and economic rights, particularly by securing more adequate representation for localities and hence greater control of public policy.

(4) There was an effort by the colonies to make good their rights within the empire.

The "compact" as an agreement among the people as the basis of government was well understood; it found expression in the Mayflower Compact and in the Fundamental Orders of Connecticut, to mention only two which preceded the great example of the Constitution of 1787. The people felt that any compact should be expressed in writing, as their colonial constitutions (charters) were, in order to minimize uncertainty; this opinion was general even in those royal colonies where the crown's commissions and instructions to the governors served as the written constitution. It was the full implementation of this compact as concretely expressed in the charters and in the "rights of Englishmen" that was the goal of the colonial political struggle.

The English governing class had historically included only those who had a "stake in society" because of their ownership of land. Now the common people of the colonies, unlike their British progenitors, had a stake in society in the acres that they had wrested from the wilderness with such labor and peril. As a consequence they had developed an independence of spirit—not to say intransigence—which made them willing to defend their hard won gains by revolution. The American society of 1776 was in large part bourgeois and at the same time leveling and democratic. This means bourgeois in the sense of owning property and respecting property as an evidence of solid worth and good citizenship, and democratic in the sense of asserting that government should be of, by, and for the people. Of course the merchant and planting plutocracy of the seaboard disapproved of the leveling aspirations of the common man, and joined in revolution in the hope of promoting and confirming their own ascendance. Still, even as they did so, they were perturbed by evidences that they were assisting in a movement that could result in their own downfall. American society had gotten too far beyond Winthrop's model to be willing to suffer any further under elite controls.

It is notable that, though the method of the democratic process was chiefly developed in England, the Thirteen Colonies soon passed the mother country in the application. The American people emerged from the colonial period with the tenets of democracy burned into their hearts far more deeply than they existed in English hearts at that time.

(1) The Americans understood the reality of the democratic process and the method of advance by persistent struggle and temporary compromise. The changing balance of social forces as expressed in the political war of maneuver was accepted as the natural and inevitable means of progress.

(2) They understood the necessity of the basic civil liberties, of popular control of legislative power, and the usefulness of the legislature's check on executive and judiciary. It was generations before they lost their fear of a strong executive and an independent judiciary.

(3) They had a deeply ingrained fear of the union of church and state. Though the union existed in nine of the Thirteen Colonies, it had been shorn of aggressive power and was to be wiped out completely by 1833. This fear was not altogether the result of the Enlightenment; rather it arose from the splintering of sects and from the growing refusal of dissenters to pay taxes for the support of an established church.

(4) They understood the economic basis of democracy and realized that democracy could not exist when economic power was concentrated in a few hands. This was the crux of the democratic battle during the colonial period, and it has remained the crux down to our own day. The main battle has never yet been against property as property, but against the abuse or potential abuse of the power which property gives.

The British policy was, as we have noted, a threat to evolving American democracy. However, it would be too much to say that the life or death of democracy was involved—at least in any immediate sense. What was at stake was the freedom of the democratic process to go on evolving in America on the pattern already begun, which, if Americans had stopped to think in those terms was to build the City of God in their own way. Perhaps the most striking distinction between Europe and America in the eighteenth century was the different roles that the Enlightenment played in them. To the Europeans the Enlightenment was a stimulus and a program for building a better society. To the Americans it was primarily a source of arguments and justifications, for they already enjoyed more liberties than any people in Europe. What they were trying to do during the Revolution was to open the way for further advancement by breaking the shackles of custom which still confined the thinking of many of their compatriots—and, of course, of the British ruling class.

Many years later G. K. Chesterton was to utter a profound truth which fits the American case exactly: "You can never have a revolution in order to establish a democracy. You must have a democracy in order to have a revolution."

On the morning of the Battle of Lexington, Levi Preston ran sixteen miles to get into the fight. Seventy years later he was asked his opinion of the oppressions that had led to the war.

"Oppressions?" exclaimed the old man. "What were they? I didn't feel any. The Stamp Act? I never saw one of the stamps. The tea tax? I never drank the stuff."

"Well," said the interlocutor, "I suppose you had been reading Sidney or Locke about the eternal principles of liberty?"

"Never heard of them. We read only the Bible, the catechism, Watts' hymns, and the almanac."

"Then what did you mean by going into that fight?"

"Young man," was his answer, "what we meant in going for those redcoats was this—we always had governed ourselves, and we always meant to. They didn't mean we should!"

Protest Becomes War

The break came with the skirmishes at Lexington and Concord in April 1775, and immediately many moderate and even-tempered colonists joined with the hot-tempered radicals in organizing armed force against the king—or as they then understood it, Parliament.

The radical members of Congress probably had been ready for independence from the opening day, but they hesitated to shock public opinion and fulfill Tory prophecies by championing it openly. As it was, before long revolution was slowing down. The chief reason for the radicals' hesitation was that in the past they had built up a popular idea of George III as a monarch who loved justice and liberty but was being thwarted in his good intentions by ministerial ogres. It had been the custom to speak of the British regulars as "ministerial troops," and some even referred to the provincial militia as "the king's troops." Though the radical leaders now knew that the ministers were nothing more than the king's clients, their problem was how to erase the popular portrait they themselves had painted.

It was Thomas Paine, a recent immigrant from England, who showed the way in his pamphlet *Common Sense*, published in January 1776. In terse, breathless sentences that still have the power to stir, Paine swept away the clouds of indecision and convinced the colonists that it was time to end doubts and suspicions by tying the colonies together in the common cause of independence. With remorseless logic he attacked the institution of kingship, and then went on to expose George III as puppeteer of a dummy ministry. To the American people *Common Sense* came like an electric spark. Undoubtedly the spirit of independence was already there: it needed only the spark to bring it to life. It is said that 120,000 copies of *Common Sense* were sold in the first three months after its publication, and half a million altogether. If that figure is correct, it meant approximately one for each family in the country.

The effect of *Common Sense* was reinforced by the events of the winter of 1775-1776, notably the burning of Falmouth, now Portland, Maine. When word came that the king was sending peace commissioners, the effect was canceled by further work that he was also sending German mercenaries. The British navy blockaded the coast, prohibited American trade with the world, seized American ships, and closed the fisheries. Truly it appeared that Britain was closing every exit but the one labeled "independence." The Continental Congress acknowledged the situation in May 1776 by advising the provinces to set up governments with authority derived not from the king but from the people, on the ground that it was "necessary that the exercise of every kind of authority under the said crown should be totally suppressed."

Before the end of winter, grassroots movements for independence had begun to appear in local conventions and provincial congresses, particularly in New England and the South. Then, on June 7, 1776, Richard Henry Lee, as directed by the Virginia Convention, introduced into Congress a resolution that "these United Colonies are, and of right ought to be, free and independent States," and called for a plan of confederation and a search for foreign alliances. On July 2 Congress voted, and every state sustained Lee's resolution except New York, which did not come over until July 15. Only July 4 a formal declaration, largely the composition of Thomas Jefferson, was adopted. It was entitled "The Unanimous Declaration of the Thirteen United States of America,"

The engrossed copy of the Declaration was signed on August 2 and was, of course, a solemn occasion. John Hancock, who signed first as president of Congress, is said to have delivered a little admonition to the effect that after this step they must all hang together. "Yes," rejoined Franklin, who was never at a loss for a quip, "we must indeed all hang together, or most assuredly we must all hang separately."

The thoroughness of Paine's preparation is shown by the fact that, though the burden of American protest up to this time had been directed against Parliament, the Declaration was directed against George III. There was also the necessity to exhibit at least a superficial consistency. Since Americans had insisted that the empire was composed of equal states joined by a common sovereign, they could hardly declare independence to escape from the control of Parliament when that control had never been acknowledged. So now the Declaration consisted of two distinct parts, each representing one of the two kinds of argument Americans had developed as a justification of their claim to self-government. The first part was based on John Locke's doctrine of natural rights, which had now become the common property of the sons of the Enlightenment. While it was given much greater appeal of Jefferson's felicitous style and by the fact that the Declaration was followed by a successful revolution, the philosophy of natural rights was regarded as basic. Indeed, it was accepted in Jefferson's day as so axiomatic that he could refer to these truths as "self-evident"—there was no need to prove them. Jefferson said quite frankly in later years that he had no intention of working up new ideas in the Declaration. Rather, he said, "it was intended to be an expression of the American mind. . . . All its authority rests then on the harmonizing sentiments of the day."

The second part of the Declaration exhibited the hereditary English partiality to concrete liberties by ticking off under twenty-seven heads the "long train of abuses and usurpations" of George III that had led to rebellion and which justified independence. These were also, of course, evidences of the way in which George had broken the compact between sovereign and people which presumably had first established government. In his evidences Jefferson pointed out how the king had confiscated property, a violation both of the Rights of Englishmen and of natural rights. Yet it is striking that Jefferson, perhaps at Franklin's suggestion, did not follow Locke in asserting the right to property but substituted "the pursuit of Happiness." This was an open omission (if not actual rejection) of Locke's assertion that the fundamental purpose of government was the conservation of property, and a reversion, whether or not conscious, to Richard Hooker's more liberal assertion that in the last analysis social welfare is more important than property. Jefferson here drew the fundamental distinction between modern conservatism and liberalism—between Locke and Hooker—and, as we shall see, between Hamilton and himself. Jefferson's Declaration is one of the most powerful and important statements in history. It filled that most vital of human needs, self-justification, by seeking to explain the American action out of a "decent respect to the opinions of mankind." And as independence was won, it became the reason for America itself. In its terse yet luminous phrases, succeeding generations of men have found the inspiring statement of why America exists. In other words, America did not begin as just another nation; it began as a nation whose very existence was explained to a "candid world" as a great demonstration that certain political ideas are true.

The adoption of a declaration of independence was too much for many moderates and they went over to the side of the Tories with the result that the cause of moderation was weakened in the councils of Congress and the states. The popular view of the Revolution is that it was a dignified and lofty crusade in which rich and poor unanimously laid aside contention and self-seeking and pulled together for the common good. Of course, there were many high-souled, self-sacrificing men in high position (Washington was an outstanding example) who worked quietly, intelligently, and patiently against desperate odds, and who triumphed, partly because they were aided by resounding luck.

But the statesmen of the new union were leading a people who were often blind to their own best interests, and whose local rivalries were often more powerful than their national patriotism. In their attitude toward the war Americans were divided among Patriots (hitherto known as Whigs), neutrals, and Loyalists (Tories). The relative strength of the factions will never be known, but the Patriots were by far the most dynamic, and they forced action or acquiescence on the others. Many

Loyalists found it unhealthy to remain at home and flocked to the cities under British control and into the British army. It should be noted that the dynamism of the Patriots was exhibited chiefly in their own neighborhoods, and that sometimes they relaxed to the extent of actual obstructionism when the war passed on to other areas.

Congress was split between radicals and conservatives—though perhaps the latter would more accurately be called moderates if we think of the Loyalists as conservatives. The radicals, based on a coalition between the Adamses of Massachusetts and the Lees of Virginia, constituted the party of extreme democracy, decentralization, agrarianism, and free trade. Such men could sniff tyranny in the conservatives' program of aristocratic leadership, centralization, commerce, and regulated trade. Normally they were dominant not only in Congress but in most of the state legislatures. The conservatives were for the most part planters or members or associates of the commercial community in the North. They were by no means opposed to human rights, nor were all of them opposed to the widespread exercise of the franchise; but they did wish to find ways to restrict power—or at least the final say in its use—to their own class.

Bickerings and intrigues in the halls of Congress were paralleled in the states, in the army, and among the diplomatic representatives abroad. Congress had no constitutional authority for almost six years of its existence, but simply went ahead and did what had to be done in the hope—frequently vain—that the states would agree. The constitution, styled "Articles of Confederation," proposed by Richard Henry Lee at the time he introduced the resolution for independence, was ready toward the end of 1777 but did not go into effect until March 1781.

Meanwhile the states had drawn up constitutions that showed the current fear of executive encroachment by reducing the power of the governors. The powers of government were carefully balanced among executive, legislature, and judiciary, and the legislatures were bicameral except in Pennsylvania. Most state constitutions included Bills of Rights spelling out the rights that the war was being fought to secure.

That many of the struggles in Congress and the states were over vital procedures, policies, and rights does not mitigate the fact that the greater struggle for independence was set back. Certainly the states must share the responsibility for Congress's shortcoming. Congressmen, of whom most were by no means financially well off, lived hungrily and worked hard. Congress was weak because the popular will behind it was weak;

finances were straitened in large part because the people were not willing to sacrifice.

We have seen that a deep fissure separated the two wings of the revolutionary movement. On one side were those who had initially wanted to settle the argument with Britain within the framework of the British Empire; on the other were those who, at least from 1775, wanted independence. When it finally became apparent that only by independence could the argument be won, the former agreed, but reluctantly. Always lurking in their minds was a realization that so extreme a step as independence would probably be followed by many other kinds of change. Any great upheaval brings to the top the radicals, the kind of men who have been calling for social and political changes all along. Men like Washington were quite happy with the internal arrangements within each colony, social, economic, and political. It was just the external argument with the London government that had to be solved. So it was only with the deepest misgivings that they chose a course of action that opened up the possibility of change in many other spheres.

The Meaning of the Revolution

As it was, the Revolution brought only one really important change—independence—but it did clear the way for more changes in the next century. The Articles of Confederation were to a marked degree the creation of the radicals, but the conservatives were still powerful, and the Constitution was to be their handiwork. They were reinforced by newly wealthy men, largely politicians, profiteers, or those who had bought up Tory estates. However, it was plain that changing times had weakened aristocratic dominance (*privilege* had already pretty much been lost) and that the new conservative aristocracy was faced by a strong democratic challenge.

What, then, was the meaning of the Revolution, if it did not appreciably alter or accelerate the course the Thirteen Colonies were already traveling? One may venture the opinion that its principal effect was to preserve the rights that Americans already had gained—in the words of Bernard Bailyn it gave them legitimacy—and in so doing cleared the way for the continued evolution of the new psychological and institutional patterns that had appeared in America. Outworn theories were sloughed off as a sycamore sheds old bark. What emerged was based on the concepts of human freedom and progress; on pragmatic compromises between the individual and society and the state and the nation; and on a new view of economics—that the people should have a chance to prosper.

Americans were pleased by what they understood was John Locke's emphasis on individualism and defense of the superior rights of private property, and so they built these into their system. (It was not the only possible democratic answer to the problem, and the English eventually adopted Richard Hooker's teaching that the welfare of society is superior to property.) Revolution had followed on the failure to solve the age-old imperial problem of how to turn colonies into an integral, equal part of the metropolis. The Constitution of 1787 was to solve this problem and make a beginning toward solving the equally ancient problem of how to reconcile local and national rivalries. Mercantilist trammels were broken by independence, not to be reimposed decisively until after the Civil War—and then in greatly altered form. The effect was not only to widen international trade but to open the way for industrial development.

The legal vestiges of feudalism could now be replaced by new views of law that would confirm freedom of opportunity and promote progress. The way was opened for economic expansion. The British Parliament in the Bubble Act of 1720 had practically forbidden the joint-stock and corporate forms of private enterprise without which this expansion was greatly hampered. After the Revolution, the corporation became legal and acceptable in the United States, even though it continued to have enemies. The Elizabethan delight in taking calculated risks had already found a new home, and that home now deliberately adopted constitutional and institutional patterns aimed at fostering it.

These were the eventual—or rather, the not-long-delayed— consequences of the Revolution; they might or might not have come without it. The immediate political and social gains, perhaps even the immediate economic gains (of which we know little), seem to sink into insignificance beside the Revolution's great work of cutting away the underbrush that clogged the path to the future.

The Revolution also had a profound influence abroad—not only on the continent of Europe but in England itself.

> The effects of the American Revolution, as a revolution, were imponderable but very great. It inspired the sense of a new era. It added a new content to the conception of progress. It gave a whole new dimension to ideas of liberty and equality made

familiar by the Enlightenment. It got people into the habit of thinking more concretely about political questions, and made them more readily critical of their own governments and society. It dethroned England, and set up America, as a model for those seeking a better world. It brought written constitutions, declarations of rights, and constituent conventions into the realm of the possible. The apparition on the other side of the Atlantic of certain ideas already familiar in Europe made such ideas seem more truly universal, and confirmed the habit of thinking in terms of humanity at large. Whether fantastically idealized or seen in a factual way, whether as mirage or as reality, America made Europe seem unsatisfactory to many people of the middle and lower classes, and to those of the upper classes who wished them well. It made a good many Europeans feel sorry for themselves, and induced a kind of spiritual flight from the Old Regime.[2]

Every nation convinces itself that it has something good to offer the world, and usually it has, though not always the thing it prizes most highly. Colonial writings, as noted in previous chapters, were studded with prophecies of the coming greatness of America. The political aspect of the American mission emerged during the Revolution, for the United States did not begin as just another nation. It began as a nation whose very existence was explained as a great demonstration that certain political ideas are true. At first the revolutionists felt it their mission merely to preserve the liberties of both England and America or see them buried in a "common grave." The trumpet call sounded by Tom Paine in *Common Sense* changed all that. These lines are worth repeating:

> O! Ye that love mankind! Ye that dare oppose not only the tyranny but the tyrant, stand forth! Every spot of the old world is over-run with oppression. Freedom hath been hunted round the globe. . . . O! receive the fugitive, and prepare in time an asylum for mankind.

Americans now regarded themselves as a chosen people, and America as the ark "in which all the liberty and true religion of the world are to be deposited." Henceforth, Americans felt that their mission was

---

[2]R. R. Palmer, *Age of the Democratic Revolution*, two volumes (Princeton, N. J.: Princeton University Press, 1959, 1964), 2:282.

to foster and preserve the democratic process and to spread the gospel that in it they had found a universally applicable way of life which the world must sooner or later accept.

George Bancroft's *History of the United States*, published between 1834 and 1874, was a paean in ten enormous volumes to the loving care with which God had fostered the American mission. Bancroft's text might have been taken from Washington's First Inaugural Address. The heart of the address was in these words:

> The preservation of the sacred fire of liberty and the destiny of the republican model of government are justly considered, perhaps, as *deeply*, as *finally*, staked on the experiment intrusted to the hands of the American people.

In casting up the balance sheets of the American Revolution, it is apparent that out of the war came both a tragedy and a blessing. The seed was sown of a long rivalry between the two nations. American development, unchecked either by experienced administrators or by a deeply rooted native aristocracy, entered upon a course of headlong democracy which was often as oppressive as liberating. Perhaps if the Americans had remained part of the British Empire and eventually become part of the British Commonwealth of Nations, the *Pax Britannica* might still dominate the world and encourage orderly growth. There might have been no world wars, no Russia and Germany resurgent in the same senses as in our time, because it would obviously have been foolish to combat so great a combination devoted to the cause of peace and law.

On the other hand, as things turned out, we have seen that democracy can appear in various forms. The United States has been a moderating influence in modern imperialism, both because of its example and because its existence has forced rulers to moderation—as Britain in Canada. It is conceivable that without independence America might have had a saner growth, but it would never have attained the tremendous power which has enabled it to cast a deciding sword into the scale against predatory doctrines.

Chapter 5
The Fledgling Republic

Proem

[The Constitution] speaks not only in the same words, but with the same meaning and intent with which it spoke when it came from the hands of its framers, and was voted on and adopted by the people of the United States. Any other rule of construction would abrogate the judicial character of this Court and make it the mere reflex of the popular opinion or passion of the day.

(Chief Justice Taney, 1857)

* * *

Some men look at Constitutions with sanctimonious reverence, and deem them like the ark of the covenant, too sacred to be touched. They ascribe to the men of the preceding age a wisdom more than human, and suppose what they did to be beyond amendment. I knew that age well; I belonged to it and labored with it. It deserved well of its country. It was very like the present, but without the experience of the present; and forty years of experience in government is worth a century of book-reading; and this they would say themselves, were they to rise from the dead. . . . I think moderate imperfections had better be borne with. . . . But I know also that laws and institutions must go hand in hand with the progress of the human mind. . . . We might as well require a man to wear still the coat which fitted him when a boy, as civilized society to remain under the regime of their ancestors.

(Jefferson to Kercheval, July 12, 1816)

* * *

Jefferson said, "The Many!"
Hamilton said, "The Few!"
Like the opposite sides of a penny
Were these exalted two.
If Jefferson said, "It's black, sir!"
Hamilton cried, "It's white!"
But 'twixt the two, our Constitu-
tion started working right.

(Rosemary and Stephen
Vincent Benét)[1]

* * *

In the emerging political system neither order nor liberty could be permitted to hold complete sway. It was necessary therefore to establish and maintain a tension between them, and this has been the fundamental problem throughout American history.

Framing the Constitution

Wounding as it may be to American pride it is not likely that independence could have been won without massive aid by France. The end of the war in November 1783 found a congeries of thirteen sovereign states linked by the Articles of Confederation into "a firm league of friendship." The more democratic wing of the new nation—if it can be called a nation—wished the states to retain effective controls and opposed the granting of more powers to the central government. Conservatives, however, were determined to have a central government strong enough to ensure order and to protect business enterprise inside and outside the country. Though the 1780's were on the whole prosperous, conservatives managed to spread the conviction that economic hardship and political collapse loomed just over the horizon. They were aided by inflation, quarrels among the states, British trade aggression, discontent in the West, and finally by the revolt of dissatisfied farmers in western Massachusetts.

---

[1]Rosemary and Stephen Vincent Benét, *A Book of Americans* (New York: Farrar and Rinehart, 1933), p. 42.

The events that followed called forth unsuspected reserves of national sentiment. It is true that there were dangerous dividing influences: rivalries between little and big states, between coast and interior, between commerce and agriculture, and the incipient quarrel between North and South over Negro slavery. But the binding influences were stronger and were daily breaking down state differences. First were common blood, language, and institutions, and the common possession of the West. Developing economic interests were already cutting across state lines. The interior agrarians from Vermont to Georgia had more in common than their condition of indebtedness: they wanted cheap land, transportation, self-government, and protection from the Indians. Even more important, Northern merchants and Southern commission merchants were finding common ground with bankers, manufacturers, and planters in a determined defense of their property. Perhaps most powerful of all was the memory of the struggle for independence: it had already become a heroic legend which bound together men from every state and region in a common determination that their sacrifices should not prove to have been in vain.

The Constitutional Convention met in Philadelphia's Independence Hall and was organized on May 25, 1787 with George Washington in the president's chair. The sessions lasted through a hot and muggy summer until business was adjourned on September 17. There were fifty-five members in attendance at one time or another, only thirty-nine of whom signed the final recommendations. Voting was by state delegations as units. The members were remarkable for their youth, ability, and property. Twenty-nine of the members were college graduates, five were college presidents or professors, eight had signed the Declaration of Independence, and more than half were lawyers. The average was forty-two, but the youngest member was twenty-seven, and the average was raised by a few oldsters like Franklin and Washington. On the whole, it was the young men who did the work—notably James Madison of Virginia, Alexander Hamilton of New York, and James Wilson of Pennsylvania.

To be successful the convention had to solve four problems. First was the necessity of reconciling the interests and jealousies of the large and small states; second was the problem of reconciling the sovereignties of states and nation; third was the desirability of protecting holders of large property without hampering or antagonizing holders of small property;

and fourth, though not yet as evident as the others, was the necessity of dealing with the growing rivalry between North and South over slavery and commerce.

These problems were solved, mainly by hard-won compromises, but the document that emerged was not entirely an original creation. It was simply the next step in political evolution. Considerable reference was made to Greek confederacies and to the Bible, to Blackstone, and to Montesquieu; but on the whole the Constitution owed its nature to the examples offered by the Articles of Confederation and the constitutions of the states and, most of all, to the Anglo-Saxon genius for compromise.

In looking at the origins of the Constitution we can see how New England's Calvinism and the deism of the Enlightenment cooperated to make what both regarded as a new start in human history. Of course, one had begun by thinking of a purer church and the other of a new political and social order, but both seem to have been convinced that the nation they were guiding was "God's American Israel." Deists, out of their belief in the perfectability of society, wanted as little government as was consistent with good order.

It is difficult to know precisely how much influence Montesquieu and Blackstone had in persuading the convention to separate the powers of government, but there is another possible source of the idea: Calvin's *Institutes*. It may well be that the members trained in theology—Baldwin, Ellsworth, Johnson, and Williamson—as well as James Madison and James Wilson, both Presbyterian-oriented by their education, were familiar with Calvin's advice that government be in the hands of many, so that "if anyone arrogate to himself more than his right, the many may act as censors and masters to restrain his ambition." Calvinistic pessimism may have triumphed over deistic optimism when the framers sought to restrain sinful ambition by setting the parts of government to keep watch on each other. Other democracies have found other means of protecting liberty, notably in Britain, but the method has worked fairly well in the United States until recently.

The Constitution that emerged from the deliberations in Philadelphia set forth the clearest framework of federal government ever devised by men up to that time.

(1) It *divided* the powers of government between states and nation. Within its powers the federal government dealt directly with the citizen ("We, the People. . . .") without the interposition of the states, as under

the Articles. Powers not granted to the federal government were reserved by the states.

(2) It *separated* powers within the federal government among legislature, executive, and judiciary, yet by a system of checks and balances made them interdependent enough so that none could become tyrannical.

(3) It *created* a Congress of two houses: the Senate, in which the states were equally represented by two members elected by the state legislatures; and the House of Representatives, in which the people of each state were represented in proportion to population by directly elected members. The Senate had a check on the President through its right to approve treaties and confirm appointments by the President. The House had the right to originate revenue bills. Congress had power to pass all laws affecting federal powers and duties; to lay and collect taxes, excises, and customs duties, and to appropriate money; to regulate commerce, coin money, operate a postal service, administer the public lands, declare war, support armed services, regulate Indian affairs; and to make laws regarding naturalization, bankruptcy, and weights and measures. Any actions which conflicted with the above were forbidden to the states, but there were also certain powers forbidden to Congress (Article I, Section 9).

(4) Executive powers were lodged in one man, the President, thus providing for efficient administration and clear-cut responsibility. He was to enforce the laws, negotiate treaties, command the armed forces, and was given the right to veto legislation. The Vice-President had no executive duties, but was to preside over the Senate.

(5) The judiciary, headed by the Supreme Court, was appointed by the President with the consent of the Senate, and its members held office for life. The judiciary exercised jurisdiction defined by the Constitution. Most important were its rights to adjudicate cases involving foreign states, between states, and between states and the United States. Treason was strictly defined and limited. Trials were to be by jury, except in cases of impeachment.

(6) Elections were to be held at stated intervals and elected officials were to hold office for definite terms—the President and Vice-President for four years, Senators for six, and Representatives for two.

(7) New states could be admitted by Congress on the same footing as those already existing.

(8) Provision was made that the states must give full faith and credit

to one another's acts, extend all privileges and immunities to one another's citizens, extradite criminals, and deliver up fugitive slaves.

The framers of the Constitution adopted or invented and used in their document the three basic American contributions to the democratic process. First, the Constitutional Convention implemented the compact theory in a practical way, and the method has found worldwide acceptance. Second, the federal system found the practical compromise between the age-old rivals, nationalism and localism, and has been one of the important factors in making possible the growth of the modern state. Third, the old concept of empire as composed of a metropolis and permanently subject colonies or possessions was done away with; the constitution-makers deliberately provided for the admission of dependent areas to the same status as the old.

When the convention was over and the members had signed their names to the document, Benjamin Franklin pointed to the painting of a sun on Washington's chair. "I have often looked at that sun without being able to tell whether it was rising or setting," he said. "Now, at last, I have the happiness of knowing that it is a rising and not a setting sun."

It was a witty observation, but the issue was not to be settled until almost fourscore years had passed. The preamble proclaimed that "We the people of the United States . . . do ordain and establish this Constitution." This has been interpreted to mean that the people were the authors of the Constitution. On the other hand, the Constitution provided that it was to be considered by especially summoned conventions, and was to go into effect on the agreement of the conventions of any nine states. The issue was thus drawn between two historic sides—the states, and the people of the nation. The enemies of the document bitterly denounced the Constitution as ignoring and attempting to supersede the states. The issue was pointed up in *The Federalist*, written by Hamilton, Madison, and Jay. Hamilton argued for the view that the Constitution set up a *nation*, and Madison for the view that it was a *compact* among the states. Their views disclosed the schizophrenia of *The Federalist* and of the country, a schizophrenia that was to lead eventually to the Civil War.

The so-called "sweeping clauses" supplied the rationale later used for the expansion of federal powers. One of them, in the preamble, declares it the purpose of the Constitution to "promote the general welfare"; a second (Article I, Section 8, Clause 1) gives Congress the power to "provide for the common defense and general welfare." The so-called elastic clause (Article I, Section 8, Clause 18) has in particular been used to further the growth of federal authority; after the enumeration of federal powers, the clause provides that the government shall have power "to make all laws which shall be necessary and proper for carrying into execution the foregoing powers."

One objection to the proposed constitution was that it had no Bill of Rights that specifically guaranteed the civil liberties of the people against federal encroachment. Federalist consent to the incorporation of such limitations helped to win the battle for ratification in Massachusetts, Virginia, and doubtless other states. The first Congress submitted proposals to the states which now appear as the first ten amendments: the Bill of Rights.

The Bill of Rights is in many ways the most striking and valuable part of the Constitution. It has become the keystone of American liberties to an extent that perhaps even its original champions did not foresee. The Supreme Court, by a process of evolution, has become the conscience of the nation; it can and sometimes does act when President and Congress are in the doldrums of indifference, or are hampered by political exigencies. In the Bill of Rights the Supreme Court finds a standard of individual liberty which it is obliged to support and which warrants it in vetoing Presidential actions and invalidating federal and state laws when they controvert the letter or the spirit of the Constitution. Nor, in case of a Constitutional showdown, can Congress very often override the Supreme Court. In cases of conflict the principal recourse for Congress is the cumbersome one of amendment.

In studying the Constitution of the United States and the circumstances of its adoption, one is impressed by the all but general dissatisfaction; no one would have claimed that it was a reliable blueprint for the construction of a City of God. The fears of the framers and the people were expressed by the many compromises, the elaborate checks and balances, and the demand for a Bill of Rights. These mechanisms were so patently intended to prevent the interference of government in individual affairs and to prevent hasty action that it is almost fair to say that the document was intended as much to circumscribe government as to implement it. This precaution was inevitable in an unformed nation which had just emerged from a war against tyranny and which was torn by rivalries among localities and between social classes and economic interests.

The framers, perceptive enough to realize that they could not do away with tensions, sought earnestly to hold them in equilibrium. The Constitution provides not only for the *division* of powers between federal and state governments but also for the *separation* within the federal government of powers among executive, legislature, and judiciary. This system, previously adopted by the state constitutions, was in line with the current (and basically erroneous) interpretation of the structure of the British constitution.

In order to maintain this balance, the Constitution and custom have provided checks. The President appoints officials and makes treaties with the consent of the Senate, and he may veto legislation. The legislature initiates bills, restrains executive and judiciary by the power of impeachment, and overrides vetoes by a two-thirds vote. The judiciary may restrain executive officials from illegal acts, and it has the right to declare legislation unconstitutional.

The framers took the opportunity to balance social as well as governmental forces. Most of the members of the convention had a profound distrust of the common people and wished to place their own social class in control. They could not go to an extreme, however, for it was evident that their document must meet the test of popular approval. They therefore sought to remove the people as far as possible from direct influence on policy. Indeed, the only direct control given the people was in the election of the House of Representatives. Senators were elected by the state legislatures. An electoral college whose members were elected by the states was to choose the executive; the man who received the most votes was to become President for four years, and the runner-up was to become Vice-President and preside over the Senate.

The Constitution was not democratic in our modern sense and was not intended to be; and yet it is important to note that, like the democratic process, it kept the way open for change. This fact is evident in the provisions for amendment and for local control of qualifications for voting. No class received any privileges or even recognition, though certainly the convention intended the propertied classes to be represented in the Senate, since it was to be elected by the state legislatures, which were rather generally composed of propertied men. When the framers sought to protect minorities from the malice of majorities, they may or may not have been thinking of big property, but the effect was to protect little property as well—not to mention a long line of dissenters. Nor, for that matter, was any easy way for any class or category of property to gain control. The Founding Fathers were plainly afraid of power, no matter who wielded it, even—or especially—the states.

One curious intention of the framers in setting up their system of checks and balances was to prevent the growth of parties—"factions," they called them. Actually, the system had produced the opposite result, for the balancing parts of government cooperate well only when they are united by party discipline in support of common policies.

The requirement of the consent of three-fourths of the states to pass an amendment would seem to have been made not only to win the good will of the jealous states which feared the tyranny of their neighbors but also to hamper change. On the whole, technical amendments made but few important changes until this century. Meanwhile the vital changes came about through interpretations, the growth of a body of political and technical customs and usages, and the arbitrament of arms, such as the Civil War's decision of certain aspects of the problem of states' rights.

The Rise of Political Parties

Washington had been the giant of the Revolution, and one is entitled to question if independence could have been won without him even with the aid of France. He had presided over the Constitutional Convention with even-handed justice, though it was evident that his sympathies lay with the conservatives. When he was called to serve as the first President of the United States, he was worn out by care and responsibility, so turned to the young and vigorous Alexander Hamilton for help. Hamilton had been Washington's aide-de-camp—really chief-of-staff—and he now became Secretary of the Treasury and assumed the task of organizing the finances of the new government. He seems to have believed that the office constituted him as chief minister, after the pattern of the prime minister in the British Cabinet, the First Lord of the Treasury.

Hamilton was a small man, with handsome features, quick energetic movements, a charming smile, and conversational fascination. There was no doubt of his willful pride and thirst to command. He was eloquent, logical, systematic, an unusually hard worker, and honest and honorable in his business life. On the other hand, he was a director rather than a leader, tactless in management, quick-tempered, and intolerant of stupidity.

He came into office at the age of thirty-four with his political philosophy already developed and with an economic plan for putting it into effect. He held to three principles: (1) government by the aristocracy—though plutocracy might be more accurate; (2) dominance of the economy by investors and entrepreneurs—that is, merchants, industrialists, speculators, bankers, and even planters, if they accepted his program; and (3) a loose interpretation of the Constitution, so that its "defects" could be overcome by "administering" its provisions to promote the power of the federal government.

The touchstone of Hamilton's life and policy was his mistrust of and contempt for the common people. One evening when flushed with wine he uttered the famous words, "The people—your people, sir, is a great beast." While he would not have made serfs of the people or excluded them completely from political rights—he even favored manhood suffrage—he proposed to, thwart their disruptive demands by seeing to it that the rich were cared for and thus, having a property interest in the government, would support it against the storms of democracy. He envisioned the United States as another England, with great industrial cities, ruled over by a privileged class which, because it had everything it wanted, would not be subject to temptation. He seems never to have understood the real nature of the democratic process though, like all democratic conservatives, he yielded to the rising counterforce.

Hamilton was remarkably successful in his policies. In 1831 Daniel Webster eulogized him in a famous passage: "He smote the rock of public resources, and abundant streams of revenue gushed forth. He touched the dead corpse of public credit, and it sprang upon its feet." Hamilton got his way with much of his program. He paid off the Revolutionary bonds at face value—a windfall for their holders. He got his Bank of the United States, intended to issue banknotes and make loans to sound enterprises. On the other hand he failed in his dream of building an industrial nation. In his *Report on Manufactures* he set forth a program for fostering the growth of industry by bounties and stiff tariffs intended to protect infant industries. His merchant followers, the bulk of his party, promptly refused to accept his recommendations except for a low tariff to raise revenue. He was not gifted in his mercantile cohorts, for they were a decaying class which resisted being turned into industrialists.

There were other dissident elements in Hamilton's Federalist Party. John Adams was a critic of his emphasis on "paper" wealth—that is, government bonds and bank stock. As Adams and other opponents of Hamilton saw it, the only real wealth consisted of precious metals and real estate, and they felt that Hamilton had subverted the order of nature by enabling the holders of "intangible" wealth to dictate to planters and farmers.

To the very last the Federalists looked on themselves not as a party but as the political instrument of the ruling class, governing by natural right because they possessed the property. They even denied with a perfectly straight face that they were organized, and carefully concealed the strings of management in order to appear consistent in denouncing the organization of their opponents. Fisher Ames of Massachusetts departed only a little from the official phraseology when he stated that of course there could be but two parties: "the friends order, and its foes."

It is well to warn against classing the Federalists as authoritarians. Despite their pessimistic view of popular stupidity and emotionalism, they would not have washed out civil liberties nor denied the people a voice in government. Fisher Ames proclaimed that "Our Government is a Democratical Republic." He is quoted as having on one occasion contrasted monarchy (absolutism) and republicanism, by which he meant representative government: "Monarchy is a merchantman which sails well, but will sometimes strike on a rock and go to the bottom; a republic is a raft which will never sink, but then your feet are always in the water." Ames described a democracy as a government subject to popular passions regardless of the public welfare; true republican rulers, on the other hand, were bound to act not simply as those who elected them *would*, but as they *ought*.

As it turned out, Hamilton's attempt to strengthen the power of economic privilege called into organized being the counterforce that was to thwart his attempt to "administer" the Constitution in accordance with his image of effective government, and was to furnish the balance to his concepts all through American history.

The leader of the rising counterforce was Thomas Jefferson, a Virginia planter whose catholicity of interests was rivalled only by Benjamin Franklin. Allied with him and a vital contributor to his political standards and program was his Virginia neighbor, James Madison. Tall, loose-jointed, red-haired, and long-faced, Jefferson was at first meeting shy and reserved. Slow and calm in manner, he was seldom irritable or emotional. Probably he lacked a sense of humor, but he possessed sympathy, tolerance, patience, and tact.

In his political methods Jefferson showed an astuteness that Hamilton tried to equal but never could. He did not make Hamilton's mistake of organizing an army of generals. He sought to arouse the common people to an awareness of the value of the vote, he sought to break down excessive property qualifications for the suffrage, and he preached party discipline incessantly. He knew intuitively what the people at the grass roots were thinking and was able to build upon it. Even more important, he had that faith in the people which was necesary to inspire them in following him toward the bright goal of human rights.

Jefferson believed in working calmly and slowly by education; and he believed that if the people saw the light, they would find their own way. Yet he recognized the danger that popular whims might institute a tyranny of majority. The minority also had rights; the majority, to be right, must be reasonable. Basically Jefferson taught that government is the natural enemy of man—hence his insistence that as many functions as possible must be localized in order that the people be able to control them directly. Since government must not be permitted to do anything for the people which they could do themselves, "that government is best which governs least."

He opposed government interference because in that era government rarely intervened in the economy except to aid wealth. Government interference meant protective tariffs, special bounties, lucrative land grants, and monopoly privileges to engage in banking or certain kinds of transportation. Jefferson believed that wealth would sooner or later breed power, and that power for the few is a menace to the liberties of the many. He had at first little comprehension of the part that capital, credit, and labor play in the creation of wealth, and did not learn it until much later. Since power and property are inseparable, he wanted property to be scattered as widely and as evenly as possible; in other words, he favored the multiplication of yeoman farmers.

Jefferson saw the social struggle as one between landed capital and business capital; Hamilton thought of it as basically between the holders of property and the propertyless. Jefferson, however, was inclined to share Hamilton's distrust of the propertyless. Great cities he regarded as great sores, and he never trusted the proletariat, because they were dependent on the good will of employers. For this reason Jefferson was willing to break his tenets and use the government to distribute land cheaply and protect the farmer in its ownership. Indeed, he believed that agriculture was the creator of national wealth and that merchants and manufacturers, however necessary, were parasites. He went so far as to hold that the American states ought "to practice neither commerce nor navigation but to stand with respect to Europe precisely on the footing of China."

In brief Jefferson took direct issue with Hamilton's objectives and taught (1) government by the people; (2) the dominance of agriculture; and (3) the literal and strict interpretation of the Constitution.

The democratic party which Jefferson now undertook to form was known at first as Democratic-Republican, a name soon shortened to Republican. (It was not the ancestor of the present Republican Party.) As Jefferson and Madison looked around for material, they saw the best prospects among the Southern planters, whose deeply rooted belief in agrarian rule was being flouted by the Federalist program of expanding the power of "paper" wealth. The prospects were poorest in New England and South Carolina, though even those in time were to be won over. Pennsylvania's Germans and Scotch-Irish, as well as Philadelphia's "mob," had reliably democratic leaders.

The history of the political conflicts in the first twenty years of the young republic is fascinating, but there is not space to deal with the details here. The events of the French Revolution roused a public interest which was quickly translated into political terms. Those who sympathized with France rallied to the Republicans, and the pro-British to the Federalists. Washington, though himself a Federalist, was distressed by the partisan political conflict, and chose to steer a neutral course between the European combatants.

His Farewell Address, published in September 1796, showed that he had not fully grasped the role of parties in a democracy and regarded them as contravening the rule of reason. Along with much other good advice, he warned against the evils of party strife; but the part of his address most frequently referred to was his warning to have as little political connection as possible with foreign nations. "It is our true policy to steer clear of permanent alliances with any portion of the foreign world.... Taking care always to keep ourselves by suitable establishments on a respectable defensive posture, we may safely trust to temporary alliances for extraordinary emergencies."

This advice was intended to apply to the peculiar circumstances of that time; nowhere did Washington intimate that he was laying down a permanent policy for future generations to follow. The phrase warning against "entangling alliances" attributed to him was not Washington's but Jefferson's in his first inaugural address.

John Adams succeeded Washington in the Presidency, but his tenure was replete with troubles—many of them inspired by Hamilton, who distrusted his economic ideas. Nevertheless Adams should be remembered for his refusal to go along with Hamilton in advocating war with France after the XYZ Affair, even though public sentiment, in the volatile fashion which was to become all too common, had swung against France. But the Federalists antagonized the public by their Alien and Sedition Acts, and with a Federalist Party weakened by faction the Republicans put Jefferson into the Presidency in 1801. There was yet another reason for the Federalist decline and fall. Their aristocratic theory of government was already outmoded—outmoded in its mercantile aspect, that is. Another fact was that Americans were getting out of the habit of voting for their "natural" leaders—except perhaps in the South.

And yet the Federalists deserve more than a parting jeer or a romantic tear from posterity. They had done a task which the Republicans, either because they were not convinced of its necessity or were not willing to take risks boldly, could not have accomplished. It was the Federalists who established the public credit, nursed the fledgling Republic through its first perilous decade of foreign embroilments, laid down precedents and customs, and set the feet of public administration on the firm upward path.

After the fall of the Federalists, most of the leaders of the party became flabby catastrophists. Out of the democratic ascendancy, they told themselves smugly, would come chaos and finally a military dictatorship—a divine retribution on the people for having cast their "natural" rulers out of power. When that day came, the Federalist political veterans would shine in a more splendid court than Washington's, while the chastened people would humbly knuckle their foreheads as they passed. Thus dreaming, they doddered off life's stage and into the wings from which no man and no institution ever returns. They deserved better of fate, but fate has no pity on those who meet the future with only dreams of the past in their hearts.

When Jefferson took up the Presidency he was favored by the fact that Europe was on the verge of a general peace, which would at least remove the occasions found in foreign affairs for party quarrels. He honestly intended his accession to begin the decline of federal power. It did not, and for three reasons: Hamilton had set the customs and precedents in the general direction of his desires, had swollen the public debt, and had taken over the judiciary, wherein judges sat for life; international problems were presently revived and so complicated the situation that they scuttled many of Jefferson's dearest plans; and Jefferson himself, as Hamilton knew, was not a man to thwart a practical solution by clinging to a theory. There is no proof that Jefferson ever changed his basic thinking, but we see in his actual policies a forecast of the characteristic modifications that inevitably come to victorious reform movements.

His principles, set forth in his inaugural address, can be ticked off as follows: a cease-fire in the party battle; strict construction of the Constitution as between federal and state powers; economy and tax reduction; and "peace, commerce, and honest friendship with all nations, entangling alliances with none." Most of these principles had to be modified in actual practice as Jefferson began to learn the facts of political life, and to yield to political pressures and his own keen sense of what was practical.

Unfortunately, events conspired against him. The purchase of Louisiana not only stretched his strict interpretation of the Constitution out of all recognition but plunged the country into debt. The Federalists had entrenched themselves in the Supreme Court and Chief Justice Marshall took advantage of a minor case (*Marbury v. Madison*, 1803) to assert the right of the Court to interpret the Constitution. The miniscule navy instead of being laid up to save money was sent to fight a war against the Barbary pirates in defense of American commerce. Then to top it all, war was renewed between France and England, and each side coolly undertook to prevent the United States from trading with the other. When Jefferson got Congress to lay an embargo on trade with the warring powers in order to bring them to terms, Jefferson became the butt of all but universal opprobrium. Thus one of the most important attempts in history to find an economic substitute for war failed dismally.

The Legacies of Hamilton and Jefferson

When he left the Presidency in 1809, Jefferson was a disillusioned man. He, like Washington, had failed in an attempt to imbue public affairs with a spirit of sweet reasonableness. Most of the Republican principles of 1801 were now unrecognizable. Instead of strict economy and tax relief, national expenditures were greater than ever; instead of a navy at the docks, it had been busier than ever; instead of peace, there had been one war and a narrow escape from another; instead of strict construction and preservation of states' rights, federal power had been enhanced. Even the hated Sedition Act had been aped by a no less tyrannical Embargo Enforcement Act. Secretary of the Treasury Gallatin, the enemy of the Bank of the United States, had become a convert to its convenience and efficiency—and Jefferson, after a mild protest, had assented. From distrust of manufactures Jefferson had come to view them (at least publicly) with pride and even to count them as a good result of the Embargo.

If Jefferson needed any proof of his basic failures, it was dramatized in the long caravans of common farmers who, in despair of relief from Republican policy, were abandoning their sour and eroded acres and wending across the mountains to the fertile bottom lands of the West. That his agrarian policies were not those of the developing future was shown by the way in which his followers, in both North and South, were furtively turning the pages of Hamilton's *Report on Manufactures* and dreaming not of a bucolic paradise but of bustling cities and whirring machinery. It was they who had pulled down the pillars of his Embargo when it was on the verge of success and ruined his hope of finding a substitute for war.

In the United States we find two great ideological streams, represented by Hamilton and Jefferson, each laying primary emphasis on different aspects of Locke—respectively property rights and natural rights. Textbooks usually draw a clear dichotomy between them as standing respectively for (1) strong government versus weak government; (2) manufactures versus agriculture; and (3) aristocracy versus democracy. Still, neither of them was thoroughly consistent even in what he may have regarded as his fundamental principles. It would be a mistake, therefore, to view American history along hard-and-fast Hamiltonian and Jeffersonian lines, for as we shall see they cross-fertilized and even traded principles.

Certain of Hamilton's and Jefferson's principles resembled the laissez faire school of economic thought which had been developed by the French physiocrats and Adam Smith. The physiocrats, who began writing soon after 1700, were searching for a means of breaking the stifling mercantilist restrictions on the landowning class. As they saw it, agriculture and the extractive industries were the only wealth of a nation—everything else depended on them. All taxes, wherever along the line they were collected, were passed back to the landowner; therefore why not do away with the tangle of taxation and lay a *single* tax on the cultivator's surplus? Jefferson long insisted that all wealth comes from the land and that manufacture and trade are parasites. He may not have copied the French physiocrats in detail, but there is a certain resemblance between them. There was a further facet of physiocracy. Following John Locke, the physiocrats held that, just as there is a natural law in morals and politics, so also there is a natural law in economics—the principle of freedom. In order to put this law into effect, all that is needed is to let individuals alone, for they will normally act in accordance witht the law. Let the government, therefore, stand aloof from economic activities and act only as a benevolent policeman to protect life, liberty, and property. *"Laissez faire et laissez passer, le monde va de lui-même."* Let goods be made freely, let them (and people) pass freely through frontiers; the world goes on of itself. The logical result should have been the breaking-down of national boundaries and the growth of European unity but, as we shall see, nationalism and imperialism intervened.

Hamilton's domestic economic policy was in some part consistent with physiocracy's child, laissez faire, but not so his international policy. He wished to put the force of the government behind a movement to industrialize. If Hamilton had got his way, the government might have felt forced to go on to subsidize manufacturers by other means (as has happened in the twentieth century). In this case the government might have overshadowed the individual entrepreneur—or perhaps in the end the great entrepreneurs would have run the government. This would have been a return to mercantilism (page 77—a kind of neo-mercantilism). Actually, Hamiltonianism, with its close relationship to government, did not come into its own until well after the Civil War, with the burgeoning of the protective tariff, of government-favored big industry, and particularly with the rise of oligopoly in our century.

We can see now that it is not quite accurate to call Hamilton conservative—that is, conserving the old—for he was certainly progressive in economics, and in those days the word "liberal" carried much the same meaning as "progressive." Nor was Jefferson altogether a liberal even in the modern meaning of the word—that is, receptive of new ideas—for he had the desire to keep power in the hands of the agrarians, who were certainly conservative.

With the above said, we can repeat that liberalism as a historical term in the United States (not necessarily in Europe) has been the political movement which expresses the needs of more or less disadvantaged groups, and so is a form of protest against established interests. In America one group has been markedly influential from the beginning: private business. Therefore, while American liberalism has had many objectives, the one that is most common, that seems to exist in any time and place, is this: to cut back or control the power of private business so that, in the view of the liberals of the day, it is helpful rather than harmful to society at large.

American liberalism, therefore, has been Jeffersonian in its goals. These goals are more a spirit than a precise set of objectives. But they are best understood as those set down in Jefferson's great statements, most notably the Declaration of Independence: equality, freedom from oppression, a concern for the ordinary man, an intense determination to safeguard freedom of thought and expression. We cannot say that the liberal always emphasizes the unity of the group and collective action. In earlier times, it happened that liberals fought against precisely these things on the ground that, under current conditions, they would increase oppression, give big business more power, heighten rather than reduce inequality, and hamper freedom of expression. The means, then, will vary from one generation to another, but the goals sought remain the same.

The people of the United States have found in capitalism the promise of popular welfare, and quite often its realization. The abundance of resources gave to their reform movements a color quite unlike that of older countries. Since nearly everyone has been able to win some property if he is willing to work and save, the historic combat has not been a straight issue between property and human rights. It would be clearer and usually more accurate to speak of the struggle as between big property and little property.

While it is true that political revolts are always in progress somewhere in the country, the Jeffersonian side of the conflict nevertheless becomes clear in the national scene only about once in a generation (1800, 1828, 1860, 1896, 1912, 1932, 1964). The Democratic Party is one with the *tendency* toward liberalism, but the opposition is never without its liberal wing, and Jeffersonian reforms may be implemented by either party. Lincoln once pungently illustrated this condition with a story: "I remember being once much amused at seeing two partially intoxicated men engaged in a fight with greatcoats on, which fight, after a long and rather harmless contest, ended in each having fought himself out of his own coat and into that of the other." Lincoln himself, though a member of the party of Hamilton, has become a legendary hero of Jeffersonianism.

American political reform movements have never been root-and-branch crusades. They have pared, and altered, and regulated, but in the end the old tree is still alive. The aim has been, not to kill basic institutions but to revitalize them. Little property has sought to limit the overwhelming menace of big property to democratic equality. Liberal political movements usually have come on the heels of notable increases in the size or privileges of big property. It is also noteworthy that in a number of cases the rebels have been bought off by a handout of public land. Jefferson had to make recourse to this evasion when he lowered the price and terms of payment of public land. Hamiltonians and Jeffersonians have historically followed pretty much the same methods. Both have desired minimum government interference, though neither has scrupled to call for government aid in a pinch—little property against big property, and big property against labor agitators or foreign competitors. The tendency in this century, however, is for the Jeffersonians to demand regulation of big property and to enforce competition.

Jefferson himself began the fuzzing process during his Presidency, and by the 1840's the two streams had greatly influenced each other—and the process has contained ever since, as it must in a democracy based on compromise. Moreover, neither has hesitated to grasp the typical weapons of the other—as is seen by the way in which the party in power, whichever it may be, tends to favor strong government; and by the way in which both parties have liberal and conservative wings. This seems illogical to those outside the English-speaking tradition, but has thus far (with the exception of 1860) prevented the division of politics into two intransigent ideologies which cannot compromise, and which therefore are always teetering on the verge of civil war.

Jefferson had not passed away before his movement showed deep fissures. He had advocated self-reliance, but by the 1830s some of his business-oriented followers drew a doctrine of rugged individualism from his doctrines. Not all farmers and laborers have been Democrats, but along with certain kinds of businessmen they have historically formed the core of the party, at least in the North and West. The aristo-agrarians, by a line of descent through John Randolph of Roanoke, John

Taylor "of Caroline," and John Calhoun, came to reject the natural rights doctrines transmitted through Hooker, Locke, and Jefferson and to stress the patriarchal order of Filmer. Perhaps this was inevitable in a slaveholding society. At any rate, the disaster of the Civil War rather than destroying the patriarchal society actually prolonged its life—though it has been forced into uneasy alliances either with the Hamiltonians or the Jeffersonians. Finally, there were the rising laborities with their penchant for hard money, free trade, and certain reforms.

The Hamiltonians also had their divergencies. The mercantile element, centered largely in New England, tended to oppose Hamilton's favorite policy of promoting manufactures by active government guidance, mainly by means of bounties and protective tariffs. Until the War of 1812 the merchants dominated Hamilton's party, but thereafter true Hamiltonianism began to forge to the front. *Began* is the operative word, for it did not reach its culmination until the New Deal—which, curiously enough, was in certain important aspects Hamiltonian.

Thus the simon-pure Hamiltonians were hospitable to government aid to industry and more than that, to government guidance. The Jeffersonian rugged individualists wanted the first but not the second, and when they joined the Hamiltonians in the Republican Party (the second Republican Party) after the Civil War the two elements were uneasy together and have furnished one of the reasons for the present-day split between the Republican left and right. The former is really Hamiltonian in its hospitality to government guidance, the latter—the advocate of extreme states' rights and laissezfaire—stems from the rugged individualists. (But note that Jefferson advocated self-reliance, not the cutthroat individualism later drawn from his teachings.) Similarly, the Democratic Party has a Hamilton wing that favors government guidance and a Jeffersonian wing that favors states' rights and laissez faire. Nevertheless, there is a difference between the two main streams, and this difference is the basic distinction between the parties.

When Jefferson retired from the Presidency he placed his own bust and that of Hamilton facing each other in the great hall of his home at Monticello, and there they still stand, opposite each other in death as in life. Their position is fitting, for they personify the two great forces of democratic evolution. As Jefferson himself said, "The terms Whig and Tory belong to natural as well as to civil history. They denote the temper and constitution of mind of different individuals." In another place he was even more explicit: "In every free and deliberating society, there must, from the nature of man, be opposite parties and violent dissensions and discords; and one of these, for the most part, must prevail over the other for a longer or shorter time. Perhaps this party division is necessary to induce each other to watch and to relate to the people at large the proceedings of the other."

We have devoted so much time to the first twenty years of the Republic because this was the period in which the nation set the direction of its development (capitalism) and the method of its development (the democratic process). Hamilton stood for a strong central government, the dominance of commerce and manufactures, and rule by the rich, the well-born, and the able; Jefferson stood for a weak central government, the dominance of agriculture, and rule by the people as a whole. During the first twenty years of the republic we find either the two leaders or their followers deliberately contradicting in word or deed every item of their trilogy of tenets, and there is a lesson in that fact. No one can be quite so pure and moral about "principles" as a party out of power; no one sees so readily as a group of men in power that facts must be dealt with on their own terms. But the original cast of mind remains, and earth will deal with a situation as nearly as possible in conformity with its basic beliefs and hopes.

The basic principles of Hamilton and Jefferson—as distinguished from the above tenets—lie much deeper. They can perhaps be best expressed in the two concepts "order" and "liberty." Hamilton did not reject liberty, of course; he simply believed that it must give precedence to good order, in the sense of stability. Jefferson did not reject order; he simply believed that order without liberty is of no value.

Both believed that where a man's treasure is, there will his heart be also. Hamilton looked on order in the sense of stability, and property as treasures that are responsibly guarded only if they are entrusted to the select few. Property, as the rock of good order and the guarantee of stability, must be preserved from direct injury or from limitations that prevent it from multiplying itself freely. Obviously, the Jeffersonians did not reject the holding of property; they simply believed that property should not become an instrument that could be used for limiting the rights, snatching the livelihood, or besmirching the dignity of the individual.

In the emerging political system neither order nor liberty could be permitted to hold complete sway. Rigid order is the bulwark erected by conservatives—including those who have "made their pile"—to protect their status or property, and inevitably it will vitiate liberty because it gives them the power to oppress their fellows. Complete liberty (individualism) enables those with luck, initiative, or shrewdness to gain an undue share of economic power—and with it will come inequality, because *they* will have the power to oppress their fellows. It is necessary therefore to establish and maintain a tension between order and liberty, and this has been the fundamental problem throughout American history.

Jefferson saw what many still fail to grasp: that to preserve this tension there must be a considerable degree of relative (*not* absolute) economic equality. If we examine his policies in that light we will see that he devoted his life to shoring up small property interests as an offset to the monied "aristocracy." He thought of the small farmers as the bulwark of democracy because in their independence and relative economic equality lay his hope of preserving the tension between order and liberty. (Equality also tends to promote mediocrity and hamper the initiative essential to progress, but that is another story.)

Hamilton sought to implant and maintain the political ascendance of an aristocracy; it was Jefferson who forced on him the pattern of democratic evolution through political conflict. Hamilton's legacy was intensely practical, mundane, and a little selfish; he lighted the furnaces of America's iron mills, hoisted the sails of its trading ships, and posted the ledgers in banks and counting houses; his was the inspiration that led to organization and technology that bred mass production and the American standard of living.

Jefferson's legacy was that of faith in humanity; he touched the moral consciousness of men with the spark of inspiration and sounded the trumpet call to battle for human rights. Hamilton was the head, Jefferson the heart. Hamilton was materialistic, Jefferson was idealistic; and though they may clash, neither can live long without the other. Hamilton was might, Jefferson was right. Might gives right the power to survive, and right gives might the moral reason to fight for survival. Thus in eternal conflict, eternal compromise, and eternal interdependence, Hamilton and Jefferson have lived since there were men on this earth and will live as long as men remain.

Chapter 6
Problems of the
Democratic Revelation

Proem

The mechanics of the United States have already outstripped the artists and have, by their bold and unflinching adaptation, entered the true track and held up the light for all who operate for American wants, be they what they will. By beauty I mean the promise of function; by action I mean the presence of function; by character I mean the record of function. We found our institutions on hope, Europeans on experience. We hoist the sail and are seasick; they anchor and dance.

(Horatio Greenough, 1852)

* * *

De Tocqueville Looks at Two Sides of America. Alexis de Tocqueville, a young Frenchman, visited the United States in 1831 and in his *Democracy in America* analyzed in depth what he saw.

American Discontent. In America I saw the freest and most enlightened men placed in the happiest circumstances that the world affords; [yet] it seemed to me as if a cloud habitually hung upon their brow, and I thought them serious and almost sad, even in their pleasures. ... He who has set his heart exclusively upon the pursuit of worldly welfare is always in a hurry, for he has but a limited time. ... If in addition to the taste for physical well-being a social condition he added in which neither laws nor customs retain any person in his place, there is a great additional stimulant to this restlessness of temper. ... They have swept away the privileges of some of their fellow creatures which stood in their way, but they have opened the door to universal competition; the barrier has changed its shape rather than its position.

Democracy Adjusts Its Errors. The difficulty that a democracy finds in conquering the passions and subduing the desires of the moment with a view to the future is observable in the United States in the most trivial things. The people surrounded by flatterers, find great difficulty in surmounting their inclinations; whenever they are required to undergo a privation or any inconvenience, even to attain an end sanctioned by their own rational conviction, they almost always refuse at first to comply. . . . Though a democracy is more liable to error than a monarch or a body of nobles, the chances of its regaining the right path when once it has acknowledged its mistake are greater also; because it is rarely embarrassed by interests that conflict with those of the majority and resist the authority of reason. But a democracy can obtain truth only as the result of experience; and many nations may perish while they are awaiting the consequences of their errors.

The Simple Mechanic

If the War of 1812 played any legitimate part in the American quest it can be no more than in conviction that more land would bring more freedom and opportunity. The conduct of the war was so mishandled that it was a debacle from which stalemate emerged only because of Macdonough's defeat of the British fleet on Lake Champlain. Most obvious results of the war were the passing of the pro-British Federalist remnants into limbo and a certain stimulus to enterprise. The reason for the delusion that the War of 1812 was a significant American victory lies in the fact that we forget pain and remember pleasure and that we interpret events to our own credit. The opinion was based, among other things, on Jackson's victory at New Orleans (actually won after the signing of the peace treaty); on the end of impressment of sailors and trade discrimination because of the end of the Napoleonic wars; and on the end of significant Indian troubles in the Old Northwest.

The postwar period has conventionally received the misnomer of the Era of Good Feelings. Actually there were plenty of ill feelings as rival politicians jockeyed for advantage, and the period is best understood as one of reorientation. In order to understand the conflict which was renewed in the 1820's it is useful to examine certain material aspects of the adolescent republic.

First of all we should mention the existence of tremendous natural resources, exploitable by the current technology, and so abundant that Americans hooted at the suggestion that they could ever be used up. Historians, especially Frederick Jackson Turner and David Potter, have taught us to believe that it has been abundance that has guided our national development and that is at the root of the world-wide revolution of rising expectations; democracy could survive and flourish only because of the opportunities afforded by our natural resources, and which enabled us to allay discontent by making cheap land available. Though this was seldom understood before our own time, American history is in a sense the history of our drive into abundance, and it has never ceased to influence our actions. We shall examine the concept in greater detail when in a later chapter we treat power and illusion.

America was a raw continent with all the heavy work of building a civilization to be done and relatively few inhabitants to do it. In these straits it was natural for Americans to see the uses of steam in lifting, moving, hauling, sawing, crushing, and grinding. Then there was the problem of distance, for the United States was not compact like England and France, but even in its infancy sprawled over nearly a million square miles.

We know the solutions. The errand into the wilderness had been transplanted from the realm of theology to the secular realm of politics. Now it was transferred to the realms of science, technology, and economics. American scientific thought bourgeoned, led by such men as Joseph Henry and Josiah Willard Gibbs, but the American genius was, above all, practical. The vision of the City of God had now become that of a society in which the common man lived in peace and plenty, and this vision was drawn closer to fulfillment by the way in which American independence had released a surge of creative activity not only in political and constitutional affairs but in technology. Within a generation after the revolution Americans began to pour out a spate of inventions: the cotton gin, efficient steam engines, the steamboat, and machine tools; and to these were presently added new printing processes, agricultural implements, the sewing machine, the electric telegraph, and numerous railway improvements.

The invention fundamental to this amazing spurt, however, was the interchangeable part, which can be attributed primarily to Eli Whitney and Simeon North. It was this invention along with the perfection of machine tools driven by water or steam power that made it possible to use semi-skilled labor in the manufacture of useful goods at prices that could be afforded by the common man. The names of inventors and improvers could be extended ad infinitum; suffice it to say that long before the Civil War the machines of the Northeast were pouring forth a steady stream of bolts, nails, tacks, screws, wire, small tools, and other objects too numerous to mention. Before the Civil War the copying lathe, the drop hammer, and the die forge had been invented. The crowning achievements of Yankee ingenuity were the turret lathe, the grinding machine, and the universal milling machine; with these it was possible to attain an automatic precision hitherto undreamed of.

One amusing illustration of the way in which new techniques were changing the competitive picture in American industry will serve to illuminate the whole. Before the 1830's wooden clocks had cost $5 and metal clocks as much as $50, but in 1838 Chauncey Jerome of Connecticut used a system of interchangeable parts to produce brass clocks that sold for fifty cents. When a shipment of his cheap clocks reached England, the British customs officials, thinking that he was trying to beat down the amount of the duty, decided to punish him by buying in the clocks at the invoice price of $1.50 each. Jerome was delighted and sent another shipment. It also was seized and prompt payment made. It was not until the third shipment arrived at the same low invoice price that the British discovered that they had been "had" by the Yankee clockmaker.

A writer in *The Economist* (London) of August 27, 1853 viewed the American industrial scene:

> The Americans seem to be an eminently practical race. Their numerous inventions all tend to the common and general advantage, to bring about equally beneficial results for all by less labour. Their intellect is exerted for the benefit of all. It is not warped to consult the gratification of a few. They open their eyes and their senses to present wants, and set all their faculties to work to gratify them. They look Nature in the face, attend to her minutest signs, learn to read quickly her directions, and they are inventive, skillful, and prosperous.... Not being an old people, their senses are not perverted, nor their faculties benumbed, by a reverence for ancient prejudices.... They unite that perfection of the senses which is proper to the savage with the knowledge and appliances of civilized men. More than any existing people ... they are free to use all their faculties to promote their worldly success, and they are eminently successful.

If Hamilton was able to look down from whatever paradise he inhabited he must have been delighted by the change in economic America, for at last an appreciable number of the merchant class were taking steps toward industry, though by and large the capitalists were new men unconnected with commerce. The growth of industry found philosophical champions in Mathew Carey and his son Henry, publishers of Philadelphia.

Mathew Carey aimed at more than profits for manufacturers, or even national self-sufficiency. If democracy were to be realized, he held, it must offer wider opportunities. As the country then was, the ambitious young man was limited in choice to a few callings; these could be increased only by industrialization, and that could come only when England's throttling hold on the American market was pried loose. Then talent and ingenuity would be rewarded, general prospertiy increased, and personal life cultivated and enriched.

According to Henry Carey, laws are unitary, and so economic law must agree with moral law. He repudiated "the invisible hand" of free trade and competition that Adam Smith had claimed would usher in peace and prosperity, and plumped for the protective tariff, and for the "principle of association"—a happy balance between industry and agriculture. He also advocated a sort of Hamiltonian form of national planning, by which each nation should shake off the shackles of England and develop its own economy and culture. The mission of the United States was to hasten this day by its own example. Only when by such means the economic problems of humanity had been solved could there ensue harmony of interests and the universal reign of tolerance, peace, and morals. Henry Clay drew from the Careys much of the inspiration for his American System, which tried to find common interests among farmer, planter, and manufacturer.

The groping which we shall find so evident among the American intellectuals of the middle of the nineteenth century was partly due to the early phases of a dilemma which was not to become clear until our own century; this was the conflict between the European cultivated tradition and the American vernacular, or native workmanship. It was basically a struggle between an aristocratic elite and the democratic engineer.

Europe's art and technology were rooted in its traditional civilization that had developed with more or less symmetry from classical times to the Industrial Revolution. To quote John Kouwenhoven, the American vernacular—that is, native workmanship—is the folk art "of the first people in history who, disinherited of a great cultural tradition, found themselves living under democratic institutions in an expanding machine economy."[1] American democracy, for the first time in history, sought a civilization built on material service to, as well as appreciation by, the people; and in pursuance of this dream many artists, engineers, and craftsmen were trying to find the way to use the material resources of America in new forms useful to the masses.

Although the political institutions of the United States were based on democracy, many of its inherited social institutions reflected distrust of the people. The inexorable pressure of democracy was shaping a machine culture to develop the nation's resources in the service of the masses, but the pressure of the American inferiority complex was calling for the absorption *in toto* of the European cultivated tradition. The conflict that grew out of these clashing pressures not only pained artists but confused the public. Nevertheless, generations of simple American mechanics refused to feel inferior but asserted that function should govern form. Devoid as they were of any training in taste, they deplored Europe's so-called "art" and "beauty" as mere artificial prettiness, though they failed to realize that they themselves had found the nub of art and beauty in their native workmanship. That they had done so is evident to anyone who examines the simple architecture of the antebellum period, such as the Shaker barn or the Cape Cod cottage, or the common artifacts, such as furniture and tools—for example, the ax, a light, utilitarian, and graceful descendant of the European's unwieldy broadax.

The European tradition and the American vernacular were quite incompatible, and each stubbornly refused to give way; it was in effect a great struggle between the aristocratic elite and the democratic engineer, who sought to exploit the machine to elevate the masses. The first promised static order; the latter intended change, with all its potential for either a better life or chaos.

Hence American intellectuals were torn between the supposed security of status and the democratic demand for change. The struggle between native and alien forms afflicted not only art, literature, and mechanics, but politics and, in one sense, the Civil War was an aspect of this conflict.

---

[1]John Kouwenhoven, *Made in America* (Garden City, N. Y.: Doubleday, 1948), p. 15.

Horatio Greenough, the sculptor, was one of the first to recognize the nature and significance of the clash. Americans, he said, founded their institutions on hope, Europeans on the past. "We hoist the sail and are seasick; they anchor and dance." Greenough also anticipated the modern role of function. "The mechanics of the United States," said he, "have already outstripped the artists and have, by their bold and unflinching adaptation, entered the true track and held up the light for all who operate for American wants, be they what they will. By beauty I mean the promise of function; by action I mean the presence of function; by character I mean the record of function." In another place he went on to say "this American people is the advance guard of humanity because it is one vast interrogation. Never affirming but when there is need for action. . . . it gives peace and good will in proportion to the universality of the wants to which it ministers."

The American vernacular influence sprang from the masses, and persisted despite the determined effort of the upper class to put Corinthian pillars on steam engines and brighten their framework with pomegranates and arabesques. Europe feared the machine and wished to hide and prettify it. The American vernacular wished to strip away unnecessary bulk, weight, and ornamentation in order to simplify, cut the cost, and increase efficiency. The difference in approach was fundamental. Europe wished to preserve the old, which itself had once been functional but was now outmoded by new techniques, because the old represented the set of values on which an age-old elite based its ascendance—values that were now obsolete but for which no sure substitute had been found. The American instinctively realized that if the machine was to serve *all* the people it must not be hamstrung by the old artistic forms. Just as the explorer had boldly set out to find new lands, some Americans boldly set out to find new social values—and to express them in all of life.

One of the most remarkable developments was the balloon-frame house, so called in contempt of its lightness, which used the plentiful nails provided by new machines to fasten together frames composed of light two-by-four studs. This was the answer to the need for cheap housing for the masses, and was an example of the way in which the vernacular overpowered the cultivated tradition. Hitherto houses had been framed of heavy timbers as much as a foot square, joined by mortise-and-tenon and held firm by wooden pegs. Apparently the first balloon-frame structure was St. Mary's Catholic Church in Chicago, designed and built by Augustine Deodat Taylor in 1833.

The New Nationalism

The Federalists had been fatally weakened by their pro-British stand during the War of 1812 and by the continued dominance of the mercantile class. Still maundering in their stocks about the inevitable catastrophe that would follow in the wake of democracy, they found their sons refusing to accept the roles of catastrophists and traitors. Young Federalists signed on with the Republican crew, bringing with them Hamilton's *Report on Manufactures*, and joined with young Republicans to pull the party ship out of the Madisonian doldrums and speed it before the winds of nationalism.

These men now led the Republican Party in pushing Hamilton's nationalist program, including the protection of manufactures by a stiff tariff; the formation of a Second Bank of the United States (called B.U.S. for short) in place of the old one, whose charter had run out; and the building of a network of roads and canals. The leaders were such men as John Quincy Adams and Daniel Webster of Massachusetts, Henry Clay of Kentucky, and John C. Calhoun of South Carolina. The success of the Nationalists consolidated the opposition among those who felt that the federal government was unconstitutionally encroaching on the rights of the states. The leaders of the opposition, among others, were Andrew Jackson of Tennessee, the hero of New Orleans, and his devoted follower, Martin Van Buren of New York.

But meanwhile the young Republicans had found a powerful ally in the Supreme Court and in the legal profession generally. American patriots, eager to be independent in all matters, proposed the passage in each state by legislative statute of a democratic code of laws to supplant the inherited English common law, but the movement was stopped cold by two great jurists. They were Joseph Story of Massachusetts, associate on the Supreme Court bench, and James Kent, Chancellor of the State of New York. Their method was to show that English common law was based on natural law (moral law to the more pious) and must therefore of course be accepted. Their lives were devoted to fitting the common law of England to the facts, at least the supposed facts, of American conditions.

Now where law is supreme, there is a tendency for the lawyer to become supreme, because the law is a "mystery" known only to the initiated. Since the law is the lawyer's life, he finds it to his interest to preserve it from heedless executive and legislative encroachments; he watches over it with a jealous care which the average citizen, even in a democracy, would never have the knowledge, opportunity, or patience to imitate.

That the law as it was being interpreted was chiefly concerned with the protection of individual rights, principally those relating to property, does not mean that the courts were consciously promoting control by big property, for their decisions were aimed at giving little business a break as well—and this was then a nation of little business. The federal government was defended against the assaults of the states because the latter were presumably more open to control by wild and subversive interests that might attack property.

John Marshall of Virginia had been made Chief Justice by President John Adams in an effort to set up a judicial roadblock behind the retreating Hamiltonian forces. No matter what fire-eating Republicans might sit on the Supreme bench, Marshall's clarity of reasoning and charm of manner steadily converted them to his opinions, and in time the Court's delaying action was to turn into an advance. Marshall did not, of course, draw these constitutional principles out of the air (though the Old Republicans accused him of it) but "found" them implied in the Constitution itself.

The two principles validated by his decisions were the supremacy of the federal government in its sphere of action, and the role of the Supreme Court as the arbiter between states and nation and of the constitutionality of legislative and executive actions.

In a long succession of decisions Marshall and the Supreme Court asserted the right of the Court to pass on the constitutionality of Congressional and state legislation and to overrule state courts. He also upheld federal sovereignty over the states in certain disputed matters by confirming Hamilton's doctrine of implied powers. Control of interstate commerce was awarded to the federal governement. Business corporations were in some measure freed from state control by the decision that state charters of incorporation (that is, contracts) once granted, were not arbitrarily subject to change. (Later generations have found ways of limiting what was for a while practically the sovereign powers of corporations.)

To the jurists of the Supreme Court goes the credit for making the slightly considered third branch of the federal government a decisive instrument for preserving balance within that government and between it and the states. The Court paved the legal road for the creation of a nation in place of the congeries of sovereign states whose rivalries among themselves and with the federal government might have torn the Union apart. It also laid the foundations necessary for the growth of industrial capitalism.

The 1820's also foreshadowed the controversy over slavery which forty years later was to split the Union and lead to civil war. The framers of the Constitution had favored the slave states by allowing them to count three-fifths of the slave population in estimating the number of men they could send to the House of Representatives. At the time there was a fairly widespread opinion that slavery was on the way out. However, Eli Whitney's cotton gin provided a quick and cheap means of removing the seeds from cotton; the result was that the profits were put back into slavery and cotton and slavery spread across the Gulf states.

When in 1819 Missouri applied for admission as a slave state the North insisted that it must give up slavery; the object, of course, was to amend the slave states' "over-representation" in the House. The emergence of the slavery issue struck a chill to the heart of every man whose first love was his country. The aged Jefferson wrote that it came "like a fire bell in the night." All over the country and in the halls of Congress the Constitutional and moral aspects of slavery were fiercely debated.

When Maine obtained the consent of Massachusetts to apply for admission as a state, Henry Clay saw that the raw materials of a compromise were available. The names of Maine and Missouri were not combined in one bill, but it was well understood that they were to balance each other. The compromise, passed in 1820, was technically the provision that the Louisiana Purchase north of 36° 30' should, except for Missouri, be regarded forever as free from slavery. However, the admission of Missouri and Maine preserved the Senate balance between free and slave states, and for the next generation this balance was preserved by the admission of states in pairs.

The immediate effect of the Missouri Compromise was to crystallize the attitude of Southerners toward their special interests, especially slavery. Though the slavery issue did not openly reappear in Congress for some time, its existence was disclosed by the stiffening of the South's resistance to encroachments on all its other interests.

These other interests were usually economic and social, though an attempt was made to veil them by constitutional arguments. The constitutional issue, of course, was states' rights versus nationalism, and the issue was never far below the surface during the early years of the republic. They were defended as abstract constitutional principles, but the defender always had in mind some practical problem or interest.

During the 1820's, nationalism was far from being an irresistible force, and at that very time was being confronted by a new rival, the democratic movement. At first the democratic movement seemed to be all on the side of states' rights but the outcome was not that simple or clear-cut. The truth is that by the 1820s the influence of Hamilton and Jefferson had cross-fertilized to a point where it is sometimes difficult to distinguish between them. We can say, however, that the Hamiltons were represented by such forces as the Second Banks of the United States, whose directors, led by Nicholas Biddle, saw "Bank and State" (meaning by "State" the federal government) as natural allies in guiding the country's economy through a course of sound—and not too rapid—growth.

The nationalist President, John Quincy Adams, deplored the increasing decay of Christian community and envisioned something very like the service state. It was to be democratic, but guided by an enlightened aristocracy—an aristocracy in the true sense of the word *aristos* (best), composed of men of character, compassion, and intellect. He would have had public needs transcend private by taxing away speculative profits and the unearned increment in land values to promote the general welfare. Of course Adams in his views was more modern than Hooker (who might be called the last of the medieval interpreters) but he emphasized freedom and constitutionalism just as Hooker did and he looked on the democratic leader much as Hooker did on the "general mover" and as Edwards did on the ruler who must have "great ability for the management of public affairs."

Adams' dream was so alien to the rugged individualists of the brash young republic that it was shouted down and laughed down, and the dreamer himself was crushed. Nevertheless, the dream persisted and was to be revived by some of the New Dealers in and out of government, at least in their aspirations.

The Jeffersonians, on the other hand, insisted that the government should stand aside and let the individual run his own affairs. Northern individualists, whether farmers or businessmen, identified democracy with private enterprise, upheld states' rights, and essentially preferred Jefferson's weak government to Hamilton's strong government. Among them were those rising businessmen who believed their interests best promoted by states' rights and who were to spearhead the attack on the Bank which they regarded as a Hamiltonian enemy.

Southern Jeffersonian was based on planter aristocracy. It was the die-hard, aristo-agrarian, states'-rights school which opposed business and insisted on complete laissez faire; it set up the Athenian ideal of a society of citizens erected on an economic basis of slavery. The two wings of Jeffersonian individualism often made common cause against the Hamiltonians.

By the 1830s there were three easily discernible sections in the country. New England and the Middle Atlantic States had hitherto been separate sections; now, they began to emerge as the Northeast. The Southeast comprised the states south of Mason and Dixon's Line and east of the Appalachian Mountains. The West, the area west of the Appalachians, was destined to split along the line of the Missouri and Ohio Rivers, but in this period it was a unit, at least in the general sense that it wanted free, or at least cheap, land. These were the general lines of division that emerged in the 1820s and lasted until about 1845. Each section tended to rally around its peculiar economic and political interests, but this was not invariably true. Above all, one should avoid the error of thinking of the sections as each adhering to a single political party. On the contrary, the parties were national. They drew their support from every section.

The Democratic Resurgence

The Jacksonian Era in a strict sense would include President Andrew Jackson's two administrations and that of his friend and successor Martin Van Buren—that is, from 1829 to 1841. However, the issues around which the conflicts of that period centered began to take first place in public attention as early as 1825, with John Qunicy Adams' first annual message. This message so clearly championed the nationalist program that it called forth the bitter opposition of the advocates of states' rights, and with the hard times of 1819 they advocated the resurgence of democracy as a remedy. The people, looking about for a scapegoat, were ready to find simple causes and to be sold simple cures. What could be more simple than to assert that the people had lost control of their government, and what more simple cure could be found than to take it back? The nationalist program, it was claimed, had all been for the benefit of business, and so democratic ardor focused upon upsetting it.

It has often been the custom to picture this democratic resurgence, called the Jacksonian Movement, as sweeping out of the West like a great wave. Actually, it came from all parts of the Union. Look at the numerous local complaints. The West was convinced that New England was blocking cheap land and internal improvements; the South blamed the Northeast for raising the prices of manufactured goods by the tariff; the Northeast blamed the rest of the country for bringing on the crash by a razzle-dazzle currency issued by all sorts of unincorporated banks and enterprises. Nearly everyone in trouble blamed B.U.S. for its attempt to gain a monopoly of currency and attacked the Supreme Court for promoting national power.

Eastern laborers complained that their wages were oppressively low and that employers could cheat them with impunity, for of course a poor man could not afford expensive legal redress. Moreover, they went on, membership in unions was punished by loss of one's job, and courts went out of their way to prevent and punish strikes. In the East and South, the commonalty complained that state constitutions preserved many earmarks of the conservative reaction of the 1780's, and suffrage was still based on property. State churches survived in New England. In six states Presidential electors as late as 1824 were chosen by the legislatures, not by the people.

The democratic wave began in the states and then invaded national politics, though it continued to swell in some of the states even after it was blocked on the national scene by the rising controversy over slavery. As in the Jeffersonian movement before it and every effective political reform movement since, the leaders were realists. It was they who developed the modern machine, fed it on the spoils of office, and manipulated it to seize control of conventions and local and state organizations from the old-line politician.

It was inevitable that a movement with so many springs should be amorphous. Nor was it by any means confined to the common people and their political leaders. The ironmasters of Pennsylvania saw a chance to trade votes for a tariff on iron. State bankers saw a rich opportunity to overthrow their enemy, B.U.S. The planter aristocracy (to some extent) joined in the attacks on their ancient enemies the merchants and manufacturers.

Plainly there were two theories of government in conflict—the positive state and the negative state. Jefferson had championed the negative state by asserting that the federal government must interfere as little as possible with the activities of the citizen and with the conduct of local government by the states. Arraigned against the Jacksonians were the advocates of the positive state—soon to be known as Whigs and later as Republicans—who approved of Hamilton's belief in government guidance of the economy. They did not, however, approve of strengthening the Presidency as was being done by Jackson. Indeed, they upheld the supremacy of Congress so consistently that the "Whig concept of the Presidency" has become the label given the view that the President is merely the servant of Congress. (Here we must inject the cautionary note that the two parties were by the 1930's to swap views on the positive and negative state all but completely, but that is a matter for later examination.)

As it was, the resurgent democratic spirit was making many men in both parties hospitable to change. In other words, both were liberal in one sense of the word inasmuch as they wished to change the old order and bring in the Good Society. Their difference lay in how it was to be done, for the Whigs favored government action to stimulate and direct private enterprise, while the Democrats wished to leave individuals to their own devices.

It is no wonder that American politics are confusing, for they follow no logical system. National political parties are created by history—frequently *local* history. The attitudes of local voters depend on a number of factors: family tradition, economic interests, constitutional theory, antipathies between churches or between immigrant elements, perhaps even the presence of a charismatic leader. The result is that national parties are composed of a conglomeration of locally based interests brought into alliance by the hope of advancing their interests or forcing the national government to adopt their theories. Sometimes when these interests are angered by the compromises essential to democratic government they break away and join the opposition or form parties of their own. National political leaders are always haunted by the prospect of such splits; only occasionally does a leader of genius succeed in welding these diverse elements into a solid national front which can put social and economic reforms into effect.

The party battle, fought on state levels, resulted in the widening of the franchise until nearly all white males enjoyed it. New and more liberal state constitutions were written. Public schools were encouraged. The last vestiges of state churches were abolished. Presidential electors were chosen by popular vote except in South Carolina. Laborers enlarged their right to organize in unions and obtained some—but not much—easing of long hours and conditions of work. Mechanics' lien laws enabled laborers to collect from defaulting employers. Public resentment against "monopoly" promoted the loosening of bankruptcy laws in order to permit the farmer and small businessman to escape from their obligations and start over. These bankruptcy laws were to prove unexpectedly welcome, however, to big businessmen with defective consciences.

It is not necessary to enter into the national political battles of the Jacksonian era, though they are no less fascinating than those of the first twenty years of the republic. Indeed the actions and their motivations are so complex that they have become the constant resource of young historians seeking recognition by presenting new and startling interpretations. The core of the period was the bitter conflict between Jackson and Calhoun. The former took the Northern and Western interpretation of Jeffersonianism. The latter took the Southern interpretation, by which he supported the right of a state to nullify federal laws and acts which it regarded as unconstitutional. Calhoun's nationalist days were over, and he had cast his lot with Southern sectionalism. Out of the melee there rose the Whig Party, devoted to nationalism, loose construction, and the promotion of industry, and led by Clay and Webster. The Democrats were an uneasy coalition of Northern farmers and laborers with Southern sectionalists, split among various interpretations of strict construction and states' rights.

Jackson was determined to stop the growing power of the federal government through the actions of the new nationalists in Congress and the decisions of the Supreme Court, and to turn all but a few functions back to the states. He had some successes, but it is not likely that he ever understood that he had failed to reach his goal of governing least. If he was not as ignorant and uncouth as his enemies claimed, at least he was naive in the field of economics and political science. At any rate, though there is reason to doubt that he ever thoroughly understood the full implications of his presidency, he vitally influenced American history in a number of ways.

(1) He made the party a definite, disciplined instrument of policy, in contrast with the old idea that its mission was to rally the unanimous support of the nation. At the same time, the party machine had to have financial support, and so the adoption of the "spoils system" was

accelerated. It was not invented by Jackson or Van Buren, but they helped perfect it.

(2) He glorified mediocrity—the millstone of democracies throughout history—by his belief that one intelligent man could perform the duties of an office as well as another; Jefferson had believed in the election and appointment of men of experience, ability, and culture to office.

(3) He forced the Whigs to beat the drum for democracy even louder than the Democrats; and indeed, the basis of the vote had been so broadened that the privileged caste could no longer cry down democracy and hope to win elections.

(4) Jefferson had distrusted the city worker on the ground that he would be controlled by whoever controlled his daily bread; Jackson shared this distrust but nevertheless welcomed the votes of all producers.

(5) Jackson's Maysville Veto put a temporary stop to federal support of business enterprise, though this support was later to be revised in the forms of protective tariffs and land grants. Meanwhile, the states took up the mission, and undertook to subsidize canal and railroad building.

(6) Not the least of Jackson's influences on American history flowed from his destruction of B.U.S. He earnestly believed in laissez faire, and he saw B.U.S. as its greatest enemy. Some historians believe that when the rising enterprisers in industry and in state banking swept B.U.S. aside, they were able to build up the country faster than would have been possible under sound banking practices; if this is true, it may still be that the price was too high. During the next century, wild speculations and cut-throat competition boomed and drained the economy by turns.

Finally, (7) Jackson "temporarily" rejected Jefferson's fear of a strong executive and used his powers to promote the public welfare as he saw it. He thus set the precedent that has enabled strong presidents to make their office an aggressive force—far more than merely the executive associate of Congress.

Chapter 7
The American Mind and Heart

Proem

We will walk on our own feet; we will work with our own hands; we will speak our own minds. The study of letters shall be no longer a name for pity, for doubt, and for sensual indulgence. The dread of man and the love of man shall be a wall of defense and a wreath of joy around all. A nation of men will for the first time exist, because each believes himself inspired by the Divine Soul which also inspires all men.

(Ralph Waldo Emerson, 1837)

* * *

One's-self I sing, a simple separate person,
Yet utter the word Democratic, the word En-Masse . . .
Of Life immense in passion, pulse, and power,
Cheerful, for freest action form'd under the laws divine,
The Modern Man I sing.

(Walt Whitman)

* * *

Scotch savants had a profound influence in America, and one illustration is seen in the way their view of the Indians was adopted to excuse American violence and injustice. Actually the Indians, though lacking in letters and technology, were in their natural state no more brutal or debased than the first whites who landed on their shores.

The rude [Indians] fond of their own pursuits, and satisfied with their own lot, are equally unable to comprehend the [learning and amenities] which in more polished society are deemed essential to the comfort of life. Far from complaining of their own situation, or viewing that of men in a more improved state with admiration or envy, they regard themselves as the standard of excellence, as beings the best entitled, as well as the most perfectly qualified to enjoy real happiness. Unaccustomed to any restraint upon their will or their actions, they behold with amazement the inequality of rank, and the subordination which takes place in civilized life, and consider the voluntary submission of one man to another as a renunciation, no less base than unaccountable, of the first distinctions of humanity. Void of foresight, as well as free from care themselves, they wonder at the anxious precautions, the unceasing industry, the complicated arrangements of Europeans, in guarding against distant evils, or providing for future wants; and they often exclaim against their preposterous folly, in thus multiplying the troubles and increasing the labour of life.

(William Robertson)[1]

The Still, Small Voice Within

After the Revolution, American intellectual and social life entered on a half-century of stormy transition during which the spirit of democracy, with its ideas of equality and reformism, fought against the conservatism of the old order. Belief in natural rights was almost universal, though its validity seemed to be challenged by the visible facts of inequality among classes and races. Environmentalism sought to explain this inconsistency by pointing to social and economic abuses and to differences in institutions and training. The belief caused some liberals to question such institutions as slavery and to hold that any violation of natural rights would poison the springs of liberty. By 1800 popular reaction against the violent excesses of the French Revolution had given Federalist thinking the victory, and we have the curious situation of a country going liberal politically and conservative intellectually.

The effects of conservative ascendancy were not long in developing. For example, though there had been much praise of secular education as necessary for training citizens in a democratic society, in practice public

---

[1]William Robertson, *History of America*, in *Works* (London, 1824); quoted in Roy Harvey Pearce, *The Savages of America* (Baltimore: John Hopkins, 1965), pp. 87-88.

education lagged. Morals became the core of the educational curriculum and gave it a distinct odor of sanctimoniousness. "Culture," says the historian Schouler "was squeamish, affected, finical, full of classical pretensions, the toadeater of the rich and patronizing to the poor, inane, wholly out of sympathy with American democracy and imitative of English authors." The literature of the early Republic has aptly been called "twittering."

After the horrors of the Napoleonic wars, the major intellectual movement which affected all Western Civilization was romanticism. Revolting against the straitjacket of natural law and the grim realities of developing industrialism, romantics muted Nature's basic savagery to a wild and melancholy music that sent delicious chills up their spines and brought tears to their eyes. They were deliberately and sometimes blindly optimistic. Armed with more clichés and soothing "romantic" ideals, they rode forth to tilt against a threatening universe.[2]

One result of the flowering of the romantic mood was that the United States shared with the rest of Western Civilization an admiration for florid oratory. Many of the Founding Fathers were men of wisdom, who spoke simply when they spoke at all. The contrast after the War of 1812 is startling. Calhoun, Clay, Webster, J. Q. Adams, and others were orators, though only Calhoun and Adams were touched with profundity. Americans had come to admire form, color, and emotion rather than substance; in general, political leaders found oratorical charm more important than ability.

Romanticism was vast, and almost neutral, in a political sense. Liberals found sustenance in its concentration on such themes as the individual and his uniqueness, the drama of the rise of the people against monarchies, the concept of moral enthusiasm, energy, and creativeness. Conservatives cherished the romantic reliance on emotions rather than intellect, its turning to a glorification of an idealized past, its dwelling on the inescapable miseries of life created by man's base passions and fallen nature. As with Darwinism in a later day, romanticism could be used by either the right or the left, depending on what was selected for emphasis from its vast corpus.

For great numbers of Americans, romanticism became a form of

_____

[2]For a definition of romanticism by a historian, see Rollin G. Osterweis, *Romanticism and Nationalism in the Old South* (New Haven: Yale University Press, 1949), pp. 235-39.

escape, a yearning for dreamy worlds and golden ages. Their nostalgia for a romantic way of life is seen in the American sale of five million copies of Scott's novels in the decade beginning in 1813. Even the Federalists welcomed Scott's work, since it portrayed the aristocratic society for which they yearned. The would-be aristocratic South took these novels so seriously that Mark Twain quipped that Scott was the cause of the Civil War. Certainly the frontier and sea novels of James Fenimore Cooper strikingly exhibit the influence of romanticism. Cooper later became a bitter critic of the excesses of democracy and denounced the idea of progress as a wishful and optimistic misrepresentation of mere change.

The romantics recognized realities but turned away to a pleasing mythus. A step lower in the scale were the sentimentalists who either deliberately refused to recognize or were incapable of recognizing reality, but embraced the mythus. It is, of course, characteristic of the mentally or psychologically immature. Cooper showed great awareness of the problems of his generation, but the historian and essayist Washington Irving passed through them with sublime unawareness. Sentimentalism became characteristic of a large part of the people (particularly the prosperous and satisfied) who refused to recognize the real sores on the American body and answered complaints with smug moral and inspirational clichés.

The United States of the 1830's, shot through though it was with romanticism and sentimentalism yet, curiously enough, also saw the rise of the most remarkable wave of reforms in the nineteenth century. The reform movements had many sources, including the humanitarianism of the Enlightenment and the Quakers. Philadelphia long the most progressive city in the country was foremost in those movements. No less significant in the long run was Unitarianism—itself an aspect of early romanticism—which appeared in New England about 1800. Unitarians held that each man must work out his own faith, that precise theologies are unnecessary, and that variation in belief means only that no one can ever grasp all of God's truth. They insisted that all are equal before God, that all men are brothers, and that we should each strive to make the world a better place to live in.

Unitarianism was a comfortable compromise between deism and the searing theology of Calvin, and it found such ready acceptance among the prosperous and satisfied that it was called the "cult of the arrived." Unitarianism, it has been said, took a great weight from the soul of New

England. Certainly it prepared the way for the flowering of transcendentalism in the next generation.

During the 1820's certain of the more liberal Unitarians were strongly affected by their studies of European and Oriental philosophies. These served to reinforce the twin streams of the American heritage: on one side, American idealism and the Calvinist conscience; and on the other, the self-reliance, common sense, optimism, and restless experimentation that were finding expression in the Jacksonian movement. The result was a kind of romanticism that went under the name of transcendentalism. The transcendentalists believed that knowledge of truth transcends experience and reason and is implanted by God in the human heart. Knowledge of the ultimate truth (the Absolute) is thus possible to the individual who will listen to "the still, small voice within."

Transcendentalism was not the creation of any one group at any one time, but it found its most famous focus in the meetings of the Transcendentalist Club, which began in 1836 in Boston. Since they were Americans, the transcendentalists felt the obligation of action, the necessity to preach and experiment and to put their God-given ideals into practice. Though they thus accepted the idea of progress, the relationship to Calvinsim's self-righteousness is apparent. It is just as apparent that the expression of unalterable moral principles would cause trouble when they reached the political arena, with its demand for compromise.

Another source of the reform movement can be traced back to the great revival of religion in the 1790s in interior New England which was carried to upper New York by migrating Yankees. The region from Vermont westward was swept by so many fires of religious emotion that it became known as the Burned-Over District. In a way, at least, these fires were a conservative reaction against the new industrialism which was forming and which was accused of concentrating wealth and power in the hands of the godless. The Anti-Masonic movement was one result, directed against the alleged "aristocratic" privileges and sacrilegious beliefs and rituals of the Masons. The movement was carried into politics by a group of shrewd young politicians, but was eventually absorbed by the Whigs.

Another manifestation was the rise of millenialism, which held that Christ would soon return to earth to reign in peace for a thousand years as foretold in the Book of Revelation. Closely related to these religious waves was the doctrine of Christian perfection whose flaming evangelist was Charles G. Finney, also a millenialist. He taught that man is the captain of his own soul, and that salvation from sin was essentially (with God's help) an act of will on the part of the sinner which led to repentance, conversion, dedication to good works, and striving toward living a perfect Christian life. Along with this striving must go an effort to show others the errors of their ways. The effect on Calvinist predestination (already weakened) and on American life was tremendous, and contributed vitally to the rising reform movement.

Ralph Waldo Emerson, the greatest of the transcendentalists, yet stood aside from its extreme manifestations. Scion of a long line of ministers, Emerson retired from the Unitarian ministry to work out his attitude toward God and his fellow men. The world, as he saw it, was throttling law, progress, and individual freedom, and he devoted his life to the battle for individual salvation. "Let men but stand erect," he said, "and they can possess the universe." Serene, high-minded, often accused of pallid thinking, he traveled and lectured untiringly. No settlement was too remote or its fee too small to divert him from his duty.

Emerson vigorously championed Jeffersonian democracy but was repelled by the "impudent vulgarity" of the Jacksonians. Nevertheless, he retained his optimism and expressed the faith that one day there would emerge from the racial and social welter of America "a new race, a new religion, a new state, a new literature, which will be as vigorous as the new Europe which came out of the smelting-pot of the Dark Ages." Concord, Massachusetts, where Emerson lived, became the home of a coterie of thinkers who warmed themselves at Emerson's flame but were in no sense subservient disciples.

During the 1830's and 1840's America entered on a period of groping (not yet ended) in which writers, artists, religious leaders, and intellectual leaders in general, sought to find the American identity and clarify its mission. The Transcendentalists professed to find guidance in the still small voice within. Reformers and religionists of a hundred varieties sought to remake society in some more perfect image by panaceas.

Scarcely a field was left untouched—hence the name Universal Reformers. Inevitably there were many cranks and extremists among the reformers, but most of them advocated and fought for the practical reforms which were to remake American society. Women's rights, institution of free public schools, reform of prisons, orphanages, poor houses, and insane asylums were all the objects of intensive crusades. One of the most significant was, of course, the abolition of slavery. Since it was so closely related to sectionalism and civil conflict, we shall discuss it in a later chapter.

Utopias: Religious and Secular

It must not be supposed that the American quest was carried on only in secular terms or even in the mystical terms of the transcendentalists. From the foundation of the English colonies we find socialistic threads running through the warp and woof of American life, and it kept cropping up, usually connected in some way with religion. However, the heyday of American socialist experimentation came during the generation before the Civil War. Developing industry had been slow in fulfilling its promise of a better living for the masses, and life in factory towns too often had the grimness of a nightmare. In Europe reaction to the French Revolution had tightened social and religious controls. Oppression and misery in Europe and bleak living and emotional starvation in America made the people anxious for any release. History shows that when society reaches the depths of economic or psychological misery, release often comes in the form of religious excitement. Pietists on both continents, longing for the day of salvation, thought they saw in Biblical prophecy the promise of the early return of Christ to earth—the Second Advent—which would begin the millennium, already defined as a thousand years during which Christ would reign in peace on earth.

The effect was to tighten the bonds of Christian brotherhood and to introduce celibacy as a sort of purification for the Second Advent. Economic distress and religious hope prompted pietists to find a way of living apart from the sinful world, and because they were poor men, their best opportunity lay in pooling their resources and (if they were Europeans) moving to the New World, where land was cheap and, moreover, government was tolerant. This type of socialism was often known as communism, because it supported community of goods; it had none of the political or terroristic earmarks of modern communism.

German pietists formed a number of successful communities. The Harmonists, or Rappites, under the leadership of George Rapp began in 1803 to build the village of Harmony north of Pittsburgh. In 1815 they moved to New Harmony, Indiana, on the banks of the Wabash, and in 1825 to Economy near Pittsburgh. The society remained in existence until 1905. The Amana Society, beginning in 1843, founded communities in New York and then in Iowa. The various communities lived quietly for the most part and prospered as the result of industry and wise leadership.

The frequent emphasis on celibacy, however, tended to drive away the young people and reduce the strength of the communities. Germans were almost uniformly successful in the early years of their socialistic enterprises because they were docile, obedient, industrious, and possessed of technical skills.

The history of the Millennial Church or United Society of Believers, usually called the Shaker Society, shows that the seeds of socialism were sprouting in America. Imported from the Rhone Valley by way of England, this pietist movement was distinguished by strange jerks and other physical manifestations. Its theology was millennial and Quaker with esoteric trimmings, and eventually its physical manifestations were subdued and formalized into the peculiar Shaker "dances." Shakerism was introduced into America in 1774 by Mother Ann Lee, who founded a community near Albany. The society soon became thoroughly American, and at one time numbered about a score of communities in seven states. Shakers lived celibate lives, wore distinctive garb, and are today remembered for their beautifully utilitarian buildings and furniture. Despite its long success, Shaker communism proved unsuited to modern society, and now has all but disappeared.

There was a natural connection between socialist experimentation and transcendentalist revolt, but none of the experiments had more than passing significance. More successful and long-lived was the Oneida Community, near Seneca Lake in New York, the creation of John Humphrey Noyes, a remarkable reformer from Vermont. The community, founded in 1848, was unique in that first reliance was placed on manufactures rather than agriculture. Equality of the sexes was emphasized and women cut their hair and wore bloomer costumes. Every effort was made to eliminate competition in both work and sexual relations, and to build up a completely cooperative, "perfectionist" way of life. For a generation, under the wise guidance of Noyes, the community was happy and successful. Nevertheless, certain practices akin to free love hampered the wider acceptance of its tenets, and Noyes' influence began to wane. In 1881 socialism was dropped, and the venture was reorganized as a corporation. It still exists as the manufactory of Community silver plate.

Meanwhile socialism as an economic doctrine began to take form in Europe. Robert Owen, an English industrialist, and Charles Fourier, a Frenchman, proposed that competition be eliminated and socialism instituted by the organization of associations (called phalanxes by Fourier) which should become the centers of their members' social and economic life. They expected to do away with competitive drives by abolishing private property, religion, and marriage. Robert Owen's purchase in 1824 of New Harmony from the Rappites gave him a ready-made town, and 'here and in subsidiary communities he gathered a thousand poorly selected idealists who engaged in cooperative enterprises. Even Owen's role as financier and leader could not prevent dissension among the rather high-brow New Harmonists; and when Owen tried to abolish private property, marriage, and organized religion, the community failed.

Charles Fourier's creation from dream-cloth of elaborate industrial phalanxes found an American propagandist in Albert Brisbane. He interested a number of "universal reformrs" in the scheme, but particularly Horace Greeley, a Vermont farm boy who was rising rapidly as editor of the *New York Tribune*. Fourierism, thus popularized, was tried out in forty or fifty places. None of the experiments was adequately financed or directed, and their citizens were too often impractical idealists or desperate down-and-outers. All of them failed.

As noted previously, the area between Vermont and Lake Erie had been swept by so many religious fires that it was known as the Burned-Over District, and New York and Vermont were seeding grounds for a number of socialist enterprises. Here gathered all sorts of religious extremists, whether sincere believers or fakers. Swedenborgians, Shakers, vegetarians, wielders of divining rods, and even a sect of men who refused to wash or shave and would wear only bearskin tunics. A curious phenomenon of this district was the "millennial dawn" preaching of William Miller, another New Englander, who prophesied the Second Advent of Christ in 1843 or 1844. Hysteria and panic followed among the poor and ignorant. When the time limit passed without fulfillment, it was natural for extremists to insist that Christ had come but had chosen to remain invisible. The Adventists are present-day relicts of this movement. Fully as remarkable was the spiritualist movement, which was set off by the pranks of two sisters named Fox who claimed to be able to communicate with the spirit world. Even when they confessed that their spirit rappings and table tippings were hoaxes, the movement refused to decelerate.

Most remarkable product of the Burned-Over District, however, and most successful of American utopian movements was the Church of Jesus

Christ of Latter-day Saints, usually known as Mormons. About 1820 Joseph Smith, born in Vermont and member of a shiftless family near Fayette, New York began seeing visions. In 1830 he published his revelations in the *Book of Mormon*, a work that shows to an amazing degree the crosscurrents and soul searchings of the Burned-Over District. Whatever his social origin or the source of his revelations, the Prophet Joseph Smith became a magnetic leader. His missionaries made converts by the thousands, both in the United States and Europe.

The two Mormon centers in Ohio and Missouri had to be abandoned because of local hostility, and a third site was found in Nauvoo, Illinois, on the Mississippi. Here the Mormons became so politically potent that they held the balance of power in the state, and their opinion that they were a people chosen by God did nothing to make them popular with their neighbors. Unfortunately they were joined by rough elements, which gave color to the accusation that Nauvoo was a rogues' harbor. Joseph Smith's announcement that polygamy would be added to Mormon practices crystallized resentments. In 1844 Nauvoo was mobbed by the uncontrollable militia, and Joseph Smith was murdered.

Mormonism was probably saved from extinction by a second remarkable Vermonter, Brigham Young, who deserves to rank among great Americans. In 1847 Young led the broken and fleeing Mormons across plains and mountains to the shores of the Great Salt Lake, then in Mexican territory. As the wagons of the pioneer band reached a point overlooking the Great Salt Lake, Young, who lay ill on a pallet, rose and said, "This is the Place."

"The Place" was a sagebrush desert, but the Mormons set to work with a will and ditched in water. By the end of 1848 about 8,500 settlers were established on the shore of Salt Lake, living meagerly and working indomitably. Salt Lake City was laid out. Land was parcelled out to families according to need. Within two years an irrigation system was operating efficiently—a remarkable feat when it is remembered that there was no precedent in the English-speaking world for sharing water. The California Gold Rush provided a profitable market for the Mormons' surplus food and stock and furnished their homes with equipment traded in by the gold seekers.

And still the Mormon immigrants came—driving ox teams, riding horses, or pushing handcarts. By 1856 some 22,000 people were living in Utah, and a number of additional towns had been founded. Brigham Young sought self-sufficiency, and he refused to let his people be swept away by the current mining craze, insisting that they stick to farming, stock raising, and simple manufactures.

Young's original plan to set up an independent nation was thwarted by the American annexation of Utah in 1848, and he next turned to laying the foundations of a state to be called Deseret—meaning *honey bee*, a word taken from the *Book of Mormon*. He planted settlements along the Mormon Corridor, southwestward as far as San Bernardino, and even planned to annex San Diego as a seaport. What he actually did was to set up a frontier theocracy in the form of a government complete with legislature, courts, and himself as governor. He failed to get statehood partly because of the gold rush, partly because of public opposition to Mormon polygamy. Nevertheless, when the Territory of Utah was erected, Young was appointed Governor by the President.

By 1857 the popular outcry against polygamy led to the so-called Mormon War, when federal troops were sent out to install a "Gentile" (non-Mormon) Governor. In the end, the Governor took his seat peaceably. without the aid of the troops. The territorial executive and courts, however, operated chiefly among Gentiles. The Mormons settled their differences in their own way.

Utah succeeded in its quasi-socialist program partly because of its religion, but fully as much because of the personality and genius of Brigham Young. The pattern in agriculture and industry was established during the lifetime of Young, and the Mormon Church still holds vast corporate interests in both lines. The City of God on Massachusetts Bay had collapsed in 1691; the City of God in Utah survives and flourishes.

If the utopian experiments proved anything, it was that socialism cannot be suddenly put into effect (at least in a complex society) except when those concerned are skillful and industrious workers ready to yield obedience to a wise and practical leader whose ascendance amounts to absolutism. Indeed, in most cases the experiments succeeded only when their idealism was sparked and disciplined by deep religious feeling. Robert Dale Owen, son of the New Harmonist, clearly stated the reasons why cooperative enterprises did not usually flourish in America: land was too cheap and wages were too high.

Van Wyck Brooks suggests that the prominence of Vermonters in the utopian movements was, after all, the legitimate offspring of New England's Calvinist theocracy, of its search for the City of God and its determination to bend mankind to conformity to the divine plan. But at the same time utopianism was the child of revolt against the individualistic transcendentalism of Concord—a transcendentalism which eventually, and perhaps unwillingly, was to become the apologist for the philosophy that "the business of the United States is business." At any rate, reformers accepted the traditional belief that the responsibility for reform lies with the people, and that it will become expressed in law only after the champions have forced it upon the public conscience.

The Emergence of American Character

During these years the composition of the American people was being radically changed by an in-pouring of millions of immigrants. They furnished cheap labor but otherwise were not always welcome. Indeed, there was a strong nativist movement directed chiefly against Catholics. European ignorance of America was abysmal in the earlier years, but around 1830 strictly factual guidebooks for immigrants began to appear, and these did much to correct romantic or hostile views. Most important of all were the letters—"American letters"—written home by immigrants. The appearance of a single such letter in a community might spread the "American fever" for emigration and almost strip it of able-bodied citizens.

In spite of undoubted drawbacks, the romantic view of America remained deep-seated. Letters are evidence of the awestruck amazement of the immigrants at the opportunities offered by America. The Irishman, lately starving on his blighted potato patch, found that he could have meat three times a day. A German farmer could sell his land, buy tickets to America, and still have enough left to purchase a cleared farm with buildings for himself and each of his three sons. The Swede could write home that "there are no large estates whose owners can take the last sheaf from their dependents and then turn them out to beg."

Faith in Europe was gone, and even those who could have lived comfortably at home often left because they felt they could do better abroad. In America there was no enforced service in the army, taxes were negligible, and so great was the government surplus that Congress was actually troubled by what to do with it. Peasants who had lived under extortionate taxes, rents, and tithes, and had been harassed by government spies were amazed to find that government cost so little and interfered so little with the citizen. One observer who asked German emigrants why they were going to America received from them all the same answer: "There is no king there." No white man in America, the immigrants found, acknowledged a master. Farmhands and housemaids sat at table with their employers, and American women were not accustomed to field drudgery. The poet Goethe summed up the usual European attitude in the simple words, "America, thou hast it better."

Few of the immigrants chose to go to the South, doubtless because they could not compete with slave labor. The Irish, in particular, went to the cities, and there they engaged in frequent and often bloody clashes with free Negro labor. Those immigrants with trades went to the cities and towns, and Cincinnati, Chicago, and St. Louis had large German elements that became significant culturally. Farmers who could afford it purchased run-down farms, and those who could not afford them went farther west where land was cheap. Foreigners were undoubtedly an important element in the West, and were quickly absorbed except when those of a single national origin settled as a group.

The West of the Jacksonian era can be rougly defined as the area between the Appalachian Mountains and the Great Plains; the West from "The River"—the Missouri—was a post-Civil War development except for the mining country of the Far West. The West had a wealth of positive qualities. One of the most noticeable was its well-nigh universal optimism. The Westerner attacked his problems with intelligence, energy, initiative, and without undue scruples; he took calculated risks, and if he lost he picked himself up and tried again. He was materialistic, as was natural, for it was a material problem he set out to conquer. The West was an economic opportunity rather than a stamping ground of freedom. Its citizens often worked hard to raise its religious, educational, medical, and cultural standards, though the standards they had in mind were imported from the East or from Europe.

The Westerner was democratic, but he did not give the vote to women, Negroes, or Indians; after the Civil War he agreed reluctantly to emancipation but preferred to leave the details to the South. The Westerner was ostensibly convinced of his own superiority, but the heat of his protestations apparently rose from a basic inferiority complex. He was jealous of Eastern and British advantages and sometimes showed it by ridiculing manifestations of culture, luxury, and good manners.

Contrary to popular opinion, the various Wests were not always areas of progressive revolt. Of course they upheld capitalism, but their intention was simply to extend its blessings to themselves by pruning off the privileges that enabled Eastern capital to drain away their surplus. While it is true that economic radicalism was nearly always characteristic of agricultural areas, it usually took the form of panaceas such as advocacy of free land. Thus the demand for a homestead law granting land to bona fide settlers was carried on intensively, and was preached with the emotional zeal of a crusade. Again, Westerners contributed few mechanical inventions, though they eagerly accepted and sometimes improved agricultural machinery. The Westerner was an expansionist but only in North America; an isolationist, but with a touchy sense of national honor; and a nationalist, but sometimes with his fingers crossed on policies (such as the tariff) which the East thought essential to national welfare.

Posterity has frequently exaggerated the individualism of the pioneer ancestor. It is notable that individualism flourished best where it was most feasible, and that where harsh conditions made it impossible—as among the Mormons of Utah—it did not prevail. Of course there were those whose individualism crossed the line into lawlessness, and who kept their communities in turmoil with stoning preachers, plaguing wedding parties, gouge fights, duels, robberies, and feuds.

The turbulent individual's demand for personal dominance was quelled in the end by social pressure. The West's demand for conformity to a pattern of equality was so strict that mediocrity was glorified. To be socially acceptable, a man could not afford to rise above his neighbors; to show the marks of education and culture, to dress well, or to build a mansion was in many communities known as "putting on airs." The dead weight of public opinion favored the stodgy, humdrum virtues, mediocrity, and complete predictability, and it made headway against the more self-assertive and lawless elements. Everyone was perfectly free—to do the socially acceptable thing. As Jefferson put it, "The inquisition of public opinion overwhelms in practice the freedom asserted by the laws in theory."

All this shows nothing if not that the West had a conservative side. Progress was a fetish, but it was strictly material progress; any other kind of change had to fight its way against general suspicion. The standard of success was property, not education, culture, travel, or work for building a better community in any except a material sense. The result was that the individualist threw himself into making money and amassing property and in the end brought about the very inequality which Jefferson had dreaded and which now in fact menaced liberty. Western equality had failed to obtain a dead level of economic conditions and was in danger of being overturned.

Though the West may not have played quite the dominant role that its admirers would insist, it nevertheless had tremendous significance. Its drama has pervaded American literature, song, and story. Its psychological characteristics have strengthened certain trends in the pattern of national thought and action which would otherwise have been less pervasive. The West turned national attention inward and bred an illusion of isolation and self-sufficiency; at the same time, the cotton and grain of the West slowed down the growth of industry which might have done more to give the country an enlightened interest in world trade and consequently in world affairs. As it was, the tremendous domestic market afforded by the West (and the South) delayed an interest in world affairs even after industry had grown to unprecendented size.

The West drew surplus Eastern farmers and thus, by lowering the pool of prospective native industrial laborers, raised wages and stimulated the flow of European labor; this action in turn bequeathed to the country the problem of the melting pot and delayed the integration of American culture and the solidification of social and economic classes. Finally, this vast agricultural empire (cotton, corn, and wheat) has been a decisive political influence. Even though the population in industrial states has outgrown that of agricultural states, the number of latter under the American constitutional system has given them great strength in the Senate. The modern traveler can have little comprehension of the terrible price that was paid to conquer the land and raze the forest. Red men were the least of the dangers. It has been the custom to speak of the pioneers as men and women with unusual health and endurance. Now we are not so sure but that their endurance rose simply from necessity. Though Western adults were younger than the national average, it would seem that they had poorer health. Disease, malnutrition, exposure, and accident always plagued the pioneer. Few families failed to lose children. Henry Clay, for example, was one of only three in a family of thirteen children to live to maturity, and of his own eleven children seven died before him. Relatively few men and women reached old age with the same spouse with whom they had begun adult life—death, not divorce, was the great separator.

The ordinary men and women of the West were heroic, but not in any dramatic sense. They lived (in the words of Thoreau) lives of quiet desperation. They were heroic because for a generation, perhaps all their lives, they doggedly fought adversity and monotony and forced both to yield a few grudging conveniences. They were tragic, also, not because they were smitten with sudden disaster but because through the years good crops and good prices seldom came together, because of the lengthening row of graves in the field beside the cabin, and because all too frequently the years bowed their shoulders without giving them their hearts' desire.

The democracy of the Jacksonian Era was an incongruous and contradictory mixture, without much philosophy or direction. In the South it tended to be aristocratic, based on slavery. In the North it was scrambling for the dollar, ready to be bent to selfish purposes. Jeffersonian democracy, suitable for a simple agrarian life, was out of date in the developing industrial society, and its doctrine of individualism was to be the support of the very interests Jefferson had sought to overthrow—the men of action, the builders and money grabbers who saw democracy as the bulwark of their own power.

Fortunately, democracy had its critics. James Fenimore Cooper, as noted above, caustically analyzed its excesses and denounced the idea of progress of wishful and optimistic misrepresentation of mere change. Edgar Allen Poe, a gifted Virginian, master of the romantic mood, inspired writer of poetry and short stories and inventor of the detective story, was the prophet of "blasted hope." Nathaniel Hawthorne, born in the decaying old seaport of Salem, showed in his novels that pain and sorrow and struggle are the human lot, and that there is no pleasant and secure railroad to the City of God. The two most slashing critics of the democratic dogma were Thoreau and Melville. Henry David Thoreau, a complete individualist, pointed with alarm at the state, nationalism, and the machine. He wanted to stop them cold, not mold them into stepping stones to a better life; and he went to live in the woods at Walden Pond near Concord in part to show how it should be done. His *Civil Disobedience* is a purge for the overly cooperative. "My thoughts," said he, "are murder to the state and involuntarily go plotting against her." He believed what he said; and when as a practical protest against government support of slavery he refused to pay a poll tax, he was thrust into jail. Emerson visited him and asked sadly through the bars: "Henry, why are you here?" Thoreau's answer was transcendentally direct: "Waldo, why are you not here?"

Herman Melville in his tremendous allegory *Moby Dick* sounded the warning that there were no automatic guarantees of human progress. Man is fate's lieutenant; good and evil are eternally with us. Captain Ahab must always pursue the white whale. Our purpose on earth is to engage in the strife; this is our delight and the expression of our individualism, even though in the end we go down, like Captain Ahab, before the fury of evil. Man's alliance with good against evil, the everlasting search for truth even though we may be destined to know it only in part—these were the facts of life as Melville saw them; the City of God will never be reached on this earth. Ralph H. Gabriel succinctly points up the two wings of democratic thought: "Emerson said: Trust thyself because God is in you. Melville replied: Trust thyself because no god will aid you."

A leading optimist was Walt Whitman, a New York Quaker and journalist. Fired by Emerson's faith in man, he applied himself to forging the declamatory poems which he set in type and issued in 1855 as the first edition of *Leaves of Grass*. No more joyous or impassioned affirmation of the credo of democracy has ever been written. Rude, impulsive, and affirmative, he lived among the people and loved them, and, as has been said, "precipitated the American character." He looked on himself as a primitive poet whose function it was to focus tribal aspirations and stir the people to action. He spurned the pallid, unimaginative, duty-bound reformism of the transcendentalists and put iron tonic in the veins of their self-reliant man. He gathered together the disparate, warring elements of democracy and gave them organic being and dynamism. There he stuck, for he was not a man of ideas and did not know how to project the democratic future. That has been the task of our century, insofar as it has been done.

One of the most striking characteristics of Americans was their ambivalence toward foreigners. No doubt among the reasons were fear of foreign power and jealously of foreign culture. The civilization of the United States obviously derived from that of Europe, particularly Great Britain, but instead of calmly accepting the fact, Americans often sought to deny or minimize the influence of Europe, even while slavishly imitating it. It was perfectly possible for the same person to do both. Great Britain became almost to a morbid degree the object of American hate and love.

Travelers, of course, each saw what it was in his nature to emphasize, just as Americans saw in travel books the points on which they were most sensitive. Frances Trollope, in *Domestic Manners of the Americans* (1832), wrote chiefly and critically of Cincinnati, then in its rawboned adolescence, where she had lost her money in a mercantile venture.

Charles Dickens was another English traveler whose criticisms were regarded as outrageous. No doubt some Britishers were alarmed by the growing power and conceit of America and slandered its democracy in order to help dam the wave of reform then sweeping Great Britain and threatening to undermine privilege in society, politics, commerce, and colonial administration.

Foreign observers could not avoid seeing the evidences of social crudeness, and they tended to blame them on democracy. Let us look at American society as some British travelers portrayed it. They saw a nation of sallow, unhealthy-looking specimens, with bad teeth, slurring nasal speech, slovenly clothes, and unclean habits, overrun with bedbugs and cockroaches, glum and frigid in manners, eating voraciously of a destructively heavy cuisine, swilling iced drinks, drunk in the afternoon, eternally whittling, rocking, staring, and chewing and spitting tobacco so liberally that sidewalks, steamboat decks, and hotel lobby floors were stained brown by the ceaseless expectorations of boot-blacks and statesmen. The American national emblem, said one humorous observer, should be not an eagle but a spittoon.

The Americans were portrayed as curious to the point of impertinence, reading newspapers avidly but gleaning more prejudices than facts, swept by religious orgies at camp meetings and revivals, brutal to slaves but moral except in matters relating to business, politics, and such items as gouge fights and murders. Women were dependent on their menfolk for all decisions, took no exercise, and possessed only ornamental accomplishments. Children were brats. American prudery was often shown in amusing ideas of propriety. For instance, the word *legs* was not used; the Englishman, Captain Marryat, told of seeing in a young ladies' academy a piano with legs modestly swathed in frilled pantalettes. (Yet Lady Gough, a countrywoman of his, laid down the rule that the books of male and female authors, unless they happened to be married, must be separated on the shelves.)

On the other hand, many foreigners—even some whom Americans resented—saw much good in the United States. Note especially Alexis de Tocqueville's *Democracy in America* (1835, 1840) and Alexander Mackay's *Western World* (1849). Of course American superficiality was recognized ("We teach all the branches of knowledge," admitted Thoreau, "and none of the roots"), but it was also recognized that the American workingman was better informed than his European counterpart. Americans were patient under the inconveniences of noise, mud, and discomfort in travel. They were genial to strangers and pitilessly hospitable. The church and the clergy were honored. Family life was full of affection and simple pleasures. Equalitarianism, while it bred mediocrity, recognized the worth of the individual rather than that of ancestors: it was what was above ground, not below ground, that counted. Foreign land-lookers were almost always pleased by what they found. The United States was "the poor man's country," where low taxes made it seem like heaven to the immigrant, and "plainness and simplicity of manners, equality of condition, and a sober use of the faculties of the mind" made classes not static but fluid—and gave promise of a bright future.

Americans shared the human tendency to be torn between opposite urges: between individualism and social-consciousness, idealism and materialism, tolerance and intolerance, optimism and pessimism. The struggle in America, however, was fiercer because the country was young and ill-balanced and because democracy insists on continual changes to meet changing conditions. These conflicts and contradictions led to vacillations between extremes.

An outstanding quality of the European peasant was love and respect for the soil. One of the most striking and significant American characteristics was rootlessness: the lack of attachment to any certain place. Americans rarely loved the soil, despite the spoutings of sentimental novelists. They "wrested a living from the soil"; they were subduers of nature, not children and partners. Because the forest and the tough sod of the plains were seen first as enemies, it was difficult to develop an affection for the acres that had been won with suffering, and they were frequently abandoned for any reason or no reason. European observers early noted that Americans' affection and loyalty turned toward institutions instead of the land, specifically toward their social and political systems.

Most Americans were full of national and race prejudices—not unique phenomena in the world even then. More obvious and universal, however, was the lick-all-creation spirit. It was a fairly common impression that America had cornered all wit, goodness, and intelligence, that all blessings rose from the excellence of its institutions, and that Europe was rapidly sinking into decrepitude and senility. "We air a great people, and bound to be tolerable troublesome to them kings," boasted one yokel. Especially marked was a sense of insecurity which imbued the nation with a strange unrest, a haste to get things done which set men chasing dollars as evidence of accomplishment and building museums and colleges as evidence of culture.

The American was a man of conscience. His history was concerned with intolerance, race prejudice, and legal and economic oppression, not because they were more common there than in other nations but because Americans refused to become reconciled to them and never for long gave up the fight against them. Conscience, in its social sense, rises from the ability to look in two directions at once—toward the practical program and toward the ideal—and from the realization that the ideal program cannot succeed unless it has yielded enough to the practical to give it a firm foundation. Hence the bitter struggle all through American history over what shall be the terms of the compromise between the practical and the ideal—how the American quest should be conducted. Hence also the necessity in the years before the Civil War for defenders of slavery to rationalize it as a public, private, and moral good. The cynic was rare in America until the twentieth century.

The American saw his struggle as part of the universal search for moral values. As we have noted, Americans believed that they had a national mission. It was obvious that God had designed North America, or at least the better part of it, which was bound together by the Mississippi River system, to be one nation. As that arch-Federalist Timothy Dwight put it in an optimistic moment:

> See this glad world remote from every foe,
> From Europe's mischiefs, and from Europe's woe.

The Calvinist concept of a chosen people flourished vigorously. "We are the peculiar people," said a Charleston editorial writer in 1845, "chosen of the Lord to keep burning the vestal flame of Liberty, as a light unto the feet and a lamp unto the path of the benighted nations, who yet slumber or groan under the bondage of tyranny." This was uttered in blank disregard of the existence in Charleston itself of a class which "slumbered or groaned" under the bondage of slavery. As levelheaded a man as Lincoln shared the sentiment. The Declaration of Independence, he said, gave "hope for the world for all future time. It was that which gave the promise that in due time the weights should be lifted from the shoulders of all men, and that all should have an equal chance."

Americans did not see themselves as merely builders of cities, factories, and railroads. Like John Winthrop they believed they were building a society that could serve as a model to the entire world. At the core of this new way of life was the belief that the nation's natural resources could and should be used to give the people an unprecedented standard of living, to afford the opportunities and advantages that only the wealthy could enjoy in the rest of the world. On the other hand, we should bear in mind the point made in the preceding chapter that Americans thought of their democratic institutions as universally applicable, and did not realize that they had flourished because of the abundance of natural resources. This gave rise to a number of ancillary illusions that can best be treated toward the end of this book.

No doubt the American sense of mission rose not solely from security but also from insecurity. Separated from the mainstream of Western civilization, Americans sought a means of unifying themselves around a concept that would give them world significance. Because they were rootless they had to build their own contribution, and (sometimes ignoring the blot of slavery) they found it in the glorification of their free and equal institutions. Until almost the end of the century they sought to teach by example. One cannot read widely in American history without being struck by the real anxiety in every time of crisis lest democracy be stamped out and the hope of the world vanish with it.

As Long as Grass Grows and Water Runs

We cannot in honesty let the matter of conscience and mission rest with the above self-gratulatory paragraphs even though they point out the irony of the Negro's exclusion from human sympathy. The truth is that conscience and mission all too often yielded precedence to the strong urge toward ruthless expansionism. The imperialist aspects of this movement can be deferred, but it is appropriate now to speak of the Indians, the original inhabitants of the land. It is true that in every generation there were voices raised in favor of justice toward them, yet it is also true that the *effective* national voice favored "clearing away the Indians"—as though they were no more than insensate trees and shrubbery that had to be removed before land could be plowed. Readers must be aware of the many massacres and counter-massacres, of the constant white demand that the Indians be pushed on west, and of the countless treaties negotiated to last "as long as grass grows and water runs" but which are faithlessly broken by whites—rarely by Indians.

Two ways of life were in conflict, and in the long run there was no possibility of their existing side by side. Western public opinion would accept no compromise and demanded that the Indian be exterminated or driven out; it did everything possible to prevent them from taking up the whites' agricultural way of life. When Indians did seek to learn white ways and to settle on the land as farmers, their simplicity laid them open to white chicanery and they often lost all they had. Indians had little comprehension of the value of money, the ownership of land, and the necessity of thrift; and so land sharks and grog sellers found it easy to mulct them of their property. When the victimized Indians left off hanging about the settlement and took to the warpath to rectify injustices whose origin they only dimly understood, the very men who had undermined their undoubted virtues pointed to their actions as proof that red men were improvident, thievish, and treacherous.

Pioneer opinion held that trees were one indication of soil fertility, and so it was natural that the explorers of the Great Plains should regard them as deserts fit only for buffaloes and Indians. There thus grew up the myth of the Great American Desert. Far from regretting the condition, many people hailed the plains as a providential limit to white settlement. The existence of this vast area, supposedly of no use to white agricultural settlers, bred the project (sponsored in 1825 by Secretary of War Calhoun) of setting it aside as a permanent home for the Indians, one to which Eastern Indians would be encouraged to migrate. Between it and the settled states would exist the Permanent Indian Frontier, marked by a road and a line of forts west of which no whites would be permitted to settle.

The Indians in the states northwest of the Ohio were pushed westward by stages until they were crowded into a few reservations in the extreme north and in what is now Oklahoma. The so-called Civilized Nations of Georgia, Alabama, and Mississippi possessed considerable improved land and stock, but their property was taken by chicanery and "legal" force. Thousands of the Indians died of hardships on the long trek to Oklahoma, but in 1840 there were about 40,000 gathered there, and though they were still wards of the government most of them handled their own affairs under written constitutions.

Of course the Eastern Indians were not welcomed by the Horse Indians of the Plains, and there was a state of endemic warfare between them that lasted until after the Civil War when the Plains Indians themselves were conquered and confined to reservations. That in itself is a long, sad tale and was accomplished only after the slaughter of the buffalo destroyed the commissary of the Horse Indians. Even as it was, an army officer estimated that it cost a million dollars to kill one Indian. Undoubtedly the whites' diseases—smallpox, tuberculosis, and syphilis—did more than military action to reduce the Indian population and end warfare.

Some of the shortcomings of federal Indian policy—here we refer especially to the Eastern Indians—rose from ignorance and political exigencies. Indian agents were often corrupt, or filled with impractical idealism, or incapable of understanding Indian psychology; it is arguable that any one of these was as destructive as the others. Some critics of Indian policy have asserted that: it was a mistake to treat the Indian nations as possessing sovereign power, when in actuality they had neither the knowledge, experience, nor political machinery to act as such; frequent removals bred social maladjustment and discontent; the great size of the areas assigned to the nations fostered the false hope that they could preserve their traditional way of life; and the system of payment for land cessions encouraged arrogance, spendthrift habits, and the feeling on the part of some Indians that the government owed them a living.

While ignorance and political exigencies were contributing factors, the major reason for the failure of federal Indian policy can be traced to the inability of policymakers to understand or appreciate Indian culture. The removals, even though they bore the curse of political expediency, were intended, by many of those who favored the policy, to improve the welfare of the Indians. Indeed, the entire policy was the culmination of a long battle on the part of conscientious men in Congress and administration to do their duty by the aborigines. Yet, in all of the contacts between whites and Indians the assumption underlying federal policy was that white cultural values (Christianity, the English language, and an agricultural way of life) were superior. These assumptions were never challenged, even by the sincere friends of Indians.

On the other hand, the recognition of the Indians' right to their land met a standard of moral obligation that conquering nations have too often ignored. The money paid for lands was invested and honestly administered. Famine and severe weather were often mitigated by government gifts, and epidemics were often fought by army surgeons. Orphans were maintained. Missionary schools were subsidized to teach the white man's ways, and tools, seeds, and livestock were distributed. Criminal jurisdiction was extended to protect the Indians, and the federal courts regarded themselves as the red men's guardians. Even the military forces, however often they were high-handed, frequently protected peaceful Indians against hostile men, both red and white.

Whatever the good intentions of government policy, they were swept aside to an alarming extent by the events of the 1850s as traders and immigrants crossed the plains and saw that they were quite suitable for white agricultural settlement. One result was cancellation of the Permanent Indian Frontier Policy, at least in its original form, and the crowding of the Eastern Indian nations together in the territory now included in Oklahoma. Western pressures forced the creation of the Department of the Interior in 1849 to initiate policies being urged by the West in the control of public lands and Indian affairs—particularly making public land more cheaply and easily available, and hastening the process already begun of restricting the Indians to reservations being continually reduced in size to make room for white settlers.

Chapter 8
Background for Conflict

Proem

The black race . . . came among us in a low, degraded, and savage condition, and in the course of a few generations it has grown up under the fostering care of our institutions, reviled as they have been, to its present comparatively civilized condition . . . I hold that in the present state of civilization, where two races of different origin, and distinguished by color, and other physical differences, as well as intellectual, are brought together, the relation now existing in the slave-holding States between the two is, instead of an evil, a good—a positive good.

(John C. Calhoun, 1837)

* * *

There is an immensity about Calhoun that compels respect. Whatever else he may have been he was not small. His aspirations were lordly, his range of thought was gigantic, his sense of honor was august, his sense of duty was sublime. And his errors were titanic. One is tempted to believe that the very excess of his virtues combined into an appalling vice. It is by no means certain that it is altogether desirable for the political leader of a population of sinful men to be stainless. It may lead to arrogant refusal to take into account the weakness of ordinary people.

(Gerald Johnson)[1]

[1]Gerald Johnson, *Secession of the Southern States* (New York: Putnam's 1933), p. 65.

I have seen Calhoun's monument. That you saw is not the real monument. But I have seen it. It is the desolated, ruined south; nearly the whole generation of young men between seventeen and thirty destroyed or maim'd; all the old families used up—the rich impoverish'd, the plantations cover'd with weeds, the slaves unloos'd and become the masters, and the name of southerner blacken'd with every shame—all that is Calhoun's real monument.

(Walt Whitman)[2]

*   *   *

The champions of the Old South claimed that theirs was the ideal social order and the only permanently founded democracy, all because it had, with God's blessing, slavery. Surely, Southerners had come a long way from Jefferson and a long way out of reality. Fighting to defend their way of life they had taken refuge in a dream world, and they insisted that others accept their castle in the sky as an accurate description of conditions in the South....[Their] minds, under the impact of a long train of bitter criticism of their region and with a realization that the power of their opponents was growing, had turned into this curious, psychopathic condition. And one thing else must be recognized. Even though the idealized portrait of the South was false, it was to be a strong and living force in the years ahead. In the long run, the vision of the perfect South was to supply a substantial element in the construction of the romantic legend of the Old South. In the nearer future, it was to give the Confederate soldier something to die for.

(Charles S. Sydnor)[3]

The Cotton Kingdom

Sectional rivalries among the states had been evident from the very first, but the Missouri Crisis of 1820 had rung up the curtain on the first act of a drama that is not yet concluded. Before that, rivalries had been most evident between mercantile New England on one side and the agrarians of the rest of the nation, whether planters or farmers, on the other, with Massachusetts and Virginia respectively leading. During the next forty years the boundaries of the sections were expanding and changing with the westward movement, and there was considerable

---

[2]Walt Whitman, "Specimen Days," quoting a hospitalized Union soldier's reply to a comrade who had told of having seen a monument to Calhoun.

[3]Charles S. Sydnor, *The Development of Southern Sectionalism 1819-1848* (Baton Rouge: Louisiana State University Press, 1948), pp. 338-39.

fluidity in the rivalries and alliances among the sections. By 1860 the slave-holding states, dominated by planters, were to be ranged on one side and the industrialists and free farmers of the North on the other.

During the 1840s the Old South took its place on the American scene. It was a great backwater wherein was being preserved the older way of life, with a certain degree of rural conservatism and stability, gracious cultural values, and relaxed social intercourse. Unfortunately, it also preserved the old agrarian narrowness, the stubborn localism of the early Republic, a considerable degree of intolerance for intellectual change, and growing advocacy of rigid barriers between social classes—especially as manifested in the insistence on retaining Negro slavery.

There was far more diversity in the Old South than is usually recognized, but the essential unity of the South was nevertheless clear. Its boundaries were set by common interests whose externals are easily discernible, however complex the pattern they formed. Foremost was the presence of the Negro both as black man and as slave, for this encouraged race and class consciousness. Ulrich Bonnell Phillips, historian of the South, found the "central theme" of Southern history in the determination of all whites to preserve white supremacy. The South was overwhelmingly agrarian, and it depended on exports and imports—that is, on the exchange of its agricultural products for the manufactured goods of the North and of Europe. Its religious life was dominated by conservative evangelical sects, and its intellectual life by conservative aristocrats. Little affected by direct industrialization or by European immigration or cultural currents, its institutions were still primarily English. Nativism, family-consciousness, and localism were still strong.

It has been a popular opinion that the antebellum South was a land of great plantations and pillared mansions presided over by a wealthy aristocracy of Cavalier lineage, broad culture, impeccable manners, and unsurpassed hospitality. The women are pictured as gracious and beautiful, and the men as equally at home in the hunt and under the dueling oaks, riding beside their overseers and declaiming in the halls of Congress, in their libraries and at fashionable watering places. Actually, only about 8,000 families possessed the fifty or more slaves necessary to rank them as magnates, and most of these must have been of the newly rich "Cotton Snobs." Most of the slave owners were small planters who lived in log or clapboard houses, struggled with failing land and falling cotton prices, and probably had to work alongside their slaves. The vast majority of the South's whites were yeoman farmers, and it was they who composed the backbone of the Confederate army.

The South clearly had a poorly balanced economy, and many of its ills arose from this fact. The complicated argument about how profitable cotton planting was cannot be settled here. At any rate, the planter was extravagant, and low prices merely spurred him on to greater production. Instead of growing all his own food, he purchased much of it; and instead of patronizing Southern yeoman farmers, he often purchased from the corn belt, whose products were brought in by water or rail and did not have to travel long distances over bad roads. Thus the poor whites and many yeoman farmers were forced to be largely self-sufficient and could buy little of either home or foreign products.

Powerful psychological considerations helped override any opposition to slavery, even if it was not the unalloyed economic bonanza that some of its proponents claimed. The cost of slaves was high and land was cheap; therefore the tendency was to exploit the land and, when it wore out, demand new lands; hence the increasingly vehement demand of the South for territorial expansion. Southern planters did not propose to chance their occupation. For one thing, planting carried social prestige, whereas trade and manufacture (even were the shift practical) were regarded as ungentlemanly. Moreover, it was believed that the breaking-up of the plantation system would remove the controls necessary to keep the Negro in order and so result in social chaos.

There have been numerous diverse portrayals of the condition of the slaves and of their attitudes, and we cannot attempt to choose among them. The bloody Nat Turner insurrection of 1831 in Virginia's Southside was followed during the next decades by a number of lesser ones. Actually, it would seem that many claims of conspiracy or insurrection are based on *rumors* recounted in Southern newspapers, and simply have no demonstrable basis of fact. Nevertheless, Southern whites lived in terror of insurrection, and it was an article of their faith that such risings were always just on the verge of breaking out. An interesting fact is that Southerners almost invariably blamed white outsiders—abolitionists, foreigners, kidnappers—for hatching these plots. The slaves if left to themselves would be happy and contented!

There is a reason to believe that the peculiar cotton economy and rural civilization of the South would have been impossible without the power-driven machines and the amazing rise in the world standard of living brought by the Industrial Revolution. The South, however, stoutly insisted that the cause lay in the other direction: that industrialization and the rise in living standards would have been impossible without Southern cotton. It believed that it had a natural monopoly on the growth of cotton and could dictate its own terms to the textile manufacturers of Europe and the United States. "Cotton is King" became the watchword of the South, and Southerners actually believed that the fall of cotton would bring down the entire industrial structure and involve the world in ruin.

The Southern way of life had a special attraction for all classes of whites, each after its own fashion but with certain fundamental values in common. It was these values that helped compensate for possible economic loss or stagnation. Southerners believed that the unique rural civilization of the South stemmed from England (a source of pride) and, furthermore, that it had been improved and stabilized in the new milieu. To the more obvious joys of politics, hunting, and social gatherings they added the rich texture of days passed in unhurried pursuit of business or of frankly relaxed leisure. Only "Southrons" knew how to "live," and they regarded any change as dangerous to their perfect existence. They had built their City of God; the only problem remaining was to get rid of the Yankee, both the abolitionist and the cold-eyed manufacturer who was gouging them.

Southerners saw themselves as individuals first and only secondarily as members of society, and they took such pride in this attitude that they formed an erroneous picture of the Northerner as a wage slave, a mere robot. Actually, the Southerner's role as an individual was severly limited. The individual was constrained to conform according to rule. He might seek to dominate those around him by violence—pistols and coffee at dawn, or a knock-down-and-drag-out fight—but his actions were subject to a certain code of behavior, and above all his actions had to stop short of an attack on what the community defined as essential to its welfare— particularly the Southern way of life. The Southerner was socially responsible, but it was a personal responsibility for preserving the status quo, not for building a better society. As he saw it, any changes necessary in the South would be made by the South in its own way and in its own good time; it was no concern of the nation. The attitude survives to this day.

The Southern sociological view was a survival of the belief in medieval England that though society was a unit—God's family—its members occupied specific places in a divinely ordained hierarchy. Seen in its simplest terms, this meant that each person's status was determined by the status of his blood family in the feudal hierarchy and by the amount and value of its land; men might or might not be considered equal before the law, but they certainly were not socially, economically, or politically equal—in short, they were not equal *as persons*. These ideas had been planted everywhere in America, but before they were well rooted they were attacked by the champions of natural rights and of the equality of man—Locke, the Revolutionary fathers, and most of all Jefferson. Both concepts survived in both North and South, but in the former the rise of cities and industries led to the triumph of equality, at least as the dominant theory.

The South, almost wholly rural and devoted to the plantation ideal, cherished the old hierarchical view. The result was a curious mixture of aristoagrarianism and Jeffersonianism—or rather, each retained a certain amount of identity while affecting the nature of the other. To see this, it is necessary only to look at the way the Jacksonian movement was sweeping the South at the very moment when the extension of cotton and slavery to the Gulf states were bolstering the hierarchical organization of society and affirming the opposite of Jefferson's assertion that "all men are created equal."

The South as a Conscious Minority

By the time of the Missouri crisis the South was well aware that it was falling behind the North in population and developed resources, and that it must find a way of countering Northern political and economic power or see its cherished way of life fall before industry and abolition. To do this, it was necessary to weld the South into a unit that could exert its political power to veto any Northern action that threatened to harm Southern interests. From now on, the South devoted itself to three quests:[4]

(1) The quest for some constitutional means of guarding its special interests. The quest passed through four stages: (a) local self-government, or states' rights; (b) the concurrent voice; (c) constitutional guarantees, and (d) independence.

(2) The moral defense of its special interests.

(3) The stabilization of the *status quo*.

---

[4]The classic treatment of these quests is Jesse T. Carpenter, *The South as a Conscious Minority 1789-1861* (1930).

By the 1830s the economic and psychological tides of the South were running in favor of Southernism. The tobacco and cotton kingdoms were drawn together, and the latter took command. Its Jeffersonianism was not that of Jackson and Van Buren which basically favored business enterprise as long as it remained subject to the states rather than the Federal government. Rather it looked to two other great Virginians, John Taylor of Caroline and John Randolph of Roanoke. They had been followers of Jefferson but soon became his critics. Taylor, the philosopher of the movement, accepted Jefferson's preachments of the paramount significance of agrarianism and of local—that is, state—government. Taylor adopted these ideas ostensibly in defense of the freeholding farmer, but actually in defense of the plantation system and slavery.

He rejected Jefferson's concept of conflict between balanced social forces and depended on the states holding the balance between a selfish financial "aristocracy" in control of the central government, on the one hand, and the chaotic tendencies of the people, on the other. The Constitution was a compact between the states, and the latter were the judges of its terms. He countered implied powers with the compact theory and asserted that the real issue in the Missouri controversy was the balance of power between the sections. It was a peculiarity of Taylor's argument that he reserved the word aristocracy for bankers and other holders of "paper" wealth, not for the planters.

Taylor's followers tended to oppose tariffs, banks, and the "paper wealth" of corporations. As the common interests of the Southern states drew them together to resist Northern attacks, the localism of Jefferson and the compact theory of John Taylor were united into the dogma of Southernism which a group of embittered Southerners, led by John Randolph preached in Congress and spread throughout the South at dinners, barbecues, and private gatherings. The rise of the young nationalists during and after the War of 1812 drew the "Antique Republicans" of the South into a desperate little band of "statriots" determined to sell their lives dearly.

Inherent in the definition of Southernism even in its earlier stage was the belief in the model of Athenian democracy—a society of aristocrats (or at least citizens) erected on an economic basis of slavery. The idea, however, did not emerge full blown until after the Missouri Crisis. This theory found ready acceptance in the Cotton South, especially after the discovery in 1822 of a projected slave revolt by Denmark Vesey, a free

Negro of Charleston. Vesey had apparently been influenced by abolitionist literature. Thereafter any prospect for the emancipation of the slaves faded.

Calhoun had begun his career as a nationalist, but as Southernism waxed in the South and he was cast off by the Jacksonians he saw that he would have to go over to the "statriots"; it was probably the bitterest choice an American politician ever had to make. The accession of Calhoun at last enabled the Antique Republicans to develop the discipline of a party and the dynamism of a political program.

Shades of Karl Marx! Calhoun saw the struggle then in progress as lying between capital and labor—that is between capitalistic planters and businessmen on one side, and on the other side industrial labor and the slaves, the latter represented by the abolitionists. His first choice would have been an alliance between planters and businessmen, aimed at ensuring Negro slavery and suppressing labor agitation. But most businessmen (at least in the North) refused to give up their advocacy of loose construction and a protective tariff. Accordingly, Calhoun felt forced to champion agriculture against business, and therefore left the Whigs and joined the Democratic agrarians in the late 1830's, losing many of his Southern Whig followers in the process. (Southern Whigs were largely businessmen, but also those planters who recognized the usefulness of a business structure.)

Calhoun and the Democrats—even those in the North—agreed pretty well on states' rights, the tariff, and the race problem, and they got along fairly well until the issue of slavery in the territories became so serious as a result of the Mexican War that it could no longer be avoided. Calhoun foresaw that this would be the result of the war and he bitterly opposed the expansionists' demand for Mexican territory.

Calhoun began his defense of Southern Rights by denying that the Constitution had divided sovereignty between the federal government and the states. Sovereignty remained indivisible and was lodged in the people of the states. The federal government had no sovereignty, but was really nothing more than an agent of the states. This was much more than a restatement of the compact theory of 1787, for it led logically to the conclusion that any state could prohibit the agent (the federal government) from violating the compact by assuming undelegated powers within the state's borders.

Calhoun was willing to agree that government should be by the majority, but held that a numerical majority might well smother the liberties of the minority. Only when every interest exercised a check on the others and decisions were compromised until they satisfied all, only then was there a *concurrent majority*, the one effective guarantee against tyranny. Thus every public decision must be tailored to the satisfaction of the minority. Of course it was possible to defend this doctrine by showing that in a democracy every piece of legislation was passed (or voted down) only after a great deal of give and take that watered it down until it suited every considerable minority.

By Calhoun's proposal no numerical majority (meaning the North) could institute a policy such as the protective tariff, which injured the interests and rights—which might merely mean desires and privileges— of a considerable minority (meaning the South).

To prevent such injury, the minority was entitled to "a concurrent voice in making and executing the laws, or a veto on their execution," and the specific mechanism which Calhoun proposed to use in finding the concurrent voice or in interposing the veto he called "nullification." This meant that any state that felt that its interests were being injured by federal acts or legislation could call a special state convention and declare the obnoxious acts or legislation null and void within its borders. The federal government could (1) yield and withdraw the offense, or (2) propose a constitutional amendment giving to itself the disputed power. If the amendment were rejected by the states, the federal government could not exercise the power. If it were accepted, the objecting state must submit or consider secession from the Union. Actually this would give the South a permanent stranglehold on the Union, which was what Calhoun basically desired.

The concurrent voice depended for its effectiveness on the balance of slave and free states in the Senate. This balance was destroyed by the entry of California as a free state by the Compromise of 1850. From that moment the position of the South rapidly deteriorated. True, the Compromise of 1850 brought in the third stage by its guarantee of the existing status, and in the Dred Scott Decision of 1857 the Supreme Court took the side of the South. Southern leaders had put their hope in constitutional guarantees and had fought to maintain national parties, but with the rise of the Republican Party (by 1856) it became evident that a sectional party, devoted to the destruction of these guarantees, was gaining ground. The Republican capture of the Presidency in 1860 caused the South to seize the last and sharpest weapon in its arsenal: secession.

The rise of abolitionism led inevitably to the second preoccupation of the South as a conscious minority: the moral defense of its special interests. This was inevitable in an English-speaking country, where in general any interest that demands a stranglehold on the majority must demonstrate that its standards are morally superior and will promote the interests of the whole. The South's principal defense lay in the assertion that slavery, far from being an evil, was, in the words of Calhoun, a "positive good." This meant that the whole system of Natural Rights had to be jettisoned. The positive-good argument rested in part on the claim that the Negro was biologically inferior (an opinion also common in the North), and in part on the assertion that human nature was not good (as Jefferson thought) but selfish and egotistical and must be subjected to discipline. Slavery was upheld as a blessing to the Negro, as a condition which gave him a bountiful and assured living and introduced him to civilization and to Christian salvation.

The last argument was particularly significant to a deeply pious generation, and to it was added the assertion that slavery had been accepted by the inspired writers of the Bible and therefore could not be a moral evil. Eventually there emerged the "mudsill theory," that democracy could exist only on the economic foundation of slavery. In theory, at least, the Athenian concept of democracy had triumphed.

Since the South could not conceive of any orderly alternative to its current way of life, it could not afford to submit its special interests to the democratic process lest it change the *status quo*. The South was opposed to practically every proposed major change that reached the arena of national political conflict. Little by little it strengthened its sanction against dissent. Laws were passed prohibiting criticism of slavery and punishing the distributors of incendiary literature because abolition literature had almost surely helped to promote Negro unrest and revolt. Citizens were prosecuted under laws limiting civil liberties. The South, while demanding a concurrent voice in the affairs of the nation, prohibited it within its own borders.

Whether there was a considerable Southern aristocracy is a problem that has occasioned a great deal of heartburning. The conservative aristocratic ideal was sought by the mass of newly risen Cotton Snobs, and after 1840 there were signs that aristocracy might flower if it did not lose its economic basis. Men born in frontier cabins to the accompaniment of Indian war whoops now sedulously nursed faint blood connections with Virginia and South Carolina Tidewater gentry. The Cotton Snob, torn between aristocratic restraint and the self-assertion of frontier individualism, was unsure of himself. The result was that his behavior ranged from the pompous to the overbearing, and the dueling pistols were put into use all too often. The would-be aristocrat was romantic, hedonistic, violent, leisurely, and wasteful, yet paradoxically terrified of the wrath of a just God. Lastly, the new man accepted aristocratic responsibility, but this was a personal responsibility, not an urge towards a united effort to build a better society. The Southern aristocrat never saw his basic responsibility for the unprogressiveness of his section.

At the same time, the South was deepening its religious conservatism. As cotton culture spread, the Episcopalian and the deistic planter aristocracy was penetrated by the more "God-fearing" denominations of yeomen who rose into their ranks. The effects of the recent frontier revivals were strengthened by the realization that the Bible, as the bulwark of slavery, deserved Southern adherence. Southerners correctly identified abolitionism with "universal reform" and endeavored to stop all "isms" at the border, with the notable exception of temperance.

On the whole, the conservative program was successful. The luxuries and necessities of the North and of Europe were imported, but not their liberal ideas. Presently the churches emphasized their stand by splitting away from their Northern brethren. Technically the splits were over slavery. Actually, they were just as much an assertion of Southern orthodox rejection of "new light" in theology. The South was now the citadel of puritanism. The angry God of Massachusetts had become the tribal deity of the South.

Since the South was perfect and its culture the highest of all time, it increasingly gave itself to political defense against the North rather than to a search for the solution that might have forestalled disaster. The aristocrat's political power declined during the generation before the Civil War, but his influence increased. Growing Northern pressure and the South's refusal to examine itself were welding Southern white men into an organic whole: a white brotherhood. By 1840 the South, at least its leaders, had become so clearly conscious of its separate interests that many observant men confidently expected the growth of a Southern national consciousness as opposed to the old states' rights.

The fact that Calhoun's fruit was borne after his death and that in the end that fruit was Apples of Sodom should not blind us to his place as one of the greatest figures of American history. Would there have been a war without him? Of course we shall never know. Nevertheless, it was he who watered the seeds of Antique Republicanism and gave form, substance, and strategy to South Carolina's order of battle. He created the South's picture of itself as an underdog. His were the voice and pen that fostered the morbid sensitivity of the South, that harped on Southern rights, white supremacy, and slavery as a positive good, and that consistently exaggerated Northern hostility to the South and to slavery. His emphasis on Southern honor was a shrewd appeal to Southern romanticism, romanticism in its most invidious sense of rejecting the distasteful fact and accepting the pleasing mythus.

Everyone with whom he came into contact was screwed up to high tension by the fierce old man. Just the same he was too much the theorist and the fanatic to win immediate general support anywhere in the South except in South Carolina. Southern politicians were concerned with preventing rather than hastening disunion. Their desire was to fight the political battle over economic issues, not over nationalism and sectionalism. "Calhoun," said one of them in 1849, "is our evil genius."

But with all this said, there remains an exception. The dilemmas that Calhoun so clearly and cogently posed to the champions of liberty, equality, and democracy were eternal. The guns of the Civil War drowned out his voice and vetoed some of his proposed escapes, and later history has even made some of them seem ridiculously naive and shortsighted. But the dilemmas remain. He grasped the truth that a strong government can as easily become the weapon of tyranny as an instrument of public good, and he chose nullification in the belief that he was protecting liberty by keeping the national government submissive to the states.

The present century has seen the rebirth of a body of neo-Calhounian ideas as the defense of the South in the battle over race equality. But beyond this is the ironic fact that the doctrines he shaped to combat "paper wealth"—corporations—are now being used by those very interests in an attempt to remove the power of regulation from the federal government, which they have difficulty in controlling, to the states, which they feel confident of controlling.

The Northern Forces Emerge

Next to industry and the free farmer, the most powerful force emerging in the North was abolitionism. When we treated Northern reformism in the generation before the Civil War, we pointedly omitted abolitionism. It is now appropriate to turn back to examine how the reformer helped change American history.

Objections to Negro slavery had been voiced almost from the time of its introduction, but the most continuous protest was made by the Quakers of the Philadelphia area. They were joined in 1831 by William Lloyd Garrison, whose weekly, *The Liberator*, started in Boston on 1 January 1831, was devoted to emancipation, immediate and absolute. The leading article of the first issue ended on this intransigent note: "I am in earnest—I will not equivocate—I will not excuse—I will not retreat a single inch—and *I will be heard*." Garrison never abandoned this note, and his quotable invective found an immediate hysterical response in the South and served to make him the symbol of abolitionism in the popular mind.

As a matter of fact, the American abolition movement owed most of its impetus first to the long and quiet work of the Quakers, and second to the British abolition of slavery in 1833. In the same year a number of local abolitionist societies were united into the American Anti-Slavery Society, formed chiefly under the patronage of the two Tappan brothers, Arthur and Lewis, pious and wealthy silk merchants of New York.

The great day of the abolitionist movement, however, owed its dynamism to a marriage of New England's transcendental reformism and the evangelical zeal of New York's Burned-Over District. A product of this area was Theodore Dwight Weld, who from 1835, using Oberlin College in Ohio as a base, conducted a powerful and effective crusade against slavery. Weld's one aim was to convince the national conscience that slavery was a sin. Regardless of whether it was constitutional, it violated a Higher Law, one before and above the Constitution, the natural right of men to own their own bodies, participate in their government, and mold their opinions and acts by the dictates of their own conscience. All this was, of course, a reversion to John Locke's doctrine of natural rights. Weld preached racial equality, not just an end to slavery. His converts included four men who were to become abolitionist political paladins: James G. Birney, Joshua Giddings, Edwin M. Stanton, and Benjamin F. Wade.

Generally, however, abolitionism was anathema, even in the North—for most Northerners did not favor racial equality—and abolitionists were made to suffer for their faith. James Birney's press was destroyed by a Cincinnati mob. The abolutionist temple in Philadelphia was burned. Elijah Lovejoy, publisher of an abolitionist paper in Illinois was shot by a mob. Nevertheless, the abolitionists continued to sow pamphlets and books filled with anecdotes about the brutalities of slavery and with arguments drawn from the Bible. Abolition journals were legion, and they gave circulation to yet another type of propaganda, the antislavery poem: John Greenleaf Whittier and James Russell Lowell were the outstanding antislavery poets.

The intransigence of slaveholders and abolitionists was so evident that many Northerners would have liked to dismiss the controversy with a "plague on both your houses." As it was, the problem refused to go away, for it was exacerbated by events. Not least was the South's insistence that fugitive slaves who had escaped to the North must be returned in accordance with the clear provision in the Constitution to that effect. Northern states, prompted by opponents of slavery, invoked states' rights by refusing to give aid to slave catchers.

The Northern coalition that was to fight the Civil War was partly pushed together by hostile forces and partly drawn together by astute leaders who realized that they could make no headway separately. Actually, the coalition was formed with the greatest reluctance, and might never have been formed at all if it had not been for Southern pressures. These, in turn, were at least partly due to Northern pressures.

Indeed, once the pressures and counterpressures started, there *seemed* to be no solution short of war. It was the abolition movement that constituted the upper millstone to the South's nether millstone. The two were to grind between them the parties of the free-soil farmers and the merchant capitalists, and to force them to take one side or the other. It is notable that right up to the Civil War many politicians in both parties objected strongly to making their parties vehicles for sectional as opposed to national interests. In the end they had to go with their section or be turned into political pillars of salt for having looked over their shoulders toward peace.

The members of the Northern coalition—the capitalists, the workers, the farmers, and the abolitionists—had very little in common at the outset except a generalized hospitality for progress as opposed to the insistence of *status quo* of the South's dominant elements. The merchant capitalists certainly distrusted the rising industrial capitalists, and only reluctantly abandoned their fellow feeling for the cotton planters and commission merchants of the South—if indeed, they ever did. Northern farmers, for the most part, saw their interests as reconcilable with industrial capitalism, though they were vigilant in protecting them from encroachment.

Most Northern whites were reluctant to join a coalition against the South. They were prejudiced against the Negro, and shared the Southern opinion that Negroes were irresponsible and incompetent. Such people believed that a tremendous social problem would follow upon emancipation in the South and so had little patience with abolitionism. Northern farmers were inclined to let slavery alone where it already existed, though they opposed its extension to the territories on the ground that it would thus exclude free farmers. Reconstruction after the Civil War was to convince most Northerners that their opinion was right, and in the end they tacitly left the management of the freedmen to white Southerners.

Basically, merchant capital feared and distrusted industrial capital as venturesome and disruptive, and as opposed to sound money policies. Moreover, the merchant, as an importer, was opposed to industry's desire for a protective tariff. New York merchants had built up the "cotton triangle"—which included rice, sugar, and naval stores. Their shipping lines carried Southern cotton to the North and to Europe, brought manufactured goods from Europe to New York, and distributed them to Southern ports. It was in considerable part the cotton triangle that gave New York its overwhelming commercial importance.

Northeastern sympathy with the South was further increased by the dependence of New England's cotton textile mills on a Southern supply and by a growing fear of inundation by foreign labor, a fear strikingly akin to the South's fear of servile revolt. Taken together, New York merchants and the New England textile manufacturers constituted a powerful interest that for a long time dominated the Northern wing of the Whig alliance. So clear was their sympathy with the South that they were known as Cotton Whigs. They fought against the formation of the anti-Southern coalition during the 1840s and 1850s, and many of them, especially in New York City, actively opposed the prosecution of the Civil War. Their Whig opponents among abolitionists and industrialists were known as Conscience Whigs because of their opposition to slavery.

Aside from cotton textile interests, Northern manufacturers rather generally opposed the South, and wanted to get rid of slavery because it was the South's economic mainstay. Rising industrialists in such lines as coal, iron, steel, machinery, and gun manufactures were hungry for capital and for protective tariffs, and wanted to smash all those who opposed them. As they saw it, they needed and deserved high tariffs, ready access to natural resources, plentiful credit and currency, and cheap labor—and until they got them the country could not be put on a sound and prosperous basis. They wanted growth—tremendous growth—and regarded the merchant capitalists as only slightly less harmful to progress than the planter South and the radical Democrats called Locofocos.

Manifest Destiny

A story is told about a party of Americans who met in Paris in the 1850's to dine and drink those sententious toasts characteristic of the day. Presently a Bostonian arose and in cultured accents offered the following:

"Here's to the United States, bounded on the north by British America, on the south by Mexico, on the east by the Atlantic Ocean, and on the west by the Pacific."

Next came a Chicagoan. "My eastern friend has too limited a view," said he. "We must look to our Manifest Destiny. Here's to the United States, bounded on the north by the North Pole, on the South by the South Pole, on the east by the rising, and on the west by the setting, sun."

Prolonged and boisterous applause followed, but the next gentleman, a Californian, considered the toast too moderate. "With Manifest Destiny in our favor," he cried, "why limit ourselves so narrowly? I give you the United States bounded on the north by the Aurora Borealis, on the south by the Precession of the Equinoxes, on the east by Primeval Chaos, and on the west by the Day of Judgment!"

The exuberance of the Californian typified the great era of American territorial expansion. The words Manifest Destiny seem to have been used first in July 1845 by John Louis O'Sullivan, editor of the *Democratic Review* of New York, in an article on the Texas annexation question which decried the attempts of European powers to "check the fulfillment of our manifest destiny to overspread the continent allotted by Providence for the free development of our yearly multiplying millions." Propaganda for territorial expansion had its appeal not only to the lick-all-creation American spirit, but to the land-hungry free farmers and to the cotton planters whose land was worn out and who hoped to move to the rich soil of Texas and beyond.

The movement was, then, basically agrarian. Of course there was plenty of second-quality land left but it was easy enough to ignore that and turn to other arguments. The planter wing of the imperialists feared that unless slave Texas were admitted the slave states would leave the

Union and unite with Texas. Proponents of state rights felt that expansion and the admission of new states would weaken Federal power to interfere with local institutions, and they pointed out that the abolitionists, the foremost advocates of Federal aggrandizement, were the bitterest opponents of annexations. The proslave argument, offered without humor or intentional deceit, was that the expansion of slave territory would also expand the territory of freedom. At any rate the acquisition of Mexican provinces in 1848 became inextricably mixed up with the slavery issue and led with seeming inexorability to the Civil War.

The second great cause of the resurgence of imperialism lay in fear— American fear of Europe and European fear of the United States. The chancellories of conservative Europe were fully aware of the sprawling inefficiency of the United States in its gawky democratic youth, but the lesson of the country's inherent power had been driven home by De Tocqueville's half-admiring, half-horrified, but altogether fascinated analysis of the American scene. The rising industry of the Northeast was regarded as a menace to Manchester and the industrial belt of Paris. The cold-eyed Yankee merchants of New York were molding a financial and commercial wall about the United States which Britishers would soon be unable to pass without their permission. The Cotton South was arrogantly boasting that it could at a word bring civilization down in chaos. Worst of all, the success of the American democratic experiment was encouraging restiveness of the European masses under their kings and nobility.

Just as strong was American fear of European interference. Industrialists feared direct competition. New York feared that Europe not only would breach its wall but would carve out private domains on the Pacific coast and in Latin America. Cotton Whigs favored annexations because the spread of cotton culture would benefit business. Too, they viewed the Pacific coast as a base for the expansion of Pacific trade and were particularly eager to get hold of the fine harbors on Puget Sound, at San Diego, and at San Francisco. The South feared that its rule of cotton would fall before the competition of the vast prospective cotton lands of British-controlled Texas. Along with these separate fears went one which shook the nation. A threat to the United States or its welfare was a threat to the existence of democracy and to the American democratic mission. The very least to be expected, proslave men and abolitionists agreed, was the weakening of democratic purity. The welfare of democracy came first; this was the "higher law" of Manifest Destiny.

This view was supported by a series of curious rationalizations: democracy's rights were superior because it was democracy; the necessity for new lands gave a natural right to them and, moreover, Americans would make better use of them than their present barbarous owners; these lands were sparsely occupied, were contiguous to our borders, and were within our "natural" boundaries—boundaries which the God of Nature and of nations had marked for our own. The last argument soon developed until its advocates likened the growth of a human political society to the biological growth of plants and animals which ruthlessly overrun or devour weaker competitors. The resemblance to the philosophies of modern dictatorships cannot be escaped. It is a psychology common to empire builders, along with the usual protraction that their political and economic and cultural institutions are superior to those of decadent peoples. From this was drawn the curiously inconsistent corollary that therefore it is the "duty" of the strong to "protect" the weak, to bring them the blessings of superior institutions, and to eliminate the international nuisances which exist in the behavior of primitive or decadent nations. Europeans and Latin-Americans were dismayed by the remorseless progress of the American pioneers, so like the march of faceless and conscienceless soldier ants.

In the Mexican War which side was the aggressor? As early as 1830, Lucas Alamán, the Mexican historian, found the common factors in the absorption of Louisiana, Natchez, Baton Rouge, Mobile, and Florida:

> They commence by entering the territory they covet, upon pretense of carrying on commerce, or of the establishment of settlements, with or without the consent of the government to which it belongs. The settlers grow, multiply, become the predominant party in the population, and as soon as a foundation is laid in this manner, they begin . . . to bring forward ridiculous pretensions, founded upon historical facts which are admitted by nobody. . . . These pioneers excite, by degrees, movements which disturb the political state of the country in dispute. When things have come to this pass, the diplomatic management commences; the unrest they have excited in the territory in dispute, the interests of the settlers there, the incursions of adventures and savages instigated by them, and the persistence with which the opinion is set up as

to their right of possession, become the subjects of notes, full of expressions of justice and moderation, until, with the aid of other incidents, which are never wanting in the course of diplomatic relations, the desired end is attained of concluding an arrangement as hard on one party as it is advantageous to the other.

On the other hand, Justin Smith, the American historian, in his *War with Mexico* (1919) recited a long list of frauds and insults on the part of Mexico. They are worth repeating because of the rather general American impression that there was no reason for war:

The American public noted in a general way the entire long series of our grievances: our flag insulted, our minister traduced and threatened, our consuls maltreated, our government officially maligned, agreements broken, treaties ignored or violated, citizens persecuted and imprisoned, property confiscated, trade hampered and ruined, complaints more or less politely mocked, positive demands adroitly evaded, valid claims fraudently defeated; and heard that such offences were not merely committed now and then, but repeated over and over again with apparent deliberation and malice. The highest Mexican authorities were found encouraging prejudice and illwill against our citizens, exerting themselves to make foreign nations distrust and hate us, misrepresenting our efforts to conciliate them, and describing our honest wish to be on friendly terms as hyprocrisy and craft. Our people saw threats of war freely made to influence our national conduct. . . .

Moreover, the United States could appeal, not only to strict law, but still more forcibly to broad equity. To sum up the case in one sentence, Mexico, our next neighbor, on no grounds that could be recognized by the United States, repudiated her treaties with us, ended official relations, aimed to prevent commercial intercourse, planned to deprive us of all influence on certain issues vitally connected with our declared foreign policy, seemed likely to sell California to some European rival of ours, made it impossible for us to urge long-standing claims or watch over citizens dwelling within her borders, refused to pay even her admitted debts to us,

claimed the privilege of applying to our government publicly
the most opprobrious epithets in the vocabulary of nations,
designed to keep our people in a constant state of uncertainty
and alarm . . . planned to destroy our commerce by
commissioning privateers. . . . [and] informed the world that it
was her privilege to keep on harrying Texas from generation
to generation; and on a broader scale, but in a manner
precisely analogous, it was now proposed to hang upon the
flank of the United States.[5]

Here, then, were the two sides of Manifest Destiny. It is impossible to
assess to each the exact justice of its arguments. One thing sure is that no
party, European, North American, or Latin-American, approached the
court with the first requirement of equity, that is, with its own hands
clean. Each party had its own "higher law," carefully tailored to its own
needs, and insisted upon its priority. Now it so happens that such "higher
laws" are in a practical sense enforced only by the judicial administration
of the sword, hence one important cause of the Mexican War. However,
in the process of adjudication by the sword there arose within the United
States a struggle over how the welfare of democracy was best to be
promised, and this is what turned the expansionist movement into a
quarrel over slavery.

The war that followed was by no means a walk-over for the United
States; indeed European experts had rated Mexico as militarily superior.
As it was, the Mexicans could only blame themselves for their defeat. The
country was designed by nature for guerrilla warfare, and had that course
been pursued the United States could not possibly have won. The
Mexican generals, bred in the martial tradition, wanted glory, and to get
that had to offer battle—and were resoundingly defeated. When they
finally tried guerrilla warfare it was too late. Benito Juarez profited by the
experience and in the 1860s defeated the French armies of Napoleon III
by guerrilla tactics.

---

[5]Justin Smith, *The War with Mexico*, two volumes (New York: Macmillan, 1919),
1:118, 156.

Chapter 9
The House Dividing

Proem

The extremists on both sides, abolitionists and proslavery men, knew perfectly well that principles cannot be compromised, and so each made it their object to convince the public that they were championing eternal moral standards. Unfortunately events played into their hands. Finally, as each partisan presentation failed to convince the opposition, the sense of moral outrage and sectional injury mounted and emotions spiraled until a tension was built up that was snapped by the attack on Fort Sumter. The breakdown of the democratic method of compromise is an instructive example and a dire warning to this generation.

*   *   *

We cannot escape history. . . . The fiery trial through which we pass, will light us down, in honor or dishonor, to the latest generation. . . . The world knows we do know how to save it. We—even we here—hold the power, and bear the responsibility. In giving freedom to the slave, we assure freedom to the free. . . . We shall nobly save, or meanly lose, the last best hope of earth.

(Abraham Lincoln, *Annual Message to Congress*, 1862)

*   *   *

Bury the bygone South
Bury the minstrel with the honey-mouth,
Bury the broadsword virtues of the clan,
Bury the unmachined, the planters' pride,
The courtesy and the bitter arrogance,
The pistol-hearted horsemen who could ride
Like jolly centaurs under the hot stars.
Bury the whip, bury the branding-bars,
Bury the unjust thing.
That some tamed into mercy, being wise,
But could not starve the tiger from its eyes
Or make it feed where beasts of mercy feed.
Bury the fiddle-music and the dance,
The sick magnolias of the false romance
And all the chivalry that went to seed
Before its ripening.

And with these things, bury the purple dream
Of the America we have not been,
The tropic empire, seeking the warm sea,
The last foray of aristocracy
Based not on dollars of initiative
Or any blood for what that blood was worth
But on a certain code, a manner of birth,
A certain manner of knowing how to live,
The pastoral rebellion of the earth
Against machines, against the Age of Steam,
The Hamiltonian extremes against the Franklin mean,
The genius of the land
Against the metal hand.

(Stephen Vincent Benét)[1]

And the War Came

We turn now to the great conflict between the sections that has been justly called the ridgepole of American history. The world today looks on it as a great struggle over the moral issue of slavery, in which right triumphed. The most difficult thing for any reader of history to grasp is

[1]Stephen Vincent Benét, *John Brown's Body* (Garden City, N. Y.: Doubleday, 1930), pp. 374-75.

that men of the past did not have our advantage of hindsight, that those who fought against what we now regard as morally right were firmly convinced that their own side was the champion of eternal truth. The annexation of Mexican provinces immediately plunged the issue of slavery in the territories into politics. The Compromise of 1850 was only a temporary respite. The admission of California as a free state upset the balance in the Senate and destroyed the effectiveness of Calhoun's concurrent voice. Calhoun had died in the midst of the debate over the compromise, but his followers were now convinced that secession and perhaps war were only a matter of time. Accordingly they devoted themselves to capturing complete control of the Democratic Party and making it the champion of their interests, and at the same time undertook to build up Southern industries and transportation in order to furnish the sinews of war, if war came.

The decade of the 1850's saw a succession of steps going down, as though inevitably leading to war. The repeal in 1854 of the Missouri Compromise with its prohibition of slavery north of 36° 30' opened a Pandora's box of woes and led to the formation of the Republican Party, springing into being like a warrior in full panoply prepared to fight against the extension of slavery in the territories even to the shedding of blood in Kansas. Though formed by farmers who wanted free land for their sons, the party was presently seized by industrialists who wanted federal favors, especially high tariffs and easy access to natural resources. The Republican Party was plainly sectional, confined to the North, and the Democrats never let their opponents forget it. But the Democrats, though still national, were chained to the sectional interests of slavery. The Whigs tried to ignore the central issue, but presently were lost in the shuffle.

In 1857 the Supreme Court declared in the *Dred Scott Decision* that the Missouri Compromise had been unconstitutional. The elated South now saw the triumph of its contention that Congress could not exclude slavery from the territories; on the other hand abolitionists and their new farmer allies insisted that the decision must be reversed; even if it were legally right, it was morally wrong, for the Higher Law (natural rights) voided even the Constitution's recognition of slavery.

One event after another troubled the waters, not the least of them the mad raid by John Brown on the arsenal at Harper's Ferry, Virginia, in a quixotic scheme to start a slave rebellion. During recent years Abraham Lincoln of Illinois had become a spokesman of Republicanism and the foremost opponent of the unhampered extension of slavery to any and all territories. The South denounced him as a Black Abolitionist and in a way he was, though without the intemperateness of the abolitionists. His assertions that slavery had become the affair of the nation, not solely of the states, and that slavery was a moral issue which flouted all principles of right and jeopardized the rights even of all free men—these were also the fundamental principles of abolitionism. Though most Republicans denied that they wished to extinguish slavery where it already existed, he denied this when he said: "Let us draw a cordon, so to speak, about the slave states, and the hateful institution, like a reptile poisoning itself, will perish by its own infamy."

The election of Lincoln to the Presidency in 1860 was taken by the South, whether or not correctly, as the signal that the North intended to abolish slavery, by force if necessary. Eleven Southern states finally grasped Calhoun's sharpest weapon—secession—and formed the Confederate States of America. It was the final step downward; the war came.

The four years of war that followed showed the fallacy of the South's arrogant belief that without cotton Western Civilization would collapse. Some cotton got through the constantly tightening blockade of Southern ports and that little was supplemented from other fibers and cotton from other countries. As the Union armies were whipped into shape and competent leaders found, the Confederacy was deliberately cut in two along the Mississippi and then from Atlanta to the sea. Its railroads were destroyed, its crops seized, its warehouses burned, and its towns laid waste.

And yet the long record of Confederate victories over the more numerous and better equipped troops of the North seemed for a while to confirm the Southern boast that "one Southron can whip five Yankees, suh!" Undoubtedly Southerners, even the yeoman farm boys, were more adaptable to military life than Northerners. And they were better led. For example the accomplishments of General Robert E. Lee were little short of miraculous. He built an army as he fought, and with it swept back in three years no fewer than four major invasions by an army that was constantly being renewed in personnel and equipment. He was bold in his plans and bold in their execution; if he had a military fault, it was perhaps his overtenacity in hopeless situations. Lee is disproof that success is the only basis for immortality, and proof that "human virtue should be equal to human calamity." Above all was his superhuman devotion to duty, which, as he said, "is all the pleasure, all the comfort, all the glory we can enjoy in this world."

The Lee Legend has risen not only from the remarkable qualities of the man but from the Southern desire to personify the chivalry of antebellum days and the glory of the struggle for the Lost Cause. The mythus of Southern chivalry was drawn from the thin line of Tidewater culture that was spread even more thinly by westward-going planters. In antebellum days it existed chiefly in bombast and the novels of William Gilmore Simms. But then came the paradox, when in such men as Robert E. Lee and his humble followers from the red fields of the South it attained in combat its richest claim to having existed. And so in perishing the South found fulfillment.

The men on both sides in the Civil War regarded themselves as crusaders for Christianity, justice, democracy, and humanity—as champions of eternal truth. Tales have been told of the prayer meetings in Stonewall Jackson's army which turned the camp into one great shouting revival. Such manifestations did not occur in the Union army— and yet hear this.

Lee's army had known a year and a half of such victory that its men never doubted of final triumph when on December 13, 1862, the Union army found it firmly anchored on impregnable Marye's Heights above Fredericksburg, Virginia. That day the Union forces proved their mettle, forming again and again for the charge, and falling in windrows with their faces to the South. Then, as they formed for the last charge, the words of a new song were wafted across the stricken field and rose above the screams of the wounded up to the listening heights.

> Mine eyes have seen the glory
> Of the coming of the Lord;
> He is trampling out the vintage
> Where the grapes of wrath are stored;
> He hath loosed the fateful lightning
> Of His terrible swift sword.
> His truth is marching on.
>> Glory, glory, hallelujah!
>> Glory, glory, hallelujah!
>> Glory, glory, hallelujah!
>> His truth is marching on.

The men is blue sang those strange and terrible words as Cromwell's

Ironsides must have chanted Psalms, like "men who made some conscience of what they did." The charge was a bloody failure: Marye's Heights was not taken. And yet that day the Confederates who listened to "The Battle Hymn of the Republic" as they crouched behind their breastworks knew their first doubt of victory.

Why Did Democracy Break Down?

In assessing the war's origins, Southerners have been confronted by one embarrassing fact: the South's support of slavery was patently against developing moral standards. The result sometimes has been a denial that slavery could have been the cause of the Civil War. Slavery, they say, was the *symbol* of sectional conflict; the real subjects of strife were labor, agrarianism, industry, the tariff and, of course, the meaning of the Constitution.

But it may be held that unless the Negroes had been slaves there would have been no plantation economy, with its effective agrarian opposition to industrialization and to the democratic process; no block to European immigration into the South; no question of white supremacy or of a Negro social menace which could bring war, for the North would not have gone to war to enforce simple race equality, and no crucial question of the extension of slavery to the territories. And since the Negro would not have been in the country except as a slave, it is almost impossible to imagine his racial influence up to 1865 apart from his "slaveship."

Slavery—not simply the Negro, but the Negro as slave—was woven into most aspects of Southern life. The *primary* basis of sectional division was slavery and freedom, not agriculture and industry or white and black labor. Nor did the division result from any deliberate Republican intention to menace white supremacy. This basis of division was well recognized in the South. In its Declaration of the Causes of Seccession the South Carolina Convention of 1860 stated that the constitutional crisis rose directly from the North's violation of the "rights of property" in slaves. Southernism and the Confederacy, as Alexander Stephens, Vice-President of the Confederate States, put it in his "Cornerstone" speech in March, 1861, were based on the "great truth" that slavery was the Negro's "natural and normal condition." The statesmen of the South frankly admitted at the time that slavery was the cause of secession. It was not until they found it necessary to woo European aid that they began to lay primary stress on constitutional and economic causes.

Nevertheless, even though slavery lay at the root, it is not our concern to place the ultimate blame, in a moral or causal sense, on any section. If slavery was a sin, that sin lay at the door of both North and South. Our objective is to try to understand why the democratic process broke down, and our analysis must include factors other than slavery. We must be careful, however, to distinguish between the causes of three separate phenomena: sectional controversy, secession, and war. They came in that order, each of the latter two growing out of its predecessor, but we must avoid the implication of inevitability. Statesmanship and restraint might have arrested or deflected the evolution, and American history might have been acted out quite differently. At the risk of oversimplification, let us note the basic contradictions between North and South.

First, each had its own definition of democracy. The North believed that democracy was majority rule, and that all subjects of dispute could be brought into the political arena if they could not be settled by other means. The South defined democracy as based on the concurrent majority, which of course put a whip in the hand of the minority. As the North saw it, the South not only refused to yield to changing economic and moral standards but sought to prevent the submission of its "peculiar institution" and its results (such as the territorial issue) to the democratic process. The North, whether or not justly, felt that it was forced to organize a sectional political party that would bring the country up-to-date, not only on the slavery issue but in governmental organization and finance, tariffs, land disposal, and education.

Second, the North saw in the Southern interpretation of democracy a menace to the civil liberties of whites. In the South the critic of slavery was driven out by riot and arson, and the spirit of free inquiry and criticism—the basis of liberty and progress—was throttled by legislative and lynch law. Furthermore, the South had attempted progressive encroachments on Northern whites. There had been the demand for the suppression of abolitionist propaganda; blocks to the right of petition; the activities of slave catchers in the North; and finally a demand that the North silence all criticism or even discussion of slavery.

Third came the issue of the nature and division of sovereignty. The framers of the Constitution ignored Richard Hooker's warnings on this issue, if they had ever read him. When they offered their solution for the problems of division of political sovereignty, they could not envision the tremendously complex economic, institutional, social, and moral problems that were to rise during the next century. Even if they had foreseen them they might well have felt that it was not the concern of the convention. At any rate, it is now evident that political federation can work best when supplemented by nationwide federations of economic, cultural, and other groups, such as the great business and citizenship organizations which now absorb some of the heat from political combat. There was no way to do this in 1860, and so the quarrel over the nature and extent of soverignty took on alarming proportions.

Was sovereignty, as Calhoun held, lodged wholly in the states, and was the federal government merely an agent without sovereignty? Was sovereignty divisible and its parts parallel, as the Constitution itself seemed to imply? Or was ultimate sovereignty in the federal government as the North claimed? Was the Union a permanent national sovereignty or a temporary league of sovereign and independent states? In the answer lay the final decision as to the exact character and the permanent value of the federal system.

Fourth, though both North and South saw the holding of property as a fundamental democratic right, the slavery issue raised the question of the meaning of this right. "Due process of law," as imposed on the federal government by the Fifth Amendment, can be *procedural* or *substantive*—that is, it can examine the procedural *how* of a law's application, or the substantive *what* it is. The first means the guarantee of a fair trial under proper legal safeguards, and this was the meaning ordinarily attached to due process before the 1850's. The second meaning was brought to the front, notably by Jefferson Davis, and was later adopted by Chief Justice Taney in the *Dred Scott Decision*. It was a positive, practical protection of the individual white man's right to life, liberty, *and property* against encroachment by the federal government.

Theoretically, Southern planters and Northern industrialists could agree on this substantive limitation of the power of the federal government to interfere with the right to hold property. The difference was that the South saw property as factories *and* slaves and the North saw it as factories but not human beings. The North insisted that even if the Constitution recognized slavery, the recognition was void because the Higher Law (natural rights) forbade slavery—and so refused to let the South invoke substantive due process to protect slave property in the territories. The South, of course, was aghast at the doctrine of the Higher Law, and Jefferson Davis may have regretted introducing the second, or substantive meaning of due process, which could be used by Northern industrialists to defend their property.

Fifth, the North saw in the Southern course a growing threat not only to the Union but to the future of democracy all over the world. Developing nationalism and democracy had become so intertwined in the North that most people in that section could not envisage the preservation of democracy without national supremacy. They felt also that the United States had a mission to furnish an inspiration and example to the world by fostering and developing democracy.

Many profound and well-balanced American thinkers, while recognizing the shortcomings of their democracy, felt that Southern independence would be a fatal blow to any hope of a democratic future for the world. Not only was the South evolving toward what the North took to be an anti-democratic goal, but its successful secession would perhaps be the signal for the breakup of the Union into its component states or sections. At best the remaining Union would be so weakened and so discredited in the eyes of the world that democracy would lose all chance of survival.

None of the problems implicit in these divergent points of view was unsolvable by reasonable men. Indeed, the world before and since has seen similar bitter differences settled without war. The spark that turned sectional differences and secession into war must then be sought in another direction, the psychological. American society wore a superficial air of broadclothed solemnity; men strutted behind an amusing variety of beard designs, spouted flowery clichés with hands smugly on hearts, leaned perilously on Latin quotations, and turned every puny public address into an impassioned oration on property, respectability, constitutionality, and the "American eagle" and the "British lion."

And yet this owlish sedateness was easily dissolved into an emotionalism that might bring on a vulgar, belly-rending guffaw or a murderous stabbing affray between men rolling like dogs in the mud. The per capita consumption of liquor was appalling, and even some revered statesmen habitually advanced from a genial glow at noon to a full conflagration at midnight. Liquor and custom and a semibarbaric demand for personal dominance led to amazingly sordid personal and political vilification, justified by neither truth nor expediency and hinging upon absurdly petty causes. The mortality among editors and politicians was something to consider before choosing journalism or politics as a calling.

Southerners especially, despite their reputation for good manners, their basic good-heartedness, and their backslapping good fellowship, were touchy and unpredictable. Northerners never knew just how to take them, for they were the most astute of political traders, claiming everything in sight, yielding a little to gain a great deal, and often flying into a rage and proceeding to direct action when they lost an argument or perceived or fancied an obscure insult. They made their bewildered political opponents and finally the entire Northeast skittish at every proposition; the Southern version of the situation, naturally, was that the Yankees were trading and squeezing the South out of everything worth having—and undoubtedly some of them were doing their best at it.

In those days Americans took their politics seriously, perhaps because there were few rival amusements. What with local, state, and federal elections, there were mass meetings, resolutions, barbecues, banquets, and toasts in almost every month of the year, the more so because elections were not concentrated as they are now but were spread out so as to occur sometimes as often as twice a year. This was partly the result of the search for the entertainment of speeches and parades, but annual elections as the safeguard of democracy were defended savagely. Politics, though it received obsessive attention, was poorly articulated: national parties were little more than state alliances, and localities and states were able to make national elections the vehicles for local feuds. Elections, as 1860 proved, thus hinged so often on local problems and animosities that they were poor indexes of popular attitudes toward national issues.

The unfortunate result of all these conditions was the continual exacerbation of party feeling. There was no way for issues to lie fallow while the electorate considered them calmly. Debates on slavery or its related problems only confirmed prejudices and rubbed salt into unhealed wounds. "Reactions," as the historian Avery O. Craven says repeatedly, "were more important than realities." Each side stubbornly interpreted every action as an assault on its rights, and with this attitude came unreasoning confusion, prejudice, and finally fear.

A pointed illustration was the speech of Robert Toombs of Georgia in Congress in 1850. "We have the right," he taunted the North, "to call on you to give your blood to maintain the slaves of the South in bondage! Deceive not yourselves; you cannot deceive others. This is a proslavery government. Slavery is stamped on our heart!" On the other side, Thaddeus Stevens spoke iron-faced in the House, lashing the "slavocracy" with the scorpions of his scorn while Southerners surrounded his desk, cursing and snarling but fearing to touch his bodyguard, the gigantic Roscoe Conkling of New York. Such episodes as these helped convince the self-righteous partisans of each section that their opponents were not so much fearful of losing their rights as sadistically bent on domination.

The essential immediate cause of the Civil War was fear, deliberately induced fear, which promoted in both sides a stubborn self-righteousness and which in turn created a political and moral hotbox. Politics became so heated that it lost its ability to function in its true sphere: the compromise and solution of conflicts. It failed to prevent economic and social factors from being transposed into moral principles. The dominant parties, instead of being instruments of compromise in the democratic tradition, were transformed into ideological vehicles bent on thwarting compromise.

We can blame this failure on the extremists of both sides. They knew perfectly well that principles cannot be compromised, and so each made it their object to convince the public that they were championing eternal moral standards. Unfortunately, as we have seen, conditions and events played into their hands. Finally, as each partisan presentation failed to convince the opposition, the sense of moral outrage and sectional injury mounted and emotions spiraled until a tension was built up that was snapped by the attack on Fort Sumter.

The breakdown of the democratic method of compromise taught Americans a lesson that has been heeded thus far—though it is in danger of being flouted in our own generation. In the main, Americans have sought ideals, but their method of attaining them has been by the compromiser's gradual and practical approach. Politics is the field in which democracies settle social and economics problems too controversial for more quiet and harmonious methods of change. The failure of the method to function in the period just before the Civil War is an instructive example and a dire warning to this generation.

The politician has made a lifelong study of methods of reconciling differences: that is why a politician as President is usually preferable to an engineer or a soldier. Politicians are paid in the coin of prestige and power; but if they make compromises regarded as ill-judged or dishonest, critics pile on abuse, sometimes even before they know the facts of the case. The politician must straddle issues judiciously in order to win enough votes to get himself elected. Heedless observers say that he is trying to deceive the people; an even better case can be made that he is trying to guess what the people want. At any rate, politicians prove their usefulness by finding the ground on which the ideal and the practical can meet.

Actually, politicians are slow to recognize any issue as moral, for of course a principle cannot be compromised. If either side in an issue insists that it is upholding a moral ideal, there can be no practical political compromise. The result is that democratic peoples are frequently plagued by guilty consciences because, no matter what rationalizations they may manufacture, they know that sometimes by compromising they have yielded on a principle.

The Tragedy of Reconstruction

After four years of fratricidal strife the Confederacy collapsed with the fall of Richmond (April, 1865) and this was quickly followed by the assassination of Lincoln. During the next decade the radical wing of the Republican Party walked roughshod over the conquered states, using the Negro freedmen and "scalawag" whites as its instruments. Meanwhile Northern industry was consolidating its control of the nation and turning the South into an exploited colony—a condition from which it is only now recovering. The nation that came out of the Civil War and Reconstruction was not the same one that had gone to war.

Examination of most of the currents of national life shows that they led, whether or not inevitably, to that grand climax. It is no less clear that the great problems and movements of American life in the last four generations have flowed out of the dislocations of that war and its aftermath or taken form because of the decisions made then. On the other hand the drama of war and reconstruction has tended to obscure the fact that the same social, economic, and political reforms might have been made by peaceful methods without bringing desolation and sectional hatreds in their train. Whatever might have been, the fact remains that there was a Civil War and there was a period of reconstruction, and both were instruments of change.

The sympathy of the European nations, especially England and France, for the Confederacy confirmed the American antipathy toward Europe and reinforced the conviction that European governments were inveterate enemies of democracy. Even the South bore a grudge against the European nations for their failure to render more positive and decisive aid. Europe's vague uneasiness at the growth of the western democratic republic was turned to alarm lest with its over-weening power and prestige it upset the uneasy political and economic balances of the world—as, of course, it eventually did. On the other hand, the strength of American federalism was an encouragement to German federation, and the victory of American nationalism and democracy gave a fillip to the parallel movements in Europe. The triumph of the Southern slave states might well have spelled disaster for the democratic movement on the European continent and might seriously have retarded it in Great Britain.

The most obvious domestic result was the amendment by arms of the Constitution to the effect that the federal government was supreme— that a state could not secede. True, the doctrine of states' rights remained an issue and still is, but there is no longer a question of where ultimate sovereignty resides. At the same time, the question of allegiance was settled. The old state pride lingered here and there, but henceforth it was generally accepted that the first allegiance of the American is to the nation, not to the state.

Irreparably linked to the prosecution of the war was the tightening of federal controls. Lincoln assumed war powers which, if they had been fully exercised, would have turned the government into a dictatorship after the pattern of the Roman Republic in time of crisis. After the war, it is true, the Radicals failed to break down states' rights by reducing the states to super-counties, and they failed to consolidate all federal functions in an all-powerful Congress. Nevertheless, the American nation was never to return to the relatively lax federal control it had known before. A social, economic, and political revolution had whirled it into the stream of change, and the current was too strong for a return.

The democratic process was inevitably affected by these changes in constitutional meaning. Northerners had fought to vindicate democracy and to open up the road to its full fruition, a road which the South had blocked. The basic tragedy of Civil War and reconstruction lay in the fact that scarcely had this roadblock been removed than another was substituted. That is, industry and finance had forged in the fires of sectional strife a control of the Union that (while far from absolute) was strong enough to thwart the democratic process for another generation. Thenceforth political and economic protest on the part of farmers and workers was directed toward clearing away this new roadblock and re-establishing the democratic balance with industry.

The Civil War brought the end of slavery, but not complete freedom and equality to the Negro. The peculiar status of second-class citizenship held by the American Negro, especially in the South but also in great areas of the North, had its origin in precisely the same fears that had done much to bring on the Civil War. Economically the Negroes entered into a condition that bore some resemblances to serfdom and some to peonage. Socially they made a few advances, but they were still the bottom layer of society. Civil liberties were drastically curtailed, generally by social pressures rather than by legal measures.

Closely related to the race problem was the phenomenon of the Solid South. Reconstruction welded the South together in a common psychological loyalty to the Lost Cause, and this was shored up by the growth of the Southern mythus, a compound of nostalgic memories of a time that never was. Reconstruction, for a while at least, tended to reinforce the survivals of antebellum conservatism. It convinced Southerners that the Negro vote was dangerous and must be met by white solidarity. Its extravagance reinforced the Jeffersonian prejudice that cheap government and good government are synonymous; moreover, the fact that there had been some progressive ideas connected with Carpetbag rule made such ideas even more distrusted.

It is difficult to think of any American problem, foreign or domestic, that has not been affected by the Solid South. The dependability of the Southern Democratic vote and the seniority of its Congressmen have given them certain valuable perquisites. Until recently they have not been able to name Presidential candidates, but until 1936 they had a veto over Northern selection by use of the Two-Thirds Rule. Southerners have been committee chairmen in Congress and have strongly influenced the policies of the party when in opposition and administered them when in power. When the Democratic Party has failed to obey, the South has not hesitated to ally with the Republican Party in Congress to get its will, or at least to thwart the Northern wing. This tactic has been particularly evident whenever the problem of equal economic or political rights for Negroes has come before Congress.

The war rose in considerable part from a quarrel between the old and the new, and the triumph of the North meant that many of the old obstacles could be cleared away. The result during the next two generations was a tremendous growth of industry, which led to an amazing rise in the American standard of living, and in time made the United States the economic giant whose world impact has profoundly affected civilization. The acceleration of technology and industry by the demands of the war itself may not have been so great as is sometimes supposed, for the country was already undergoing tremendous economic expansion in the 1850's. Nevertheless, it is probably accurate to trace to the war some of the growth in mining, heavy industry, and agriculture; and progress in mechanization was marked. Tariff protection became a permanent policy, and the income tax and the internal revenue on luxuries were added to the American way of life. Northern capital made its entry into the South and won a great measure of Southern support and protection.

The Southern alliance with capital has made it a considerable obstruction to the rise of labor, for capital has been able to take refuge in the South, where labor has historically been cheaper and more docile. Too, the South has prevented the full development of the American standard of living because it has been an economic weak spot and has not been able to buy its share of its own products. Of a piece with this is the Southern championship of states' rights, for within this refuge economic concentration has found such free expression as would have scandalized the Founding Fathers of the Confederacy.

Southern conservatism fought against the evolutionary change of society and for this reason long pledged itself to the type of Christian orthodoxy which bases itself on a presumed knowledge of absolute truth that admits no room for adjustment. The effect on the American religious picture has been marked. No less obvious have been the social effects (and in recent years the political effects). Southern Congressmen are often aligned with the opponents of social legislation, even though Prohibition, the most drastic example of social legislation, was largely the gift of the South. Southern Congressmen certainly have a point when they attribute this opposition to fear of the centralization of political power, but it would be more convincing if they showed a more practical fear of economic centralization.

Not the least of the psychological results of the Civil War was the creation of the Lincoln Legend; over much of the country at least, the kindly, homespun Lincoln receives more worship than the aloof patricians Washington and Lee. The revolution against the rather common portrayal of the ugly man from the prairies of Illinois started the poets and other creators of folk myths upon their task, and even sneering *Punch* regretted its failure to recognize "this rail-splitter as true-born king of men." In life Lincoln was the most complex of men; along with his attributes of greatness he was skeptical, brutally realistic, acute to the point of foxiness, coarse to the point of vulgarity, and indifferent to cultural nuances.

After his assassination, the other side emerged to form a monolithic image. Lincoln became the patient, tolerant, innately dignified, melancholy, yet whimsical man of the people agonizing over the travail of his country like a modern Christ. "New birth of our new soil, the first American," he became the typification of American opportunity, the model boy who was bound to rise. Born in a log cabin, he studied before a flickering fire, learned to write with charcoal on a slab, and walked miles to return a few cents over-charge. He split rails; lifted out hogs when they were stuck in the mire; never drank or swore; told off-color stories only as parables; and spent his years in the White House snatching widows' only sons from the firing squad.

The Lincoln image has concentrated in it the heroic essence of the war years as emancipator and savior of the Union, and finally has become the exemplar of the best in democracy, the proof that the democratic process can stand the test. And yet there is truth in the statement that "Lincoln is not so much the type of democracy as he is an abstract embodiment of the ancient and cosmic forces of genius and wisdom."

Each year we repeat in February the ritualisitc observance of the birthday of the folk hero. No visit to Washington is complete without a pilgrimage to the classic marble structure over whose portal we read: "In this temple as in the hearts of the people for whom he saved the Union the memory of Abraham Lincoln is enshrined forever." There are his greatest speeches which the commoner reads with reverent, moving lips, while a shaft of light falls upon the white statue of the pitying hero. Nothing can be clearer than that here Americans find the sanctuary and embodiment of their dreams of the sacredness of human dignity and of the American mission to point the way to a better life for the world. When in the hungry winter of 1931 the American people were beaten down by forces which seemed about to shatter the American dream and Lincoln's successor in the White House recommended a diet of faith, a minister lifted his prayer to the folk hero: "Oh, Lincoln. Arise! Stand forth that we may gaze upon thy furrowed face. Look upon us; pity us; speak to us as thou didst at Gettysburg; stretch forth thy hand; point the way of destiny and duty that America may be thy living monument down to the end of time. Oh, Lincoln, come down from thy summit of bronze and march."

Events in the present century have thrown some doubt on the familiar claim that we learn from the study of history. Actually the origins, progress, and aftermath of the Civil War should have taught us two lessons which would have been invaluable in our generation. The first is that democracy is not automatic, that it depends for its successful operation upon our courage and restraint. The two extremes can work havoc, if they refuse to compromise, by grinding away the moderate center as though between upper and nether millstones. It is open to question whether we can stay the march of evolution, but there is no doubt about our ability to increase confusion and to breed oppression and injustice.

The second lesson concerns our policies toward defeated nations. War destroys, but its aftermath can be even more fruitful of dislocations and hatreds. A defeated people does not automatically yield the principle (good or bad) for which it fought. Economic and territorial concessions may be enforced, but the deeper psychological values are almost impregnable. The belief that democracy can be implanted in short order in Germany or Japan is a delusion; the best that can be hoped for is the first step in the right direction. Many years will pass, perhaps many generations, before democracy becomes second nature in those countries. Let the doubter look at France, in the eighteenth century the exemplar of absolutism, and now, after a dozen or so of revolutions, wistful of democracy but still under the shadow of the man on horseback. Only time can work a change, and this truth we should have known from the history of our own sectional controversy.

Chapter 10
The Gilded Age

Proem

Dangers in the Age of Transition. The new epoch introduced by the manufacture of power must from its very nature destroy many of the conditions which give most interest to the history of the past, and many of the traditions which people hold most dear, not because the things which are destroyed are themselves bad, but because however good and useful they may have been in the past, they are not adaptable to fulfill the requirements of the new epoch. It must destroy ignorance, as the entire world will be educated, including savage and barbarous races, and one of the greatest dangers must come from this very source, when the number of half-educated people is greatest, when the world is full of people who do not know enough to recognize their limitations, but know too much to follow loyally the direction of better qualified leaders. Some time may elapse after the old has gone before the new is established in its place. The danger is that the destructive changes will come too fast, and the developments which are to take their place not fast enough. The next two or three centuries may have periods of war, insurrection, and other trials, which it would be well if the world could avoid.

(George S. Morison)[1]

---

[1] Adapted from George S. Morison, *The New Epoch as Developed by the Manufacture of Power* (1898).

The Age of Confidence. I believe that there were values in that period called the nineties . . . which were as worthy (greatness aside) as any cultural period has ever developed, and which are now lost, perhaps irrevocably. . . . But I believe also that no one can fail to see in looking back the seeds of dissolution, the shame, the animated corpses of belief, the diseases of culture, which were also coexistent with this pausing time in our American history, when there was such real content, and such a complacent yet enviable and sometimes splendid trust in the future; when for the last time in living memory everyone knew exactly what it meant to be an American. . . .

Creative wildness, that longed to shape and invent, to make life richer or better balanced . . . was regarded as eccentricity or weakness. A few such eccentrics found an outlet in the expanding industrialism of the age and flowed into it. The vitality of the others was dammed up, diverted, or turned inward to grow sour and stagnant. We acquired a neurosis which was to be like a familiar disease in American life for the next decades. Those who aspired to the arts generally suffered from an infantile paralysis contracted in their youth under the dominance of business, from which they are only now beginning to recover. This is what happened to the young in the age of confidence who soared or flapped instead of taking to the nest to lay a golden egg.

(Henry Seidel Canby)[2]

Removing the Invisible Hand

The close of the Civil War brought in a period of social tinselry that Mark Twain appropriately called the Gilded Age and which lasted for a third of a century. Indeed, much of its spirit spilled over into the twentieth century. A period of the ascendance of the middle class, it partook of the virtues and vices that go with a bourgeois society. There was a certain contentment in mediocrity, a worship of material success, and a failure to see things as they were.

Nevertheless, the Gilded Age was a time of experiment and uncertainty, when both farmers and workers were searching for the weapons with which they were to triumph in the next century. In the struggle, Jeffersonian agrarianism was submerged, and labor was defeated. No less evident was the failure of reformers to make more than token headway against the political corruption and social injustice that

[2]Henry Seidel Canby, *The Age of Confidence* (New York: Rinehart, 1934), selections from pp. 242-46.

were all too common. The so-called Mugwumps labored diligently for reform, but their genteelism was offended by the raucous outcries of the "wild asses" from the plains and the labor "skates" from mine and factory. As a consequence they were never able to summon mass support, and their reformism flagged under what they took to be the threat of agrarian and proletarian revolution.

Since the bourgeoning of industry was the most striking phenomenon of the period it is useful to begin with it. The corporation had not been widely used before the Civil War, and it had been deplored by the public when it was used in banks and transportation companies. Nevertheless, as business enterprises increased in size the many advantages of the corporate form appealed to the emerging class of enterprisers known as the Great Entrepreneurs. It was obviously useful as a means of raising capital; its limited liability feature appealed to the investor; and because of its status as a legal person it could sue and be sued. Perhaps most important of all, the Great Entrepreneurs who controlled the great corporations wielded such financial power that it was all but impossible for labor and local governments to challenge them.

The world of that day accepted the concept that there could never be a sufficient supply of goods to fill all human needs. Therefore, the producer felt that his interest and, indeed, his only salvation lay in approaching a monopolistic position in his field; the practical effect was that competition (and laissez faire) would last only until one producer or a few producers managed to swallow or destroy the others—that is, gain a monopoly. Free enterprise meant the right of a man to risk his stake in the competition—and the right of the victor to keep the spoils. The result frequently was over-expansion, wastefulness, and mutual destruction. In the end the solution would have to be oligopoly—the control of production by a few corporations.

The alarming state of the economy spurred a demand for federal regulative legislation and a reluctant Congress passed the Interstate Commerce Act (1887) and the Sherman Antitrust Act (1890). Neither of them was very effective (nor was intended to be) until the reforms made a generation later as the result of the political progressive movement. As a matter of fact the states were much more successful in legislating for the regulation of corporations and the protection of the rights of labor.

In this extremity the corporations turned to the Supreme Court. The best source of power against the states' corporation and labor legislation turned out to be the Fourteenth Amendment. Among other things, it states:

> No State shall make or enforce any law which shall abridge the privileges or immunities of citizens of the United States; nor shall any State deprive any person of life, liberty, or property without due process of law; nor deny any person within its jurisdiction the equal protection of the laws.

During the 1880s the Supreme Court began to rule that the word *person* in the Fourteenth Amendment included corporations, which were *legal persons*, thus limiting the states' exercise of police power whenever it interfered with property rights. This interpretation opened up a long road down which business enterprise could jog without fear of interference by state laws. Here, at last, business found a way to invoke for its own protection that substantive due process which Jefferson Davis had found in the Fifth Amendment and propounded as a defense of the Southern right to take slave property into the territories (see above, page 182).

The courts also developed interpretations that enabled them to limit or forbid actions by labor unions of individuals. The common-law interpretation of the strike as a conspiracy in restraint of trade had been weakened in Massachusetts by Chief Justice Shaw's decision in 1842 that labor unions and the strike were legal. Other states yielded slowly, until it became evident that the injunction was a more expeditious and thorough weapon against labor. An injunction is a court order requiring a party to do or refrain from doing certain acts; violation of the order entails trial and punishment, not for doing the acts (which may be perfectly lawful) but for contempt of court.

The Supreme Court was clearly engaged in preventing the erection of obstacles to industrial centralization. The significance to the growth of American economic power is clear. In its early stages the campaign was directed against the states, but presently, when Congress set up obstacles, these also were ruled out. Critics felt that there was an increasing tendency on the part of the Court to judge expedience as well as constitutionality. This was seized upon by injured parties to carry practically every important economic act of Congress to the courts for adjudication. By the beginning of the new century this had become so confirmed a custom that the Supreme Court had become in effect a third legislative chamber. The situation was to continue until our own time.

Finance capitalism means control of enterprise by banks and other financial institutions; some prefer the term *security capitalism*, since capital takes the form of securities—that is, stocks and bonds. The movement toward finance capitalism was hastened by the crisis which was being brought on by business tactics and market raiders. By the 1890s there had appeared propaganda for a live-and-let-live policy based on the "community of interest" among businessmen, but especially among the new captains of finance capital. The doctrine envisioned a monopoly (or near-monopoly) in each field of production, and in natural monopolies (such as railroads) the formation of common policies and a division of the traffic.

The program of consolidation and monopoly that soon began to be put into effect under "community of interest" was held to be vital to the salvation of business. The reasons behind such a program were roughly as follows. First, business had to be saved from itself—that is, from the reckless financial policies, irresponsible raids, and cutthroat competition that were ruining it. Second, the rise and fall of prices must be minimized and the disastrous effects of the business cycle mitigated. Third, the rising power of labor must be held within some limits, if capitalism was not eventually to give way to socialism. Finally, if entrepreneurs were to increase profits, they had to make savings in buying and manufacturing processes, and to control prices. Adam Smith's "invisible hand" had assumed that the economy would be automatically controlled by competition; the move toward finance capitalism quietly sought to remove the invisible hand and make arrangements among corporations that would minimize competition.

The consolidation of Republican power by 1897 cleared away the political obstacles to the rise of corporate concentrations, and the years from 1898 to 1902 were to see the movement reach its climax. The dominant leaders were J. Pierpont Morgan and John D. Rockefeller, and they headed two great financial empires, which, however, did not succeed in gathering all American industry into their folds.

By 1900 the Great Entrepreneurs and the Finance Capitalists had brought in a degree of centralized organization and relative economic stability, so that mass production could lay the foundations of a vastly increased national power and a higher standard of living. The new technique was a revolution as important as the Industrial Revolution. Mass production is the manufacture of large quantities of goods by the use of (1) machine tools, (2) driven by power, (3) to make standardized, interchangeable parts; and (4) the whole process being organized efficiently by the principles of scientific management.

It was a Philadelphia engineer named Frederick Winslow Taylor who took advantage of this knack for teamwork to add the fourth step in mass production—scientific management. Taylor saw two primary new industrial needs: efficiency at every step, since the ever-all means of mass production is efficiency; better human relations, not only as one element in attaining efficiency but as compensation for the performance satisfaction lost when a complete, coherent task is fragmented in the interest of efficient production.

The logical outcome of "Taylorization" was the assembly line, and it was only natural that it should first be perfected in the automobile industry, then the least enslaved by tradition. The man responsible was the genius of the industry, Henry Ford. The first automatic conveyor went into use in January 1914, and within three months a Model-T car was being assembled in ninety-three minutes. The assembly line was the culmination of this phase of mass production, though around 1950 automation was to introduce methods as revolutionary as any of those that had gone before.

The City: Its Problems and Protests

At the base of the Statue of Liberty, Bartholdi's heroic bronze of "Liberty Enlightening the World," contributed by the people of France and placed on Bedloe's Island in New York Harbor in 1886, were inscribed these lines by Emma Lazarus:

> Give me your tired, your poor,
> Your huddled masses yearning to breathe free,
> The wretched refuse of your teeming shore
> Send these, the homeless, tempest-tost to me;
> I lift my lamp beside the golden door.

During the half-century after the Civil War, nearly 25 million immigrants came to the United States, most of them to stay. In 1870 one person in seven was foreign-born, and in 1900 the ratio was still almost as high; though the number of foreign-born residents had almost doubled, the population of the country had also jumped about 100 percent—from 38 million to 76 million. In 1890 the foreign-born in New York-Brooklyn were two-fifths of the population, in Philadelphia one-fourth, in Boston one-third. At one time New York City boasted (whether or not correctly) that it had more Italians than any other city except Rome, more Irish than any other city except Dublin, more Germans than any other city except Berlin, more Greeks than any other city except Athens, and more Jews than any other city in the world. The foregoing graphically illustrates the changing nature of the immigration, except that there were in addition millions of Slavs from southern and eastern Europe who were brought in to service mines and factories.

The United States of 1870 was still overwhelmingly rural, but the cities were growing by leaps and bounds, faster than the technology needed to solve their problems and the ability of those in local government to foresee problems. Traffic congestion, water famines, fire hazards, sanitary failures, and the growth of slums were well-nigh inevitable. Crime and disease abounded. The new problems puzzled even the most upright and sincere civic leaders; as it was, the guidance all too often fell into the hands of political bosses and businessmen who used improvements as a means of lining their pockets.

The most disheartening aspect of city life was the corruption in politics. The city was a shapeless conglomeration of clashing races, nationalities, religions, and classes, but most of its dwellers exercised the vote. As a politician, the aim of the political boss was to win votes, but aside from that he performed the function of bringing some order into urban confusion, both for the good of the citizens and to serve the bourgeoning industries. Order meant welding together the inchoate masses. This the political boss achieved by giving out five-dollar gold pieces for votes and organizing picnics and parades, but even more by furnishing the social services that public opinion did not yet permit states and cities to provide. He provided for the widow and orphan, aided the man out of work, helped the boy in trouble with the law, and looked after the newly landed immigrant.

All these things took money. Therefore the boss collected a percentage of the salaries of municipal employees, and took a cut from each contract awarded to city contractors. Too, the power of the boss rested on a mutually beneficial arrangement between him and businessmen. He found ways for them to get around the law or to change it—for a price. While corruption was most obvious in the cities, this does not mean that it did not also exist in rural areas; control of counties by "courthouse gangs" was a familiar condition.

The cities were inevitably the centers of much of the protest and progress that marked the era. Reformers borrowed certain ideas of public ownership and control from the radical ideologies then rampant in Europe. It is appropriate, therefore, to look at some of these ideologies and at their struggle to get Americans to give them a hearing. Any outlines of radical ideologies given here is certain to be simplistic, for it would require weighty volumes to explore their ramifications.

The idea that certain economic functions, especially production facilities, are so important that they should be owned and operated by the community goes back for centuries. Most socialists—at least in Europe—prefer to speak of themselves as Christian Socialists, and this was essentially the character of many of the American utopian communities. Certainly modern socialists are best understood in the light of the Judaeo-Christian ethic, for they usually derive their inspiration from its teachings of brotherhood and equality and its strictures against greed. They emphasize that changes must be made by the democratic process—by evolution, not revolution—and this view predominates among British and American socialists.

We may understand better the reasons why Americans of the Gilded Age feared socialism if we note the way in which the theory differs from capitalism. There are two main distinctions between capitalism and socialism. First, capitalism is private enterprise, and socialism is state ownership and management of what are felt to be the key segments of the economy. The second distinction lies in the theory of income; capitalism says "from each according to his ability, to each according to his *work*"; socialism teaches "from each according to his ability, to each according to his *need*." Actually, socialists split among several theories of income, but even those who now admit that payment must be made according to work usually look forward to the day when payment can be made according to need.

Socialist experience in Britain has been so disheartening that its theory is showing a tendency to shift from government *ownership* to government *control* of private enterprise. Indeed, the so-called socialist nations of Africa and Asia are adopting a *mixed economy*, which has both public and private enterprise, but is all more or less subject to government controls and planning.

In 1848 Karl Marx, a German political philosopher, and his friend Friedrich Engels published the *Communist Manifesto*, a call to the workers of the world to unite—they had nothing to lose but their chains. Marx then proceeded to elaborate his doctrines in a long book called *Capital*. What he set forth was *revolutionary* socialism, and he appropriated the name *communism*, a word which hitherto had been a synonym for *socialism*. The appropriation led to further confusion about the meaning of a doctrine (socialism) which was already confused by clashing theories. But in a general sense, *socialism* still includes all the theories that uphold government control of production; in a specific sense, it opposes the revolutionary method of communism and is designed to attain its result by democratic and evolutionary processes.

Marx preached *economic determinism*, which speaking strictly, means that economic conditions (materialism), such as methods of production, inexorably shape society and its ideology. But as economic changes evolve they cause a conflict (the *dialectic*) between the old and the new, between *thesis* and *antithesis*. At a certain time in the conflict there will come a moment when men can influence its course. The result is revolution and the formation (*synthesis*) of a new set of economic conditions, which in their turn shape a new set of economic conditions, which in turn shape a new society and a new ideology. The whole process Marx called *dialectical materialism*. In effect it denied the interposition of a deity, and indeed gave economic determinism the role of a deity— hence, Marxism is often called a religion. Marx taught that the holding of private property was the basic sin of history from which all evils flowed, and which had given rise not only to wars, famines, and poverty, but to bitter class conflict. Revolution was inevitable, and it would lead to a perfect, classless society in which there would be no conflicts and no political state. History would then cease to be made.

Another radical doctrine was anarchism. There were so many forms of anarchism that it is almost hopeless to sort them out, but we may risk the statement that anarchists held extreme ideas of the rights and dignity of the individual, deplored and sometimes denied the necessity of government, but usually sought to organize the world into small independent geographical areas, each of which would be a social democracy and would trade as it pleased with other areas. Anarchists are usually idealistic dreamers like Leo Tolstoy. Another brand of anarchist, inspired by Michael Bakunin, was seen in the Black International which intended to throw enough bombs to force society to adopt their plans. In addition to Marxists and anarchists, there were the syndicalists, who proposed that the trade unions destroy all national governments and themselves own and manage industries.

Most of the European radical ideologies found adherents in America, chiefly German or Eastern European in origin, always few though typically vigorous and vocal. Considering their expenditure of energy, talk, and printer's ink, it is remarkable that they influenced American labor history as little as they did. Anarchists were fairly common during the period after the Civil War; though they were very much divided, they caused a good deal of public concern. Socialism's political activities in the United States were carried on by numerous societies and workingmen's parties, but in 1901 the moderate socialists, led by Eugene Debs, united to form the Socialist Party.

American labor fought its way upward during the Gilded Age against the stiff opposition of both industry and public and had won the right to organize—but only after a series of great strikes—most of them bloody failures. Just the same, labor's condition was being ameliorated by state laws, basically because it was able to wield political power with the increase of the industrial population. Moreover, it stilled the fears of business by accepting capitalism and agreeing that management and profit and loss were the function of business; its own function was to insist that labor receive some of the profits in the form of wages and suffer none of the losses in the form of wage cuts. Samuel Gompers, pragmatic leader of the American Federation of Labor, when asked to state his objective gave the classic answer, "More."

It should also be borne in mind that the exploitation of labor was relative rather than absolute. The American laborer had a high ideal of freedom and welfare, and he had a tendency to compare his working conditions with what he though they *ought* to be rather than with those of workers in comparable European trades, as his employer exhorted him to. Corporations could afford concessions because little of their resources went to pay income taxes, nor did they have to support huge military and naval establishments, as did European taxpayers.

The growing efficiency of the factory system, already moving into full-blown mass production, was cutting the cost of goods and increasing the number of semiskilled workers, who traditionally were better paid than the unskilled, and even the marginal workers often shared in the improvement. Finally, politicians needed labor's votes and so supported one move after another to assure labor's rights and improve its conditions.

The Garrison South

With the withdrawal of Union troops from the South in 1877 the area fell under the political dominance of the Bourbons, so called because like the French Bourbon kings "they never learned and never forgot." Actually the cognomen was not quite fair for they did promote some progressive measures. They might or might not have done more, but the South had fallen under the domination of Northern banks and industries which did not propose to see the region rise above helotage.

When Negroes refused to work in gangs because the system had been used in slavery days, a substitute was found in sharecropping. Plantations were divided into one-man farms, operated by the freedman and his family and usually planted to cotton. Because of its exploitation the South was in a permanent depression and the sharecropper rarely managed to emerge from debt, so was in fact a peon. During Reconstruction the Negro had enjoyed civil rights and the vote; now they were gradually withdrawn. In 1883 the Supreme Court by the Civil Rights Cases denied that it was the business of the federal government to guarantee to the Negro equal use of privately owned public facilities; the result was a rash of "Jim Crow laws" segregating Negroes from whites, and this was soon extended to schools.

The most prominent Negro leader of the era was Booker T. Washington, educator and lecturer. He believed it impossible for the Negro to attain equal rights suddenly; a long period of apprenticeship and adaptation must come first, and this must be approached not through the white man's classical curriculum but through mechanical and agricultural education. In his "Atlanta Compromise" speech in 1895, Washington said, "The opportunity to earn a dollar in a factory just now is worth infinitely more than the opportunity to spend a dollar in an opera house." Perhaps the light emphasis on the *just now* was intended to deceive; at any rate, Northern humanitarians and Southern white upperclass advocates of "parallel civilizations" understood him to be counseling patience in inferiority, and so were ready to help him.

Washington's "reaslistic" approach was bitterly denounced as "Uncle Tomism" and "appeasement" by a group of Negro leaders, chiefly Northerners, led by William Edward Burghardt Du Bois of Massachusetts, a brilliant scholar and historian. Du Bois denied the validity of Washington's vocational approach on the ground that only the usual classical education could provide the "Talented Tenth" necessary to lead Negro advance. He demanded equality in all respects, supported his stand in a long series of powerful books, and was an organizer of the National Association for the Advancement of Colored People (NAACP), which led the long struggle for Negro rights.

The unfortunate truth is that white hostility to Negroes had become more intense. This was true not only in the South but also in the North as more Southern Negroes appeared in Northern cities, and these saw numerous bloody riots. Whether Southern courts were disposed to deny equal justice to Negroes has been disputed, but there can be no doubt that the white populace resorted to violence to keep Negroes "in their place." Of the 4,672 known victims of lynching between 1882 and 1936, three-fourths were Negroes—most of them, though not all, in the South. Rape, arson, and attempted murder of whites were frequent excuses for lynching, but many a Negro met death because of some trivial offense or simply because he tried to rise out of his caste or was not properly humble before whites. Lynching occurred most frequently in rural areas, where the races were most evenly divided and came most into competition.

By about 1900 the agrarian and industrial interests of the South had worked out a *modus vivendi* which suited them fairly well and which was to survive deep into the new century. Southern Negroes had no choice but to accept their assigned role. The rural areas, especially the cotton, rice, and sugarcane regions, relied largely on Negro labor. The factories, with some exceptions, preferred white labor. Negroes could hold land, but on the whole it was not wise for them to show marks of expertness or prosperity. In the cities Negroes received less pay for the same jobs than white artisans, and the threat of Negro competition was useful in hampering unionization and holding white wages down.

Rural and city interests had their clashes, but these were fought out in white primaries, and when the general election came, the interests formed a solid front. After all, they had one common meeting ground: white supremacy. In a general sense, the ruling class succeeded in its original objective of preventing white and black workers from uniting, and the policy of race division suited Northern investors very well. It was not the first nor the last time that local conditions had lent themselves to the illustration of the motto "Divide and rule."

There was a curious contradiction in ideals. Lip service was still given to Anglo-Saxon civil liberties, but they were for the white man; their denial to the Negro was interpreted as the very substance of morality.

Blood was the basis of society; any attempt to change the pattern of segregation would, therefore, destroy the whole pattern of society, ethics, and politics. The worst crime that could be committed was a Negro man's assault on a white woman, for that defiled the very foundation of white society, the blood line. A white man's assault on a Negro woman, by some sort of twisted logic, did not defile the blood line!

The Civil War and reconstruction solidified the South's traditional conservatism and paternalism, convinced it of the rectitude of the aristo-agrarian ideal, and made white supremacy the standard around which all loyal Southerners must rally. The South's leaders were more than ever determined to protect the citadel of white supremacy by imbuing their people with the psychology of a closely disciplined, beleaguered garrison. They made internal politics a means of enforcing that discipline, and external politics a continuation of Calhoun's search for a veto on the nation in any policy that affected Southern interests. They found this in the Southern ability (until 1936) to veto the Democratic Party's selection of Presidential candidates, and in the ability of its Senators to block legislation by means of the filibuster.

W. J. Cash has described the mythus that now took over the mind of the South, and to a considerable extent was believed in the North.

> Like many another people come upon evil days, the South in its entirety was filled with an immense regret and nostalgia; yearned backward toward its past with passionate longing. And so it happened that, while the actuality of aristocracy was drawing away toward the limbo of aborted and unrealized things, the claim of its possession as an achieved and essentially indefeasible heritage, so far from being abated, was reasserted with a kind of frenzied intensity. It was in this period that the legend of the Old South finally emerged and fully took on the form in which we know it today. With the antebellum world removed to the realm of retrospect, the shackles of reality, as so often happens in such cases, fell away from it altogether. Perpetually suspended in the great haze of memory, it hung, as it were, poised, somewhere between earth and sky, colossal, shining, and incomparably lovely—a Cloud-Cuckoo-Land wherein . . . life would move always in stately and noble measure through scenery out of Watteau.[3]

---

[3] W. J. Cash, *The Mind of the South* (New York: Random House—A. A. Knopf, 1941, p. 124.

The Agrarian Crusade

Railroads and new agricultural methods and machinery had opened up vast new lands. The result was glut and depression, conditions worsened by the stranglehold which New York and Chicago banks held on rural areas by their control of credit, grain elevators, and rail transportation. The farmer bought in a home market protected by high tariffs from foreign competition; he sold in a world market where prices were depressed by world competition.

There seemed to be no effective way to cure the farmers' problems. A tariff would not help much, for little agricultural produce was imported. Reduce production? There would have been a storm of protest at such a violation of the law of supply and demand. Labor would have objected because of the price rise; anyhow labor was suspicious of the farmer's petty captialism, and the two never succeeded in getting together for long, even under the New Deal.

At this point it will be useful to call attention to certain inconsistencies in the behavior of American economic interest groups. Business leaders regarded themselves as foresighted and benevolent in so far as natural economic laws would permit; and the middle class generally agreed, at least until the turn of the century. Farmers and laborers, however, were quite generally convinced that business had instituted a double standard of morality—one for itself and one for them. When they protested to the businessman that the effect was to turn them into exploited dependents, he answered simply that if there was any villain it was the "law" of supply and demand.

And yet, as labor and agrarian critics did not fail to point out, the businessman was daily violating that law with such bland assurance that one could only judge that it was not intended to apply to him. He expected government favors in the forms of tariffs, handouts of public lands, and police protection as a natural right; but any move to protect the farmer or the laborer and to raise his income or working conditions was denounced as a violation of the Constitution and of all American traditions. The businessman organized trusts and monopolies to regulate prices and markets, but he held that labor unions and farmers' alliances were subversive, and demanded that the courts treat them as such.

The businessman held that business property was the source from which all economic blessings flowed. Therefore it was sacred, and its right to multiply itself freely must be protected by the full might of the law. At the same time the laborer's property in wages and the farmer's in prices must be protected only by the "law" of supply and demand! Finally, the courts and the legislatures were regarded by the businessman as his perquisites, his because he knew how they should be used. Let the farmer and the laborer keep their noses out of economic matters of which they knew nothing; and if they must have a political outlet, it should be confined to torchlight processions, to voting for a pre-selected slate, and to criticizing foreign ways and actions—as by twisting the Bristish lion's tail.

While capital's rulers cannot be cleared of having used their control of bank credits, tariffs, and transportation to squeeze agriculture and labor between high costs and low incomes, they were by no means to blame for all the shadows in the panorama. Fundamental to the situation was the traditional Jeffersonianism of the American people, which caused farmers and laborers to help create their situation by their headlong individualism.

There was a good deal to be said in support of the accusation that they, too, were violating the "law" of supply and demand. Farmers expanded heedlessly into new territories and glutted the market with cotton, wheat, and meat which there was not purchasing power to absorb. The urban labor supply was increasing by leaps and bounds as farm boys poured into the cities and hundreds of thousands of immigrants flooded through the portals each year. Laborers failed to protect their common interests by effectively uniting to form an economic and political pressure group which might have bettered their conditions in the democratic manner. Farmers and laborers, in their turn, were advocating a double standard of morality in their own favor. They expected to be protected in their own runaway individualism from the far more effective and efficient individualism of entrepreneurs.

The farmers' discontent had taken the form of various political revolts, and some progress had been made in forcing the farm states to regulate railroad and warehouse rates. A cycle of drought years in the West coincided with the hard times of the 1880's, and the drastic deflation of farm prices led to the spread of organizations called Farmers' Alliances, and in 1891 they founded the People's or Populist Party.

Populists favored an economic program which now seems moderate. They advocated an expanded currency, government control of railroads, the initiative and referendum, the direct election of Senators, enforcement of the rights of labor—for Populists often felt a kinship with labor—the imposition of an income tax, and the breakup of monopolies. The movement also asked for direct government help for the farmer. It desired to put into effect a "sub-treasury plan" by which the farmer could deposit his grain and cotton in federal warehouses and borrow up to 80 percent of their value in specially issued Treasury notes.

Populism cannot be understood except in the light of its psychological background. It was a symptom of rising rural alarm at the growth and emerging power of great new cities in American life. Certain of its ideas had been brought from Europe and preserved as part of the rural heritage. Christianity was deeply ingrained in America, but so were some of its medieval prejudices—as against Jews and usury.

Christianity had grown up in the midst of what it interpreted as a gigantic conspiracy against God and those who sought to do right; here was an obvious source not only of the accusation of a bankers' conspiracy but of the isolationism and nativism so characteristic of America's rural areas. Finally, Christianity posited an apocalypse that would result in a judgment against sinners and the emergence of a new heaven and a new earth on which Christ would reign; here was an obvious parallel with the populist dream of building the City of God by freeing all toilers, purifying American institutions, and fulfilling the American mission in one apocalyptic stroke.

Populism had a certain kinship with the Jacksonian movement, and for a few years it swept the South, but only so long as its leaders remained Democrats. When by 1892 it became evident that the success of populism as a party would divide whites and turn the balance of power over to black voters, the white electorate refused to go along. The Populist Party in the South thus foundered on the shoals of race conflict.

The Populists then turned to the economic panacea of free silver. Free-silver propaganda, as set forth in speciously simple terms by such writings as *Coin's Financial School* (1894), explained deflation and hard times as the result of a conspiracy between British and American financiers led by the Jewish Rothschilds to control the world's stock of gold and thus take over and govern a distressed economy and reduce farmers and laborers to virtual serfdom. The cure was equally simple: resume free and unlimited coinage of silver dollars at the old value of sixteen ounces of silver to one of gold—the historic "sixteen to one."

Because of a number of silver strikes in the West the price of silver had declined to the point where the silver in a dollar was worth only fifty cents in gold. The claim was that a free-silver policy would result in a degree of inflation, and would be a boon to debtors and a stimulus to the national economy. Greenback inflation might justly be regarded as dangerous because it was limited only by available paper and green ink; but silver inflation was drastically limited by the amount of silver.

The latter, it seemed clear to the Populists, should be acceptable to reasonable conservatives—certainly to Eastern workers who were being crushed by deflation. Actually, many Eastern workers, being consumers, were so in favor of sound money—in this context, gold—that they even thought of the Republican promotion of banknotes as a soft-money policy. On the other hand, the deep distress of labor, as evidenced by the great strikes, and the resentments caused by their forcible suppression, did give inflationists some ground for their optimistic belief that they could carry the East.

Whatever the reasons, it soon became evident that free-silver's simple cure-all was rapidly becoming the one issue that could invoke the enthusiasm of the rank and file voter. The campaign for "the people's money" was not waged solely by the embattled farmers. The advantage to silver-mine owners was obvious, and they poured hundreds of thousands of dollars into propaganda, both printed and spoken. One favorite tool was the American Bimetallic League, and its favorite orator was a young Nebraska lawyer and politician named William Jennings Bryan.

President Grover Cleveland was a Democrat and had been responsible for many reforms, especially in the administration of public lands. On the other hand he was pro-business and he refused to champion free silver. The result was that the bulk of his party repudiated him and nominated Bryan on a free-silver platform, and the chagrined Populists had to accept him also. The Republicans put up William McKinley, and "gold bugs" rallied to his support and filled the party coffers and brought every possible pressure to bear on businessmen and workers.

The Boy Orator of the Platte—he was only thirty-six—threw himself into one of the most impassioned crusades in American history. Hitherto most Presidential candidates had remained sedately at home while batteries of politicians did their campaigning. Bryan kicked over the precedent, traveled 18,000 miles, and talked to an estimated 4,800,000 people. The summer melted into autumn, and the national temperature mounted as Bryan trumpeted his message: "The people have a right to make their own mistakes." It was quite in the Jacksonian tradition, but conservatives shrieked of socialism, class conflict, and tumbrels rolling toward an American guillotine. McKinley himself remained on his front porch in Canton, rocking and fanning through the heat of summer, delivered carefully prepared little speeches to bands of pilgrims who came from afar, then excused himself and went upstairs to read the Bible to his invalid wife.

In the election Bryan was defeated, though not resoundingly. Nevertheless, the Populist Party faded and died. It is easy to say that the Populists were ignorant men given to crank theories and economic fallacies. No doubt this was true of part of their program—but some of the opposite beliefs of their opponents are just as clearly open to challenge. Many of the Populist proposals needed to be brought before the people, and the soundness of a number of them is shown by the fact that they have long since been put into effect. The Populists, like most political pioneers, had to suffer contumely—and then see other men put their ideas into effect and get the credit.

As it turned out, prosperity returned for a variety of reasons, none of them the result of Republican policies. Gold strikes and the cyanide process increased the supply of gold, and new technical uses for silver increased its price. The drought cycle ended in the West, crops failed in the rest of the world, and wars boomed the demand for wheat.

The so-called Battle of the Standards was one of the most important campaigns in American history. The fact that free silver took the place of vital issues may seem to argue that its importance has been over-rated. On the other hand, Tom Johnson, reform mayor of Cleveland, wrote in 1911 that it was the first great protest of the American people against monopoly—the first great "struggle of the masses in our country against the privileged classes. It was not free silver that frightened the plutocrat leaders. What they feared then, what they fear now, is free men."

Certainly it was a victory for Big Property, as Morgan and the rest of the Wall Street stock waterers soon began to prove, and a defeat for the dirt farmers. Jefferson and Jackson had sought to seize the central government in order to weaken it; now their heirs had been thwarted in an attempt to seize the central government in order to force it to give positive aid to the Jeffersonian ideal of small property. Bryan, as unerringly as though he had been hired to do it, crushed that hope, stamped out the Populist Party, and turned the country over to Wall Street—by simply dramatizing a quack comedy.

The weakness of free silver lay not in its promise of inflation (perhaps an expansion of currency would have been beneficial) but in its cruelly false promise to bring the New Jerusalem. Jeffersonian agrarianism went down to destruction in a battle waged over a will-o'-the-wisp—an end strangely in contrast with its hopeful origins. It was not, of course, the end of agriculture. During the next two decades agriculture enjoyed a wave of prosperity. The original Populist program was to appear in refurbished form and was to triumph in the next century. Agrarian leaders learned from their defeat to operate within the framework of the old parties, and a generation later were to get much of what they wanted. But it was to be a new form of agriculture which emerged—the commerical farm. The family farm, the backbone of American democracy, was already passing, and the Battle of the Standards was only a last despairing gesture.

The Faith of the Gilded Age

Americans of the Gilded Age accelerated the tempo of certain of their traditional quests: for wealth, for respectability, and for culture—and in the process often failed to assure the fourth, a viable democracy. Many of them succeeded in the first, and even more were able to put on the outward signs of the second. The fact was that Americans were a people in search of their identity and, like the adolescent dreaming of the future, they tried on many faces and agreed on many self-complimentary and self-confident myths. Still, just as the boy is father of the man, Americans of the Gilded Age were laying the foundation of future national character and accomplishments.

The standards of the old aristocracy emphasized character—character in the sense of reliability, respectability, and devotion to duty—and these standards were shared by millions of men and women unknown to history. But various factors, including the reaction from war and the effects of the long battle against the wilderness, threatened to make cleverness and love of power more important as American traits than character. The task of making character a part of the American grain was an absorbing and invaluably constructive interest of the Gilded Age.

There was a tendency to confuse gentility with character, but perhaps gentility is a mask that must be worn while character is being developed. The gentility of the Gilded Age led to an attempt to deny or at least conceal anything regarded as "unbecoming" according to the rather prissy standards of the time. Unpleasant social facts were ignored or glossed over. Genteelism afflicted literary and artistic circles. Never before or since have English speech and writing been so smothered by euphemisms, those greatcoats and mufflers of language.

There was thus a tendency to confuse respectability with character. Still, this was in the spirit of the hoary English motto "Manners makyth man." The attempt to implant a respect for the humdrum virtues was perhaps a healthy sign and a necessary step in the building of both culture and social-conscious wealth. It was perhaps also necessary in preparing the nation for the responsibilities that were to descend upon it in the twentieth century.

Those who belonged to the Cult of Respectability were "good providers" for their families, went to church, contributed to charity, committed their sins in private or in discreet company, and kept within the letter of the law, even seeing to it that the special privileges granted by kept politicians were garnished with all due formality. Gentility was diligently cultivated; men became "gentlemen," and women "ladies"; even the working classes assumed the titles.

Appearance, manners, and behavior became second in importance only to sound financial standing. The book of etiquette was more diligently read than the family Bible, however prominently the latter was displayed on a marble-topped table. Women were models of prim decorum and became helpless without proper male escort. Little girls were taught to model themselves on their mamas, and little boys in their Fauntleroy suits were reproved for unseemly noise. Bearded paterfamilias comported themselves with a painful dignity, which they flattered themselves was quiet elegance.

Gold watches, Malacca sticks, neat clothing of good quality, punctuality, reserve without coldness, and refinement without artiness were the marks of the devotee of the cult of respectability. Regularity was prized. One moved week after week on the same unvarying round; sat in the same pew on Sundays, ate with the same relatives on holidays, went to the same resort every summer, lived in the same house and sat in the same chair of an evening during the whole of his adult life.

The antebellum struggle between religion and science ended in an uneasy truce by which the churches recognized the conclusions of science as disclosures of God's "design" for the universe. But theology's stubborn insistence that man was the center of the universe had received a powerful blow when in 1859 Charles Darwin's *Origin of Species* offered natural selection ("survival of the fittest") as the method of evolution for which scientists had long been seeking. Before long evolution was to open a can of worms—naturalism, pragmatism, relativism, and communism, and to authenticate change by revolutionary violence; in a word, the chaos of our own time. On the other hand, it also pointed out some of the remedies, if we will only use them.

The immediate result was the emergence of the philosophy of Naturalism which regarded all phenomena as subject to natural law, and so tended to find a connection among physical, biological, and social manifestations. True, this hypothesis had been posited by the Enlightenment, but the eighteenth century thought of the universe as static, and with regard to society transformed natural laws into natural rights. Naturalism thought of the universe as dynamic (evolutionary) and of the moral and social orders as subordinate parts of the natural order.

Naturalists thus came to look upon natural law as wielding a power over social and individual action that was almost, if not fully, coercive. It can readily be seen that Naturalism, starting from evolution as its basic assumption, could move quite easily through Marx's economic determinism and then into totalitarianism. It assumed that men could exercise considerable freedom if they only learned how to conduct themselves within the limits laid down by natural law. This was essentially the ideal of Herbert Spencer, the English philosopher, who proposed the "survival of the fittest" as nature's way of weeding out those who transgressed natural law or who were not properly adapted to it. It may be pointed out that Spencer did not regard this brutal competition as a permanent state of society, but looked forward to a perfect society in which evil and immorality would disappear. There were in this certain parallels to the Marxist dream.

Spencer's doctrine was seized upon by certain Americans as an explanation and amoral justification for the overweening power of the Great Entrepreneurs. Spencerianism, or Social Darwinism, as it came to be called, ordained that the superior (the successful) must not be burdened by having to support the inferior (the unsuccessful). This was an obvious discouragement of reform. Exploitation of labor fulfilled the grand purpose of the cosmos by weeding out the unfit. The state must confine itself to the function of an occasional umpire. It could not even operate hospitals, schools, roads, and fire departments; they should be supported by private charity or thrown into the competitive struggle.

In effect, Spencer stripped the ethical system of many of its inconvenient prohibitions and cleared the way for material aggrandizement. Social Darwinism was also related to the growing conviction that Europeans were a "master race," destined to rule the world. One form this took was Teutonism, the belief that the Germanic peoples of Northwest Europe and their emigrant descendants were the master race; another form was Anglo-Saxonism, in which the English-speaking nations constituted the master race.

There was a widespread opinion that the pursuit of wealth was not only consistent with morality but was itself a part of the moral code. The Gospel of Wealth preached that the country's salvation lay in amassing riches and in proper respect for riches. It would be a mistake to label as conscious hypocrites either the overlords or the ministers of the Gospel of Wealth—which, by the way, took its name from an article by Andrew Carnegie, the steel magnate. Indeed, it was a flowering of one of the basic tenets of Calvinism that wealth has a responsibility for guiding society and promoting its welfare.

As rich men saw it, the brutal economic struggle bred leaders who, because of their economic power, could and would do more for the masses than corrupt political leaders. The successful individual was the key symbol of a successful individual culture; success thus became the symbol of morality even though it might have been gained by immoral means. The wreckage in unsuccessful lives that might lie behind the rich man and around him should not claim attention (they were merely unfortunate incidents in the inevitable operation of Natural Law), only the fact of his emergence. As John D. Rockefeller, Jr., remarked, the American Beauty rose was created only by snipping off all the smaller buds below. To serve the ends of fostering the successful, it was imperative that state and federal governments provide tariffs, cheap raw materials, and favorable currency and banking laws. Beyond these the state must let wealth alone while it made America into the City of God.

The industrialist was now trying to join the aristocracy, but the "society" that emerged was plutocratic rather than aristocratic, and the "cult of conspicuous consumption" was frequently the substitute for culture. Conspicuous consumption, while carried to the superlative in America, was a feature at this same time of Europe; on both continents it bred resentments which fostered radical movements. There was evidence that the rich were in some measure washing their hands of their responsibility to improve the communities which had made them wealthy. In America *Life*, then a humorous magazine with rudiments of social conscience, satirized the contrasts in the social scene. The "yellow press" played up the rivalries among hostesses and hinted at the scandalous orgies of the rich. Popular resentment at some of these extravagances rose so high that the perpetrators felt compelled to exile themselves to Europe.

There was a saying at the turn of the century that the United States imported art and exported artists. Young artists could expect recognition only after a term of study in Paris, Munich, or Rome (and here the word "artist" applied not only to painters but to sculptors, architects, writers, and musicians). The popularity of the European flavor in American art, fiction, poetry, and historical writing must have betokened a desire to escape from the present and the real.

Such absorption bred in them a nostalgia that gilded even the lampposts of Paris and made it impossible for them to distinguish between the good and the mediocre—let alone to appreciate the promise of their own country. Like Henry James, who gathered "a golden-ripe crop of English impressions" as soon as he crossed the threshhold of his inn, the American exile wistfully endowed Europe's trifling mannerisms with an aura of leisure, charm, and grace, without sensing that underneath ran a current of brutality as cynical as that in the United States—moreso—and without the American promise. If only America could have these mannered traditions! It was William Dean Howells who answered with gentle irony that perhaps it was well that we had no sovereign, no court, no aristocracy, no clergy, no church, no country gentlemen, palaces, nor manor houses—but simply the whole of human life left!

The expatriates failed to see that a new America—a new world—was being formed, an economy and a culture devoted to the welfare of the masses. When the architect Louis Sullivan raised his affirmation that "Form follows function," he was saying that the machine age with its inexorable demand for new forms in art and life was offering to creative artists an opportunity never before matched in the history of the world. It was their tragedy and perhaps that of the world that so many of them fled, leaving to their less sensitive but more vigorous fellows the task of adjusting creative art to the new day.

Henry James had fled from the turmoil and what he viewed as the crass materialism of America. Mark Twain solved the difficulty by wielding two pens. One of them he sold to the Gilded Age—but saw to it that it left plenty of blots on the gilded escutcheon. The other pen he did not sell—nor did he sell his soul. Apparently on one side he worshiped a completely conventional wife and reveled in the Great Barbecue around him. On the other side he was tormented by the misery and injustice of the age. His humor was a vehicle for the portrayal of democracy's courage and its seaminess and at the same time his pessimistic contempt for "the damned human race."

His genius was observed in his own generation, and today he is generally recognized as America's greatest prose writer. His importance is twofold. He created almost single-handedly modern prose style, stripping his prose of formalism and introducing essentially the rhythm of speech. Practically every writer since his time has been influenced by his style. His work, especially *Huckleberry Finn*, is the finest expression of Jeffersonian democracy in literature. Without being blinded to the meanness and corruption that surrounded him, Twain nevertheless holds to the faith in the common, untutored man that is the very base of the democratic system. Huck and Jim are all the apostles of democracy that any sensible person needs to have. Cynic and all (and cynicism is a good part of it), Mark Twain is the great democrat.

Among those who stayed in America, or returned, was a galaxy of painters, sculptors, and architects. A notable pioneer among the last-named was Louis Sullivan. He found in the skyscraper the "emotional synthesis of practical conditions." His guiding rule came to him one day in the quiet of the Vatican's Sistine Chapel, when Michelangelo seemed to be audibly saying, "Form follows function." Sullivan looked on architecture as a social manifestation and read in it the social state of mind. His functionalism, cool and terse, whether in skyscrapers or dwellings, was in striking contrast with the garrulousness of the average American architect.

Sullivan and those others who were probing beneath the clamor and din of the Gilded Age to find their identity were joining the battle between the American *vernacular* and the European cultivated tradition first noted on page 215. As we pointed out there, European art was rooted in its traditional civilization, which had developed with more or less symmetry from classical times to the Industrial Revolution. The American vernacular, on the other hand, to quote John Kouwenhoven again, is the folk art "of the first people in history who, disinherited of a great cultural tradition, found themselves living under democratic institutions in an expanding machine economy."

Hitherto the prestige of the cultivated tradition had drawn American artists to Europe, and many of them had stayed there because there was not enough sand in their souls to face life in the sprawling, formless, noisy country of their birth. As a result, the vernacular had been relegated to the common craftsmen and to a few rebel artists, architects, and engineers. Artists had always had the vision of instructing the tastes of the masses, and at times had attained some degree of success. Now, however, certain American artists and engineers were seeking a broader aim—a civilization built on material service to, as well as appreciation by, the people; and in pursuance of this dream they were trying to grasp the way to use the material resources of America and to express its values in new artistic forms.

The American was short-cutting European evolution and entering the era of mass production; the same struggle went on in Europe, but the European was more firmly rooted in the past. Thus, about 1870, Americans used a cast-steel plow which weighed forty pounds, while the British clung to a wrought-iron plow (intended to do the same work) which weighed two hundred and fifty pounds. Even though the ornamental lines and coruscations of the European tradition were then sadly afflicting American machines, the most impressive treat at the Centennial Exhibition of 1876 was the enormous, starkly functional Corliss steam engine. Even Europeans recognized its artistic quality. The London *Times*, little inclined to praise things American, noted that "the American mechanizes as an old Greek sculptured, as the Venetian painted."

The cultivated tradition refused to adapt itself to the vernacular, and the result was for a long time the sterilization of both on the American scene: drab cities dotted with pompous classical monuments. Even the vernacular builder was too often affected (when his patron could afford it) and broke his vernacular plane surfaces with the jigsaw lacework called Carpenter Gothic.

The rebel artists and writers were indications of the deep undercurrent of criticism of the Gilded Age. Foremost among the critics of the age and among movements for reform were the four Adams brothers, grandsons of President John Quincy Adams. Here our concern is with Henry because he was the most deeply interested in why Americans had failed to build the City of God. His search for the key to history as an exact science led him on long travels into the realms not only of history but of theology and science. On the way he examined intensively the democracy of the Jeffersonian period. In it he saw a unifying ideal—that of belief in human perfectability and of what we can define as the American ideal: that cultural and material resources shall no longer be the exclusive property of a chosen few but shall become of service to all.

In his monumental *History of the United States*, devoted to the administrations of Jefferson and Madison, Adams proved to his own satisfaction that the ideal had been betrayed by compromisers, largely because it was impractical—human nature and the logic of events being what they were. Failure had overtaken the attempt of his grandfather, President John Quincy Adams, to introduce a welfare state (in the context of 1825) built on the Puritan ideals of truth, duty, and freedom. The next step (in the history of democratic degradation, not in the order of publication) was depicted in *Democracy* (1880), a novel that devastatingly portrayed Washington in the age of Grantism, a place where power was exercised for its own sake, and therefore corruptly— the ultimate outcome of democracy once it had lost its Jeffersonian idealism.

This pessimistic conclusion did not fit into any historical scheme until in 1900 when, at the Paris Exposition, in viewing the display of forces in the great Hall of Dynamos, he glimpsed an awesome future governed by radioactive energy. He then came to the realization that force was the key—that is, the unified world view that attracts the loyalty of men and summons them to creative effort. In *Mont St. Michel and Chartres* (1904) he saw this force—personified in the Virgin—as a spiritual energy that absorbed the faith of men and led them to build the great cathedrals, the concrete embodiments of medieval ideals of faith, harmony, and unity.

The next step was *The Education of Henry Adams* (1906). The book is an autobiography only in the sense that the author uses the events of his own life to string together his analysis and judgment of his times. *Mont St Michel* presented a world of "unity, simplicity, morality"; *The Education* presented a world of "multiplicity, contradiction, police." What unifying force in the twentieth century could attract the loyalty of men, furnish an object and a meaning for existence? The problem was especially acute in America, where religious faith as a constructive force no longer existed and the democratic faith (as Adams saw it) had been degraded into a mere instrument of power.

The works of Henry Adams, taken together, constitute a *tour de force* in the philosophy of history, and the chronicle of a search which always ran into the second law of thermodynamics—a blind alley which denies the truth of human progress because available energy one day will be dissipated into the outer universe and no longer sustain life. (The "cheery" universe which, according to Hoyle and Lyttleton, perpetually renews its energy, was as yet unheard of; in any case, its cosmic optimism bodes destruction rather than survival for that minor planet, the earth.)

Intellectually, Adams found no escape from his blind alley, but the result of his intuitions and speculations—however faulty, and at times even absurd—was that history could no longer be mere chronicle. He had pushed the search for the law and meaning of history beyond the social, economic, and political realms to a fusion with art and science—even with mathematical physics. As Adams himself put it, the task before the historian required another Newton.

Chapter 11
The Imperial Thrust

Proem

British rule had its faults, but in retrospect its virtues shine brighter. Where the Union Jack flew, there were trade and good order, there were schools and local assemblies of the people, there were missionaries and technicians bringing the arts of Western Civilization. Britain's power was based (among other things) on her realistic acceptance of the commercial standard of success that, after the first years, promoted the welfare of both rulers and ruled; on a certain flexibility that made it possible to meet special situations with special measures; and on a "sense of the limits of power," which meant that those who struggled for self-rule would sooner or later be accepted as equals and partners. Here were the reasons why the British Empire was self-liquidating, why its rule was doomed from the day its flag was run up an alien pole.

* * *

The White Man's Burden—written in 1899 by Rudyard Kipling to help persuade the United States to annex the Phillipines.

> Take up the White Man's burden—
> Send forth the best ye breed—
> Go bind your sons to exile
> To serve your captives' need;

To wait in heavy harness
On fluttered folk and wild—
Your new-caught, sullen peoples,
Half devil and half child.

Take up the White Man's burden—
The savage wars of peace—
Fill full the mouth of Famine
And bid the sickness cease;
And when your goal is nearest
The end for others sought,
Watch Sloth and heathen Folly
Bring all your hope to naught.

Take up the White Man's burden—
And reap his old reward:
The blame of those ye better,
The hate of those ye guard—
The cry of hosts ye humour
(Ah, slowly!) toward the light;—
"Why brought ye us from bondage,
"Our loved Egyptian night?"

Take up the White Man's burden—
Ye dare not stoop to less—
Nor call too loud on Freedom
To cloak your weariness;
By all ye cry or whisper,
By all ye leave or do,
The silent, sullen peoples
Shall weigh your Gods and you.

Origins of the New Imperialism

Imperialism, says William L. Langer, is "the rule or control, political or economic, direct or indirect, of one state, nation or people over similar groups—or perhaps one might better say the disposition, urge or striving to establish such rule or control." Mr. Dooley bluntly called it "hands acrost th' sea an' into somewan's pocket." Actually imperialism is not confined to capitalist countries: the Soviet Union is the most ruthless imperialism since Rome.

Imperialism, after all, can be nationalism projected beyond the national border. Nationalism is the community of basic ways and beliefs within a political entity, or a would-be political entity. It carried with it a worship of those ways and, oftentimes, a belief in the nation's mission to rule over lesser peoples, or at least to give them the benefit of superior culture and institutions. The nation is not necessarily the creation of blood, but of history, geography, ideas, and usually culture and language. Nationalism finds expression in several ways: ideologies, the cultural, political, and institutional beliefs and way of life—of which democracy is one; militarism, by which everything is subordinated to the military search for strength; navalism, in which the navy is the weapon of might; irredentism, the propaganda for the recovery of "lost" provinces; and, of course, the active thrust of imperialism.

The loss of the thirteen American colonies came at the moment when the Industrial Revolution gave promise of making England the workshop of the world. The result was the growth in England of the idea that colonies were not paying investments, especially since in time they would break away from their political allegiance. The burden of governing a people with an advanced civilization (as of the Thirteen Colonies) was arduous, thankless, and sometimes unprofitable. Why not, therefore, abandon the mercantilist policy of annexation, sell goods wherever possible, and leave the political headaches to the peoples of the land?

Out of this philosophy there emerged a British economic empire which was as important as the British political empire. The Union Jack did not wave over the vast stretches of China and South America, but they were nevertheless British to all intents and purposes and at the time fairly free to experiment with revolutions, war lords, and constitutions. During the nineteenth century the United States was also a part of this economic empire, led by loose financial strings which were not finally severed until World War I turned us from a debtor to a creditor nation. Another dependency was the Dutch East Indies, especially the liberalization of Dutch rule in that area before 1900.

Hispanic America was in a sense peculiarly fortunate. There the Monroe Doctrine, the British emphasis on economic empire, and the stalemate among rival European powers resulted in all but complete freedom from alienation of territory except to the United States. The political and economic chaos during the last century was appalling and it is only within this generation that some semblance of order has been restored.

The conditions outlined above underlay the *Pax Britannica*—the British Peace—which made the century from 1815 to 1914 a period of peace and progress such as had not been known since the *Pax Romana* of the palmy days of Rome. There were many reasons, of course, for this happy state of affairs, but most important was the world balance of power maintained largely by the mild ascendance of Great Britain in international councils, the economic strength of her bankers, her manufacturers, and her traders, and the rule of her navy over the principal paths of commerce.

Modern imperialism is basically the foreign phase of the same expansion of the control of capital which we have seen in the democratic homelands, and it may be significant that Soviet writers use the word imperialism as a synonym for capitalism and colonialism. Both at home and abroad capital has utilized the power of government to enforce its will, and in both places the growth of democracy and of humanitarianism gradually set a limit to its power. This development was slower in the colonies than at home because there the people, even if they had been given civil liberties, had to learn to use them and, moreover, they depended greatly upon the pressure of liberal opinion in the homeland. Such opinion grew slowly because the average homelander saw little of the colonies, and what he heard was often obscured by the same moral veil which we have seen so often in our study of democracy. Moreover the plain man was at intervals bitten by the bug called "pride of empire" which is a cousin of the bug that makes men struggle for personal power.

Soon after 1870 it became evident that a resurgence of imperialism was under way. Nationalism was making strides with the unification of Germany and Italy and the stirring of national consciousness among the Slavic peoples. The kings and nobles of Europe had seen how the Industrial Revolution and rising democracy had destroyed the old political order in England and France, and how the logical result of their influence would be to break down economic and eventually political barriers between nations.

The counterattack is seen most clearly in Germany. The junkers sought there to bind the Industrial Revolution and the rising bourgeois to their own interests. They succeeded. The internationalizing influence of the Industrial Revolution was thwarted by restoring a modern version of mercantilism, that is, making it dependent on government favors such as tariffs and trade blocks and by using its strength primarily to build up military power rather than to raise the standard of living. Popular discontent was allayed by measures of state socialism. A subtle propaganda was begun about the mystic ties of blood and *Volk*. Then presently the search for power began to take on imperialist color as the Pan-German movement attempted to unite all Germans politically and sought to bolster economic power and prestige by acquiring overseas colonies.

The rise of neo-mercantilism was fostered by a series of economic changes which stemmed primarily from technological development. Manufactures were now much less expensive, especially the textiles and hardwares desired by less advanced areas. The revolution in transportation and communication had also cheapened the processes of collection and transportation so much that colonies could afford European goods, and European workers could afford colonial goods. Business became more efficient and began to pile up surpluses of goods and capital. Now we know that in such a case the pressure can be relieved by raising wages, reducing interest rates, developing new processes and industries which will employ more men, or by investing abroad. All of these relief valves found some favor, but the last most of all; the difference between three percent income on French railway bonds and ten to twenty percent on Indo-Chinese railway bonds was a persuasive argument. Investors demanded overseas investments for their surplus capital, then demanded political control in order to protect it and to exclude foreign competitors. Industrialists with surpluses made similar demands.

Another economic change that became evident to the observing after 1870 was the decline in Britain's proportion of world manufacture and commerce. It was clearly losing out to younger and more vigorous rivals and was being forced to live more and more off its fat—that is, existing investments. It was not mere desire to maintain prestige that led to its participation in the resurgence of imperialism after 1870; it was dire necessity, at least by the standards of the time. By 1890 British statesmen began to feel that the empire was like an old stag that lives in continual danger of being pulled down by wolves. The logical step, then, was to look around for friends. We shall return later to this search.

Imperialism was thus impelled to action not by the nation as a whole but by certain interests which obtained an "effective majority" and utilized the collective power of the nation despite some compromises made to satisfy dissidents. It is the fashion to blame business altogether for imperialism; this indictment is too sweeping, for certain business interests were among its most inveterate enemies. Wisconsin dairymen and Southern cottonseed oil men would naturally oppose the acquisition of colonies which produced copra for making margarine and soap; Louisiana sugar growers opposed the acquisition of new sugar sources in Hawaii, the Philippines, and Puerto Rico. All three interests would support Philippine independence in order to do away with the competition.

However, business supporters of imperialism would include importers and exporters, and importers and users of colonial raw materials. Shipping interests would welcome enterprises likely to furnish cargo and would demand coaling stations, naval bases, subsidized immigration, and sometimes protection from foreign shipping. Bankers would be involved in all of the above interests and would prosper with them, and would therefore naturally do everything possible to promote them.

The pressure of nonbusiness interests, however, was probably even more effective. Explorers and adventurers were always calling the attention of governments and businessmen to golden opportunities. Military and naval men took pride in their conquests and did everything to justify them and to retain and defend them. Diplomatic and colonial officials naturally defended their profession of manipulating or governing "backward" races. Politicians advanced their own interests by promoting the public dither which the cable enabled the penny press to make over colonial affairs. Then there were the missionaries. Their very promotion of order enabled white traders and other exploiters to make entry, bringing with them the vices and contentions of Christendom. In desperation the missionaries then sought annexation to the countries of their origin in order to impose restrictions on vicious whites.

Propaganda for empire was usually based upon certain dynamic ideas. The appeal to national honor and prestige at times made the home taxpayers consent to wage war to seize colonies or to support vigorous action in defense of compatriots' lives and property. There was fear of aggression, to which the natural response was the aggressive defense: the seizure of naval bases, coaling stations, and colonies as posts for defending trade routes by ensuring naval supremacy. The American demand for control of the Caribbean and for the digging of the Panama Canal was more for strategic than economic reasons. Then there were the arguments that an industrial nation must control colonies for their trade and raw materials and as outlets for surplus population. Actually, trade and emigrants stubbornly go where they please, while overseas raw materials are utterly useless without absolute command of the ocean highways.

The most popular defense of imperialism, however, was "aggressive altruism." Imperialism was exploitative and therefore inconsistent with Christian morality, which had made great progress during the nineteenth century; so it was necessary to find good moral reasons whenever it was proposed to do something immoral. Kipling made the point in 1899 when he admonished the United States to "Take up the White Man's Burden" and retain the Philippines. Hence we had in Britain and the United States the White Man's Burden, in France the *mission civilisatrice*, and in Germany the mission to spread *Kultur*. It was the use of "brutal force to impose on unwilling peoples the blessings" of one's own civilization: the willingness to fight other civilized nations on behalf of the imposition of one's own superior civilization.

British rule had its faults, but in retrospect its virtues shine brighter. Where the Union Jack flew, there were trade and good order, there were schools and local assemblies of the people, there were missionaries and technicians bringing the arts of Western Civilization. Britain's power was based (among other things) upon her realistic acceptance of the commercial standard of success which, after the first years promoted the welfare of both rulers and ruled; upon a certain flexibility, which made it possible to meet special situations with special measures; and upon "a sense of the limits of power," which meant that those who struggled for self-rule would sooner or later be accepted as equals and partners. Here were the blessed reasons why the British Empire was self-liquidating, why its rule was doomed from the day its flag was run up an alien pole. The British economic empire, as indicated at the outset, was even more important than its political empire.

It is now apparent that there was no reasonable excuse for imperialism. It was the least intelligent of several alternative ways of solving the economic problems that confronted the industrial nations. Its appeal to national pride was to an expensive delusion. Its strategic arguments were logically valid only if a nation could attain unchallenged supremacy on both land and sea; this was impossible. Finally, the argument of altruism was a rationalization; and even at that it was more honored in the breach than in the observance. In any case, even though Western culture and institutions might win admiration and be imitated, Western rule was more likely to breed distrust than goodwill. Human nature being what it is, good government is no substitute for self-government.

And yet the fact remains that imperialism was the road chosen by the nations, and it tremendously influenced modern history. What were its effects? Critics have almost invariably judged colonial administration not by the historic norm but by the *best* Christian standards. But it should be said for Western imperialism that, by and large, it governed less harshly than the old native regimes. Moreover, whether or not for altruistic reasons, it sought to raise the local sanitary, technical, and educational standards. Nowhere does history show such tremendous cultural changes in so brief a time. The stamp of Western Civilization was placed irrevocably on the world, whatever compromises may be worked out in the end. The proof of its success lies, paradoxically, in the ability of the rebels against imperialism to use the arguments, the ideals, and the methods of the West against their Western rulers—and find the latter agreeing with them!

The Rise of Inevitable Destiny

Before the present generation came upon the scene there was a rather smug tendency to echo George Harvey's famous witticism that the foreign policy of the United States was "to have no foreign policy." Few generalizations have been less accurate, for the United States did have a fairly well defined foreign policy based upon enlightened self-interest and the national concept of the American mission. Allan Nevins points out that these found expression in four objectives that were followed as consistently as most other nations have followed their objectives. One of these objectives had been the avoidance of entangling alliances with foreign powers—an objective attributed to Washington but which actually originated with Jefferson. The second objective was freedom of trade, which led to the historic policies of defense of freedom of the seas and championship of the Open Door in trade. The third objective was to prevent (for security reasons) the further extension of European power in the Western Hemisphere; this found expression in the Monroe Doctrine. Lastly was the American predilection to support democratic aspirations wherever they appeared, usually by popular opinion, sometimes by financial aid and diplomatic pressure, and finally by war; these actions were regarded quite simply as inseparable from the carrying-out of the American mission.

The old imperialism of the sixteenth to eighteenth centuries was primarily aimed at building up trade and acquiring settlement colonies. That of the nineteenth century, especially after 1870, was aimed primarily at the exploitation of foreign resources and manpower. Not only did the United States begin its imperialistic adventure later than other powers, but it was not pushed by any dire necessity to obtain raw materials or to dispose of surplus goods and capital. It was animated by the *hope* of trade, by the desire for prestige, by a sense of moral responsibility, and most of all by strategy. Indeed, when it began its great adventure, it was still heavily in debt to Europe and had less than half a billion dollars invested abroad—and two thirds of that in Canada and Mexico.

American ideology presented a clash between the democratic doctrine of equality and the heritage of a people who had been accustomed to regard Indians and Negroes as inferiors. Thus it did not need the rising racism of Europe to implant the concept of a master race in America, but many Americans welcomed the "scientific" demonstration of the master-race theory. This demonstration stemmed from two sources: the idea of natural selection as expressed in Social Darwinism; and the racism of Gobineau and Houston Stewart Chamberlain, brought back from Germany by American graduate students. The first was most likely to take the form of an Anglo-Saxon mythus; the second expanded the master race to include the Teutons, whose purest representatives were found in Germany but who (it was claimed) had carried their blood and their genius for mastery to surrounding nations. Popularizers in the United States did not always clearly distinguish between the two ideas, but Anglo-Saxonism was the stronger because it was reinforced by a common language with Britain and by long familiarity with English literature and institutions. The publicists of expansion may have had their private quarrels with British snobbery, but in other things they were Anglophile.

The Monroe Doctrine as enunciated in 1823, was a simple warning to European powers not to colonize further or to annex any more territory in the New World. The embarrassing fact is that it was enforced, not so much by the United States, as by Britain, which found it a useful device in enforcing the Pax Britannica. During the next century the United States expanded it to prohibit transfers of territory, coercion of American nations, and finally to forbid oppression—as by Spain in Cuba. European statemen looked with some alarm on these expanding interpretations, partly because the Monroe Doctrine was never twice the same, partly because they denied its assertion that different interests and institutions existed on the two sides of the Atlantic. They defied it, but cautiously, and preferably at times when the United States was involved in a crisis—as in the Civil War.

The more Europe challenged the Monroe Doctrine, the more convinced Americans became of its utility and validity, and the more real its shape became to them. This can be seen by an examination of public reactions at certain times when the Doctrine was called in question by either word or deed. The baffling thing, however, was that in some cases there was a public reaction and in some cases there was not.

By the 1890s it was clear that thinking men in Britain and the United States were seeking to weld the interests of the two countries. When in 1895 Britain refused to submit to arbitration a boundary dispute between Venezuela and British Guiana, Secretary of State Olney brusquely declared that "the United States is practically sovereign on this continent, and its fiat is law upon the subjects to which it confines [directs] its interposition." The American public was roused to belligerence, but business and cultural leaders refused to back strong action, and the British public refused to consider war.

At this time Britain stood in "splendid isolation," without allies and without powerful friends and, moreover, was engaged in colonial disputes with France and Germany. The latter even showed signs of interfering in the developing quarrel between Britain and the South African Boer republics. The British retreated from their Venezuelan stand and began to build up a special relationship with the United States. Outstanding differences such as the Alaska boundary were settled in favor of the United States. The prior interests of the United States in the Western Hemisphere were quietly acknowledged, and the British navy was withdrawn save for a few guard vessels. In her secret negotiations with other powers, Britain repeatedly stipulated that nothing should obligate her to take sides against the United States.

The propaganda for Anglo-Saxonism in the United States was seized upon by a growing group of scholars and politicians who advocated expansion. However, the outstanding advocate of American expansion in the 1890's was Admiral Alfred Thayer Mahan. The publication in 1890 of his *Influence of Sea Power Upon History* launched him into a career as the historian and protagonist of sea power; before the decade was out, he was to add a powerful impetus to the navalism already growing up not only in the United States but in other nations. Mahan's thesis was that sea power had been the chief factor in making and breaking nations and empires, and he drew chiefly on England for proof. The significance of sea power was that it fostered and protected commerce; hence a navy, merchant marine, bases, and coaling stations were essentials of national greatness. In 1890 the United States was lacking in all of these, and Mahan demanded that it supply the realistic basis for its destined expansion. Not only must it build up the navy and merchant marine, but it must dig an isthmian canal and acquire bases and colonies in the Caribbean and the Pacific. He believed that the United States and Britain were agents of the divine will, and that they must prepare for the coming struggle with the Yellow Peril—meaning China and Japan.

Despite this pious obeisance to Providence, Mahan approached his problems in a notably realistic manner, basing his recommendations upon power rather than sentiment. He recognized that England's naval power rose from the facts that it was an island, rich in coal and timber, and situated so as to block the Atlantic entrances to France and Germany. His disciples in Germany ignored these factors and confidently counted on beating England at its own game; actually, the United States and Japan more nearly met the requirements of the Mahan strategic concept. While he analyzed correctly the reasons for the rise of England, there is wide argument that Mahan's glorification of sea power has not stood the test of time as a historical generalization. Not only have commentators pointed out historical inaccuracies in his thesis, but geopolitical extremists have tried to show that the land mass of Eurasia cannot be dominated by sea power. Certainly the growth of the land-sea-air team (not to mention pushbutton warfare) has put a different face on the power picture.

Whatever history's decision may be on the validity of Mahan's thesis, the fact remains that it had tremendous effect upon succeeding thought and action. Congress began to provide for the construction of a modern navy. Propaganda for an isthmian canal and for the annexation of Cuba and Hawaii was stepped up; and there was talk that, while Cuba was being taken from decadent Spain, the Philippines might as well be taken also as a foothold in the Far East. The effect upon politicians was notable, not least on Theodore Roosevelt. Expansion suited his gospel of the strenuous life and his opinion that war was a beneficial stimulant of the national glands, so he poured out articles and reviews urging America to seek a place in the sun. He and other politicians, all Republicans, and most of them alarmed by the populist movement, not only favored expansion for its own sake but expected to make it a counter to the swelling chorus of radical and popular protest.

In the light of the usual accusations that businessmen lead in imperialism, it is interesting to note that in the United States they violently opposed it, at least up to May 1898. It was the scholars, the publicists, the strategists, and the politicians who espoused it. They sometimes spoke of the commercial advantages of imperialism, but when it came down to actual argument they stressed the White Man's Burden and the historic American mission to spread democracy. The new Manifest Destiny, it was claimed, had about it a certain fatefulness which could be resisted successfully neither by the aggressors nor by their victims. America, they said, had an "inevitable destiny" to expand and bring light to the world, then quite without humor beat the alarm lest we come short of that destiny. In the Calvinist tradition that the elect must strive to fulfill the will of God, they devoted themselves unstintingly to helping "destiny" fulfill itself.

Their opportunity was not long in coming. The endemic unrest in Cuba had broken into revolt, partly due to the hardship that followed upon the withdrawal of Cuban raw sugar's privilege of free admission to the American market. Friction followed between Spain and the United States, and it was promoted by the American yellow press and by the expansionists. When on 15 February 1898 the battleship *Maine* was sunk by an explosion in Havana Harbor, Congress used the incident as a partial excuse to force war on Spain. The Spanish-American War was a brief chronicle of glories and absurdities. In retrospect it is evident that the Spanish would have had no chance of success even under less inept leadership. Its tin-pot navy was sunk in two actions on opposite sides of the world (Manila and Santiago) and American troops were in Cuba, Puerto Rico, and the Philippines when the war ended after less than four months of combat.

Becoming modesty struggled with pardonable pride when President McKinley told a group of clergymen how he decided to "take" the Philippines:

> I walked the floor of the White House night after night until midnight; and I am not ashamed to tell you, gentlemen, that I went down on my knees and prayed Almighty God for light and guidance more than one night. And one night late it came to me this way—I don't know how it was, but it came:

(1) That we could not give them back to Spain—that would be cowardly and dishonorable [*national honor theme*];

(2) That we could not turn them over to France or Germany—our commercial rivals in the Orient—that would be bad business, discreditable [*economic nationalism*];

(3) That we could not leave them to themselves—they were unfit for self-government—and they would soon have anarchy and misrule worse than Spain's was [*racial superiority*];

(4) That there was nothing left for us to do but to take them all, and to educate the Filipinos, and uplift and civilize and Christianize them as our fellow-men for whom Christ also died. [*Altruism, the "white man's burden" and missionary zeal. The Filipinos, by the way were already Christians, Roman Catholics, with the exception of a small number of Mohammedan tribesmen.*]

And then I went to bed, and went to sleep, and slept soundly.[1]

The Spanish-American War stands with the War of 1812 and the Vietnam War as the most unjustified among American major conflicts. It had no excuse in international law, and the humanitarian arguments seem weak when placed beside our own treatment of the Indians and our later treatment of the Filipino insurgents. Undoubtedly there was a strong psychological impulse to war. Young men had listened to their elders' tales of the Civil War, and wanted a war of their own. Such emotions supplemented the propaganda that urged the United States to take a strong line among the nations. Spain's tyranny and ineptitude in Cuba afforded the opportunity to follow the European example of imperial expansion. On the other hand, there was a strong idealistic current running through the pattern. Even Bryan, a bitter opponent of imperialism, believed that our mission was to champion justice. Most powerful argument of all, however, was the strategic. With European imperialism resurgent, it was felt that we must control the southern approaches to the United States. The Monroe Doctrine, of course, was

---

[1]Parker T. Moon, *Imperialism and World Politics* (1927), pp. 394-95; as quoted in Charles S. Olcott, *The Life of William McKinley*, two volumes (Boston: Houghton Mifflin, 1916), 2:109. Words in italics are Professor Moon's comments.

wrested to serve as a handy justification of American domination of the Caribbean.

By the Peace of Paris (10 December 1898) the United States annexed the Philippines (paying $20 million conscience money for them), Guam, and Puerto Rico, and assumed responsibility for Cuba. Meanwhile, in the rush of imperial events, Hawaii had also been annexed. The occupation forces were withdrawn from Cuba in 1902, but the so-called Platt Amendment was a leading string which gave the United States the right to intervene in case of civil disorder; the right was exercised three times, in addition to sundry diplomatic interventions.

The annexations of the late 1890's were bitterly opposed by many intellectual and reformist leaders. In 1899 they formed the Anti-Imperialist League, and the next year supported Bryan when he ran on an anti-imperialist platform. Bryan lost. At the moment the people were basking in the pleasant consciousness of being a world power and helping to tote the White Man's Burden. Instead of hearkening to anti-imperialist orators they preferred to watch the troops marching off to embark for the Philippines while the bands played "There'll Be a Hot time in the Old Town Tonight."

Nevertheless, anti-imperialism must have had some effect, for the imperialists recoiled from further annexations and have added only the Canal Zone and a few odd islands since. Our early annexations at least had the virtue that they could be made into integral parts of the Union, but this was not likely to be possible with Puerto Rico and the Philippines. Our guilty conscience was shown by the way in which ever since we tried to pretend that we were not an empire, by refusing to set up a cabinet post for the government of possessions.

It was possible to get away with this in a realistic world because we discovered that an empire did not have to be political, but could be economic. Even there it took a generation for us to learn that the marines were not subtle agents of economic imperialism. There was something wrong with the motto:

> Underneath the starry flag,
> Civilize 'em with a Krag.

It was some time before we discovered that people like their own ways best, and that if they must have tyrants they prefer them native-born.

It is difficult to conceive of a nation with the power and dynamism of the United States remaining permanently aloof from world affairs in any case; nevertheless it was the Spanish-American War that saddled the country with the two specific responsibilities that were to mold future American foreign policy. First, the expansion of American strategic and economic interests to the Philippines brought us into vital contact with imperial Europe and Japan; the effect in the long run was to place our western frontier on the China coast. Second, the expansion of our strategic and economic interests into the Caribbean made another vital contact with imperial Europe, especially Germany, which was edging toward a strong position in Latin America; the effect in the long run was to place our eastern frontier on the Rhine. These assumptions of responsibility, unfortunately, were not understood by the people at large nor even by Congress, and the Executive was left to handle them as best he could without their comprehension or support. Therein lies much of the reason for the ridiculous inconsistencies and the repeated and resounding failures of American foreign policy between that time and this.

It was evident from the first that except for Hawaii the United States had no intention of including the tropical possessions in the City of God. It was no less evident that the Philippines, at least, had no desire to be included, for the so-called "Philippine Insurrection" lasted for nearly four years and was finally suppressed only after barbarisms of which the former Spanish masters would have been ashamed.

The annexation of the Philippines precipitated the United States into the affairs of the Orient, just as the anti-imperialists had predicted. Its traditional policy had been to seek equality of trade and to oppose Western annexations in the Far East, a policy which was now jeopardized by the rush of the powers to mark out Far Eastern ports and spheres of influence as their own. The United States was eager to preserve freedom of trade (the Open Door) in the Far East, and it was probably with some regret that the State Department was obliged to turn down Britain's offers of common action on the ground that they were certain to rouse political opposition. However, in 1900 Secretary of State John Hay suddenly circularized the Great Powers with the proposal that they agree within their leaseholds and spheres of interest to treat each other's nationals equally, and to respect the Chinese right to collect customs. The replies were notably chilly, but Hay calmly announced (1900) that the consent of the powers had been "final and definitive."

Later in the same year the Chinese antiforeign society, miscalled Boxers, killed scores of foreigners and besieged the foreign colonies in

Tientsin and Peking. Hay sent troops from the Philippines to join other national contingents marching to the scene. He took the occasion to state that the expedition was to "preserve Chinese territorial and administrative integrity." The Open Door was thus extended to include a guarantee of Chinese territorial integrity. This was to play a part in the American entry into World War II.

Problems of the Latin-American Frontier

The greatest weakness of the Caribbean countries at the turn of the century lay in their dependence on one crop—usually sugar, bananas, or coffee—or at the most two or three. This made Caribbean prosperity dependent on outside countries, especially the United States, which even before World War I was taking half the exports of these countries. The danger lay not only in their dependence upon the American economic situation but in the ease with which they and other tropical countries could glut the market. The condition has been only partly remedied by the guarantees to them of a certain percentage of the American market. The practice of democracy is partly dependent upon a rather widespread ownership of property among a country's citizens, a condition which has never existed in Caribbean states except, significantly, in Costa Rica. Moreover, national incomes were low, and still are, at least in the Central American states. The effect upon government budgets, education, welfare, and internal development is obvious.

Caribbean development of mines, railways, and even of plantations therefore largely depended upon foreign loans and investments. This practice meant that the Caribbean dictators, called *caudillos,* were in a position to treat their countries as private possessions, to spend borrowings as they pleased, and to force investors to purchase justice in addition to their physical assets. Foreign investors were frequently (they felt) compelled to finance revolutions in order to put into power governments which were benevolent toward their interests. Investors, it must be acknowledged, did not always seek to benefit the countries in which they operated. They sometimes imported Jamaican Negro labor, evaded their welfare responsibilities, exploited the soil, and sought special legal privileges and tax exemptions. Between them investors and bankers were draining away the economic life of the state without making adequate return, and few local patriots were ready to acknowledge that the *caudillo* was at least as much to blame as the foreigners.

It was quite usual for European governments to back up their nationals who were jockeying for Caribbean perquisites, and sometimes this interference extended to the use of force. The United States now looked upon these activities with disfavor lest they lead to permanent occupation, and undertook to impose order on revolution-prone "banana republics" and to install officials to collect customs and pay off foreign debts.

Jefferson had laid down the "will of the nation" test for deciding whether to receive envoys from revolutionary governments; the result had been that de facto governments were recognized, regardless of the crimes which had brought them into power. President Wilson, however, was nothing if not moral, and he sharply reversed the historic policy of recognition by holding that the United States had a duty to look after the morals of its neighbors. He could not, he said, recognize "government by murder." When he sought to lessen Caribbean chaos by prohibiting revolutions—the so-called Wilson Corollary to the Monroe Doctrine— the curious result was that the marines were busier than ever, both as bill-collecting agents and as discouragers of revolution. The situation certainly was not one to make a Caribbean patriot happy, for revolution was literally his only way of cleaning house. Wilson's toughest problem arose, however, from Mexico, and two interventions occurred; the only result was to add to the mounting chorus of Latin-American protest.

A retrospect of American imperialism in the Caribbean brings to light certain facts which were not clear to contemporaries. True enough, Cuba, Panama, Haiti, the Dominican Republic, and Nicaragua had treaties of protection forced upon them, and all the Central American republics had been subjected to the pressure of Dollar Diplomacy or had unwillingly entertained marines. But these protectorates were nothing like the pattern set up by European empires. They were limited in duration, their citizens could not be drafted to fight the protector's wars, and they conducted their own foreign affairs even though certain rules were laid down by Washington. Even in domestic affairs American control was usually confined to the fiscal administration and to supervision of elections. The era of political and fiscal protectorates was ephemeral and passed away as the Caribbean states became more orderly and as the overwhelming power of the United States made it useless for Europe to threaten its strategic security. Such control as survives is based upon economic treaties and common strategic interests, but unfortunately these have frequently been used to implant fiscal or economic control by corporate investors.

American influence on South America was up to World War I more institutional than economic. The framers of the Latin-American constitutions found that the Constitution of the United States was a handy pattern, particularly because their local diversities frequently necessitated the adoption of federalism. While the United States wielded few cultural and literary influences, its educational contributions were large. As it was, Latin America became economically complementary to Europe rather than the United States because at that time the latter could furnish most of its own raw materials. Moreover, Latin America was culturally closer to Europe than to the United States, with Hispanic and French cultures ascendant. It was basically Catholic, even though much of the thinking element was strongly tinged by French liberalism and Freemasonry, which were regarded as connected. European ideals of aristocratic and authoritarian ascendancy were honored, at least in practice.

Latin-American suspicions of the United States found their origin in the long series of seizures and enforced purchases by which the latter had expanded its territory. The war of literary propaganda was waged by a group of poets, historians, and publicists, some of them the undoubted intellectual leaders of Latin America. The basis of their challenge was the contrast between American materialism and Hispanic spirituality. Outstanding among these critics was José Enríque Rodó, the literary philosopher of Uruguay. In his *Ariel* (1900) he drew, on one hand, a striking analogy between Shakespeare's airy sprite Ariel and the graceful, imaginative, and idealistic Hispanic peoples and, on the other hand, between the brute-like malevolent Caliban and the vulgar, sordid, materialistic Anglo-Saxons. True, he was willing to award to the latter energy, enthusiasm, the urge to action, and a sort of blundering moral capacity. But, and only the Latin American could perceive how damning was the judgment: they had no poetic sense.

Now of course the Latin-American nations have their rivalries, and each of them has its own characteristics, some of them vitally influenced by the Indian and the Negro, or by later comers, chiefly Italians and Germans. The Cuban, it is said, is an inveterate gambler, full of gay defiance and a persistent sense of disproportion (*choteo*). The Mexican is given to opposite drives which lead to contrary moods and actions (*vacilada*). Despite national differences the inescapable fact is that Hispanic culture reigns more or less completely from the Rio Grande to Cape Horn. More than this, Hispanic psychology has given to these nations their one most outstanding common characteristic: intense individualism. Only recently has it been altered as modern influences have begun to break down the old self-contained ways.

Once the premise of complete individualism was established, there followed a stream of practical deductions. Since not everyone could rule, it was necessary to find ways of saving face, to give the appearance of belonging to the ascendant group. Many a man remained contented in a subordinate clerkship because he could wear a white collar and shuffle papers rather than wear a black shirt and wield a shovel. Contempt for manual labor was a blighting heritage from Spain which was reinforced by the exploitation of Indian and Negro labor.

The existence of this rabid individualism lay at the basis of caudillism, for general order could be brought only by a man who was strong enough to force submission and yet knew how to enable his countrymen to save face by preserving their individual dignity and the appearance of sharing the trappings of power. The result was a sentimental regard for liberty and democracy, but their growth was hampered because the method of change through successive social and political compromises was unknown. But change made inroads as science and industry and modern influences began to break down the old self-contained ways. The gradual rise of mass purchasing power has had a profound effect in awakening individuals to the fact that each has a stake in the welfare of all. Industrial and agricultural progress carried with it the requirement of literacy. Even the *caudillos* strove to promote national wealth and knowledge. Perhaps they did not wish to promote popular control, but the very necessities of modern life forced them to take the steps to that goal one by one.

The persistence of Hispanic psychology has served to give an air of unreality even in recent decades to relations between the United States and the countries to the South, especially to the once highly praised policy of the Good Neighbor. The North American concept of the good neighbor—the *buen vecino*—is of people who live in adjacent houses and who visit back and forth, play gin rummy together, borrow flour and sugar, and take turns at baby-sitting. The Hispanic concept of the fortress family envisions a relationship between acquaintances much like the relation between patron and client inherited from the Romans; essentially it is a hangover of the age of aristocracy.

The Good Neighbor Policy announced by President Franklin Roosevelt in 1933 appeared to be giving away more than it actually was. The treaties of "protection" were abrogated, the marines withdrawn, and the right to intervene was renounced. When Mexico expropriated foreign land and oil holdings Roosevelt made no threats but negotiated a treaty by which the claimants were given token payments. Just the same, economic and diplomatic pressures continued.

The superficial improvement in inter-American relations was not solely due to changes in *norteamericano* policy, but rose fully as much from conditions outside the United States. We shall refer presently to conditions to Europe but here it is sufficient to say that Catholic conservatives in Latin America were deeply troubled by the waves of fascist and communist statism in Europe which, perhaps erroneously, they likened to the Indian communalism that was rising from the grass roots in their own countries. They had long despised the United States for its "materialism" and its headlong mass democracy, but now to their own amazement they found that its conservative capitalism and religious tolerance were far more congenial than the statism and antireligionism of the Soviet and fascist regimes. Latin-American democrats, for their part, found new comfort in the reforms of the New Deal and the high intentions of the Good Neigbor policy.

Conditions were also changing in Latin America. The 1930s had seen wide defaults of government bonds in Latin America, and American banks were shy about handling further loans. American capital had gone into Latin America only because it could counterbalance the risk by large profits and the prospect of State Department support. With Latin-American governments rigidly controlling foreigners' labor policies, limiting their profits, and blocking the removal of profits from the country where they were earned, American capital was not eager to make new ventures. Indeed, it was often glad to escape from the old ventures even with a loss. Henceforth, American firms were willing to sell goods and furnish technical aid, but serious financial commitments were frequently avoided or hedged except in quick-return enterprises such as petroleum.

The above discouragements to American private investments constituted a threat to the Good Neighbor Policy, for it was quite naturally regarded as useful only in so far as it promoted their security and economic well-being. This led to a program by which during the war years the United States government stepped into the financial breach left by private capital and at the same time gave aid to the Latin-American countries in the exercise of their public functions by lending funds and experts and purchasing raw materials.

A series of conferences opened the way to patch up some of the rifts among the Good Neighbors and to win Latin-American approval of the United Nations. The Latin Americans set their price high, but by the Act of Chapultepec (1945) the United States paid it. Among other provisions it made the Monroe Doctrine multilateral; gave Latin America a virtual veto on any actions of the United States within the hemisphere; and provided so fully and securely for the settlement of all hemisphere problems by the American nations that there would be no excuse for the United Nations to interfere. The last proviso was insurance against Russia, for the Latin Americans were fearful of Soviet aggression. The Act was later confirmed by a conference at Rio de Janeiro in 1947. The United States was now bound to a mutual defense pact far stronger than anything ever envisioned by the Monroe Doctrine or any of its interpreters.

Latin America massed a considerable reserve of dollars during the war, but postwar inflation in the United States quickly reduced its ability to purchase needed goods, and reduced demand for raw materials caused such unemployment that there was general misery. An appalling proportion of Latin-American wealth was in the hand of men not interested in *productive* enterprise, but who were politically powerful enough to keep their governments from confiscating their capital and devoting it to such purposes.

The situation was ready-made for communist infiltration, and to counter this one government after another fell into the control of generals who might or might not be sympathetic to reform. The United States was confronted by the dilemma of power: it was damned if it interfered and damned if it didn't. The dictators at least gave some promise of imposing order and protecting economic enterprise, so in all too many cases the United States leaned toward them.

It should be emphasized once more that the United States was not consciously promoting tyranny. Rather, it was trying to apply in Latin America its own technique of evolutionary adjustment—quite unconscious that circumstances alter cases. This tragic lack of empathy— of imaginative insight into the nature of others and the nature of their problems—was all too general in United States attitudes toward Latin America and has since permeated its relations with the remainder of the world. Revolution was literally the only means by which Latin America could make the social and economic advances necessary to cure its dire problems of poverty—nor could political democracy be extended by any other means. With the bottling up of reform (let alone radicalism), pressures were building up in the countries and around the Caribbean which would lead eventually to explosions.

East Meets West

When we consider in detail the impact of the West upon the Far East prior to World War I, it becomes evident that by far the greatest influence was wielded by Great Britain. Nevertheless, the United States was a factor in the "awakening" of Asia, and though its political control was limited to the Philippines, its merchants, teachers, and missionaries profoundly affected nearly every country. It is therefore useful to consider the nature of the Oriental world and the effects of the Western entry.

Western interest in the Far East was based more on the hope of a vast trade than on actual accomplishments. The hope of trade, however, was reinforced by a struggle for power which might have occurred in any case. Russia and Japan both had their eyes on Manchuria, whose resources were definitely worth having, and their struggle affected all those powers which had territory or interests in the Far East. Prestige as well as trade was at stake. Just as important in the long run was missionary interest. The Open Door was in Britain and America as much the creation of missionaries as of businessmen, and, indeed, the missionaries (who were part and parcel of their pragmatic civilization) had been partly responsible for the false hopes of the businessmen. Indeed, Westerners, whether traders, colonial administrators, or missionaries, were frequently prevented by ignorance, prejudice, or laziness from forming a just understanding of the people among whom they lived, and so they carried home fables and snap judgments which crucially influenced Western political and economic decisions.

Just what was this Western Civilization which traders, missionaries, colonial administrators, and Asian students carried to the Far East? Judging by the highest ideals it was an attempt to master nature by learning her secrets ("truth") through the use of experimental science; its material object was to harness power to industry and transportation in order to utilize land and resources efficiently; at the same time it attempted to war against disease through medicine and sanitation. Its social object was the search for greater security and a higher standard of living for the masses as well as the classes. Its political object was to entrust the masses with their own government at the same time that it attempted to promote equal justice and freedom of opportunity and a high standard of public morality. Its intellectual object was to strike off the bonds of superstition through education and the search for truth, and to use popular enlightenment as a means of advance and of preserving a balance in politics and economics. Its moral object was to preserve and extend human freedom and dignity, which it regarded as the applicable-on-earth part of moral values. Yet there had always been a stiff conflict within Western Civilization as to its true meaning, and its intolerant aspects have frequently impressed the Oriental observer more than its virtues.

Asians naturally resent the idea that the West is superior and the East inferior. They point out truly that Western Civilization in its origins vitally depended on Eastern contributions; that it has no consistent meaning or acceptance in the West—a statement which is not quite accurate; that it has no characteristic altogether confined to the West; and that it is the creation of yesterday in what we smugly call its home. In short, they prefer to call it Modern Civilization, and they are probably right. At any rate, certain limits must be borne in mind:

(1) Its roots are universal and its nourishment also.

(2) It has been a method and process rather than a structure.

(3) Its characteristics are not unique to the West, nor are they nontransferable; any institution or idea that we regard as Western had its parallel in the East—and that includes activism, individualism, pragmatism, and experimental science.

(4) It is of recent growth; probably a man from Mars would not have recognized it as a separate civilization before the fifteenth century.

(5) Its shoots are being scattered and grafted everywhere, with what results remain to be seen.

The Orient had known for thousands of years heights of art and luxury whose satisfactions perhaps we do not know yet—despite our gadgets. Moreover it had reached a fairly satisfactory state of balance with nature, which perhaps could have continued indefinitely. This balance was maintained at vast expense of human misery at the bottom of the social scale, but even the peasant often knew how to live and die graciously and could find in religion and contemplation the consolations which society refused him. Still the fact remains that the Orient failed to conquer nature and provide its people with an abundant life. As Hu Shih, the Chinese statesman and philosopher, has pointed out, the Orient has a truly materialistic civilization because it is limited by matter and is incapable of transcending it. Its contentment with little and its fatalistic resignation are more materialistic than its actual hovels and images of the gods. Only the civilization which uses its full ingenuity to overcome and utilize the material in service to mankind is—or can be—thoroughly idealistic and spiritual. That is, if it can utilize the material without worshiping it.

Asia had chosen to get along with nature rather than to conquer and exploit her. The Easterner understood the value of psychological satisfaction, the importance of being wanted, appreciated, and understood by those around him. Hence his stress on the family; on courtesy as lubrication for the social wheels; his desire to have time to enjoy living; and his frequent refusal to work harder than was necessary to furnish the minimum means for simple enjoyment—a sort of materialism in itself. But this did not mean that Asians became alike. Quite the contrary, as we can see by looking at the three principal civilizations before the coming of Westerners. India was a congeries of independent states ruled by a military aristocracy and socially organized in castes; its outlook on life was otherworldly, metaphysical, pessimistic, quietist, and docile. China was historically united, ruled by an arisotcracy of learning, and socially organized in clans or families; its outlook on life was this-worldly, ethical, and optimistic; its people held a nice balance between submission to fate and a practical belief in taking their own part—a close approach to the Greek ideal of moderation. Japan was technically a centralized state ruled by a descendant of the gods but actually a feudal state ruled by a military aristocracy and socially organized in clans; its outlook on life was this-worldly, opportunistic, and aggressive, but it acted as a rigid unit which brutally inhibited individual action or responsibility and was in consequence continually in danger of blowing up. The above is necessarily an oversimplification and ignores the numerous exceptions in national character as well as the nuances of thought and behavior; so also does what follows.

The impact of Western ideas and methods was bound to strike Easterners differently. The Indians, absorbed in eternal values, were troubled and resentful at the intrusion of the practical and material West. It took two centuries of British example and education to prepare them to live in the modern world. On the other hand, the Japanese, alive to facts, saw that they must at least adopt modern technology if they expected to survive; accordingly they took it in suddenly and as a national unit, but they tried to reconcile it with the preservation of their rigid social order and their concepts of divine origin and destiny to rule the world. The result was heightened frustration and an increase of internal turmoil in the individual. The Chinese, arrogantly sure of their values, saw no reason to substitute efficiency for learning, law for custom, brusqueness for manners, haste for leisure, force for reason, factories for handicrafts, or Christianity for the ethics of moderation. As for democracy, they already had something resembling it in village life, where democracy really mattered; moreover, in *yin* and *yang* they had a satisfactory philosophy of change and compromise far older than the democracy of the West. Therefore China balked at change and for a hundred years fought a stubborn rear-guard action against it.

Asian conquerors had seldom attempted to make the conquered over in their own image; they had been content to collect tribute and bask in power and glory; usually in the end they were absorbed by the conquered. The irruption of the West into Asia was explosive because of the demand that the status quo be broken up and centuries of evolution suddenly by-passed. It is the Oriental belief that Western imperialism rose from greed and violence and from a feeling of inferiority and uncertainty, as witnessed by our intolerance and the self-defensive, crusading fervor of Christianity. Certainly Western imperialism was accompanied by use of military force; seizure of territory; humiliation of native governments; political domination, however concealed or indirect; economic exploitation with its control of tariffs, markets, and prices, and its forced labor; the deliberate destruction of indigenous and sometimes superior civilizations; and an intense racial arrogance, which was all the worse because it struck at the self-respect of the conquered.

The inevitable result was that resentment grew and festered under the continual charges that the Orient was inferior and unfit to manage its own affairs. There was a growing cynicism toward Western professions and institutions; the treatment of Chinese and Japanese in California was apt proof. When Westerners did good in the Orient there was immediately a search for the hidden joker. Christianity was denounced as an opening wedge for exploitation, as unfortunately it often was. Arrogance and oppression became the special province of the Westerner.

If only he would leave, Asians would be like brothers; and Indian communal riots and Japanese sharp practices were excused as having been stirred up or made necessary by Westerners. They emphasized the horrors of Western history and romanticized their own past. There had been no greed, cruelty, disease, superstition, no religious and economic rivalries—indeed, to speak in hyperbole, no death or taxes until the Westerner introduced them!

Western methods were now coming in but in many cases served only to reduce the Eastern commoner's standard of living further and to quicken his pace and steal from him the ability to savor living. Why then, he asked, was he doomed to toil at starvation wages in factories and on plantations when there was a way to better his standard? Simple enough, replied the local entrepreneur, it is Western imperialism that is to blame; cast out the West and everything will be wonderful. This he said knowing that he as well as the West was to blame, but hoping to succeed to the political and economic controls and investments abandoned by the departing West.

There were three opinions among Orientals as to how Western Civilization should be utilized. Some wished to adopt it entire; some favored adopting its science and technology only; while others wished to reject mechanization but to accept nationalism and democracy. Those who studied the West with honest intent to learn were struck by its political concepts and stirred by the ideas of men like Edmund Burke and Abraham Lincoln. Nevertheless, too many of them either failed to understand the delicate balance necessary to make democracy work or those to whom they taught it thought that the democratic method could be applied without training. The result was that the Orient came to interpret democracy, not as government by the people but as independence from foreign control. From that point it was easy to go on to aping the nondemocratic wing of Western Civilization, as when Japan modeled its constitution on that of Prussia, and when China adopted one-party government.

What the future brings in the Orient may depend not merely on the rise of Western-educated leaders, in the growth of mechanized industry, and in the creation of unified governments. At present it would seem that much of the Orient has decided that democracy as we understand it is not suited to its way of doing things (not only in Asia but in Africa as well). Certainly there is a trend toward some form of totalitarian control. The unfortunate truth is that Oriental and African societies are not spiritually geared to appreciate or accept democracy because they have minimal understanding of the Western concept of the unique value of the individual. Their "dignity" is centered on the family, the tribe, or, in Japan, on the nation. Moreover, communism appeals to many Orientals because of its promise of a time of completion, of rest, of justice, while democracy posits eternal struggle.

This may well mean that the *ci-devant* colonial world is rejecting the two fundamentals of Modern Civilization: the spirit of critical judgment and experimental accuracy; and the fostering of the personality of the individual and of groups under objective laws. The result may be a civilization with the discipline and mutual support of an ant hill, but it can bear little resemblance to the western City of God, either religious or secular. The potential effect on the course of history is portentous.

Chapter 12
The Pragmatic Impact

Proem

New occasions teach new duties;
Time makes ancient good uncouth;
They must upward still and onward
Who would keep abreast of Truth;
Lo, before us gleam her campfires!
We, ourselves must Pilgrims be,
Launch our Mayflower and steer boldly
In the desperate winter sea,
Nor attempt the Future's portal
With the Past's blood-rusted key.

(James Russell Lowell, *The Present Crisis*)

* * *

The end of life is life. Life is action, the use of one's powers. As to use them to their height is our joy and duty, so it is the one end that justifies itself.

... Life is a roar of bargain and battle; but in the very heart of it there rises a mystic spiritual tone that gives meaning to the whole, and transmutes the dull details into romance.

... Man is born a predestined idealist, for he is born to act. To act is to affirm the worth of an end, and to persist in affirming the worth of an end is to make an ideal.

(Oliver Wendell Holmes)

As a young man Rexford Guy Tugwell, later a member of Franklin Roosevelt's Brain Trust, wrote a bit of free verse that portrayed the enduring spirit of the quest for the City of God.

> I am strong,
> I am big and well made,
> I am muscled and lean and nervous,
> I am frank and sure and incisive.
> I bind the forces untameable;
> I harness the powers irresistible—
> All this I do; but I shall do more
> I am sick of a nation's stenches,
> I am sick of propertied czars
> I have dreamed my great dream of their passing,
> I have gathered my tools and my charts;
> My plans are fashioned and practical;
> I shall roll up my sleeves—make America over!

The Pragmatic Revolt

The United States had no sooner entered upon the era of economic and political concentration than deep-seated tendencies in American life rose to the surface to combat the new order and force modifications upon it. This was Progressivism, by Populism out of Pragmatism. Its leaders were the crusading realists whom by now we should recognize as typical of the American scene. Lincoln Steffens, the demon muckraker, confronted the ruthless reformer U'ren of Oregon with the accusation that he had made bargains with the devil to get his support. Like Moses he had broken the covenants of the Lord, and though he might see the Promised Land he would not be permitted to enter it.

"You may have saved the people of Oregon," urged Steffens, "but haven't you lost your own soul? Won't you go to hell?"

U'ren considered for a moment, then raised his clear gaze. "Well," he answered, "I would *go* to hell for the people of Oregon!" Sometimes it is the duty of the democratic leader to suffer damnation that the people may live.

The pragmatic revolt, which arose out of American dualism, challenged the new order of selfish nationalism and isolation by seeking either to break up the "monopolies" or to subject them to strict regulation—it never quite decided which. Toward imperialism it was also ambivalent, first finding a mission to assume the White Man's Burden, then turning it into a new and altruistic phase of the old mission to spread democracy, this time by means of war and world organization. It was Pragmatism's search for a method of reform which would not scuttle the middle class—for a compromise between ethics and the Gospel of Wealth.

Originally pragmatism was formulated as "a method of logic, a method of determining the meanings of intellectual concepts," by a mathematician and logician, Charles S. Pierce. It achieved widespread notice through the advocacy of its most prominent formulator, William James, Harvard professor and brother of the expatriate novelist, Henry James. Unlike his brother, William delighted in the turmoil and clamor of America. He saw its "tough-mindedness"—that is, acceptance of the fact that change is a constant of life—as the hope of the future, and he sought to find ways to use its fighting instincts in building a better society.

James, like most other Americans, was an optimist, a believer in progress; yet he could not accept progress as inevitable. Society could advance or deteriorate; accident, community decisions, and the acts of individual leaders would all enter into the equation and determine the outcome. James accepted science as a tool, but not as a master. Ideas were meant to be put into action. Truth must be tested by experience, and if there was any Absolute—final, perfect, divine Truth—it was unknowable. This was all to the good, for it gave humanity scope to strive to better itself.

Pragmatism was applied to education by John Dewey under the name of Instrumentalism. To Dewey ideas are useful only if they are instruments that aid in solving problems. The greatest hindrances to social good are the prejudices, slogans, and myths that bar our road to control of our moral and social environment and allow natural science to outdistance social science. Dewey emphasized the learner rather than the subject taught; preached the value of learning by doing (hence the blossoming of laboratories and vocational training); and sought to instill the ability to examine and evaluate ideas and facts.

Dewey made enemies in practically every ideological camp. In championing a democratic society in which cultural and material assets should become of service to the masses, he rejected the intuitive absolutes on which the elite based their ascendance. If, as Dewey advocated, these mystic insignia of class (the absolutes) are displaced by science and experiment, the preferred position of the elite is lost.

It would seem, as so often happens with intellectual pioneers, that his teachings have been misused to make science master rather than tool, to cultivate vocational and professional skills rather than "creative intelligence," and to jettison standards of accomplishment in a misguided effort to award success to every child. Be that as it may, there can be no doubt of Dewey's permanent influence. Alfred North Whitehead, who certainly did not always agree with him, believed that he will rank with the greatest of the philosophers, because like them he will give an impulse of enlightenment to civilization for many generations. He was, concluded Whitehead, the chief intellectual force providing Americans with coherent purpose.

The American is dualistic—torn between good and evil, the ideal and the material. Hence to the materialistic, the material consequence indicates truth; to the idealist, the idealistic consequence indicates truth. The theory of evolution had introduced the belief that everything is in process of change, and it suggested that morals and laws are in each generation the product of social consciousness. Pragmatism, like Anglo-Saxon behavior and institutions, refuses to choose between alternatives, but straddles. In reality it was no more than a new formulation and explanation of the way of life that had existed in America from colonial times. The transcendentalists had assumed that good and bad were not only distinct from each other but clearly identifiable, and this sort of thinking had for a while overridden the traditional American method of experiment and compromise and helped bring on civil war.

The pragmatists took the view that it is often hard to know, just by thinking about it, whether a course of action is right or wrong. In large part, this new formulation of America's traditional way of thinking had grown out of such fundamental shifts in our body of knowledge as those involved in evolutionary scientific concepts, which suggested that all ideas, morals, and laws are constantly changing, evolving from generation to generation as the product of social conditions and needs. The implication was that truth is not an absolute, unchanging thing.

The pragmatists said simply this: man's intelligence is not powerful enough for him to find out immutable truth by reasoning alone. The consequence is that absolutist philosophers who believe that disciplined thought can open the doors to truth by following the rules of logic simply do not understand how inexact a tool man's reason is. While we must always develop ideas by the most careful use of the scientific method available to us, there is only one ultimate test of whether or not the idea is a true one: how it works in practice.

Pragmatism does not ask how the idea fits in with hallowed and revered practices and concepts. Rather it asks three practical questions: (1) Will it work? (2) Will it be good for the individual and/or society? (3) If the effect is not completely desirable, what compromise can be drawn in order to keep as much as possible of the practical program and the ideal good?

This is hard doctrine for those who demand certainty. Even the pragmatist is puzzled over precisely what constitutes good, and he has some royal tussles with his fellows over what should be done. He always ends, however, by attacking confusion bit by bit rather than by sweeping generalizations, because our reasoning process is so limited that generalizations are almost always wrong. He settles each case on its own merits and according to its own necessities and peculiarities. This is exactly what democracy does, and when we come to examine pragmatism and democracy side by side, we find that they have the same attitudes and methods. Indeed, democracy is only the political expression of the age-old method that was now called pragmatism. They operate through compromise between extremes—through the experimental search for a practical solution. The rise of pragmatism in the 1890's marked the reassertion of the democratic spirit that had been blighted by the crisis of secession and the power of the Great Entrepreneurs.

Trace philosophical and religious structures to their foundations and we find that they are derived deductively from certain assumed generalizations or dogmas, such as the Marxists' belief in economic determinism, or Descartes' assumption "I think, therefore I am." Their comfort lies in their certainty that they have the applicable-on-earth part of the Absolute (eternal) Truth, and that since they know good from evil there can be no compromise and everyone must meet their standards; it is the impregnable ground for action.

When pragmatism's democratic method is traced to its source, it also is found to be based on an axiom: faith in human dignity and freedom, as William James, the greatest pragmatist of them all, so luminously testified. The Christian too believes in human dignity and individual responsibility, and so in daily life pragmatism is reconcilable with Christian ethics. The pragmatist, however, does not know eternal truth, and so he cannot try to apply it. Each generation brings up new crises which, he feels, the old rules may not fit, and to meet them new policies must be evolved. The pragmatist's only guide is the firm faith in human dignity and freedom, and he examines all crises and programs with that faith in mind. Said William James, "The practical consequence [of pragmatism] is the well-known democratic respect for the sacredness of individuality—is, at any rate, the outward tolerance of whatever is not itself intolerant."

The pragmatist operates inductively, using his reason but testing it, feeling his way by successive compromises and referring constantly to experience, to the existing social context, and to the ideal of human welfare toward which he strives. He believes that we must preserve and federate the rival sovereignties and moral values of the individual, on the one hand, and of society, on the other, as positive aids toward a higher moral order. He espouses what he sees as a process rather than as an absolute—but if the continuance of that process is jeopardized, he will fight as fiercely as any convinced believer in the absolute.

The above outline undoubtedly oversimplifies, but it is necessary to simplify to avoid metaphysical subtleties. Of course, even the most rigid idealists have always made compromises in their daily living, and the most confirmed absolutists have always understood perfectly well that they could not know all that was in the mind of God, who alone has the right to be the Absolute.

As pragmatism evolved during the Progressive Era, it simply gave intellectual respectability to an approach that is as old as humanity. Pragmatism was in the American air; the conquerors of the wilderness had judged programs and actions by their consequences, and it was natural that many teachers, thinkers, and reformers should do so.

Pragmatists claimed that they rejected Spencer's Social Darwinism, but accepted what they understood to be Darwinian concepts. They simply shifted the emphasis. Society, they insisted, was the unit that Darwin had in mind—not the individual man, as Spencer had said. Society is an organism; it has a collective mind, and a real existence. The test is to see whether *it* survives, by using its wits. Developing Reform Darwinism, as differentiated from Social Darwinism, pragmatic reformers held that American society would fail in the struggle for survival if it did not heal its inner ills—if men did not band together, use their joint strength and wisdom, and create health and vigor in the body politic where there was now sickness and decay.

Joint activity, community action, are not violations of science;

Darwinism, properly interpreted, triumphantly justified them, pragmatists insisted. Above all, collective actions to solve social ills would put back into human society the one element that most distinguishes mankind from beasts, the element that Social Darwinism would eliminate: mind. We must purposefully direct what we are doing, not passively let the anarchy of undirected greed destroy us.

Pragmatism with its implication of relativism—that is, truth is relative to the needs of the times—was roundly attacked as destroying what the masses allegedly need: assurance of a body of dependable axioms—a theology or a moral code. Horace Kallen pointed out that pragmatism "dissolves dogmas into beliefs, eternities and necessities into change and chance, conclusions and finalities into processes. Men have invented philosophy precisely because they . . . desire infallible security and certainty." Pragmatism is disillusioning and offers only the scantiest of guides. Since democracy is pragmatic and experimental, politicians and people must have steady nerves and a superb sense of balance to walk the tightrope over the gulf of uncertainty.

It is certainly true that relativism is often misused to define truth according to one's desire, thus seeming to justify expediency or selfishness. The ideal of the good of society may be subtly rationalized into the good of one's self or one's class. There is danger that not only does the end justify the means, but that (as Dewey warned) the means "becomes the end." We have recently seen examples of this in high places.

Before long, conservatives and liberals alike were entrenching themselves as champions of their latest respective absolutes, and accusing their enemies of being cynical relativists. As J. Allen Smith, the political scientist, admitted later, "The real trouble with us reformers is that we have made reform a crusade against standards. Well, we smashed them all and now neither we nor anybody else have anything left."

The confusion rose in large part, from relativism's emphasis on the influence of environment. Analyze the environment and you explain the boy and then the man he becomes. Certain it was that the new generations as they arose were confused by the clash between old and new standards, the changes brought in perhaps by relativistic ideas, perhaps by the mere rapidity of technical changes and its effects, perhaps by both. At any rate, these were called upon to explain loose sexual standards, juvenile delinquency, crime in the streets, and deceitful and slippery business methods. The assumption was, of course, that the past had been both staunchly based on a moral code and purer in its behavior.

The struggle between absolutes and relativism has broadened down through the twentieth century despite the astounding effects of the pragmatic movement in nearly every aspect of American life. This struggle is notable particularly in the churches, in clashing theories of education, in interpretations of economics, in diplomatic theory and practice, and finally in the great struggle between democracy and totalitarianism. Few of the major problems that we will examine from this point onward were unconnected with the struggle.

One of the points we have made is that pragmatism, though it might adapt the old wherever it remained useful, yet sought to work out new forms that suited the needs of the new age and best expressed its spirit. In addition, pragmatism sought always to point to facts. It was this constant emphasis on studying the world as it actually is that became the dominant theme of the social sciences in these decades. The studies of education, economics, sociology, anthropology, and history were revolutionized. The Protestant churches undertook by their Social Gospel to ameliorate some of the appalling social and moral conditions that were plainly the outcome of industrialism. On the other hand, the Social Gospel's acceptance of evolution widened the split between Conservatives and Fundamentalists. The Roman Catholic Church promulgated a constructive social program, encouraged by papal encyclicals, and Msgr. John A. Ryan spelled out some of the doctrines that later found expression in the New Deal.

Charitable organizations were reorganized, and a new breed of social workers sought to help their clients to help themselves. A group of magazine writers called Muckrakers investigated economic and political corruption. Lincoln Steffens, the greatest of the Muckrakers asserted *everyone* was to blame for the corruption in society. This was a democracy, Americans were professedly a moral people, and ultimate control lay in their hands: hence, if they did not have a clean society, it was because they shamefully looked the other way, ignoring the corruption that surrounded them. Americans should learn, he said, that the pressures inherent in business life meant that men felt driven into corrupt practices; that a link had been established between government and business that, long ignored, had ripened into an immoral relationship with which men had lived so long that they regarded it as "right." Only a moral revival by the people, a determination to take over the government and *keep* it clean by maintaining a constant interest in what it was doing, could solve the problem.

The rise of the pragmatic spirit led to increased public censure of the origins and disposal of the fortunes of the Great Entrepreneurs. The entrepreneurs believed that their tremendous development of national wealth was sufficient justification for their own wealth. Nevertheless, they grew restive as they became increasingly aware of public antipathy, and they began to counter with gifts to worthy objects. One millionaire after another warned his fellows—and took his own advice—that the amassing of wealth without purpose must be stopped, or the public would stop it. Carnegie besought his fellow Pittsburgh millionaires not to die "without leaving behind them some evidence of love and gratitude for the city in which they had made their fortunes." Here and there misanthropists denied the sincerity of the new reformism and harked back to Roman aristocrats who imported shiploads of Egyptian wheat to feed the mob and stave off revolution while they sought out, and destroyed the leaders.

Regardless of the motives, these gifts wrought enormous public benefit in a day when custom did not permit government to take much interest in scientific and social advancement. They have even, perhaps, enriched the lives of all Americans in ways that government gifts could never have done. By 1910 the outpouring of money into public-spirited enterprises had reached an amazing magnitude. Foudations, institutes, universities, libraries, research institutions, medical centers, and other benevolences proliferated across the nation.

These enormous gifts changed the ownership of the stock (though not always the control) of some of America's greatest corporations. It would not be unfair to say that many of these bequests were made in the hope that they would make more secure the owners' hold on the remaining millions. It is certainly conceivable that the hope was realized on a short-term basis; yet these gifts sowed the seeds of the millionaires' downfall. Research raised the standard of life and health, and education, bred shrewd and intelligent leaders of the masses who gave direction to the movement for expropriation by taxation or wage raises. Finally, and perhaps most significant of all, the millionaire himself changed—or at least his grandson did. There was a new spirit of responsibility and sympathy among men of wealth which gave them the attitude and standards of the steward of a trust fund.

We had occasion in a previous chapter (page 80) to show how law had come to be regarded as the expression of natural moral law; law was not *made*, it was *found*. It was the task of Supreme Court Justice Oliver Wendell Holmes, tutored by the early Harvard pragmatists, to overturn this attitude in his treatise *The Common Law* (1881) and to show how law is molded to the changing needs of an evolving society— in other words, is an "organic" growth. Law is not an abstraction, but a code of behavior in the real world; not logic, but experience. The Constitution is not ultimate, unchanging, absolute truth; it evolved through centuries, and that growth continued after 1787. Its nature was determined by facts; the United States, originally a congeries of states, had now developed by one means or another into a nation in which the federal government was supreme.

Holmes demanded that the federal government take up the battle for the rights of the individual and of freedom of opinion and adapt these principles to an industrial society. This campaign soon rallied around him a group of brilliant young men. The new school of legal realism was willing to keep captitalism but insisted that it be regulated for the protection of the people. Yet, in the traditional way, the reformers had to find excuses in the old Constitution—else they would seem to be promoting revolution, not evolution. They took over for their purposes the conservatives' own instruments—the interstate-commerce clause, the elastic clause, and the Fourteenth Amendment—and proceeded to demand that conservative decisions be reversed.

Holmes was joined on the Supreme Court bench by Louis Brandeis and Harlan Fiske Stone, and they stood together through long years of conservative ascendancy. Their trademark was usually found on reactionary decisions in the words "Holmes, Brandeis, and Stone dissenting." In the end, their views were to prevail.

The thinkers of the dawning progressive era were seriously disturbed by what was gradually coming to be regarded as a fearsome dilemma. Mankind had always lived in an economy of scarcity in which supply could not overtake human needs. The producer wished to get control of all the production in his field in order to control supply and set prices as he chose. Society, on the other hand, wanted plentiful production and low prices. The interests of the producer and of society seemed to be irreconcilable. It was this impasse that had plagued liberals from Jefferson on down and had lain at the bottom of many a political battle.

The classical economists got around this impasse by their philosophy of competition, but by the twentieth century the American economy had begun to grow away from the competitive model—especially in the newer industries such as steel and petroleum—toward a system in which one corporation, or a few friendly rivals, would control each field. As they saw it, industry must seek monopoly in order to keep from being wrecked by competitors; as society saw it, it must prevent monopoly in order to keep from being exploited. Either situation was regarded with alarm, and this alarm was not lessened by the way Big Business, perhaps quite sincerely, regarded itself as abiding by such classical rules as the law of supply and demand.

American reformers basically had been conservatives—that is, they had traditionally sought to return to a purer age of competition by pruning away the monopolistic practices that they regarded as evil and artificial; such men wished to break up the "monopolies" (in practice they meant any large corporation) and force the pieces to compete— hence they are called Atomists. On the other side, men like Theodore Roosevelt regarded large corporations as a legitimate product of evolution; they merely wished to regulate them as far as seemed necessary to protect the public—hence their name, Regulationists.

Though the differences between the two kinds of reformers were not immediately apparent and they cooperated for a number of years, they became increasingly suspicious of each other. Indeed, they seemed to face a dilemma. If the conservative Atomists had their way, they would destroy progress by returning to the competitive model of the classical economists; the end might well be chaos—or at best economic stagnation. If the Regulationists had their way, America might end up either with the state governing business or business governing the state—ends equally repugnant not only to the Atomists but to the Regulationists themselves.

No doubt the corporation was inevitable, and no doubt it was inherently oppressive in the context of the times. But it was not realized that certain tendencies within the corporation and within the mass production process were to be sparked by the restoration of democracy in the early 1900 s, and were in time to create a new atmosphere for capital and labor, for producer and consumer.

Entrepreneurs gradually awoke to the fact that expansion must depend primarily on the existence of effective purchasing power in the hands of laborers and consumers. That is, production of shoes should depend not on the number of people who need shoes but on the number of people who can pay for shoes; the only way to sell more is to pay the shoemaker enough to enable him to buy shoes for all his children. The capitalists who squeezed their labor were in effect limiting the purchasing power of the only people who could buy their goods and enable their overexpanded industries to escape disaster.

A thoughtful view of mass production will show that there is far more to it than careful blueprinting and management. It is even more basically a social effort, and in a pragmatic society it must use pragmatic means and serve pragmatic ends. Now the success of a social effort depends on the cooperation of the participating individuals. It is perhaps true that machines and many aspects of scientific management could have been developed without the inspiration of democracy. Nevertheless, the ultimate secret of the American know-how lies not in machines or scientific management or even financial and corporation organization. Basically it depends on the fostering of the spirit of freedom, co-operation, and *esprit de corps* on the part of workers, engineers, management, and capital.

Not only is the corporation a social institution and its mass production a social effort, but together they offer a solution to the rivalry between producer and consumer. Now we live in an economy of mass production, in which the supply is prospectively unlimited, but demand is limited only by effective purchasing power. For the first time *maximum profit can be obtained by maximum production at minimum cost—* exactly what both producer and society have always wanted. We have not worked out all the details but the broad outline of the future is clear. Mass production can introduce an economy of plenty, the utopian dream.[1]

Nevertheless, there is no indication that the economy can be self-regulating. Though the broad outline of the future seems clear, the details are not. For example, the key to successful operation has long been regarded less as the redistribution of what goods exist than as the manufacture and distribution of additional goods. But lately we have become aware that unchecked production will result in depletion of irreplaceable resources and pollution of the environment. Mass production's prophecy of an economy of plenty, of the attainment of the

---

[1]On the above see especially Peter F. Drucker, *The Concept of the Corporation* (1946).

utopian dream, is not self-fulfilling. The City of God is in sight, but at the moment it lies across a seemingly impassable gulf.

Progressive Politics

During the first third of the twentieth century, pragmatism in its political aspects—and to certain extent in all others—became popularly known as progressivism. A progressive is one who, as Allan Nevins put it, "favors the gradual introduction of wholly new processes of government intended to achieve novel aims." He is distinct from the mere reformer of the Cleveland type, who seeks—again in Nevins' words—"to purify the existing process of government in order to effect more completely its traditional aims."

The Progressive Era, defined as strictly as such an inchoate movement permits, extended from about 1901 to about 1916. Progressives, found in both parties were, at least in some ways, the children of pragmatism. They accepted its concepts of equality, responsibility, and environmentalism, and they learned from it a realistic view of what had to be done and how to go about doing it. They did not ask for violent monetary changes, for government ownership of railroads and utilities, or for wholesale rearrangements of land ownership. But they did work for numerous reforms in cities, states, and nation. They were most successful in the cities. Elsewhere they were never able to get uncontested control of legislatures or Congress, so had to settle for compromises.

One wellspring of progressivism was the important social change then under way with the rise of the Great Entrepreneurs and of labor as represented by the unions. The middle class thus felt caught in a power squeeze. As inheritors of the American tradition of individualism, they were worried by the changing pattern of society—not only corporations and labor unions but the urban political machines based largely on control of the immigrant vote. All this meant that the individual was being replaced by large collective units in the cities. The democratic mythus held that cities were evil and corrupt; the middle class was horrified to find that all too often this was true because urban politicians and corporations ran things to suit themselves.

The progressive movement was not animated by desperate necessities but by civic consciousness, by the conservative fear that old values were being subverted, by the pricks of guilty consciences, and by personal ambitions. It was overwhelmingly moralistic, no matter what arguments it might use to win the votes of farmers, laborers, and white-collar workers. Though the middle class, long the backbone of the Republican Party, was angered by the current evidences of corruption in politics and business and alarmed by the rising cost of living, it was still unwilling to relinquish its faith in the mythus of laissez faire and run the risks of root-and-branch reform. Probably it feared that serious reform would mean the end of its pleasant reign and its replacement by the common man—probably under the guise of socialism.

Keeping the old values of individualism would have meant sacrificing the material gifts of the new technology—which no one wished to do. Under the circumstances, there seemed to be no alternative—the corporation was inevitable. At such times men tend to accept the inevitable but to deceive themselves by adopting a "ceremonial solution"—going through the form of cleansing out abuses but not really changing the substance. This is essentially what progressivism sometimes did, and in so doing served as a national moral catharsis.

Theodore Roosevelt, the Republican progressive President, saw all this and recognized the dilemma in which it placed him. Accordingly, after the manner of politicians from time immemorial he took refuge in sound and fury, and in moral rationalizations. He was thus able to work up among his followers a fine crusading glow without seriously endangering the fairly satisfactory status quo. Before criticizing him it is well to recognize his belief that the country was not ready for drastic action.

TR's significance lay in two things: his popularization and redirection of progressive issues, and the start that he gave to the conservation of natural resources. That he actually accomplished little may be attributed in part to his own doubt and hesitancy, but perhaps even more to the political situation: he had to keep East and West together, and he would have been helpless without the aid of some of the more tolerant members of the Old Guard (the ultra-conservative wing of the Republican Party) and even some of the more susceptible Democrats. "A lot iv us," confessed Mr. Dooley, "like Rosenfelt that wudden't iver be suspicted iv votin' f'r him."

TR was clearly alarmed by the lawless ways of some members of the plutocracy and the growing desire of resentful labor to get something for nothing—two ends of the same game. The Republican Party had built its strength on the rising power of Big Business in days when the people approved of that growth. Roosevelt saw that the people were changing their attitude, and he warned the party and Wall Street that if they expected to remain in power they must yield to the rising popular demand. So keenly did Roosevelt blame Wall Street for the situation that it is said that at the Gridiron Dinner in 1907 at which Morgan was present, TR during an exposition of his policies shook his fist in the Magnifico's face and shouted, "If you don't let us do this, those who come after us will rise and bring you to ruin." He and his advice were rejected, and conservatism enjoyed a few more years of untrammeled power. But in the end the Democrats under TR's great kinsman mounted the wave of protest and rode to victory.

However, even in Theodore Roosevelt's time the "ceremonial solution" was not all. In the midst of the progressives' moral ritual certain voices were raised in favor of what was essentially a completely new approach—the partial discard of conservative laissez faire and the acceptance of direct government intervention on a large scale. Populism had foreshadowed this program, and in certain ways it proposed steps toward socialism. Theodore Roosevelt's was—eventually—the most powerful of the voices favoring a new approach, and he stated the case in his later messages and in his campaign for the New Nationalism in 1912. Whether he knew what he owed to populism and socialism is uncertain.

Progressives like Robert LaFollette were able to make reforms in many states, but they lacked the dramatic appeal and the political skill to charm the new generation of urban sophisticates, whose support was necessary to win national attention. Roosevelt knew how to charm. These two men represented the opposite wings of progressivism and were to move from uneasy co-operation to open enmity. LaFollette, as an Atomist, was deadly earnest in his trust-busting program, too earnest to see certain pitfalls evident to the more sophisticated Roosevelt. The latter accused "Battling Bob" of advocating "a form of sincere rural toryism" that was essentially conservative because it was attempting to block progress. TR also pointed out that if the corporations obeyed the law and competed sincerely, they would either kill one another off or one would be left to monopolize the field—which was against the law. When TR asserted that the great corporation was here to stay and that the only way to deal with it was to regulate it—to regulate monopoly—LaFollette accused him of favoring Big Business. This split and the long effort to find grounds for accommodation between the two camps have been a major preoccupation of American politics ever since.

When Roosevelt sundered the Republican Party in 1912 he ensured that the presidency would fall to the Democrats. The beneficiary was Woodrow Wilson, governor of New Jersey and recently president of Princeton. In campaigning he had sought for ways to defend the middle class—the modern version of Jefferson's small property. These as well as political expediency forbade the aping of Roosevelt's Regulationism, and he modified his past preachments about Atomism trying to force a return to the eighteenth century. After all, by now Hamiltonian centralization had triumphed to the extent that the issue of whether or not government should interfere in business had dropped from the political scene; even the Old Guard's President Taft had interfered.

Wilson sought to hold a position between TR's Regulationism and the extreme view held by Justice Brandeis that mere bigness was bad. He took a firm stand in favor of enforced competition—"a body of laws which will look after the men who are on the make"—and he opposed the corporations "growing big by methods which unrighteously crushed those who were smaller." He denied that the death of competition would increase efficiency, but he was ready to admit that bigness might have been gained by intelligence and efficiency. "We mean," said he, "to make little business big, and all business honest, instead of striving to make Big Business little, and yet letting it remain dishonest." He agreed that the corporation was the inevitable form of business enterprise and that it was impossible to return to the old order of individual competition. Whether or not Wilson foresaw and favored the growth of rival giants—oligopolies—in each industrial field may be open to argument, but it is probably fair to say that he implied this growth. Government action has helped it along, but perhaps it was in the cards anyway.

Wilson had defined his New Freedom as a movement to "purify and humanize every process of our common life." Government now had a positive function "to cheer and inspirit our people with the sure prospects of social justice and due reward, with the vision of the open gates of opportunity for all." His inaugural address was a clear, calm call to duty that came with soothing coolness after the fevers of the Roosevelt era. It also outlined a program of reform legislation, the principal items of which were a lower tariff, renovation of the banking system, a strong antimonopoly act, and agricultural aid.

Wilson apparently failed to see that the very success of capitalism was preparing for its transformation into another economic form. His antitrust policy was defending the passing small competitor from being crushed less by the big competitor than by historical forces, which gave a chance (if properly handled) of bringing a higher material and intellectual standard to all mankind. In the same way the League of Nations approved and imposed a passing economic and political order which was probably not in keeping with the spirit of evolution.

Wilson led in reforming banking and currency but otherwise was inclined to adopt toward corporations a policy somewhat like LaFollette's Atomism. It was not until he reversed his stand in 1916 and embraced Roosevelt's New Nationalism that federal social legislation began to make real headway. Still, as an intellectual and a member of the middle class Wilson was not willing to go too far; at any rate the coming of World War I diverted his attention.

Chapter 13
The Great Crusade and After

Proem

Why Wilsonian Idealism Broke Down—

It was not merely upon Europe that Wilson was making impossible demands: he had pushed the idealism and the resolution of his own people . . . beyond the breaking-point . . . . His effort to give to the idealism an internationalist form reckoned without the fact that his country was not, even in the remotest sense, a country with an internationalist outlook. The traditional American idea had been not that the United States was to lead, rescue, or redeem Europe, but that it was to take its own people in a totally different direction which Europe was presumably incapable of following. The United States was to be a kind of non-Europe or anti-Europe. Where European institutions were old, static, decadent, and aristocratic, American institutions were to be modern, progressive, moral, and democratic. . . . In repudiating Wilson, the treaty, the League, and the war itself [the electorate] repudiated the Progressive rhetoric and the Progressive mood—for it was Wilson himself and his propagandists who had done so much to tie all these together.

(Richard Hofstadter)[1]

---

[1]Richard Hofstadter, *The Age of Reform* (New York: Knopf, 1955), p. 278.

De Tocqueville Contrasts Russia and America, 1835 —
    There are at the present time two great nations in the world which started from different points, but seem to tend towards the same end. I allude to the Russians and the Americans. Both of them have grown up unnoticed; and while the attention of mankind was directed elsewhere, they have suddenly placed themselves in the front rank among the nations, and the world learned of their existence and their greatness at almost the same time. All other nations seem to have nearly reached their natural limits, and they have only to maintain their power; but these are still in the act of growth. . . . The American struggles against the obstacles that nature opposed to him; the adversaries of the Russian are men. The former combats the wilderness and savage life; the latter, civilization with all its arms. The conquests of the American are therefore gained by the plowshare; those of the Russian by the sword. The Anglo-American relies upon personal interest to accomplish his ends and gives free scope to the unguided strength and common sense of the people; the Russian centers all the authority of society in a single arm. The principal instrument of the former is freedom; of the latter, servitude. Their starting-point is different and their courses are not the same; yet each of them seems marked out by the will of Heaven to sway the destinies of half the globe.

Saving the World for Democracy

Our moral judgment on the origins of World War I and on what transpired after it began should depend upon whether human rights were really at stake. Actually the problems of Europe in 1914 were probably not unsolvable, provided its statesmen had realized the terrible alternative that faced them. Even after the war began destruction might have been forfended by a negotiated peace. It seems true that as late as 1916 Germany was ready to negotiate, and it seems equally clear that the Allies refused because the actions of the State Department gave assurance of effective aid or even hope of American entry into the war on their side, so they continued to hold on until the war became hyperbolic, until civilization almost broke down—indeed, did break down in some countries.

No one can say now what steps the American people would have permitted, but there were a number of courses open to Wilson if he had been determined to halt the war. He could have laid an embargo on munitions. He could have threatened to use, and if necessary used, naval force to prevent Allied breach of the old laws of neutrality; the British foreign minister later admitted that the Allies would have had to yield. He could have joined the Allies at the time of the *Lusitania* crisis but firmly and intelligently used his power to bring about a negotiated peace.

The entry of the United States into World War I had so many motivations that it has been possible for historians to approve or criticize as their prejudices dictated. Wilson's own reason—to "make the world safe for democracy"—covered it as a "big tent" covers a three-ring circus. Perhaps foremost in his mind and certainly foremost in his propaganda speeches was the concept of the American mission—the old, old belief that it was our duty to advance the building of the City of God. His call, of course, was to expand the method of crusade adopted in the Spanish-American War and in the subsequent Caribbean adventures, this time to the continent of Europe, the very seat of the evils from which the ancestors had fled. Moreover, it is probable that the American people acceded to Wilson's call to duty because of the current impact of pragmatism and of the political progressive movement.

It was deceptively easy to ticket Germany as tyrannical and predatory, and so make national security a second motivation. As a result of the Spanish war the United States had pushed out its strategic frontiers westward to the coast of Asia, southward to the Caribbean, and eastward to Europe. On the west Japan had expanded its power in China, and its appetite for further expansion was a problem to Wilson all during the war. On the south, there was fear that Germany would move into the West Indies—at least would set up a submarine base—and this fear motivated the landing of marines in Haiti and Santo Domingo and the purchase of the Virgin Islands from Denmark. On the east, there was a real danger that German victory would give the Atlantic a new master, one harder to convince than Britain of the sanctity of the Monroe Doctrine; and the United States would have no allies, for Britain and France would blame America for their defeat.

Finally there was a congeries of economic causes. Both sides had violated neutrality and restricted commerce, but German submarine warfare was more dramatic and destructive of life than Allied searches and seizures. A German victory would doubtless cause an economic collapse in the United States; certainly international trade patterns would be violently disrupted, and it would be years before new paths of commerce could be grooved.

In his approach to war and entry into it Wilson's competitive philosophy was extended to his conduct of foreign affairs. The nation, after all, was but a larger competitive unit; and, while it should live and let live, it should never lose its competitive identity in an international political and economic monopoly. In terms of British economic liberalism, Wilson believed that if a world-wide Open Door could be guaranteed—that is, free trade, freedom of the seas, and equal access to raw materials—the result would be the end of wars. He saw international relations as a "handsome rivalry," a "rivalry in which there is no dislike, this rivalry in which there is nothing but the hope of a common elevation in great enterprises which we can undertake in common." This belief led him to refuse to clap an embargo on shipments to the warring powers of Europe and to deny the right of the powers to interfere with American trade. It led both to his espousal of the self-determination of nations and to his refusal to recognize governments which seized power by force. Even the League of Nations, while reflecting in its formation many conflicting pressures, accepted his concept of national competition. It was in effect a sort of super-Federal Trade Commission, which should express the "organized moral force of the world."

It should be possible even in the jaundiced view of the post-Vietnam era to recognize Wilson's sincere idealism when he proclaimed "that America will come into the full light of day when all shall know that she puts human rights above all other rights and that her flag is the flag not only of America, but of humanity." The belief that national honor and international morality were at stake was why Wilson without hypocrisy and with no sense of naivete could call on "the conscience of the world." This was not consciously a cloak for economic materialism; rather he saw the material as a subordinate but essential part of the triumph of idealism.

The Long Armistice

The mistakes of Versailles are now readily apparent, and there is little to be gained by recounting them. The League of Nations was certainly defective, but it was improvable. The brutal fact is that neither Europe nor America was realistic. If ever the world needed a planned economic effort, it was after World War I. The war had destroyed much of Europe's wealth and its productive facilities, and recovery was handicapped by lack of capital, by fluctuating currencies and trade wars, and not least by revolutions. The world's financial capital had moved from London to New York, and the United States was now the only country with the abundance of credit necessary to world economic recovery. But the genius of laissezfaire still hovered over the nations and prohibited anything as unprecedented as mutual aid.

The United States had now reached the stage of economic maturity where it should have loaned generously and collected interest in the form of an excess of imports over exports, but it still thought like a small trading nation, unwilling to import large quantities of foreign goods and to export capital in proportion to its resources. In short, it had no vision of the world responsibilities imposed by its wealth, and no realization that its own peace and prosperity were bound up with those of the rest of the world.

The reasons are painfully clear: continued fear of slowing down the rhythm of production; *relative* self-sufficiency in agriculture, raw materials, and industry; opposition of business and labor to the introduction of competitive goods, whether or not they were cheaper; and survival of the old mercantile psychology that even a rich nation must sell more than it buys. The result was that, in one way or another, the United States stubbornly subsidized foreign purchases by loans instead of taking goods in exchange, and in the long run this exacerbated the financial imbalance. The idealistic side of Wilson's international program was jettisoned and the nation devoted itself to the economic expansionism inherent in its other part.

What the United States really needed was an orderly world in which to trade its enormous production for the many foreign products it needed or could use. And yet the nation with one third the world's developed economic wealth deliberately walled itself off from the goods of the world. *Economic* imperialism was growing; yet at the very time that American investments were invading the world, the nation refused to safeguard them either by treaty or by military preparedness and was actually scuttling its navy, dismissing its army, and plumping for pacifism.

American policies impinged at many points on world problems during the twenty-year interwar period. Europe's desperate economic plight led immediately after the Armistice to a demand for the cancellation of the war debts owed to the United States, but American public opinion was so hostile toward Europe that this was plainly out of the question. A long and bitter argument followed. On the whole, the attitude of America was economically indefensible, since it refused to accept payment in the form of goods, and payment in gold was clearly impossible. In such an impasse, the whole problem of the war debts was quietly shelved during World War II and has never revived.

The renewal during this period of the prewar diplomatic struggle among nations let to numerous crises and a general deterioration of international relations. Western Germany was the production center of Europe, and the Continent could not prosper until Germany recovered. The Allies reluctantly ameliorated the provisions of Versailles and restored German industry, but she, like all other countries, suffered by the depression of the 1930's and this helped to convince her that her economic problems arose from the Treaty of Versailles. The result was Hitler, with his demand for drastic revision of the remaining provisions of the Treaty, and when this failed rearmament of Germany.

The European of 1920 visualized the American as a gaudy figure, cocktail in hand, bestriding the narrow world. It is true that the United States had long filled the Old World with unease, but this unease was quite out of proportion with America's actual impact. Nevertheless it was evident that the dawning age belonged to America. The American was as ubiquitous in all parts of the globe as the Roman had once been in the Mediterranean. Tourists, salesmen, engineers, bank representatives, exporters and importers swarmed everywhere. Herbert Hoover's Department of Commerce boys invaded the world with their slide rules and statistical abstracts and probed shrewdly for openings into which goods and investments could be poured. But it was the machine that was the true invader, either actually or by its products and methods. It refused to be impressed by international boundaries but regarded the world as an integral market. American corporations crept under national barriers by buying or building factories in the desired marketing area, and their backlog of expensive research, designing, and business and production techniques made them almost unbeatable.

The superiority of American goods in quality, attractiveness, or cheapness forced European competitors to adopt American methods or eventually face ruin. But Europe did not have the capital, resources, or market to build up native mass-production industries; and, even more to the point, it could not adjust itself psychologically. Its social ideals clashed with the acceptance of higher labor costs which were necessary to build a market. There was the typical petty official's affinity for red tape and ritual, and the thrift which made it impossible to throw away a fairly new but still obsolete machine and replace it by a better one. Most important of all was the failure to put into effect the spirit of freedom on the part of workers and engineers which is the core of the American know-how.

Germany sought to impose what it called Fordism as a national sacrifice to augment its power, and it is said that the government devoted a quarter of the national income to the changeover. All it did was to create labor dislocations, lose foreign trade, and hasten the coming of Hitler. The result was that German industry (with a few exceptions) remained based on the skilled worker. German engineers consequently sank into pessimism and warned that in case of a second conflict with America, Germany was doomed to defeat.

Russia was the closest approach to an exception to the rule of European inability to adopt American methods. Later on the USSR sought to claim credit for all the great inventions. In 1930 even Stalin was properly humble. "We have never concealed," said he, "and we do not intend to conceal the fact that in the sphere of technique we are the pupils of the Germans, the English, the French, the Italians, and first and foremost, the Americans." Throughout the 1920's American engineers, either hired singly or representing engineering or manufacturing firms, swarmed into Russia, and some of them remained through the 1930's.

During the seventeenth and eighteenth centuries Europe had flattered the French by imitating their ways, and in the nineteenth century Britain had become the model. Now the prestige of the United States was evidenced by a superficial imitation of things American. Bars, cocktails, jazz, dances, food, clothes, and card games imported from America became the mode. Before the war the plump Viennese woman had been the ideal of Paris fashions, now the slim American woman became the standard of fashion—if not exactly of beauty. Bobbed hair made its way across the Atlantic. American slang "permeated society from below" and found a reception among would-be smarties all over the world. The typical British sports, except soccer football, were not as adaptable to the common people as some of the American competitive sports such as basketball, and it found considerable vogue over the world.

The effect of the American moving picture is hard to estimate with accuracy, yet the bitterness with which many Europeans resented it gives evidences of its significance. Hollywood put out a superior product (or at least a smoother and more highly polished one), and, moreover, it had the cachet of showing American scenes, fashions, dances, and living conditions. It was not intended as propaganda, but European politicians and businessmen rightly regarded it as that, for it spread dissatisfaction with living and working conditions. Presently the reaction came, as European leaders sought to build up their own cinema industries and launched a campaign of defamation against the American product. The efforts often backfired. When the Soviets imported *The Grapes of Wrath* to show how meanly Americans lived Russians were fascinated, not by its portrayal of poverty but by how American peasants wore shoes and drove a car.

From the viewpoint of Europe's old elite it must be admitted that there was an American menace. America's overwhelming economic power (aided by the war) had displaced Europe's world economic supremacy, had saddled it with debt, and threatened its very daily bread. It contributed to the ruin of European prestige in colonial areas, by the infiltration both of American economic controls and of economic and institutional ideas. The American example of a high standard of living was spreading discontent among Europe's workers, all the more so since emigration to the United States had been limited after World War I. Even more serious, the American example of democracy was contributing powerfully to the clearly approaching political and social crisis. Beyond all of these was an uneasy feeling that if economic leadership was lost, the leadership in the arts and sciences would soon pass to America.

The European movement to restore its position of world preeminence or at least to stave off further American encroachment took on two principal forms, one propagandistic and the other financial. Propaganda was carried on in Europe itself, in the United States, and in the traditional colonial and other marketing areas. The arguments presented to Europeans stemmed chiefly from the assertion that American government and capital were engaged in a deliberate plot to conquer the world economically and culturally. Germans had given the name *Amerikanismus* to the process of Americanization; to Europeans it meant (as Eric Fischer has expressed it) the "conversion of the world into a purely materialistic state, where economic interests and power prevail." Americans admitted the fact of the Americanization of the world, but they saw it as the spread of the creative urge and a willingness to experiment with the new and to trust the people with political power and with a high economic standard; it is not likely that they thought of it as building the secular City of God but the animating spirit was the same. Without any Wilsonian moral trimmings they saw themselves as engaged in a great crusade for the salvation of the world.

When hostile European critics analyze American "ideals," they are not likely to select the ones noted above which *we* regard as most characteristic. Rather, they are inclined to take three others, which they insist are dominant if not all-inclusive: materialism, standardization, and quantitativeness. The accusation of materialism had a superficial validity, especially when the accusers chose to ignore the long history of American idealism and social progress and stress the burgeoning of commerce and industry and the uniquely high standard of living even of the masses.

As for standardization, it is difficult for Americans to realize that in the eyes of many intelligent Europeans we are as much "faceless men" as the subjects of any dictator. Standardization, they say, not only prevents the preservation of precious diversities and the discovery of new values but promotes mediocrity and shoddiness: not only does our ruthless efficiency promote the standardization of goods, but (they say) it arose from a standardization of soul which was evident well over a century ago. There is some proof for this, however directly it may contradict the mythus of the pioneer individualist. On the other hand, the purchasing power provided by standardization is boosting the American market for specialty goods to the point where it has become a mainstay not only of importers but of domestic manufactures.

The third accusation, that the United States possesses a quantitative civilization in comparison to Europe's qualitative civilization had and has considerable truth. Critics assert that this rises from democracy's gospel of equality, which has been forced to sacrifice the esthetic because the masses cannot understand or appreciate the fine and the beautiful; therefore the fine and the beautiful will perish unless there is an aristocracy to cherish them. This is the accusation that hurts the most because it conceivably could turn out to be true. America is built upon a splendid faith that, given time, the masses can become aristocrats in the best sense of the word. If we fail, all that can be said is that at least it was worth trying once in history.

European propagandists against America frequently used the same arguments in their imperial possessions, and because they were appealing to a native elite of nobility or education they had considerable success. It was possible also to use the argument there that squeezing of wages and inflation of prices were due to American economic imperialism. The argument had some success and may have helped to delay the crest of the wave of native revolt until after World War II. The native elite who then came into control found the argument useful in hushing the murmurs of the masses. The bogy of American imperialism was also invoked in the Latin-American nations.

The European propaganda directed at the United States had considerable success not only because it was aided by many gaggling Americans but by the American's inner uncertainty and his usual respect (willing or not) for the old centers of Western Civilization. Abusive literature poured from the press and was reprinted and eagerly read in America. André Siegfried's *America Comes of Age* (1927) may well stand for this whole liturgy of abuse which surely must have been inspired by fear. Siegfried saw civilization as the sole possession of France. The United States was placed outside; so were Britain and Germany, though they were permitted a place closer to the fence where they could peer longingly through the pickets. Siegfried's was only one of a flood of anti-American books, which one commentator estimated at about five hundred.

Dominant as the United States was in the economic field, there was only nonsense in the accusation that it had reached that place and was maintaining it by a carefully prepared plan. If, as Coolidge averred, the people had awakened to the drumbeats of a new destiny, their march was strangely out of cadence. For one thing, if the United States was officially reaching for economic power, it refused to assume the accompanying political responsibility. It kept the psychological attitudes of a debtor nation and of a petty merchant. It refused to regard World War I as an organic part of American evolution but insisted that it was merely an unsuccessful moral crusade, a temporary aberration. It reacted sharply against government controls. It rejected credit or production planning and made no surveys of world conditions save such as Herbert Hoover offered. Even capitalistic combinations conducting the invasion of other countries were neither consistent nor cooperative in policies and aims.

There can be little doubt that this fact was well known to the men who inspired the propaganda, but they had a purpose to fulfill. At the outset it was Europe's intention to capture American economic power and use it as her own, but any chance of success which this program might have had was killed by American disillusionment. Europe than passed to a propaganda of vilification. This also failed, and was promptly followed by economic warfare with all the weapons of commerce. This is not the place to examine the details of the economic battles of the interwar decades, but the greatest struggles were waged over the control of raw materials, especially metals, rubber, and petroleum. Despite American advantages Europe was on the whole able to hold its own. Private citizens of the United States had no more invested abroad during the interwar years than had Britain, nor did they have as much invested in Europe (outside of the war debts) as did Europe in the United States. American technology and know-how made great strides in Europe, but they did not remake European industry in the American image. American cultural and institutional standards also made headway, but it is even more clear that they did not remake Europe even though their prestige excited much superficial imitation.

The Day of the Dictators

The basis for World War II had become clear by 1933. To the people who had been submerged by defeat, economic stress, or a long history of tyranny, two new totalitarian ideologies—communism and fascism—were promising a higher standard of living and a renewal of power and prestige. In the light of these new menaces the reigns of kaiser and czar seem almost puerile, for neither of them had managed to suppress a strong undercurrent of liberalism.

Dictatorship is not new, but most of the dictatorships in the past were what we call *authoritarian*. That is, they exercised certain aspects of authority strongly, but as long as people submitted quietly, paid their taxes, and served in the army, they were left to do pretty much as they pleased in other matters. *Totalitarian* dictators are different in that they exercise *total* control. No aspect of the citizen's life is left untouched. Not only must he conform in every respect, but he must give every evidence of enthusiasm for the system. He is never allowed to forget that "Big Brother is watching," as George Orwell put it so graphically in his novel *1984.*

Fascism claims to be a capitalist dictatorship run by an elite on behalf of the people; communism claims to be a socialist dictatorship run by the workers. Both claim to be "democratic" and to follow the *true* will of the people; never mind that the masses do not know their true will until they have been indoctrinated. Russian communism in its theory is government ownership of the means of production and of distribution, and control of consumption. Control is to be in the hands of a dictatorship of the proletariat exercised through local and federal soviets (committees) of the Communist Party. Actually, the Soviet Union is in control of a group of administrators committed to certain intellectual positions, and its current stage of development is called "building socialism."

Marx had proclaimed that the ownership of private property is the source of all evil; do away with it and after a period of adjustment the world would see the ushering in of the perfect society, a City of God, built on secular and determinist lines. The doctrine was upheld and spread with such faith and zeal that it has rightly been called a religion.

Marxists readily agree that communism could not exist were it not able to stand on the shoulders of capitalism—that is, profit by the technologies developed under capitalism and by the habits of precision and responsibility developed through the centuries. The West built its economy by centuries of scraping and saving: the Soviet Union undertook to make itself an industrial giant within a single generation by regimentation of population and resources. Instead of mortgaging itself to Western bankers it found the capital for its industrial expansion by trading raw materials for machinery. One of its actions was to trade wheat, thus consigning millions of people to starvation.

The leader of the Russian communist revolution was Nikolai Lenin. Improving on the dialectical materialism of Marx, which posited the "inevitable" collapse of capitalism, Lenin proposed to hasten the collapse by using the technique of world revolution. He presented communism as a vast scheme for doing good; the world was to be saved by force in spite of itself. Marx had regarded the proletariat as the foundation of communist power, but Lenin looked to the intellectuals and proposed that the workers and all other classes be regarded as nothing more than tools.

Lenin's desperate haste to industrialize had two explanations. It was a means of organizing and disciplining the workers in the effort to raise their standard of living, and it was essential to build military power, first to withstand and then, if necessary, to conquer the bourgeois world. He taught that the capitalist nations would be hostile—in fact, they had to be in self-defense.

Lenin was not only a thinker and a man of will, but the founder of what was in effect, as said above, a new religion. In his grand crusade to save the world he set up a super-morality when he said "Morality is that which serves to destroy the old exploiting society and to unite all the toilers around the proletariat, which is creating a new communist society." In so saying he stripped the movement of Judaeo-Christian ethics and exhorted his followers to "resort to all sorts of cunning, schemes, and stratagems, to employ illegal methods, to evade and conceal the truth." The struggle must continue until capitalism was overthrown; there could be between the two sides no enduring compromise, no honesty or good faith. He turned tactics into dogma—that is, the tactic feasible at the moment must be unflinchingly supported by all good communists until circumstances made it essential to change the approach. The new approach in turn became an article of faith.

One might find a theoretical justification for Lenin's rugged evangelism as a means of imposing the discipline necessary to modernize a nation like China, which was sunk in ancient apathy and putrescent poverty. Unfortunately, it was imposed on a nation that, though not yet industrialized, belonged to the Western tradition—even though a heretical aspect—and which quite naturally fought against being chained. The result was twenty years of chaos, purges, liquidations, and famines, and though order was eventually imposed dissidence has remained just below the surface.

The springs of Soviet policy have been much the same as governed Russia for centuries under the czars. They were shaped by an isolation from the world that on one side partook of the smug self-satisfaction and pathological suspicions of the backwoods villager, and on the other of claustrophobia. Russia had long thought with some justice that western Europe was trying to keep it penned in, so it strove all the harder to get out. It broke out to the Baltic, to the Pacific, to the White Sea, but all of these had the handicap of ice or strong guardians; hence the Russian desire to dominate Scandinavia and Turkey, with their outlets to the Atlantic and the Mediterranean.

In this search, communism's doctrine of world revolution proved to be a welcome addition to the Russian nationalist and imperialist arsenal. After the Bolshevik Revolution communist parties were founded all over the world, with Russian funds and guidance, to pave the way for revolution. Frequently they took the guise of nationalist and nativist groups in countries not yet prepared for communism's dialectical materialism. Lenin just may have believed his own propaganda about the rugged altruism of communism, but one can easily doubt it of his successor, Joseph Stalin, who was in every sense the acme of Oriental despotism.

Fascism sprang in part from revulsion against the threat of communist revolution—hence its frequent characterization as counterrevolutionary. Its original backers were members of the elite classes—aristocrats and industrialists—who were seeking a means of preserving their privileges. In time they were joined by the lower middle class ("petty bourgeois"), which in Europe was being squeezed between big business and labor but was most fearful of the latter. During the postwar disorders the capitalists financed nationalist and terrorist gangs engaged in political agitation and in harassing communists, and finally backed them in seizing political power.

The first of the fascist leaders to emerge was Benito Mussolini, who in 1922 forced himself into the position of premier and dictator of Italy. Though he was something of a "sawdust Caesar," Mussolini dreamed of a restored Roman Empire that would dominate the Mediterranean.

German fascism had a tinge of socialism—hence the name National Socialist, shortened to Nazi—and in the Jews it found a helpless minority to blame for the national ills. Adolph Hitler was a mentally ill Austrian sign painter who had served as a corporal in the German army. Orators are rare in Germany, but Hitler was a spellbinder, and this helped him to take advantage of the depression and ride into power in January 1933. He promptly summoned a corps of financiers and industrial managers and put them to work laying the economic basis for Germany's reassertion of its place as a world force.

On the other side of the world, Japan, though technologically modernized, actually had never emerged psychologically from its peculiar form of feudalism which subordinated the individual. At the same time, "emperor worship"—the peculiar reverence paid to the Mikado—had precluded the rise of overwhelmingly powerful individual leaders, such as Hitler, and had historically placed leadership in the hands of an oligarchy. Japan felt that it had been denied its just claims in East Asia by the Versailles and Washington conferences. It now planned to seize the minerals and manpower of China and use them in ousting the imperial powers from what it called its Greater East Asia Co-Prosperity Sphere, the vast area extending from Siberia to Australia. Hitler insisted that his greatest objective was the overthrow of Russian communism; this was not merely for ideological reasons but also to gain control of the Eurasian land mass which he believed would give "a thousand years of empire" to the Teutonic master race.

Attempts have been made to distinguish between fascism and communism, as by pointing to the cynicism of the fascists and the messianism of the communists. Nevertheless, it is difficult to distinguish between their effects on the man in the street. William H. Chamberlin has listed ten ways in which the two totalitarian ideologies resemble each other.

(1) The all-powerful and supposedly infallible leader.

(2) The single ruling party.

(3) Government by a combination of propaganda, terrorism, and flattery of the masses.

(4) Full government control of the national economy.

(5) Government control of labor.

(6) Widespread use of slave labor.

(7) Hostility to religion.

(8) Resort to large-scale atrocities.

(9) The cultivation of fear, hatred, and suspicion of the outside world.

(10) A primitive tribal form of chauvinist nationalism which finds vent in an exaltation of militarism and an almost paranoid conviction of a world-conquering mission.[2]

Russia and the democracies were the chief obstacles to the expansionism of the fascist powers; so it was natural that they should cooperate. First of all, they needed to test the cohesion of the democratic powers. Three questions must be answered. (1) Would the League of Nations enforce collective security? (2) Would the European democracies support one another? (3) Would the United States come to the aid of the democracies as in 1917?

Why did the democracies take no resolute action to prevent the rise of the dictators and the triumph of their aggressive policies? First of all, it is difficult for democrats to understand the nature of aggressive power; they are so used to the constitutional process of change that they are slow to recognize a threat of violence. Second, the democracies had lost their dynamism, partly as a result of World War I, partly as the result of a failure to reformulate the democratic faith in the light of the age of transition. Third, there had developed among the democratic peoples a guilt complex over the Treaty of Versailles. Fourth, the fact that there were two totalitarian ideologies confused and split the democrats. Some liberals believed against all evidence the none too subtle communist preachments of universal peace and good will; some conservatives were so frightened by the Red menace that they accepted against all evidence fascism's claim to be the champion of capitalism. Hitler knew his humankind when he said that a lie would be believed by those who wished to believe it, and the bigger the lie, the easier believed. Fifth, and

---

[2]William H. Chamberlin, *America's Second Crusade* (Chicago: Regnery, 1950), pp. 31-39.

as cogent a reason as any, the dictators rose basically from economic stress, and economic means were essential to combat them. These the democracies did not have, at least so long as the United States washed its hands of responsibility.

Between 1933 and 1939 the fascist powers by carefully orchestrated aggressions became convinced that the democracies, including the United States, did not have the will to block them. We can see now that each step led a little farther down the path to war, but it did not come until September 1939. Britain and France had guaranteed Polish security and when Germany invaded Poland they went to war. Two weeks later Russia also invaded Poland, but the Allies were not disposed to declare war on Russia, perhaps hoping that the Russians would eventually become the enemy of Germany—as they did.

This is not the place to go into the details of World War II. Roosevelt may have been convinced from the first that the United States must enter the war or see the Allies defeated, but there was a strong body of American opinion that believed Germany and Russia would eat each other. Roosevelt's problem was solved by Japan's flouting of the Open Door by its sweeping conquests in East Asia, and finally by its attack on Pearl Harbor, December 7, 1941.

Chapter 14
The Drive into Abundance

Proem

The New Deal was confronted by a double threat: the breakdown of democracy, and the breakdown of the economy. By one means or another, it maintained and strengthened democracy in a world from which the process was rapidly disappearing; and it shored up American economic power so that when the crisis came, the country was ready to serve as the arsenal of democracy.

* * *

We do not see faith, hope and charity as unattainable ideals, but we use them as stout supports of a Nation fighting the fight for freedom in a modern civilization.

Faith—in the soundness of democracy in the midst of dictatorships.

Hope—renewed because we know so well the progress we have made.

Charity—in the true spirit of that grand old word. For charity . . . means love . . . that does not merely share the wealth of the giver, but in true sympathy and wisdom helps men to help themselves.

We seek not merely to make Government a mechanical implement, but to give it the vibrant personal character that is the very embodiment of human charity. . . .

Better the occasional faults of a Government that lives in a spirit of charity than the consistent omissions of a Government frozen in the ice of its own indifference.

There is a mysterious cycle in human events. To some generations much is given. Of other generations much is expected. This generation of Americans has a rendezvous with destiny.

(From Roosevelt's Acceptance Speech, 1936)

* * *

At least since 1930, it would seem that the bigger the political entity the more likely it was to favor doing something for its underprivileged. A few of the larger states, such as New York, Pennsylvania, and California, fostered some aspects of social, economic, and ethnic progress, but over most of the nation these were brought about only by federal pressures. On the other hand, even liberals were coming to see that to cure social ailments it was not enough to make lavish appropriations and leave the administration to federal technicians. It simply would not work in a country of this size. The result was a dawning liberal willingness to make federal appropriations but to devolve most of the responsibility on the states. But there was the dilemma: most of the states were not geared either psychologically or technically to administer reforms. By and large, they were artificial creations without economic or social unity. Moreover, such viability as they may have had, had been swamped by the effects of antiquated constitutions, crumbling tax structures, and the dictation of courthouse gangs and vested economic interests. Would reform bog down again if its administration were turned over to the states and cities?

The New Deal

It is not always wise to separate the treatment of domestic from foreign affairs, for they inevitably affect each other. On the other hand, since our entry into World War I it is possible to see Americans as engaged (outside certain moments of quietude) in two giant activities: the drive into abundance on the domestic scene; and a crusade to make the world hospitable toward democracy and its political and economic practices as they understood them.

When their venture into World War I ended in disillusionment, Americans retreated to a more narrow and intolerant nativism and nationalism than even that of Andrew Jackson. This was the period of Normalcy, when Progressivism and altruism were in disgrace. The "common man" had failed to bring the City of God; now let the businessman and the engineer take over. Normalcy was on the surface a return to the Gospel of Wealth, but actually it was a desperate effort to forestall reform by proving that the businessman and engineer could bring the utopia which Progressivism had sought. As a matter of fact the 1920's did see a considerable degree of flamboyant prosperity, but in the end this proved to be superficial; certainly it did little for farmers, unskilled workers, and the disadvantaged black and brown minorities.

The collapse of Normalcy in 1929 and the coming of the Depression toppled idols on every side. The psychological effects were tremendous. It was a period of economic desperation and personal humiliation. Some men suffered from a new disease known as "unemployment shock" which robbed them of initiative and pride and made them let the wife and children scrabble for a living. Especially noticeable was the blow to American optimism. Hitherto depressions had been limited in duration and usually they had been softened by the half-rural conditions under which millions of the workers lived. Moreover, the economic mythus had assured people that depressions brought their own cure, but this no longer seemed to be true.

With such widespread misery and frustration, it was inevitable that the electorate should blame the Republican conduct of policy since 1920 and that the Democrats should be swept into power in 1932. Franklin D. Roosevelt's New Deal is far too complex to be followed here in detail, but it fell into three phases insofar as one can divide it.

The first New Deal was based on the thesis that the American economy was mature and that agriculture and industry were overexpanded. As a cure it sought both to reduce the budget and to promote national self-sufficiency, efforts now almost forgotten. Along with these efforts, in the First New Deal the administration essentially adopted Regulationism—a course certain in the end to antagonize Big Business. The aim was to confirm business in its old primacy and to refurbish its reputation by asking it to give some sympathetic attention to the interests of labor and agriculture. When by 1935 business refused to go along with this request, Roosevelt instituted the Second New Deal. Many policies were reversed as the administration abandoned some features of Regulationism and moved toward Atomism. Among other things, attempts were made to "clean up" business, and a start was made at seeking international cooperation.

Even this did not bring the desired recovery, and the administration (in the phase sometimes called the Third New Deal) settled into a permanent policy of pump priming. This simile is taken from the old-fashioned water pump in which the water was drawn up by a leather suction valve. When the valve dried out water was poured in at the top to "prime" it—that is, to swell the leather to fill the cylinder and create the necessary suction. Thus large government expenditures would serve to "prime" the economy and start credit flowing.

This operation, which found favor with many New Dealers, was part of the new theory of "compensatory spending" proposed by John Maynard Keynes, a British economist. Keynes held that in time of depression the slack in private spending could only be taken up by the government's expenditure of borrowed money. Taxes and expenditures should benefit the poor most and the rich least, on the ground that the former must spend all they receive and in this way stimulate production. Then when good times returned, the government should raise taxes and pay back what it had borrowed. Keyne's doctrine was, of course, much more complicated than this simple statement makes it seem.

There were budget deficits during Roosevelt's New Deal period, but they were hardly sufficient to end the depression. FDR's major advisers were not greatly influenced by Keynesian economics until late in the 1930s, and there is no evidence that he ever accepted the principles of deficit spending, unbalanced budgets, or a large national debt. Consequently, from a Keynesian standpoint, the New Deal demonstrates that economic policies that are too timid and too contradictory will not expand employment and income sufficiently to restore prosperity. The New Deal did not bring the United States out of the depression; only the masssive deficit spending connected with World War II was able to turn the trick.

The failure of the New Deal to solve the problem of economic depression does not mean that it was a failure in other respects. The political and social changes (revolution would be too strong a term) wrought by the Roosevelt administration have had a lasting impact on the nation. Not only did the New Deal counterbalance the power of business by elevating agriculture and labor, but it marked the point in American history when the government assumed responsibility for the majority of its citizens.

Historically, Republicans had believed in the positive use of the state to foster progress and the Democrats had supported the hands-off policy of the negative state (see above, pages 127-29). Now the parties reversed principles as the New Deal boldly used the power of government to solve the problems of the Depression and of the wastage of natural resources.

Many thoughtful businessmen agreed that the government should impose a control of competitive practices to save business from itself, but others did not think that the basic trouble was maldistribution—or, if they did, blamed antitrust legislation for it. The way to bring recovery, these said, was to encourage investment and profits, not petty consumer spending. This argument, of course, was essentially a repetition of the old "trickle-down" or "shower-of-economic-grace" theory—that the economy would recover only when business recovered, and only then would labor be helped. Labor was badly split between those who would have been satisfied with wage raises and those who demanded not only that wages be raised but that profits be lowered. For the most part, farmers were short-sightedly content to get higher prices for their products and did not seem to realize that at the same time the prices of what they bought would rise. Atomists and Regulationists, of course, continued their historic feud.

The New Deal was confronted by a double threat: the breakdown of democracy, and the breakdown of the economy. By one means or another Roosevelt built up a political coalition of workers, farmers, and idealists which maintained and strengthened democracy in a world from which the process was rapidly disappearing. No less important, he shored up American economic power so that when the crisis came, the country was ready to serve as the arsenal of democracy.

The shift of the Democratic Party to use of the positive state as the protector of the citizen entailed a number of new departures. One of them was the enlargement of the old definition of democracy as a political process by the acceptance of the belief that the citizen also has economic rights. Up to 1932, economics had in general wagged politics; now it was necessary for politics to wag economics—merely the American phase of what was going on all over the world. Jeffersonian ends were now openly being sought by Hamiltonian means—the use of the positive state.

To implement this, it was necessary to oil the creaking wheels of democracy by resuscitating the party system, restoring the atrophied powers of the President, and altering and extending the administrative bureaucracy so that it could cope with its problems. The purpose of all this was to undertake at least a moderate degree of planning, both social and economic. With decreasing opportunity, the average man saw no other way to assure himself of reasonable security than to further undermine laissez faire.

A serious obstacle to reform was done away with when the Supreme Court accepted the New Deal and began to remove one by one the dams of substantive due process which it had so laboriously erected against further change. It acceded to the view that Congress could exercise unprecedented powers over agriculture and labor, could delegate administrative functions, and could subordinate private property to social ends. Without relinquishing its duty to interpret the Constitution, it acknowledged its further duty to find legal ways of enforcing the popular will as expressed in election returns.

Business objected to the Regulationism of the First New Deal on the ground that it was "creeping socialism." On the other hand, the New Deal has been criticized on the ground that it was simply another in the long line of evasions of problems which had marked American history, made possible by our abundance of resources—that it was not really reform, but merely a grudging redistribution of goods by a government serving as cat's-paw for the capitalists and aimed at bribing the most vocal of the malcontents. Even if this were admitted, the redistribution of income was so vast that it can scarcely be rated as a "ceremonial solution" but should be honestly called reform. True, the New Deal did not cure the fundamental problem of poverty which—say the critics—could have been done if it had boldly and at one stroke instituted socialism. Under the circumstances, this claim is subject to doubt.

Be that as it may, business should have considered, while it was crowing over the Supreme Court's decisions against extension of government power, that many laborers and tenant farmers have a weak sense of the sanctity of property. If the anchors of the middle class and the owner-farmer are dragged, some later wave of reform may well wash the economy upon the rocks of socialism. There is some logic in the judgment that FDR was the greatest conservative since Hamilton.

In demanding government aid, business lost part of its independence. It became necessary for the federal government to assume control of credit, to tinker with the gold standard, to finance exports and imports, and to enter even the fields of private, state, and local finance. The government thus necessarily became responsible for and responsive to economic ups and downs as never before. Not even today do more than a handful of businessmen seem to grasp the fact that it was the New Deal that saved private enterprise. Perhaps its most enduring reform was its attempt to pacify public resentment and yet preserve the bigness necessary to mass production by encouraging oligopoly—the growth of rival giants in industrial fields where they did not already exist. Doing so was an attempt to solve the dilemma posed by Atomism and Regulationism.

The New Deal was well aware that capitalism was committing suicide, and its attempts to redistribute economic power were intended to reinforce the declining middle class with new blood—to endow workers and tenant farmers with enough property to ensure that property would become at least a little more sacred to them. Thus the Second New Deal's partial return to Atomism was a successful attempt to revive the middle class and to strengthen it by adding to it the mass of well-paid workers as an element in the balance of social forces. This was perhaps the real reason why Roosevelt was so hated by the comfortable: he destroyed the bases of their feeling of superiority. Nevertheless, he was not a man to upset the fundamentals of the existing order, and his pragmatic experimentation may have been a salve more appropriate to the times than the sweeping collectivism and Christian brotherhood upheld by some of his supporters.

It may be suggested that even with Roosevelt's seeming conservatism the New Deal, either because of him or despite him, was in keeping with one very deep current of Anglo-Saxon history. Even the more radical aspects of the New Deal had been inherent in TR's New Nationalist doctrine that property was held "subject to the general right of the community to regulate its use to whatever degree the public welfare may require it," and in its use of Hamiltonian means to serve Jeffersonian ends. Whether or not he knew it, TR had foreshadowed the eclipse of John Locke and the rise of Richard Hooker in twentieth-century America. But we can find antecedents earlier than Theodore Roosevelt.

Perry Miller has demonstrated that the keynote of Edwards' preaching was the promotion not so much of morality as of the public welfare, in which effort he denounced the "narrow, private spirit" represented in the "river gods" of the Connecticut Valley—the merchants, traders, and land speculators. In the end the "river gods" blasted him out of his pastorate, and Edwards died, as it were, in exile. Franklin has popularly been cast as the great spokesman of that same "narrow, private spirit," now called bourgeois. And yet, if one looks deeper he can see in Franklin not only an enlightened civic uplifter but something more—an attitude that is abhorrent to the marketplace mentality. "Private property," said Franklin, "is a creature of society and is subject to the call of the society whenever its necessities shall require, even to its last farthing."

A century before the New Deal, John Quincy Adams had proposed to introduce the service state (see above, page 125) and in so doing had ended the Era of Good Feelings. It was pointed out in that connection that Adams was acting in the spirit of Richard Hooker rather than John Locke.

The Winds of Change

Practically nothing remained untouched by the winds of change as the country entered the last quarter of the century. While it is true that many of the concerns of the United States after 1945 were centered on questions of foreign policy related to the Cold War, it was also a time of unparalleled domestic economic prosperity. These economic gains were mainly a result of population growth, greater governmental expenditure, a boom in housing construction, and increased agricultural and industrial productivity. By the decade of the Kennedy-Johnson administrations this drive into abundance had progressed to such a high plateau that many optimistically assumed that continued economic growth would solve the problems of poverty and would soon raise even common labor to a dazzling level of abundance. With only 5 percent of the world's population and 7 percent of its land, the United States possessed almost half the world's tangible wealth. It was easy, ignoring other factors, to extrapolate unwarranted conclusions from such statistics.

The years after World War II saw a technological revolution perhaps as significant as those of the age of steam and the coming of mass production. This was the introduction of automation, apparently named in 1946: the use of machines to run machines. It depends on the application of techniques brought into being by the new science of electronics. There are several methods of control, but the one most commonly used is to guide the machine by a tape punched in such a way as to direct it to perform certain operations. But there is more to it than this, for the technique can be applied to business procedures, transportation, agriculture, and to planning, stockpiling, and marketing. Without it rocket missilery and space exploration would be practically impossible. Automation requires data, and the provision and processing of data has become a tremendous business in itself. Electronic, "self-programming" computers now memorize, calculate, talk back, and help design new computers. *Cybernetics* is a new word coined to include both self-controlling machines and self-programming computers. No corner of American life has escaped its effects, and it has caused a shift from blue-collar to white-collar workers—from the production-line worker to highly skilled technical and professional workers. A revolution as profound as this not only opens up boundless opportunities but poses countless problems that only time can solve.

The drive into abundance has not changed the superficial aspects of the capitalist system, but closer examination shows that we have moved away from the competitive business society associated with capitalism to a managed economy. Government has redirected some of capitalism's energies, trimmed away many of its abuses, and regulated it by threats, orders, and favors. It places a cushion under agricultural prices. It protects labor by wage-and-hour laws, social security, and favors to unions. It sweetens the disposition of bankers by allowing the banking system to create the credit which it borrows, actually a subsidy. Directly or indirectly, it subsidizes transportation, scientific research, education, and certain types of publishing. Federal services have burgeoned. Manufacturers and petroleum companies receive tax favors to encourage expansion, and Congress writes down the costs to national defense. They receive cheap hydroelectric power and purchase war-surplus plants and machinery at rock-bottom prices.

Several features of the present American business system indicate the extent to which the country has moved in the direction of a managed economy.

(1) Although the number of individual businesses in the United States is in excess of 8 million, a handful of giants dominate the entire system.

(2) A number of industries continue to be characterized by "competition among the few," that is oligopoly. Moreover, another trend—diversification—has become evident as numerous firms have acquired interests in many different industries.

(3) In the several hundred large corporations that form the core of the American industrial economy, ownership has been largely divorced from control. Because the people who own these corporations (the shareholders) have little control over their property, it is misleading to call the system "people's capitalism."

(4) Increasingly the dividing line between public and private enterprise has narrowed. Many firms in the private sector are to a degree

wards of the government (public utilities, common carriers, telephone and telegraph), trading government regulation for monopoly or near-monopoly conditions. Other private firms, particularly those in defense related fields, sell the greatest share of their output directly to the government. Still other private firms are used by the government to conduct various public programs. Thus, in a number of cases the public and private sectors of the economy have become increasingly amalgamated.

(5) One of the most startling changes in the American business and political scene has been lowering of the protective tariff, begun in 1934 by the Trade Agreements Act and extended time after time. Postwar economic stress convinced many nations that trade must be encouraged by lowering tariffs, and this was done in successive steps, though at times reluctantly and with many reservations.

Mankind had now reached the point where it was exploiting physical forces which may or may not have been the greatest it could ever hope to control—forces capable of either destroying life on earth or blessing mankind with health and abundance such as had never before been dreamed of. And yet, in the immediate context, the new physical forces were used primarily for national and ideological purposes. The fundamental military and political fact of the postwar decades, then, was the translation of the new physical forces by the United States and Russia into a mutual nuclear deterrent—"the balance of terror." No previous generation in history had lived under such a sword of Damocles. Perhaps at last this apotheosis of physical force could demonstrate not merely that war is futile—this had long been evident—but that, since it had reached what seemed its logical ultimate, it could be suicidal on the grandest scale in history.

It has become a truism that the world that has been unfolded since the fission of the atom in 1938 would be unrecognizable to the scientist of 1900—let alone the man in the street. This is true not only of physics, biology, meteorology, and perhaps other sciences which only specialists could name, but, most astounding of all, philosophy's view of the universe.

The medieval world and that of the religious reformers was purposive—that is, governed by the will of God, who had a grand design that He was gradually unfolding to mankind. The scientists of the Enlightenment changed all that, and philosophers learned to follow Descartes' view that the universe is intelligible—that knowledge of things (science) could be discerned by their causes, and that it was possible to measure these things. The whole was equal to the sum of its parts, and the whole was determined by the nature and relationship of its parts. These were the terms which were drilled into the young for almost three centuries and are the terms in which most of us still think; we would be lost without them.

The revolution began with the holism of that astounding South African, Jan Smuts, when he proposed that the determining factors in nature and evolution are wholes, such as organisms, and not their constituent parts. In other words, the parts exist "in contemplation of, if not for the sake of, the whole." The biologist talks of immunity, metabolism, ecology, syndrome, homeostasis, and pattern—all terms that describe not a property of matter or quantity, but a harmonious order. Psychologists have their jargon; economists their patterns; anthropologists their cultures; and physical scientists their systems, and their quanta in which mass, energy, time, and distance are all expressed in a single entity. Even teachers of language no longer stress the parts of speech (grammar) but teach communication, the whole of speech including unspoken nuances and the atmosphere in which words are said and heard.

The over-all effect is to restore purposiveness, but not purposiveness in the medieval sense. That lay outside the material universe and anything that man could do or see; ours is in the physical configurations—"not the purpose of the universe, but the purpose *in* the universe." These new concepts are dynamic, that is, they are process, as contrasted to the static concepts of the Enlightenment. In a real sense our world is factual, not rational.

These new concepts have become the reality of our work and world. They are "obvious" to us. Yet, though we take them increasingly for granted, we do not fully understand them. Though we talk glibly of "configuration," "purpose," and "process," we do not yet know what these terms express. We have abandoned the Cartesian world view; but we have not developed, so far, a new tool box of methods or a new axiom of meaning and inquiry. We have certainly not produced a new Descartes. As a result we are in an intellectual and artistic crisis. . . . In the social sciences this shows itself in the glaring discrepancy between our talk of "culture," "personality," or "behavior" and our inability to produce much more than vast collections of empirical data about particular—and therefore largely meaningless—manifestations.... As a result, the very disciplines that are advancing the fastest [as medicine], in which therefore there is the most to learn, are rapidly becoming unteachable.[1]

There is thus a confusion of terms and symbols among the many disciplines because there is no "philosophical synthesis appropriate to the world we inhabit." When it comes it will doubtless not repudiate Descartes but will overcome and encompass him as Einstein's relativity encompassed Newton's gravity. The duality between matter and mind will vanish, if only because of our discovery that by the act of observing a phenomenon we alter it.

While relatively few Americans had more than a vague perception of the nature of the scientific and philosophical changes going on, the uncertainties and confusions frequently affected their daily lives. Consider the polarization of politics that endangered the very existence of the system of political parties.

The genius of American politics lay in the fact that both parties followed the democratic pattern of agreeing on fundamentals, and they were less interested in ideology than in winning elections. Radicals and reactionaries normally remained on the outside, perhaps in small parties composed of their own ilk, leaving the great middle to the two major parties. Within each major party opinion stretched across the ideological spectrum from liberal on the left, through moderate, to conservative on the right. To organize conservatives in one party and liberals in another would, by polarizing them, reduce the necessity for compromise within and between each, increase their intransigence, and bring on an irreconcilable conflict between idealogies. As it was, "principle" was a relative term.

The various elements in each party were enough alike to enable them to unite for a political campaign without leaving very many members in a permanently discontented minority because some "eternal principle" had been rejected by the party. The two-party system, then, can exist only when the reasonably harmonious middle prevails. Of course, the center

---

[1]Peter F. Drucker, "The New Philosophy Comes to Life," in *Harper's Magazine* (August 1957). Much of this treatment is drawn from the article.

shifts to the left through the generations as reformers manage to get their ideas adopted and the struggle passes on to new issues.

Democracy depends for balance on the reciprocal endeavors of liberals and conservatives. The function of liberals is to legislate reform and that of conservatives is to temper and rationalize it. The tragedy of the postwar decades was that the conservatives failed in their mission; instead of offering reasonable amendments they "stood pat" or even joined the reactionaries in seeking to return to the past. The result was that the liberal ideas that had been written into legislation and foreign policy often had rigid, even destructive, results. Indeed, the American party system was becoming decrepit, but no viable alternative parties seemed in sight; the prospect of a division on ideological lines raised the spectre of another 1860.

The assumption by federal and state authorities of ever-increasing responsibilities for public welfare leads into the plain fact that the nation was slowly moving toward socialism—which, by the modern definition, is not the destruction of private enterprise by the imposition of government controls. As pollsters well knew, Americans would often accept something they detested if it were given a harmless name. Accordingly, capitalism was preserved, but at the cost of letting the socialist camel's nose into the national tent under the name of social welfare and federal regulation. Respect for property was bolstered by strengthening unions to the point where the laborer now had a property in his job. Labor had now become conservative and was at times one of the strongest obstacles to making much-needed changes.

During the "Great Debate" that preceded the American entry into World War II, Senator Robert Taft had warned that if the liberals succeeded in their program of aiding Britain the result would be war, a backbreaking debt, commitments to help bring order out of chaos in all the world, and the end of democracy and civil liberties. What was the alternative? The best Taft could offer was Fortress America, an obvious absurdity in the modern world. As it was, not only did most of Taft's prophecies come true but, ironically, the war—and the sweeping assumption of world responsibilities that followed—strengthened the very forces against which the liberals had fought. The alliance between industry and national defense created a "weapons culture" which devoured an outrageous precentage of the federal budget, and had a vested interest in the arms race and in perpetual preparation for war. More than that, as President Eisenhower warned, the nation was in serious danger of being governed by a "military-industrial complex" dedicated to the rape of foreign resources and the hyperbolic amassing of armaments.

Many idealistic liberals in the 1930's had been taken in by Moscow's glowing promises of Utopia, but had been alienated by Stalin's repeated trials and bloody purges. Once bitten, twice shy. It was in great part the horror-stricken moral reaction of both liberals and conservatives to the British and French surrender to Hitler at Munich that implanted "appeasement" in the American mind as not to be permitted under any circumstances. This penchant for taking moral stands also *contributed* (for it was not the only reason) to making anticommunism the shibboleth of American diplomacy and the touchstone by which every public policy was tested.

The result on the part of both Democratic and Republican politicians had been over-promise and under-performance, with consequent loss of credibility. When at last the Vietnam War made clear that the liberal dialectic was sterile and that there was a limit to what American power could encompass, both extreme Left and extreme Right recoiled and adopted something very close to simplistic isolation.

Unfortunately, the words *conservative* and *liberal* had fallen from pedestals of honor into the mud of political contention. The world of this century is as frustrating as any in history and, as it has been said, frustration which produces tantrums in babies can lead to equally irrational fits of rage in adults. The result was seen in the behavior of the Radical Left and the Radical Right—often miscalled Liberals and Conservatives. The Radical Right showed the classical reactionary pattern of desiring to return to the past, and so could more accurately be called Radical Reactionary. The offensives from both extremes threatened to polarize and idealogize American politics and destroy both political parties. It was the most serious clash of extremes since abolitionists and pro-slavery men brought on the Civil War.

These two extremes bore a startling psychological resemblance to each other. They were angry to the point of incoherence. They were morally arrogant, certain that anyone who disagreed with them was evil, or at least deluded by evil men. This made them subscribe to the conspiracy, or devil, theory of history, which held that things went wrong because evil men planned them that way. They believed that it was moral to tell lies in order to advance a moral cause, so their literatures were tissues of falsehoods. they had a simplistic yearning to see all problems as black or white, all choices as "either-or," and to reduce all complexities to least-common denominators. A current quip had it that if a man was concerned about flouride in the water, he was a Radical Reactionary; if about strontium-90 in the milk, he was a Radical Leftist.

To define these extremes as communist or fascist is by no means accurate—at least not in all cases. Actually, most of the extremists knew little about political parties and political and economic theory and cared less; they drew recklessly on the techniques and slogans of either camp; and they used one term or the other as a smear on anyone who disagreed with them. Neither hesitated to undermine civil liberties in attaining its end, which in both cases was the destruction of democracy and the ushering in of its version of the City of God.

Closely related to the propaganda of the Radical Reactionaries, and often a part of it, was the fear-hate relationship of whites toward other races, which inevitably stirred up a similar response on the other side. The United States was to a considerable extent created by minorities— racial, religious, and social—each of which had suffered in one way or another from the legend of inferiority and the blight of prejudice. The fact that a number of the earlier minorities coalesced to form the "white, Anglo-Saxon, Protestant majority"—the WASPS—by no means proved that it would act together; indeed it was rent by rivalries, chiefly social and economic. The existence of minorities had at least contributed to a sort of crude balance in American society and politics. Therein lay a curious paradox that had run through American history. Minority groups were not freely accepted as equals by the majority (and at times actually were deprived of economic and civil liberties), yet they singly or in alliance exercised such powerful and at times decisive political pressures as to make the majority seem like merely another minority.

No less true were the facts that these minorities were sometimes suspicious of one another and were torn by internal rivalries. Each of them in its struggle to win equality for itself tended to try to hamper the others' freedom of expression. Thus no politician was free from such pressures—as for or against Negro segregation, an independent state of Israel, or the appropriation of tax money for direct or indirect use of parochial schools. Except in the South, the "white, Anglo-Saxon, Protestant majority" was reduced to public silence except in matters that could be given an economic slant. This meant only that its private protests and antipathies became more bitter.

The word "discrimination" had come to refer only to the unequal treatment of equals. Discrimination was not confined to the elite. The white laborer and the white sharecropper and tenant farmer feared Negro economic competition and also feared to lose the prestige attached to his whiteness. It was clear, moreover, that discrimination could also arise from religious or social rivalries, fear of strange customs, and the many obscure factors that rise from the dark pool of the subconscious.

Discrimination was "circular" in its effects—that is, it tended to deepen and confirm the traits on which the supposed inferiority was based, with apparent justification for continuing discrimination. Thus there was among the majority a stereotyped view of each minority. The stereotypes for Jews, Japanese, Chinese, Indians, Puerto Ricans, Mexican-Americans, and Negroes differed enormously, but they were still stereotypes. Those for the last two named were rather similar—lazy, untrustworthy, and incapable of acquiring skills. The same stereotype, though few whites realized it, had been in past generations applied by factory owners to their white labor.

It is easy enough to see that the New Deal did not cure all social ills—indeed no "deal" ever will. The New Deal only ameliorated ills to the extent that they did not for some time to come threaten to overturn either democracy or capitalism. Reform was no longer a primary public concern as was shown by the failure of Harry Truman's Fair Deal and, on the domestic front, the quiescent, almost catatonic, years of Eisenhower's administration. No doubt this interval was chiefly due to the renewal of prosperity after World War II and the renewal of the drive into abundance. Nevertheless, these years were marked by the beginning of the Negro Revolution with its non-violent sit-ins and protest marches, and by rumblings of discontent among other minorities—all of them frustrated because of their poverty, their deprivation of civil rights, and their lack of opportunity to share in the promise of America.

The failure to hearken to these rumblings played a part in the Supreme Court's decision to act as the nation's conscience. Since the 1930s the Court had been moving toward greater protection of civil rights, but with the appointment of Earl Warren as Chief Justice in 1953 the Court undertook to move into fields which neither President nor Congress had dared to enter. The Court's decisions particularly affected three areas: (1) widening the civil rights of individuals, including criminal procedure; (2) striking down segregation of the races, especially in schools; and (3) expanding federal power, including the power to enforce legislative apportionment in the states.

As might have been expected the Court's decisions stirred up bitter criticisms. One familiar complaint was that it was not interpreting the true meaning of the Constitution. Rather, it was imposing its own "sociological" view of what form law and society ought to take. The same sort of charge had been made in previous generations when the Supreme Court permitted big business to operate almost unhindered in the twilight zone between nations and states. Strangely enough, the loudest current objections to the Supreme Court's protection of individual rights rose from the Radical Right, which professed to be most concerned with protecting the individual citizen from the encroachments of government. The claim was made that the Court had hampered the police in enforcing the laws, and by the 1960s this had come close to being an item of the general folklore. Certainly it contributed to the rising fear of "crime in the streets."

It made little difference to the public that careful studies by legal bodies and district attorneys disproved this, and that the real problems lay elsewhere. Legislative inertia had prevented bringing the definitions of crime up to date. The result was that many laws were obsolete, unenforceable, or downright unjust. A second problem lay in the failure to put enough money into law enforcement—into professionalizing the police and raising their standards, and overhauling procedures in the courts and district attorneys' offices. Another serious drawback to law enforcement was the way in which it was divided not only among federal, state, county, and municipal agencies, but in which the last named were splintered among an excessive number of jurisdictions in adjoining localities.

The Great Society

John Kennedy entered office in 1961 proclaiming that "we stand today on the edge of a new frontier. . . . The New Frontier of which I speak is not a set of promises—it is a set of challenges." Nevertheless his program took the form of promises: not merely to land a man on the moon, but to renew the war against poverty and disease at home and against tyranny abroad. He faced down the Soviet program of placing missiles in Cuba, but was assassinated before he could do much about his other promises.

His successor, Lyndon Johnson, adopted Kennedy's program and expanded it into what he called the Great Society. For a brief time he was favored by a liberal Congress brought in by the election of 1964, at least partly because the Republicans staked everything on a counterrevolution intended to shear the federal government of power. They sought the support of the states' right South, the "white backlash" in the North, and the "hate groups" of the radical right. They lost.

Johnson was a master politician, skilled in Congressional negotiations, and even before the election he had pushed through various items of Kennedy's program, including a sweeping Civil Rights Act (1964). He now undertook further advances in civil rights, education, health care, and in the war on poverty. Nothing like it had been seen since the first Hundred Days of the New Deal.

Unfortunately, economic troubles began to multiply at home and abroad, then the election of 1966 restored control of the House of Representatives to the Old Guard-Bourbon alliance. Now the Great Society was in deep trouble. Times had changed ominously. National attention was turning uneasily to the escalating war in Vietnam, and to the price inflation which was attributed to the exactions of labor and to the expenditures necessitated by the war and by the Great Society. The Democratic Party was deeply divided, not only between North and South, but over the war in Vietnam.

Another ground for criticism was the plain fact that the Great Society was suffering from indigestion, and there were those who blamed Johnson's administrative ineptitude. A report in December 1966, noted that there were 21 different health programs, 17 for education, 15 for economic development, 12 dealing with urban crises, four for manpower training, and 17 for preserving national resources. The report went on to say:

> The new programs have brought with them a baffling welter of funds, agencies, bureaus, offices, departments and regional representatives within the Administration. At the moment some $15 billion in federal aid is available to state and municipal governments, but it is practically a life's work figuring out where to go for what. The money is distributed among 170 separate programs, funded by 400 different appropriations, administered by 21 departments and agencies, assisted by 150 bureaus. Such is the confusion that when Attorney General Nicholas Katzenbach was asked during a

recent Senate hearing how much federal aid was available to cities, he said $13 billion; the next day Housing and Urban Development Secretary Robert Weaver gave the figure as $28 billion. State and municipal officials find themselves all but buried under paperwork; the city of Oakland, California alone runs 140 federal-grant programs, must keep separate account books for each.[2]

Nevertheless, the Great Society did not collapse because of its organizational failures nor because it was too costly. The country had enjoyed uninterrupted prosperity for the longest time in its history, from mid-1961 to the end of 1968. The gross national product had risen by two-thirds, stocks had risen by half, profits had doubled even after taxes, and the number of millionaires had doubled, from 50,000 to 100,000— but that made all the more tycoons to abhor Johnson. Even the floor under those rated as poor was higher than ever before. No, the collapse had psychological causes—from the frustrations noted above, from the sense of privation among the poor who saw through the television screen into a world of affluence and opportunity denied to them, from the resentments of status groups, and from a revulsion against the Vietnam War.

The President had clearly reached the end of his tether. He had expended his political IOU's, the liberal majority was gone from the House, and Congress (it may have felt) had done sufficient penance for having blocked President Kennedy's program. Johnson was also opposed by the liberal intellectual clique that saw in him the coarse, ribald Texan of legend come to life. Even Johnson's massive liberal accomplishments did not win them. It has been said that liberals distrust nothing so much as success, and love nothing so well as a fallen hero.

Incidentally, a serious effort to extend the Great Society to South Vietnam by trying to give it much the same ideal and material values was a miserable failure; the Vietnamese simply did not have the background that would enable them to appreciate and profit by it, even had they had more time.

The dilemma of Vietnam was not all the creation of Johnson, but was in some part brought about by inherited circumstances. Americans had made it politically perilous to be accused of "appeasement," and the

---

[2]*Time* (9 December 1966), p. 25.

Democratic Party was dedicated to intervention wherever necessary to assure the security of the free world. Previous presidents had set the example of escalation in Vietnam, and in the end, the war got so far out of hand that frustrations, both real and artificial, overshadowed Johnson's social accomplishments by destroying the sense of movement and excitement that had a generation before worked so powerfully in favor of the New Deal.

Presidents Kennedy and Johnson did manage to advance the cause of civil rights for Negroes. But when this did not create educational and economic opportunity the emerging New Left—black, brown, and white—denounced liberalism as outworn and hypocritical and began rioting in the streets and burning down their "ghettos." The excuse was that "nobody listens unless we make the front pages." Their rebellion was against too much central control, and they demanded something called "participatory democracy"—the right to control whatever affected their personal and neighborhood interests—as, for example, to decide whether black children should be bussed into a white community to meet the courts' demands that schools be integrated.

In their campaign against poverty the liberals had stressed the Negro community almost, though not entirely, to the exclusion of the white poor. The latter felt that they labored under much the same lack of educational opportunity and inability to hold well-paying jobs as Negroes, and presently they began to drift away from the Roosevelt coalition. At the same time the blue-collar workers, whom Roosevelt had lifted into the middle class, became fearful of losing their gains. The result was the destruction of the Roosevelt coalition as the dissidents joined the Radical Right in its opposition to "rewarding rioters" by antipoverty programs, and supported "law and order," which to them plainly meant white supremacy.

Once again the quest for the City of God had foundered on the reefs of war. President Nixon was brought into office by a desperate public desire for new answers and because of his promise to put a prompt end to the war—which he did after four years of lackluster negotiations by accepting a cynically undisguised defeat. Aside from this his chief interests were in the Arab-Israeli imbroglio and detente with Russia and Red China.

A serious economic recession began at the same time he came into office and deepened throughout his five and a half years (1969-74). He moralized frequently about domestic problems but did little about them, and that largely devoted to putting the "trickle-down theory" into effect.

The paradoxical inflation that accompanied the recession was less his fault than that of the Vietnam War and perhaps the ineptitude of Congress and the bureaucracy; to be just, inflation was an even worse problem abroad.

Nixon's disgrace and resignation because of the Watergate and concurrent scandals changed nothing on the national scene beyond bringing in a wave of moral outrage which struck out more or less blindly at any target of opportunity. Optimists pointed to this sense of outrage as proof that the American heart was sound and that constitutional guarantees still prevailed. Perhaps so; nevertheless it was obvious that in less than two years after the great denouement the wave of morality was wearing thin.

Chapter 15
The Cold War Era

Proem

The history of the United States in the postwar world was its attempt to escape from the dilemma of power by finding a truly multilateral means of assuring the triumph of its ideals. It had undertaken a lonely responsibility, for even the democracies—whenever the danger seemed to recede from their doorsteps—derided the American attempt and at times actively blocked it. There was a certain plaintiveness in Secretary of State Dean Rusk's question, "Who speaks for Europe?" Perhaps, in looking back, the real motive behind the American effort to unite Europe was not merely to contain Russia but to create a like-minded great power with whom a lonely America could talk.

* * *

Could Americans define their existence without recourse to the expanding frontier [the Open Door] that had formerly provided them with the private property, they used to prove their existence? Could they, in short, define their existence and conceive grand ideas and great ideals without recourse to private property as the sine qua non of democracy, prosperity, and the general welfare? It just may be that the Age of Corporation Capitalism has created the conditions that will enable Americans to answer the question in the affirmative.

(William Appleman Williams)[1]

---

[1]William Appleman Williams, *The Contours of American History* (Chicago: reprint by Quadrangle, 1966), pp. 477-78.

The American, Archetype of the Modern Man. He is mobile, restless. He has largely broken with status and moves . . . up and down the ladder of wealth and class rank, as he moves over large areas, conquering space. He rifles the sciences as he opens up the continent, quenchless in his thirst for experience. He is this-worldly and not other-worldly, with a sharp sense of time and its uses: the objects of his ambition are secular rather than sacred. Accustomed to thinking in terms of the attainable, he is optimistic, with a belief in progress and a respect for technical skills and material success. He is *homo faber*, stamping his imprint on products and on machines that make products and on machines that run machines, and increasingly in the same spirit on art and ideas. He believes in whatever can be touched, grasped,measured. He is a technical man, whose absorption is not with *to what good* but *how*. He is nonascetic, with a taste for comfort and a belief that the means, if not the goal, of life are found in a higher living standard. . . . He is an amoral man of energy, mastery, and power. Above all else, he is a man for whom the walls have been broken down . . . breaking the taboos against knowledge and experience, even at the cost of his soul. Thus the great themes of the Renaissance and Reformation are fulfilled in the American as the archetypal modern man—the discovery of new areas, the charting of the skies, the lure of power, the realization of self in the works, the magic of science, the consciousness of the individual, the sense of the unity of history. These are the themes that have left their mark on modern man.

(Max Lerner)[2]

The Springs of the Cold War

There has been a great deal of argument about the nature of Russian imperialism: is it primarily ideological or nationalist? Regardless of the answer there can be no doubt that the Soviet leaders intended to make ideology the instrument for the subjection of the world, perhaps eventually without the use of military force. It any case it seems certain that Russia was not prepared for war in 1939 and had every desire to avoid it or at least postpone it. The favorite dream of the Soviets was to have the democracies and the fascists kill each other off, but the invasion of Russia by Germany in 1941 put an end to this. All through the war Russia was not only suspicious of and uncooperative with the Allied powers, but was laying the groundwork for seizing control of as many as it could of the nations that lay between it and the Atlantic.

---

[2]Max Lerner, *America as a Civilization* (New York: Simon & Schuster, 1957), pp. 62-64.

The Americans—and the Allies—made a number of blunders during World War II, such as an undue measure of tenderness toward Russian feelings and a sentimental willingness to believe in Russian promises. Roosevelt's insistence that the war was against imperialism was denied by Churchill, who had no intention of presiding over the dissolution of the British Empire. The worst blunder of all, however, was the utter smashing of the German and Japanese economies. These were the two powers most willing and able to resist Soviet imperialism, and the result was that both of them had to be reconstructed so that they could form parts of the wall of containment.

On the other hand Roosevelt must be credited with a list of accomplishments. It was in large part the popular faith in Roosevelt that obtained backing for a war effort the necessity of which—save as a reaction to Japan's attack on Pearl Harbor—a great many Americans never clearly understood. Roosevelt consistently backed the responsible military chiefs, and it was he who had the courage to undertake the development on the atom bomb, one of the major and yet vitally necessary gambles of the war. It was Roosevelt, almost alone among the first-line Allied leaders, who saw that exploitive imperialism must go or the fruits of the war be lost.

It was Roosevelt who wrote *finis* to the historic American policy of isolalation—though in so doing he was reaping the yield of the seed planted by Wilson. Whether or not this was wise is still debated. Finally, the United Nations was the creation of Roosevelt more than of any other man. But, like Wilson, he failed to realize that the success of such an institution depends (like democracy) on fundamental ideological agreement among its members.

Lenin had made it an article of communist faith that imperial aggression is the final stage of capitalism, in which the dying order goes abroad in search of investment opportunities and markets. Of course, in Lenin's view communist imperialism was not only self defense but the inevitable working out of dialectical materialism. This lay behind the Soviet intransigence which by 1947 had clearly assumed a form of aggression that was not open warfare but certainly was not peace, and that was aimed, among other things, at preserving its hegemony over Eastern Europe by ringing down what Winston Churchill called the Iron Curtain. This twilight zone between war and peace was given the name of Cold War by Bernard Baruch.

Despite all the moves toward "peaceful coexistence" and "detente" the condition still persists. Detente, as it has developed, means that *we* stop trying to aid and influence others while the Soviets remain free to stimulate and support communist subversions and "wars of liberation." There is no end in sight; it can come only when the mellowing process now evident in some parts of the communist world becomes an authentic willingness to live and let live. As it is, the Soviets still adhere to their Brezhnev Doctrine, that they have a right to interfere in any socialist country that strays from the path of Soviet communist orthodoxy.

One did not have to be a communist to believe that economic aggression—the world-wide Open Door for trade—had been a motivating factor in America's foreign relations. As certain historians saw it, American capitalism, the most dynamic the world has ever seen, had from the first been faced by the necessity of expanding or perishing, and had used government to that end. A primary need of American capitalism (they said) had been to avoid socialism and preserve the run-away democracy which made possible rugged capitalism with its accumulation of power and pelf. The American forms of capitalism and democracy were grossly wasteful and could be preserved only by continual accretions of resources; moreover, it was essential to furnish a high standard of living to the people in order to assure a stable domestic base for foreign ventures.

By the above thesis, Hay's Open Door Policy and Wilson's struggle at Versailles for freedom of trade guaranteed by a League of Nations were merely attempts to hold world markets open to competition because they knew Americans could dominate them. Far from supporting self-determination of nations, the American objective for more than half a century had been to impose on the world its own form of economic liberalism (oligopoly), which differed markedly from classical liberalism's assumption that free competition would bring about harmony of interests among nations. All this being true, it became evident that American opposition to Japan's Greater East Asia Co-Prosperity Sphere, to German Nazism, and to Russia's communism rose basically from their threat to close large areas of the world to American enterprise.

To maintain its position in the world, it was held, American capital supported whatever regimes would assure stability and permit American exploitation. Obviously, in a precipitously changing world there would be revolutions, and since they were overwhelmingly socialistic and threatened to block private enterprise the United States developed a pathological fear of revolutions. The tendency, therefore, was to assure stability by supporting dictators who would block change. Also, under the guise of assuring freedom and democracy, it occupied countries like South Vietnam which were rich in rubber, tin and tungsten.

The foregoing analysis of the springs of American expansionism was used in whole or in part by the historians who attributed the origins of the Cold War to the United States rather than to Russia. As they saw it, the non-Western world was bound by the chains of ancient social forms and inertial psychologies which must be broken if it was ever to conquer the problem of poverty. Russia was the spearhead of this transformation and must maintain its freedom of action at any cost. Now the United States was giving Russia little choice but to stand up against American expansionism if it was to maintain its social and economic gains and avoid becoming a part of the bourgeoning American economic empire.

As a result they interpreted (and misinterpreted) a number of American moves during and since the war as a part of their view of America's historic pattern. It is entirely reasonable to concede that there were misunderstandings, and that the United States might at times have been more conciliatory. But if one tries to throw the entire blame on the United States he is confronted by a string of inescapable considerations.

The first is contained in Churchill's suggestion that Russia was "a riddle wrapped in a mystery inside an enigma," but that the key might be Russian national interest. It is a credible thesis that the Soviet leaders were far from being the cosmic altruists portrayed by their apologists, but were basically nationalists. The totalitarian practices of the Soviets at home were so different from the Marxism they preached outside that the former could more accurately be called Sovietism. It is therefore quite reasonable to assert that the Soviet leaders saw international communism not as a means of creating a utopian world but as a means of undermining the Western imperial powers and promoting Russian national imperialism. Not since the Moslems swept out of Asia in the seventh century had there been such a menace to civilization, and just as the Moslems inspired the reaction of the Crusades so the Reds stimulated, if they did not actually inspire, the reactions of fascism and the American "rigidity" expressed in the policy of containment of communism and in American thinking during the Cold War.

Second, if one persists in believing in Russian altruism, and so justifies the right of the Communist Revolution to pursue its totalitarian course unhampered, then he is placed in what should be the uncomfortable position of denying the democratic values which the West had been painfully evolving ever since the Middle Ages. Those values have never been completely put into practice, but they do have the virtue of being open-ended so that we can learn to do better.

One need not stop there. The widely acclaimed "brilliant" self-defensive Soviet forays of the Cold War when viewed from another angle were pure aggression: subversions and guerilla wars in numerous countries, the various blockades of Berlin, the seizure of Czechoslovakia in 1948, the invasion of South Korea, the overturning of what could have been a promising balance of power in Vietnam. All these and more—besides the many interferences with legitimate military air flights, the harassing of commerce, and the kidnapping and murders of refugees and others in the West.

Even the Left's charge that American policy was based on cold-blooded and selfish expansionism had its flaws. If this were true, why did the United States seek so diligently to unite Europe? It must have been obvious that a United States of Europe would have its own economic policies, and would be in an excellent position to thwart penetration. Why did the United States retreat from China? Even if control of China did not bring control of Asia it could still have been used to harass Russia. Why did the United States make a stand in South Korea, which in itself was not worth risking World War III? Regardless of his criticisms of American moralism and of its at times regretable results, the objective observer must recognize that the United States was deeply sincere in assuming the responsibility of shoring up democracy against the erosions and assaults of totalitarianism.

Regardless of the validity of the Open Door thesis, the United States gave at the end of the war evidence that it distrusted the Soviet Union by refusing to continue lend-lease or to promise a thumping big postwar loan, and by seeking to erode the system of satellite states the Soviet was building between itself and western Europe. Incidentally, there is here a certain irony when it is remembered that at that very time critics of Roosevelt and Truman were attacking them on the ground that they were selling out Western interests—an attack that by 1950 was to burgeon into McCarthyism's reckless and unfounded accusations that Roosevelt and Truman were secret agents of communism.

Where leftist critics of Roosevelt and Truman erred was in assuming that the Soviets would act like a traditional national state. On the contrary, its Leninist ideology posited that it was a universal state—

therefore any other state that refused to yield to it was an enemy. This was particularly true of the United States because it was a capitalist power, so by Leninist logic was bound to be hostile, devoted to encircling and destroying the Soviets. There was no escape. Even if the United States had adopted Soviet totalitarianism it would still be an enemy unless it were completely subservient to Moscow. The experience of Red China was to demonstrate this.

George F. Kennan, an expert on Russia and later Ambassador to Moscow, forecast Russian attitudes as early as May 1945 in a remarkable paper,[3] and the forecast has been borne out. Russian policy, he said, would seek to obtain Western material support to repair the damages wrought by war and by its own disruptive political and economic actions; and to get the West to recognize its puppet states and thus cooperate in maintaining the fiction of their independence.

In accomplishing these ends the Soviets planned on using Allied— particularly American—illusions as a sailor uses winds; "if he cannot sail directly against them he can at least use their power to tack in general directions contrary to that in which they blow." The Kremlin knew that American views of the Soviets (in 1945) were unsound, but could use them without having the least intention to alter its own attitudes and actions which were based on discourtesy, suspicion, hostility, and arrogant violation of agreements.

Kennan realized that Western illusions and war-weariness were trumps in the hands of the Russians, and apparently had no confidence that the Allies would refuse to give the support the Russians wanted. In fact Molotov at the founding congress of the United Nations at San Francisco warned that if the conference did not give Russia peace and security on its own terms it would seek them elsewhere. That is, it would loose its minions in a reign of terror calculated to bring down the democracies. This was no idle threat, even though military advances toward the West were impossible because they would over-extend Russia's scant resources. The United Nations caved in and gave Russia what it wanted, and the Kremlin did not play its "last real card."

As it turned out Russia was already over-extended and it did make a

---

[3]The paper is printed in the appendix to Kennan's *Memoirs 1925-1950* (Boston: Little, Brown, 1967). The second paper referred to below was anonymously published in Kennan's *American Diplomacy 1900-1950* (Chicago: University of Chicago Press, 1951), under the title "The Sources of Soviet Conduct."

partial retreat by abandoning Greece and Yugoslavia. By 1947 Kennan was urging a policy of "containment" of Russia on Washington. This was set forth in a paper which was not published until 1950, and then anonymously. He pointed out that the Kremlin was swayed only by facts. It was in no hurry, but could take its time, acting with circumspection and, of course, always ready to deceive. It moved constantly toward the goal of world domination and would fill every crevice in the basin of world power, but if there were insurmountable barriers in the way it would wait patiently, meanwhile exploiting every weakness in the opposition.

Kennan's theory was that containment, backed by collective pressures, would make Russia recognize facts and back down. It would also increase the Soviet's internal strains and force it to exercise moderation and thus "promote tendencies which must eventually find their outlet in either the breakup or the mellowing of Soviet power." In time, sovietism would lose its dynamism, and the world would be saved—just as Christendom had been saved by the loss of Moslem dynamism. One part of the containment program was to rebuild Germany and Japan as components of the wall of collective security.

The Truman Doctrine and the Marshall Plan put containment into effect, and it was confirmed by the North Atlantic Treaty and other alliances. When the United States entered on these arrangements based on military and economic aid, it is tenable to suppose that they contributed to Russia's alarm and to its harsh repressions and military adventures by proxy in Korea and Southeast Asia. In any case, containment could succeed only over the long haul; therein lay its weakness, for Americans were not accustomed to patient and long-continued effort in foreign affairs—and the Russians and Chinese knew it and relied on it. As for Kennan, he was appalled by the Truman Doctrine's sweeping promise to oppose communism wherever it appeared and by its reliance on military force. He felt that the most effective and least dangerous way of containing it was by reliance on diplomatic and economic measures.

Dilemmas of the Atomic Age

The Marshall Plan, instituted in 1947, showed that the democracies had learned at least one lesson from the failures suffered after World War I. The plan undertook to rejuvenate Europe's industries, and it succeeded because Europe's nations were already industrialized. The Latin-American demand for a Marshall Plan was treated coolly because the method gave no promise of aiding states that had barely begun to industrialize.

As indicated above, the American postwar aim was to find a multilateral means of defending freedom by reconstructing Europe economically, persuading it to unite in a single trading unit, and eventually in a political unit. Only by integration, it was held, could Europe lay a sound basis for mass production; as for the United States it would thus gain not only a trading partner but an ally in containing the Soviets. A promising beginning was made by the organization of the European Economic Community (EEC) with its Common Market, but Europe refused otherwise to do more than enter the North Atlantic Treaty Organization (NATO) aimed at mutual defense. Eventually Europe's support of even these institutions flagged, and all hope was lost of forming a United States of Europe.

Nevertheless, it seems likely that Truman will be remembered as a great President because he grasped the nettle firmly with a series of remarkable actions intended to gain time—time for Russia to mellow. These actions were the Truman Doctrine, which shored up the strength of Greece and Turkey; the Marshall Plan, which restored the productive capacity and the courage of Western Europe and initiated the drive to unite its economy; the North Atlantic Treaty; the Point Four Program; and the firm resistance to communism by the Berlin airlift and then by the Korean War. Some of these were ventures into fields of international cooperation never before attempted.

Despite these accomplishments, Americans were deluged with complaints about their lack of tact and their aggressive use of power in war, diplomacy, and trade. Europe feared the United States because of its self-confident belief that since it had conquered nature it could also master history, and also because its exercise of power was so often swayed by popular passions and prejudices. If our technology had given us the illusion that we could master history we were disillusioned by the Vietnam experience.

The American economic expansion which accelerated so markedly in the 1920s was resumed after World War II. Backed by mass production's know-how and plentiful capital, it grew so enormously that it seriously alarmed even the democracies lest their economies become mere adjuncts to that of the United States. President de Gaulle of France led the anvil chorus. No doubt animated by personal pique and an inflated view of the significance of France as the rightful leader of the world, he announced that America's economic and military power was so overweening that it had become the world's prime menace. He acted accordingly. He refused to permit Britain to enter the Common Market on the ground that it would serve as an American Trojan Horse, withdrew from NATO's military arrangements, and ordered American troops out of France. Furthermore, he even sought to find ways to tie the Soviets to Western Europe so that the two could act together to trim the eagle's feathers.

DeGaulle may have been an ill-mannered and ill-tempered old man, but he did have some cause for complaint. There can be no doubt that America's efforts to rally support were frequently inept and ill-directed, but there also can be no doubt that even among those presumed to share the same interests the United States had to contend with a point-blank refusal to give anything but advice; the only exceptions were the English-speaking nations, and even they were niggling and halfhearted. The inevitable result was that normally such multilateral means as were found were little more than shams. It was much easier for the democracies to let America shoulder the responsibilities while they stood around and criticized. Not even in the Korean War did they give more than token help, nor did they ever stop trading with the enemy.

The remarkable thing is not that the United States has done so badly but that under the circumstances it has done so well. Regardless of massive waves of abuse and even hatred, it has cleaved to its purpose of protecting freedom—including, of course, its own—its only consolation being that the foreign leaders who abuse it in public very often retract in private. The question is, how long can this go on? Will the time yet come when military disaster or sheer disgust will cause a retreat to Fortress America, leaving the European democracies to shoulder their own burdens?

The postwar period opened with the assumption that the atomic bomb, presumably the ultimate weapon, would enable its possessor to wield unchallenged control over the nations of the world. Accordingly, it was something unprecedented in international power politics when the United States in the Baruch Plan offered to surrender all information and controls over atomic energy to the United Nations.

Apparently Russia accepted the thesis that the Bomb could exercise control of the world, for it rejected the Baruch Plan and strove to hold all the world's communist parties in one hand while it developed nuclear fission with the other. But the 1950s saw the destruction of faith in the Bomb. For one thing, Russia's acquisition of the Bomb produced a "balance of terror" in which neither super-power dared to use it; that weapon, it was to be hoped, would be used only if and when there was a last apocalyptic struggle between the super-powers. The result was seen in a chain of crises in which small nations—Yugoslavia, North Korea, North Vietnam, Israel, and the Arab states—defied the massive retaliation that could be visited on them by the superpowers. And with these defiances it became clear that communism, far from being the private weapon of Russian imperialism, was as many-headed as the countries that espoused it.

Eisenhower's Secretary of State, John Foster Dulles, had threatened massive retaliation (presumably by the Bomb) in case of war. By the 1960's this threat had lost its credibility simply because of its potentiality of destroying civilization. In an attempt to escape from this frightening problem the Kennedy Administration adopted the doctrine of "limited war" and began to rebuild more or less conventional forces. Indeed, this was the theory that had been applied in Korea, though opinions differed as to whether it had been successful; Eisenhower had attributed the end of the war to his atomic threats, while others thought that the death of Stalin was the real reason for the willingness of the Reds to sign an armistice.

The concept of limited war was an attempt to use power in a gingerly manner, and it carried the connotation of "graduated deterrence" or "flexible response." The theory was the "brush-fire" wars being fought by Soviet proxies could be met by just enough military force to quench them before they could spread—or, alternatively to force the enemy to negotiate terms. But, limited war, like massive retaliation, had a built-in fallacy. Since the threat of Soviet nuclear power loomed behind the "brush-fire" wars, the United States faced in only slightly different terms the same dilemma as before—that of yielding supposedly vital spots until it again came up against the choice between total surrender or total nuclear war.

Another fallacy lay in the fact that to the small opponent the war was not limited, but was war to the death. Victory was thus withheld from the superpower unless it would remove the limits—and that would in the end have forced it to face the other superpower with the Bomb. Thus limited war is feasible for a superpower only if it fights by proxy against the proxy of its great rival. Its proxy may be defeated, but that is better than invoking the mutual holocaust brought on by use of the Bomb. If it truly cannot afford to have its proxy defeated, then it must reconcile itself to using its last and most destructive weapon and accepting certain destruction. This was the dilemma that Khrushchev invoked in Cuba in 1962—and backed away from.

Here also was the dilemma faced by the United States in Vietnam, but not recognized until too late. The war lasted for twelve bloody years (the longest war in American history), and graduated response by sophisticated weapons failed to bring a relatively primitive foe to negotiate in any effective sense. The best that could be gotten was an almost cynically disguised withdrawal that was quickly followed by an undisguised communist take-over of South Vietnam.

It is of course possible to say that the United States was handicapped by idealistic scruples and by opposition at home—that it could have won had it exercised its full power. It is also possible to blame defeat on the corruption and weakness of will of the South Vietnamese. In any case one must recognize the significance of Mao Tse-tung's theory of wars of liberation which Ho Chi Minh applied over a stretch of thirty years, first against France in North Vietnam, then against the United States in South Vietnam.

Mao's theory was based on guerrilla revolutions, essentially rural uprisings that would conquer the "reactionaries" of the cities. When communism had taken over most of the nations it would then proceed to "wars of annihilation" that would swamp the industrial powers. The conquest of each rural nation was to be made from within, though of course with aid and direction furnished from outside. Basic to all this was the confidence that, if the democracies should intervene, their people did not have the patience or stamina to see a long struggle through, and would finally agree to a peace, no matter how humiliating.

The gradual disengagement of the United States from Vietnam did not obscure the realization that the country had been involved in a war that had little relation to its national security, and no relation to national survival. The reasons for American intervention will doubtless be argued by historians and others for decades. Close to the event, arguments focused around polar positions: (1) that American intervention in the war was a logical outcome of the warped values of American society, the expression of a sick society; (2) that American intervention was the result of a well-meaning, but misguided, attempt to help the South Vietnamese and contain communism; consequently it was not an indictment of the whole of American society.

Aside from the discussion over the reasons for American

involvement, it was already clear that the war had had a profound impact on American society. By the time of the withdrawal in 1973 the war had cost the United States over 46,000 combat deaths, more than 303,000 wounded, leaving a legacy that will remain with the country for decades. In economic terms the war by one estimate had cost the nation $138 billion and a severely strained economy. Beyond these measurable costs, the war alienated the young and helped turn their energies to a number of anti-institutional movements; convulsed the American system of higher education; turned many Americans—young and old—from idealism to cynicism; and eroded the trust and confidence of the public in the workings of government.

The United States had dedicated itself to the preservation of freedom and democracy and had been forced to use power to that end. Any other course would have been suicidal. Nevertheless, it was continually confronted by dilemmas that, whether it acted or not, earned distrust, if not hatred. If it did not intervene to support democratic elements, it was accused of injuring the democratic fight for security and supporting fascism or communism; if it did intervene, it laid itself open to recriminations by all those who felt themselves injured.

The history of the United States in the postwar world was its attempt to escape from the dilemma of power by finding a truly multilateral means of assuring the triumph of its ideals. One American purpose, of course, was to use the most effective means to save itself and its democratic way of life. Few Americans believed that the world would suddenly go democratic, but they hoped to block totalitarianism so that the nations could move gradually and peacefully toward democracy and the conquest of their tremendous social and economic problems. In line with democratic tolerance of everything that is not itself intolerant, an intolerant totalitarianism could not be permitted to grow and spread.

Americans had feared power, perhaps because of a vague feeling that ideals imposed by force result in their negation. At any rate Americans had often viewed the use of power as immoral, even before the Vietnam War taught that power not only had its limitations but could have immoral results. Unfortunately this sense of the ironical results of the use of power did not always influence policy, but in a surprising number of cases the United States did seek to limit the use of its power lest it promote jealously and frustrate essential cooperation among nations.

Most American policies were voluntarily subjected to the searchlight of world opinion in the United Nations. Inter-American conferences, long criticized as rubber stamps for United States policy, were becoming, though not consistently, more nearly representative of hemispheric opinion. Every effort was made to unite Western Europe, not merely to confront Russia by unassailable power, but because a united Europe could represent continental interests in democratic councils better than could a score of weak states. Moreover, a united Western Europe should be better able to carry the responsibility which must go with the independence (from America) to which Europeans aspired.

And here may have been a little-recognized key to American actions. The United States had undertaken a lonely responsibility, for even the democracies—whenever the danger seemed to recede from their doorsteps—derided the American attempt and at times actively obstructed it. There was a certain plaintiveness in Secretary of State Dean Rusk's question, "Who speaks for Europe?" No meaningful dialogue could be carried on with a Europe divided among rival states, even though they may have shared the same basic principles as the United States. Perhaps, in looking back, the real motive behind the American effort to unite Europe was not merely to contain Russia but to create a like-minded great power with whom a lonely America could talk.

Technological Imperialism

"Fifteen years from now it is quite possible that the world's third greatest industrial power, just after the United States and Russia, will not be Europe, but *American industry in Europe.*" Thus did J. H. Servan-Schreiber, the French publishing tycoon, begin his book, *The American Challenge* (1967). And yet American investments in Europe amounted to only about $20 billion and U.S.-owned companies did only about 5 percent of Europe's business. In theoretical science and engineering Europe could, it was often said, do more with bits of wire and glass than America could do with its up-to-date laboratories. It was Europeans who had made most of the basic advances in physics, chemistry, and medicine, and had given the world the automobile, radar, jet engines, helicopters, hovercraft, vertical-take-off planes, dacron, stretch hosiery, and a thousand other things that the average American thinks of as his own invention, including atomic energy.

Why then this European alarm? In an earlier chapter we examined the interwar aspects of the American economic invasion of the world and named some of the reasons why Europe lagged behind. Above all, it became evident that Europeans often did not know how to translate their scientific discoveries into practical sellable products, and even when they accomplished this they did not know how to organize and market. It was in these fields that the Americans laid the basis for the acute stage of the invasion which Servan-Schreiber warned would take over the continent.

European businessmen, of course, had long been aware of their handicaps, but the dead hand of the past held them down. Even when they adopted American methods it seemed to be the Americans who profited. Was no European country large enough to offer a mass market? Very well, six of them joined in the Common Market: Americans welcomed this, for it enabled their factories in one country to sell in the others. Did France prohibit Americans from buying into one of its industries? The Americans cheerfully bought into one of Germany's— and sent its goods across the border. Did de Gaulle put a stop to American investment in France? The Americans simply sold stock to willing Frenchmen—and dried up capital resources for French enterprises. Did a socialist state nationalize a U.S.-owned industry? The managers and technicians emigrated and set up shop elsewhere, their skills thus lost to the former host. Was there complaint that American companies brought over too many American managers? The Americans recruited the cream of Europe's young men, trained them superbly in the United States and other parts of the world, gave them unexcelled pay and fringe benefits— and sent them back to Europe to cut the business throats of their countrymen.

What could Europe do? Servan-Schreiber proposed an all-out effort to copy American oligopoly, basing it on combinations of the largest corporations. This would mean making Britain the industrial headquarters of Europe; de Gaulle took care of that by vetoing Britain's entry into the Common Market (it was admitted after de Gaulle's death). As a matter of fact, Europe was not badly off for the moment, for the threat was primarily to its prestige, and American-trained managers and specialists might well in the long run accomplish for Europe the very ends of that Servan-Schreiber desired. Americans may not have had a well-rounded view of capital's duty to society, but they had learned thoroughly Henry Ford's dictum that if a manufacturer wished to sell his product he must create a market by paying his workmen enough so they could buy. Europe's standard of living and its base of capital equipment were rising at a more rapid rate than those of the United States, though they still had plenty of room for improvement. Meanwhile, the United States was blowing up its production in warfare, or spending it in space programs of doubtful value to the taxpayer and consumer.

The real danger to Europe lay in the fact that this economic explosion sought out the highest profits, blissfully ignoring the dangers of imbalance. Unplanned and uncontrolled, it had found national and international authorities much the same sort of twilight zone between states and federal government that it had enjoyed in the United States until the New Deal. The result might well be a crash like that of 1929— only so catastrophic that mere national adminstrations could not deal with it. Year by year American enterprise continued its reckless expansion, relentlessly accumulating an annual surplus of about $30 billion, but refusing to invest a reasonable part of it in building a sound social base either at home or abroad—that is, in the low-income business of rehabilitating cities, providing low-rent housing, and restoring forests, fields, streams, and air. Here, it was feared, was a classical illustration of power without responsibility, which Servan-Schreiber warned would be "dangerous for America and disastrous for the world."

Still, there was another side to this; indeed, there was a considerable dichotomy between American official policy and that of its business operators. Unlike traditional imperial powers, the United States strove earnestly to prevent American enterprisers from unreasonable exploitation of foreign resources and labor. On the contrary, because of its faith that the emerging nations could be modernized peaceably it exported capital—much of it donated—and technicians. Naturally, the intention was not purely altruistic. American business and labor leaders approved of this because they wished to maintain production by opening markets for goods, and there was an overall desire to strengthen the free world against communism. But there was a growing realization that American economic health was dependent on the economic health of the world, and vice versa. And it was realized that only in a healthy world can freedom survive.

True enough, there were blind spots, and there were failures in creativeness and performance. Many Americans assumed that because capitalism had worked for them, it must work for everyone else. They identified capitalism with democracy, and socialism with communism. They often failed to realize that America was great because it had long had open-ended freedom to change and develop.

This new form of imperialism, as had frequently been pointed out, was one of attraction far more than of force. (Some elements of the same phenomenon were evident in the great days of Rome, France, and Great

Britain). The American might be distrusted, even hated, but he was admired and imitated, and by no one more than by his mortal enemy the Russian. To be an American, said Max Lerner, "has become, along with Communism and in rivalry with it, a key pattern of action and values. So summary a conquest of the world's imagination, never before achieved without arms and colonization, is proof of an inner harmony between America and modern spirit."

Chapter 16
Power and Illusion

Proem

The Lockean concept of property as the rock of good order and the Marxist concept that it is the root of all evil are equally erroneous. There are other sources of unjust and overweening power than property, as we are beginning to realize. The present challenge is to find new ways of ensuring the tensions so essential to limiting power and to the survival of democracy.

*   *   *

Abundance Revolutionizing the World. We have been historically correct in supposing that we had a revolutionary message to offer but we have been mistaken in our concept of what that message was. We supposed that our revelation was "democracy revolutionizing the world," but in reality it was "abundance revolutionizing the world"—a message which we did not preach and scarcely understood ourselves, but one which was peculiarly able to preach its own gospel without words.

(David Potter)[1]

---

[1]David Potter, *People of Plenty: Economic Abundance and the American Character* (Chicago: University of Chicago Press, 1954), p. 134.

The Twentieth Century Revolution is far more than a demand of the peoples of the world for self-government. It is also a demand that cultural and material resources shall no longer be the exclusive property of a few people or a few nations but shall become of service to all. Not only did the United States father this concept, but its story has been the history of the quest to fit the evolution of the idea to the moral values of human dignity and freedom which it shares with the democratic wing of Western Civilization and which it believes are eternal.

* * *

History does not forgive us our national mistakes because they are explicable in terms of our domestic politics. If you say that mistakes of the past were unavoidable because of our domestic predilections and habits of thought, you are saying that what stopped us from being more effective than we were was democracy. If that is true, let us recognize it and find something to do about it [before we excuse ourselves] into complete disaster.

(George Kennan)[2]

Abundance and Power

The clearest statement in the eighteenth century of the idea of progress was set down by the Marquis de Condorcet (Marie-Jean-Antoine-Nicholas Caritat), the child of the Enlightenment who perished a victim of that other child of the Enlightenment, the French Revolution. As he saw it, mankind, led by France, England, and America would approach perfection. Americans agreed with him that they were "acting for all mankind"—that on them rested the hope of liberalism. And yet in their thinking they sometimes confused progress with prosperity and power.

Marx and Lenin regarded the private holding of property as the basic evil throughout history and preached that perfection would come with its abolition. Lenin held that since communist societies are unselfish they cannot be oppressive, cannot build empires, and cannot begin wars; it is the capitalist enemy which forces them to these extremes. Hence when Russian and Chinese communists split (at least for the nonce) it was essential for each to accuse the other of having departed from the true faith.

---

[2]George Kennan, *American Diplomacy 1900-1950* (Chicago: University of Chicago Press, 1951), p. 73.

The fathers of communism had quite ignored the fact that there is no such thing as a completely disinterested self—that fear, envy, hatred, desire for prestige, and, especially, avidity for power can be even more corrupting than the craving for pelf. Liberals get around this fact by seeking a balance of competitive interests in the search for both power and pelf, and our educational system is directed to teaching the young to accept this as a means of social discipline.

This has become so routine that we may even have lost sight of the reason behind it. Our successess have all too often blinded us to the truth that they have been due in large part to factors outside ourselves. Ever since the founding of the English colonies Americans have been given to proclaiming their freedom from Old World ills—that here we are making a new start, building a society free from the old trammels of privilege and the corruptions of power. Not only did this ignore the real advances toward freedom being made in Europe, but it ignored the dilemma inherent in any attempt to use power to live up to our claim. We had inherited enough of Europe's ills—or rather of original sin—to subvert our boasted innocence if we honestly tried to be guided by it; if we did not try, then we only proved ourselves no better than the world from which the ancestors had fled.

The result is that our loud claims of innocence failed to conceal our doubts, and doubt and guilt have become familiars of our history. The framers of the Constitution were more realistic than their successors. They accepted the proposition that human beings are filled with depravity, and they sought to block its expression.

It may well be questioned that American ingenuity and private enterprise—and consequently power—would have exceeded those of half a dozen other nations had it not been for four advantages which it is too often the custom to ignore or play down.

(1) The settlement of the English colonies came at a moment when European institutions and technology had evolved to the point where it was possible to undertake the political unification and economic development of a continent.

(2) The United States, even in its infancy, had ready to hand a rich and virgin realm which could be exploited by the available techniques.

(3) The comparative isolation of the United States from the disruptive and expensive rivalries of the rest of the world gave it the time in which to work out its own destiny.

(4) The relative weakness of federal and state governments and the

absence of certain restrictive European institutions, such as mercantilism and the guild system, which strait-jacketed European commerce and manufactures. In other words, the relative lack of privileged classes (either of politics, capital, or labor) in the new continent and the superabundance of natural resources operated together to build up a social and political system which not only promoted the skimming of the cream but measured it out for a large proportion of the people.

The natural riches of the North American continent have vitally influenced American psychology. The first and most obvious effect was the growth of what Stuart Chase called the concept of infinity. Until the verge of our own century Americans were literally incapable of grasping the idea that there is any limit to our natural resources. The challenge to Europe's prodigal sons was irresistible. They were possessed of a furious yearning to conquer and strip nature, to reduce it to order and usefulness.

In Europe developing capitalism found savings essential for the purchase of machinery, raw materials, and transportation equipment, and so glorified thrift as the road to wealth and the respect of the community. In America, however, the concept of thrift and the concept of infinite resources have been at war. Those who favored thrift found themselves undersold by those in haste to be rich. Regulation of such wasteful methods would have seemed wise, but our federal and state governments had been deliberately molded to prevent them from interfering with private business. The concept of infinity won. Thrift was found chiefly in activities where cash had to be paid out for materials, and even there its hold was tenuous. Its safest retreat was found in children's copybooks.

Americans think of themselves as liberal and forward-looking. This concept is ordinarily true in the material aspects of our life, but it does not contradict the basic conservatism of our society, made possible because our abundance does not force us to find fundamentally different solutions to our problems. We change our machines and our styles of dress more easily than our mental and moral and social outlook. Our political rivalries have not been between conservatives and true liberals, but in a sense between conservatives and ultraconservatives. Our ancestors sensibly asked themselves why they should plump for great changes when moderate changes in the distribution of our great natural wealth would solve their problems.

Conservatism had other legitimate origins. The Calvinist point of view dominated the colonists, whatever their theology. With a continent begging to be raped they could scarcely avoid regarding themselves as chosen of God, and they desired only to be let alone to exercise the individual responsibility that Calvin had made the basis of his system. Calvinist standards of success could apply only to a limited few in the bitter European economic struggle, but America's riches made possible their attainment by more people. John Calvin and not Adam Smith deserves to be canonized as the patron saint of American chambers of commerce and businessmen's clubs.

Our conservatism was strengthened in yet another way by our environment. The isolation and insecurity of the first settlers bred within them a fierce desire to hold on to the habits and beliefs of the homeland, altered only by the particular theologies or ambitions that had brought them to America. They clung to the moral and emotional content of their heritage long after material conditions had outmoded them, by setting up a tight little society, based on state churches and a landed and merchant aristocracy that attempted to enforce religious dogmas and social distinctions. The battle was joined from the beginning over the degree of change that was necessary and advisable. The defeated in any generation found it possible to move on west to new scenes where perhaps they in turn could become the successful and relatively privileged ultraconservatives.

This desperate clinging for comfort to the old ways in the midst of new conditions has accentuated the natural tendency to hold to a body of theory that is obviously contradicted by practice. On the frontier, where life was so radically different that it dissolved the social pattern into new and more democratic forms, people desperately sought an anchor in the religious dogmas and emotions and the antiscientific prejudices that they had brought with them. The split between ideas and realities led to astounding illogicalities directly traceable to wishful thinking. When morality loses vital connection with facts, there is a tendency to offer legality as a substitute. Legality becomes a matter of technical adherence to laws, while at the same time it shrewdly defies their spirit. Injustice can then be rationalized on the ground that no law is being violated. The history of our ancestors' relations with the Indians is a case in point.

Closely related to the phenomenon of conservatism is the failure of Americans to develop hard and fast class consciousness, at least outside the slaveholding areas. Abundance made possible an expanding economy, and this multiplied opportunity and minimized the class struggle even after the rise of industry. It remains to be seen whether the looming end of our economic expansion will impose the Marxist class struggle on us, or we will find a way around it. Certainly mass production gives us the means if we have the will and intelligence to use it.

Of course the problem of property may never be settled. The Lockean concept of property as the rock of good order and the Marxist concept that it is the root of all evil are equally erroneous. Jefferson's belief that a citizenry should be made up of small landholders is no longer feasible, at least in the sense he meant. Anyhow, there are other resources of unjust and overweening power than property, as we are beginning to realize when we look at executive aggression on the rights of the citizen, at soulless bureaucracies, and computerized prying into private affairs. The present challenge is to find new ways of ensuring the tensions so essential to the survival of democracy.

Abundance had another effect on American psychology. As we have suggested before, our social problems could be ameliorated by drawing on our abundant resources so that it was not necessary to redistribute goods on an equitable basis. This bred the illusion that problems are easily solved, when actually they were only put off, so that today we are faced by the problem of how to deal with an apparently irreducible class of paupers.

There was another and even more appalling penalty. The illusion that problems could be easily solved convinced us that they could be just as easily handled in other societies. This illusion lay, in considerable part, at the root of the tragic belief that if democracy could be exported it would prove to be a panacea for all the world's ills. It is only recently that we have become aware that democracy in itself is no immediate cure-all for either domestic or foreign ills.

Worse yet, every scientific and technological triumph only thrusts on us the necessity of making choices—foreign and domestic—that seem to contradict our fundamental democratic beliefs. Domestically we seem unable to reconcile individualism, freedom of opportunity, and the work ethic with the existence of a large class of unemployed and unemployables. The traditional pursuit of happiness is for an unattainable goal because it can be realized neither in nor out of society. In society we are subjected to spiraling pressures such as the military draft, computerization, and the heavy hand of bureaucracy. Out of society, the pursuit is even more hopeless because the individual cannot survive without the mutual aid of companions.

Scientific and technical triumphs and the power they bring carry yet another penalty. Responsibility for world order, security, and economic health are made increasingly burdensome not merely by communist intransigence but by the resentments of those who envy our power and prosperity but carp at any and every move we make. Moreover, every step toward carrying out our responsibility for world order and security imposes the necessity of creating more power in the form of bigger and sharper weapons—another reason for bitterness both at home and abroad.

The clear, and unfortunate, fact is that the supposed mission to implant democracy throughout the world was based on a fallacy. Our own democracy, if viewed dispassionately, is seen to have reached its high degree of fruition chiefly because of our abundant resources—only partly because of our institutions. David Potter suggested that the real message we had to offer was "abundance revolutionizing the world."[3] This does much to explain why we have all but universally failed in our efforts to implant democracy abroad. Even where the abundance of land and raw materials exist the people are not psychologically adjusted to exploit them in the American manner, nor will they be for a long time, if ever.

The conditions outlined above give pause to our belief in progress, and make us give uneasy heed to the philosophers of history who have warned that every empire, every culture, is doomed to decay. The thoughtful man is forced to wonder whether there is such a thing as progress, even in the cosmic sense.

It seems reasonable to attribute to the environment much of the American penchant for violence both individually and as a nation. The struggle against the Indian was not only violent but it warped the pioneer entrepreneur's views of morality and property. Even apart from that, nature itself was violent and had to be met with violence. When law had not been implanted men had to find justice for themselves—to carry their law on their hips. Many Americans thus formed the belief that "nothing living can cross me and get away with it." Such a psychological state is not to be overcome in a single century. Beyond even these factors was the *anomie* bred in immigrants by their frustrations in battling with strange surroundings, hostile neighbors, and unknown customs. All in all, it is no cause for wonder that in adjusting to the world around them

---

[3]*People of Plenty*, p. 134.

with its insistent pressures for conformity, many Americans flouted the law or found ways to circumvent it.

It is ironical that this nation was born in a violent effort to confirm or implant institutions that would make violence unnecessary, and that in so doing it fostered the irrational violence of modern warfare. The careful, almost chivalrous, parade-ground battle tactics of Europe had been developed to substitute etiquette for the indiscriminate slaughter of the religious wars; with these had come the rule that war was a test of strength, not of right and wrong, for it was evident that wars fought for principles could end only with complete collapse. War was the business of professionals, and civilians were excluded.

The Americans, both Patriots and Loyalists, fought for principle and fought with the complete lack of comprehension to be expected in such a wilderness, tossed civilized rules aside and returned to the savage sixteenth century. Like the Indians, they refused to stand up and be shot, but hid behind trees and fences. All too often they flouted professional courtesies and fought to kill; they hanged civilians on the opposite side and plundered civilians on both sides. Civilians, in fact, took pot shots at the regulars and gathered in guerrilla bands to fight and plunder. Prisoners of war were sometimes slaughtered or abused, and conventions regarding prisoners were broken. Worst of all they revived the horrors of ideological warfare. War was no longer a chivalric game for a mere test of strength, but was fought to win. One can see how the practices of the American Revolution led on one hand to the moralism of Woodrow Wilson and on the other to the subversiveness of the Central Intelligence Agency.

To sum up, we have become apostles of waste and superficiality because these have at times actually been practical, workable national programs. The consequent drain on our natural resources is rightly viewed with alarm by an increasing number of observers. But what is the significance of all this? Paradoxically, it means that for the first time in history democracy has a fighting chance to win in the age-old battle with tyranny. The riches of North America bred a society in which abundance took the place of scarcity; for the first time privilege could not snatch all the economic power for itself and tread down the common man.

Democracy came into its own, and with it came the atmosphere of freedom in which science and technology find the best climate for growth. Until 1900 the United States was too busily engaged in conquering the wilderness to do much in science, but it did excel in technology. However, the riches of America operated to extend much of the same atmosphere of freedom to the rest of Western Civilization, and there science flourished amazingly. Moreover, these riches gave to England, the champion of emerging democracy, the strength to survive.

Europeans have been among the most dynamic people known to history, and they profoundly affected the Americas—not merely the United States—and in turn were profoundly affected. The result was to give to Western Civilization some of the characteristics which distinguish it most sharply from the Africa and the Asia of the recent past. Here are some of the ways in which the Americas have influenced Western Civilization:

(1) Their gold and silver paid for the rise of the Spanish Empire and precipitated the early stages of modern struggle between autocracy and developing democracy.

(2) Their resources promoted the rise of the British Empire and brought its first phase to a close with the independence of the colonies.

(3) They furnished an escape for the surplus and discontented population of Europe.

(4) They furnished the atmosphere of freedom which fostered democracy, and gave the first serious blow to special privileges in government and society.

(5) They applied scientific technology to the enormous natural resources and developed modern mass-production methods, which make possible a higher standard of living.

(6) They twice interfered decisively in world wars and today furnish such force as is being brought to bear in the struggle for democracy.

The United States has played much the most important role in all but the first of the above six areas of influence. It originated largely in the attempt, conscious or not, on the part of its people to realize the utopian dream of building a perfect society—what the first settlers thought of as the City of God. The dream can never reach full realization, but the objective has been a stimulus to unprecedented experiments and accomplishments. With its mass-production techniques and its insistence that the end of government and industry is to serve the whole community, the United States has permanently revolutionized the ways of the world.

From the 1600's when the settlers began to build their City of God, Americans have believed that they had a world mission. By 1776, when Tom Paine struck off his impassioned plea for American independence, he was able to define this mission as one to provide a refuge for freedom and prepare an asylum for mankind. From this it was an easy step to the historic definition: that in the democratic process Americans had found a universally applicable way of life and that their function was to perfect it and serve as an example that could eventually be followed by the rest of the world. It was inevitable that there should be aberrations, especially those in the 1840's and 1890's, and also the perilous attempts in this century to impose democracy on others.

But out of all this had come the Twentieth Century Revolution, which is far more than a demand by the peoples of the world for self-government. It is also as we have said before—a demand that cultural and material resources shall no longer be the exclusive property of a few people or a few nations but shall become of service to all.

History Does Not Forgive Us Our National Mistakes

In 1947 the United States began for the first time in its peacetime history a policy of positive cooperation with others in the search for active means of preserving freedom. Its actions so frequently have been denounced as shortsighted, aggressive, or downright diabolical that it is worth repeating the words of the London *Times*, no uncritical admirer of the United States:

> No nation has ever come into the possession of such powers for good or ill, for freedom or tyranny, for friendship or enmity among the peoples of the world, and . . . no nation in history has used these powers, by and large, with greater vision, restraint, responsibility and courage.

Alexis de Tocqueville, writing in the 1830's, had an encouraging word about our democracy—and a word of warning. As he put it, the people of a democracy, surrounded by demagogues, refuse to undergo privations or inconveniences even to attain the rational ends to which they agree. However, once the democracy realizes its mistake it can regain the path of reason because the majority rules. Then came the caveat: *"But a democracy can attain truth only as the result of experience; and many nations may perish while they are awaiting the consequences of their errors."*

The foregoing is intended as a bittersweet opening for what follows. Despite our successes—and they are many—our direct problems in foreign relations have, as George Kennan points out, risen from our national mistakes. Let us state at the outset some of the sources of our national misunderstandings.

(1) Ideology, idealism, morality—call it what you will—is not an infallible guide to a just society or a peaceful world and, ironically, can result in its opposite; its true role is to serve as a reference point as we engage in give-and-take with others whose opinions and cultures when rationally upheld are as much entitled to respect as our own.

(2) Mistakes cannot be cancelled out; they set forces in motion and create new conditions that have to be met on their own terms. We must live forever with the consequences.

(3) Raw power is not a reliable substitute for thoroughly informed intelligence; indeed power can be turned into a self-defeating force as in jujitsu—as we learned in Vietnam; so can rigid morality and raw, uninformed intellect—as Wilson learned, or should have learned, at Versailles. Decisions should be made with a full understanding of all the factors and possible consequences, including a calculation of the rationally acceptable costs—economic, psychological, and moral.

At no time in this book has the claim been made that democracy is a cure-all. More than that it depends on perilously delicate tensions that are dangerously subject to destruction by enemies, by selfish interests, by blunders or miscalculations, or by the operation of more or less accidental forces. Perhaps the chief danger among these arises from the fact that in a democracy decisions may be made, or put off, by the lowest (or a low) common denominator of the electorate—that the will of the people is followed even when it expresses a shortsighted demand for present pleasure at the expense of eventual disaster.

This is illustrated with alarming clarity in the conduct of democratic diplomacy in this century, and this deserves more than a modicum of space. World War I was the fatal act that destroyed the delicate balance of power and seemed to predetermine World War II. But the sole responsibility was not Europe's. The American illusion of isolation caused us to ignore the signs of coming world conflict and to do nothing about it during the twenty years that the world hung on the edge of the abyss. But this was not all, for we may be justly accused of having made positive contributions toward bringing on the age of conflict. The American democratic ideology played a share in creating unrest among the European masses. Its food and raw materials sometimes undercut those in Europe and bred economic dislocations. The threat of mass production techniques, which demanded great reasources and marketing areas and called for the integration of nations, imperiled Europe's existing political structure and helped to convince its statesmen and financiers that they must insulate their countries by conquests of territory, raw materials, and strategic bases.

But putting all this aside there remains the fact that the tremendous power of the United States thrust responsibility upon it whether or not it recognized the fact, and to the United States must go a share—perhaps the biggest share—of responsibility for not having acted to prevent the war or, once it started, not having moderated its course and consequences. Unfortunately, the United States did not recognize that its welfare hinged on peace and stability as vitally as did the welfare of Europe—that the mere possession of power cast a burden of responsibility on the nation. Neither the American people nor more than a few of its leaders were even aware that there was danger of war.

It had long been supposed that a bankrupt nation could not carry on war, and this disposed Japan to peace in 1905. In World War I it became evident that war could be prosecuted as long as raw materials held out and the military organizations could be preserved. Indeed, World War I demonstrated that so far as these factors were concerned war could be carried—and was being carried—to and beyond the point of irrationality. The only limiting factor was what the people would bear. Hitherto foreign affairs had been shaped by the heads of states and political leaders, and representative parliaments had usually followed their judgment. Now the governments of the democracies faced the test of whether they could actually continue on the course they had begun. Walter Lippmann[4] laid his finger on "the malady of democratic states" which made a rational peace impossible. This was the "devitalization of the governing power." By 1917 the Allies were making sacrifices so irrationally beyond possible gains that the weaker governments faced collapse and even on the more powerful the strain became unbearable.

War had become hyperbolic, yet the leaders were unwilling to negotiate peace. They therefore asked the people for yet greater exertions and sacrifices, "democratizing the conduct and aims of the war by pursuing total victory and total peace"—unrealistic aims that catered to the unsophisticated emotionalism of the masses.

---

[4]Walter Lippmann, *Essays on the Public Philosophy* (Boston: Little, Brown, 1955), refer to chapter 1.

Lippmann went on to point out that the mass of people are not qualified to govern and cannot govern. All they can do is say Yes or No. Mass opinion is too often shaped by emotions, prejudices, and bad advice, so that where it dominates there is "a morbid derangement of the true functions of power"—which is to exercise judgment, moderation, and foresight. If this is not remedied it may well bring about the downfall of the West.

The effect of this derangement was seen at the Versailles Conference of 1919. The Allies had obtained public consent to prosecute the war by making it a war of vengeance dedicated to the utter destruction of Germany. Wilson had sold the war to the American people as a great moral crusade, and so—at least for the moment—they demanded a Wilsonian world, governed on revealed moral principles as formulated and enforced by international agreements. It is difficult to say which program was the more destructive; at any rate the world fell between the two stools and the effect was perhaps even more destructive than either alternative would have been.

We Americans knew little about foreign conditions, so regarded them as simple, and consequently amenable to simple moral solutions. When this was proved to be wrong the American people washed their hands of responsibility and the European peoples returned to their quarrels. During the Long Armistice chaotic political and economic conditions strengthened the totalitarians and encouraged their aggressions. They could have been stopped, but only by armed action or its threat, and the people of the democracies refused to bear the burden of armaments—nor did any outstanding democratic leader demand it except Winston Churchill.

In World War II the democracies again cited "the people to paroxysms of hatred and Utopian dreams." Once again the promise was made to destroy the evil enemy. The fatal choice was made between victory with unconditional surrender or a negotiated peace aimed at reconciliation. We know the result. Europe had to be reconstructed economically, and Germany and Japan had to be restored to power as parts of the wall of containment around Russia.

Now of course the masses can and do make right decisions—such as approving the Marshall Plan—but their opinion is normally formed with glacial slowness unless suddenly made incandescent by some Pearl Harbor. On the other hand such instances of incandescence are just as likely to result in wrong decisions, as after the blowing up of the Battleship *Maine* in Havana Harbor.

Oftentimes even the leaders fall prey to moralism, as did Wilson; or to sentimentalism as did Roosevelt in viewing Stalin and the undoubtedly heroic defense of the Russian people. Another of Roosevelt's sentimentalisms was about Chiang Kai-shek; eventually the China experts who reported the truth were to fall prey to Joe McCarthy's vendetta. It is worth observing that Churchill did not share Roosevelt's sentimentalism about Stalin or Chiang; his sentimentalism was directed at prolonging the rule of empire, and in the end this also had a destructive effect.

The foregoing treatment of unrealistic emotionalism, prejudice, moralism, and sentimentalism leads us to the examination of a disheartening paradox in the history of democracy. Over two thousand years ago Plato advocated what he called the Noble Lie: that the people must be deceived for their own benefit. Indeed there are times when deception must be used if the democracy is to follow a line vitally necessary to its survival. Note how in 1940 and 1941 Roosevelt took one step after another toward war, each one solemnly proclaimed as the last and each one grudgingly approved by the people, until suddenly the Japanese swoop in Pearl Harbor cleared the scales of sentiment and of good intentions from American eyes. Another instance is seen in the way in which both Davis and Lincoln stoutly denied for so long that slavery was the cause of the Civil War; the former because he did not dare to alienate foreign sympathy, and the latter because he did not dare alienate the border slave states.

Two more instances come to mind, not of the Noble Lie but of deliberate violation of democratic principles. One was John Adams' sturdy refusal to yield to the overwhelming public clamor for war against France. The other was Lincoln's unconstitutional suspension of the writ of habeas corpus, asserting that he would not let the Constitution stand in the way of the freedom it had been established to preserve.

It is hopeless to expect to get agreement on a solution to the above dilemmas. Whatever is done to avoid disaster, we will be afflicted in conscience for compromising the moral order. We cannot avoid "the lie in the soul." As was remarked in connection with Lincoln Steffens' anecdote about U'ren of Oregon (page 256), sometimes it is the duty of the democratic leader to suffer damnation that the people may live. Our never-ending problem is to find the path that leads between the lions of morality and rationality. And the lions are not always chained as the lions were in Bunyan's *Pilgrim's Progress*.

The prevailing view of Americans that diplomacy must be based on morals has had some curious and disturbing results. As we have noted before, Americans give pejorative meanings to socialism, appeasement, and communism. These are all immoral, but the most immoral act that can be performed is to appease communism. Since in the postwar world the United States was engaging in a moral crusade against communism it was entitled to the support of all right-thinking nations. Those who supported it were good; those who opposed it or remained neutral were bad. This bipolarization was bitterly resented by most of the nations, who have not hesitated to point out that the United States had a long history of neutrality and isolation, and as late as 1941 had reserved to itself the right to refuse to take sides.

The United States was founded on revolution and long upheld the right of revolution and of self-determination. Now, in its support of stability and the *status quo*, it in effect argued that change should not be permitted—at least not outside the Iron Curtain—unless it was peaceful. The United States was thus driven more and more frequently to support conservative or reactionary factions wherever it had interests, and this further alienated the more liberal and possibly more constructive elements.

This may be the place to bring up a subject that has greatly exercised the American public. The agreements with Latin America at Chapultepec and Rio had handicapped the State Department in exercising pressures on behalf of American investors and to line up the Western Hemisphere nations in support of American policies. The marines were not as available now as of yore, but there was the Central Intelligence Agency (CIA) which not only gathered information but undertook covert operations, chiefly against communist governments and parties. As early as 1954 it backed an army of exiles that invaded Guatemala and overthrew its communist regime. Cuba's miseries had brought into power Fidel Castro who, when the United States made clear its refusal to let up on its economic pressures, turned to Russia and accepted such massive aid that in effect he was turning the country over to the Soviets.

In 1960 the CIA organized a small army of Cuban exiles, and in April 1961 the army landed at the Bay of Pigs and was promptly surrounded and captured by Castro's Russian-trained and equipped army. By this time John F. Kennedy was President, and the failure was a severe blow to his prestige, which was not mitigated until the next year when he forced the Russians to remove their ballistic missiles from Cuba. Less than three years later President Johnson landed marines in Santo Domingo to prevent a communist take-over, and managed to persuade the Organization of American States to assume responsibility.

It was not until a Congressional investigation in 1975 that Americans clearly learned something of the extent of CIA covert operations over much of the world—particularly in Southeast Asia, where it literally supplied and directed military operations in countries supposed to be neutral. Of course its operations were paralleled by—sometimes were responses to—similar communist operations. In the CIA's Operation Phoenix, mounted in retaliation for communist murders of village chiefs, it is claimed that as many innocents as guilty were killed. There were accusations, apparently unsubstantiated, that the CIA had assassinated foreign leaders, but it was proved that it had tried to influence foreign elections by covert means, possibly in contravention of American public policy.

Just how far its activities had been approved by the various presidents was unknown, but there seemed to be a likelihood that it had on occasion embarked on its operations without their knowledge. This may or may not have been deliberate, in order to enable the presidents to clothe themselves with "plausible deniability."

It now seems to have been the case that the CIA usually supported dictators, doubtless in the conviction that the order they imposed was more beneficial to American economic and political interests than would have been leftist revolutions or even democratic revolutions. This cannot be excused, but the blame should be laid where it belongs—on the lack of oversight by presidents and Congress and, basically, the public's unawareness of world realities because it lacks decisive and informed leadership.

The Soviet Union openly adheres to its Brezhnev Doctrine—that it has the right to intervene in any socialist country to support its version of communist orthodoxy. Perhaps what we need is a similar doctrine to defend democracy. In a world where subversion has become a normal arm of statecraft the United States cannot dispense with the covert operations of the CIA. The rise of the totalitarians in the 1920's and 1930's should be a lesson to us that there are times when the democracies should interfere collectively and vigorously to prevent subversion—all the more so today when terrorism has actually become institutionalized as a multinational big business and probably has nuclear capabilities. If that is impossible, then a properly run covert operation may turn the trick, as it seems to have done in preventing the communists from taking over Italy immediately after World War II. The tragedy in the present situation is that the democracies seem unable to work together either overtly or covertly, and this may well lead to our downfall.

Of course morality and idealism have a place in the conduct of foreign affairs, yet it must be recognized that diplomacy, like politics, is the art of the possible. Americans rather generally have failed to realize that statesmanship is not the art of doing the best or most moral thing, but of picking the best or most moral course among unsatisfactory alternatives. We have failed to distinguish between short- and long-term policies, so frequently we adopt a short-term policy which is ruinous in the long run. Above all, Americans have a distrust of power and tend to regard its exercise as immoral; herein lay the origin of many a postwar American dilemma. Of course, as we have pointed out before, American leaders use power, but hesitantly and therefore often ineffectively—all the more so since they have the peculiar belief that morals are incompatible with national interest. We seem to believe that morals are apart from and superior to the necessities of diplomacy, and so must take precedence.

The result is a notable failure to practice the first essential of practical statesmanship: a cold assessment of our own capabilities and those of our opponent, and a decision on how far we are willing to go to get what we want—whether moral objectives or national interests. The result is confusion, self-deception, verbalization, and a measure of cant which justifies foreign accusations of hypocrisy.

The tendency, therefore, has been to pose as champions of morals and to try to force others to solve problems by legal and moral rules. There are several results. One is that when the moral solution has been accepted, Americans consider themselves freed from further responsibility. Another result is the acceptance of nations as instruments of international action, thus arresting the process of organic change which is essential to adopt the world to changing times; in a day when great producing and marketing areas are essential to well-being, the multiplication of nationalities is dangerous.

Then there is the assumption that a nation's internal problems are its own business; we need not go into the numerous cases in which they have burst across national borders to plague the world. Let it be repeated here that covert measures can often solve problems before they lead to disaster, but such measures must be taken only after careful weighing of every condition and alternative.

The problem is that democracy formalizes the social conflict by laws and customs, with the consequent faith that force is unnecessary. Democratic peoples usually fail to see that a little force exerted at the right time and place (as against the nascent dictatorships during the Long Armistice) may prevent a world war later on. The curious result is that when the war does begin, we are less angered by the cause of the aggression than by the provocation that made us break our rule and use force. This anger over Japan's sneak attack on Pearl Harbor was far greater than over the long course of aggression which finally culminated in the attack. As a result, democratic wars become moral conflicts; and since morals cannot be compromised, they cannot end until the immoral enemy is completely crushed.

The Limits of Power

The Vietnam War has led an increasing number of thinkers and publicists to point out that the lessons to be learned from it can as profoundly affect foreign policy as the Depression affected domestic policy. They hold that the United States is overextended and must find ways to contract the enormous responsibilities accepted by the Truman Doctrine and Kennedy's New Frontier. There are, they say, four principal lessons to be taken to heart:

(1) *Revolutions are Inevitable.* Most of the world is swamped in such a putrescence of disease, misery, and degradation that Americans abroad are often so overcome by the horror that they have to be hospitalized. To cure this it is not enough to contribute capital and technicians; the entire social structure has to be *modernized.* Western technology was made possible only by the slow historical development of certain character traits: a readiness to cut loose from old taboos, to accept reason as a guide, and to cultivate a Faustian drive to learn, to acquire, and to master. Russia and Japan have developed enough of these traits to industrialize and even Red China has overcome its ancient torpor and has conquered the worse aspects of its age-old poverty and official corruption. But the fact remains that the privileged classes in most of the nations of Asia, Africa, and Latin America pride themselves on their "spiritual superiority," and refuse to undergo the fundamental psychological transformation necessary to modernization.

Abhorrent as it may be to democratic theorists, there is only one way to quickly break through the incrustation of entrenched privilege on one hand and the lethargy of the multitudes on the other: revolution in one form or another. It is not necessary for revolutions to be brought in by war, for *coups d'etat* and gradual assumption of authority are old methods. Nor do they need to be communist—they have not been in Japan, Mexico, and Turkey—but they do have to be authoritarian and decisive, operating on the rich and poor alike. Point Four's optimistic program of gradual and peaceful change has not done much to bring about the psychological transformation so essential to modernization. If any proof is needed, it is found in South Vietnam where even during the American occupation corruption, privilege, and apathy still ruled despite earnest American efforts to introduce some aspects of the Great Society. So evident has all this been that a discouraged Congress is cutting back on Point Four programs and openly discussing their discontinuance.

(2) *Power is Limited.* There is a limit to the power even of the most powerful nation in the world—certainly a moral limit. The time will come when revolutions cannot be prevented short of literally destroying the country, which is morally indefensible and would also risk bringing on World War III. But even within the *feasible* limits of power there is frightening capacity to misuse it. The United States has in effect taken a stand aginst revolutions, regardless of their merits.

But more than this it has used diplomatic and economic pressures to hold much of the underdeveloped world in a straitjacket which is accused of having prevented the emergence of vigorous and farsighted leaders. For example, American aid has fed India and managed to preserve the hollow shell of democracy under a group of mild and futile leaders—while its problems multiply. Is India any better off than it would have been under a group of ruthless, authoritarian leaders brought to the top by revolution and dedicated to the task of transforming the country, whatever the means necessary? Just how much of the world's present misery can be laid at the door of American policy—despite its good intentions?

(3) *American Policy Is Estranging the World.* The United States has largely failed in its attempt to block the admittedly brutal revolutionary method of modernization and to promote it by gradual and peaceful means. The ironic result is that the United States is being viewed with horror by a distressingly large part of the world as a benighted and tyrannical reactionary bent only on preserving order as an aid to its economic exploitations.

Thinking about American policy begins with one fact generally recognized by Europeans but by few Americans. Whether or not because of Truman's policy of containment of merely the passage of time, communism has begun to show cracks in the monolith. Yugoslavia, Albania, and China have broken away from Soviet control, and some of the European communist states have begun to mellow. The masters of the Kremlin seem at times to be on the defensive behind their iron curtain, not only because of the growing thrust of the satellites toward liberalization but because of the more frequent surfacing of the underground current of liberalism in Russia itself. In Western Europe the communist parties are openly breaking with the Kremlin line. Of course, no outsider can predict what course will be taken by the Kremlin. It might yield slowly and grudgingly or it might try to reassert its old dictatorship over the satellites even at the risk of World War III. But meanwhile the economic practices (though not necessarily the theories) of both the communist and capitalist states are changing, and seem to be moving toward new "mixes" of socialism and capitalism.

Under these circumstances, American national interests could be cautiously reassessed in a manner that would include a more sympathetic understanding of the rights and needs of other nations. There could, for one thing, be a change in attitude toward revolutions, including a willingness to recognize that not all of them are communist inspired, and that even when they are they do not necessarily work against American interests. Now that it has been demonstrated that communism is no more a monolith than capitalism, and that communist nations can quarrel among themselves there is less reason to fear communist revolutions. Indeed, the Yugoslav example has shown that they can be moderated and their legitimate aims promoted by discreet American aid once they are in power; the result should be to hasten the liberalization to which it is now evident even communist peoples aspire.

Another key to a rational foreign policy, say the critics, is to take sympathetically into account the natural resentment against absentee domination. Such controls had been feasible (though unwise) in past centuries when the dominated countries had no recourse but to submit. American investors came on the sence at the end of that period, but many of them have refused to recognize that times have changed and that host countries have rights—even the right to be unreasonable. Now it is time for the United States not only to moderate its own official interferences, but it is time to force American corporations operating abroad to exercise good manners. The government should not be so ready to get favors for them or to rush to their rescue when the host country seeks to discipline them—even unreasonably—or to expropriate their holdings. Indeed, an observance of this rule might well have prevented the Cuban imbroglio and its swing to communism.

(4) *The American Mission Is Passé*—at least in any crusading sense. The thinkers who rejected the Open Door abroad did not necessarily deny that there had often gone with it a sense of idealistic mission. They pointed out, however, that—with doubtful exception of India—no attempt to implant democracy by the imposition of democratic institutions had ever succeeded; as soon as the colony became independent it reverted to some form of dictatorship. Even in the Caribbean, where the United States had diligently sought to export its economic and political ideals, the states had gone back to the Hispanic pattern of caudillism as soon as the marines were withdrawn.

It is now possible to hold that the Open Door aspects of the American mission were aberrations—that the true American mission was to teach by example; it may have been bumptious but it was not aggressive. Certainly when the United States was riding forth to impose economic controls or to save the world for democracy there was no lack of voices warning that these courses were fraught with disaster. The nation should have been skeptical of the idealistic arguments used by the crusaders and the advocates of economic expansion; they knew very well that a moralistic people could not be convinced without moral arguments.

The core of the above lessons was the belief that it was time to stop basing certain aspects of American foreign policy on the brutal defense of private property, which had so long been one of the springs of expansion. It was time to turn to internal construction, trading freely with foreign nations but without financial or political pressures, and standing ready to expand our fiscal and technical institutions which have been set up to help them to help themselves. Hitherto Americans had usually rejected the charge that economic determinism had been the spring to their expansion, but there was nevertheless a certain credibility to the thesis that it had made our foreign policy a less beneficent influence than we had supposed it to have been. In any case, the day of the wide Open Door abroad is passing as the producers of pertroleum and raw materials take charge of their own resources, and declare economic and ideological war on the United States.

By 1980 at least 110 sovereign nations had been added to the sixty or so existing in 1945. Many of them are miniscule, but they are clamant voices in the United Nations Assembly where they form a bloc devoted to thwarting the desires and interests of the West, above all the United States. Ironically we are hated most for the economic achievements of which we are so proud, but which are regarded as proof positive of sin.

No doubt much of their clamor arises from their desperate problems at home and the need to find a devil to beat. In their zeal to find their own identity, the emerging nations seek out and romanticize their distant past, casting the white man in the role of serpent in the Garden of Eden. In any case, they have not yet adjusted to industrial civilization, and this task—quite rightly—they regard as their first order of business. To take part in the struggle between democracy and communism, to arraign themselves on one side or the other, would be to run the danger of being torn apart and having their own progress delayed indefinitely.

The leaders of the emerging nations are in a difficult situation. They had united their people in "nationalist" demands for independence, but as soon as the pressure of the occupying powers was removed, some of the nations tended to fall apart into their tribal or other components. There is a tendency, therefore, to try to hold the country together by insisting that the imperialist threat still exists. Moreover, few of these nations are economically viable. They do not have the knowledge or self-discipline essential to industrialization, nor in many cases the resources or population base. The tragedy lies not so much in the fact that they have become independent prematurely, but in their hopeless fractionating as tribal or geographic entities unsuited to the realities of the modern world.

There exists no easy way to satisfy their clamor. Their demand that industrialized nations drastically reduce their standard of living and pour their goods and food into the emerging societies gives little hope. Doubtless it can be done to some extent, but not much. Even if it were feasible to the extent demanded it would be futile, for it would only be another demonstration that Malthus was right; a booming population would push ever harder on food and resources. Not even the American cornucopia of food could fill the demand; sooner or later the malthusian limit will be reached. (We are assured that the tropics, where much of this burgeoning population lives, can by no stretch of the imagination become an efficient producer of vast quantities of food.) The logical answer, of course, is to limit population growth, but thus far the world refuses. Will the only solution be found in world holocaust?

The spirit and techniques of democracy may not at this moment be applicable to the world as a whole, but as pointed out earlier in this chapter the experience of the United States in exploiting abundance developed the atmosphere of freedom that gives hope to the world, and the techniques such as mass production of food and goods that promises (if properly used) to resolve the age-old conflict between producer and consumer. Out of the blood and oppression of the Anglo-American sweep to the Pacific and out of the rape of this splendid continent has come the opportunity that the world holds in its hands today. One can only stand in awe before the mysterious processes of history. It is more than mysterious—it is mystical.

Chapter 17
Reflections on the American Quest

Proem

The dogmas of the quiet past are inadequate to the stormy present. The occasion is piled high with difficulty, and we must rise with the occasion. As our case is new, so we must think anew, and act anew. We must disenthrall ourselves, and then we shall save our country.

(Abraham Lincoln)[1]

* * *

Pressure groups have their functions in a democracy but of late they have trangressed all reason. They take advantage of the intricate interdependency of our society and they threaten to wound the entire society unless they get their own way. What is new is that there are now no income or social barriers to the exercise of these threats—they are used by policemen, firemen, operators of essential public utilities, teachers, and doctors. As Carl Becker pointed out long ago, when democracy loses its tensions it can fall prey to exploiters as vicious as those in a communist society.

(Hugh Sidey)[2]

---

[1]From Lincoln's annual message to Congress, 1862.

[2]Based on Hugh Sidey, in *Time* (8 September 1975), p. 7.

Two years of national agony followed on the Watergate break-in and the subsequent cover-up and related actions. Finally President Nixon was cornered by inescapable proof of his duplicity and had to resign. Thereupon there went up a chorus of hosannas to the effect that the Constitution had definitively refuted any claims that it was not suited to the twentieth century. *Quite the contrary!* Surely there is some defect in a fundamental law that cannot solve palpable executive malfeasance—or even nonfeasance—without going through years of trauma.

* * *

When forced to choose between the polarizations of chaos and tyranny, the overwhelming majority of people will take the latter. In the danger that democratic tensions may be destroyed by a violent polarization lies the chief threat to progress in the world and the great hope of revolutionists. The institutionalization of terrorism and the probability that it will use nuclear weapons may yet confront us with this choice. To counter the real threats to our way of life we must evolve new techniques and inculcate a new devotion to duty and to public service, and these must be confirmed in our souls and our national habits. Only thus can we learn to preserve the tensions and equilibrate the uncertainties essential to our democracy.

Rectifying the Balances

We have previously suggested that there is in American life a considerable amount of what for lack of a better term we can call Antinomianism not only in religion but in many of our beliefs. Consider the differences between our ideals and our practices in tolerance, equality, civil liberty, freedom of opportunity, and sharing in government. We as democrats see the ideals; the rest of the world either through ignorance of the ideal or through malice sees our imperfect applications. *We* know that the democratic process will eventually get around to rectifying injustice, but humanity doesn't want to wait. It is no wonder that the promise of the communist absolute is more attractive to much of the world.

The above list of shortcomings is far from complete. The businessman prates of his allegiance to free enterprise; what he really wants is government favors for himself and strict regulation of his competitors. The labor unionist wants to be protected by the closed shop even while he wrecks the employer and the consumer by arbitrary raises in wages and fringe benefits. The farmer gluts the market with his produce but screams for supports when the price goes down. The populist ignores the truth that an excess of democracy can be suicidal, and wishes to warp our political processes by diverting them to a paranoidal persecution of big business. The liberal gives lip-service to freedom even while tightening the screws on individual action. The conservative digs in his heels against progress and piously affirms individual rights even while they are being undercut by his "corporate socialism," by the White House, and by security agencies. Most of us demand law and order but do not hesitate to commit minor infractions (such as exceeding the speed limit) even though we may not commit felonies.

It is a truism that we cannot get a completely accurate view of our own times. Nevertheless, we must try to learn wherein we have fallen short, and above all we must avoid an easy optimism that refuses to consider facts. Voltaire's Candide, in looking at pre-revolutionary Europe, observed that optimism is a mania for declaring when things are going badly that all is well. James Branch Cabell remarked that "the optimist proclaims that we live in the best of all possible worlds; and the pessimist fears this is true."

If there is anything to the American belief in freedom of the will, that is, if humanity exercises any control over its own destiny, it would seem that we have begun to fail in preserving the balance in our values. Material pursuits are good, and money can be a great liberating force and has done much to liberalize American society, but we must recognize that its value lies not simply in itself but in the basis it affords for the pursuit of nonmaterial aims. It is a fact that with most of us a reasonable amount of material security must be gained before we will concern ourselves with nonmaterial pursuits. Nevertheless there is on the other side the fact that if we fail to use material progress to promote adequate nonmaterial progress as well, our civilization is bound to fall. The course between the two requires a delicate sense of balance, and it is to this problem that we shall devote the remainder of this chapter.

The foregoing analysis of the American conduct of foreign affairs should lead to the realization that the sentimentality, moralism, and economic aggression shown there arise from the same failings on the domestic scene. In other words, as was pointed out in Chapter 14 there has often been a hardening of alternative choices to the point where they have been converted into principles. The situation has more than a vague resemblance to the same phenomenon in the 1850s that resulted in the Civil War.

This condition doubtless arises in considerable part from a defective sense of duty. The sad fact is that our society has overwhelmingly emphasized rights at the expense of duties. The imbalance cannot be rectified by adopting the warped view of duty so characteristic of bigots and zealots as found on both extremes of Right and Left. To do so would inevitably destroy the tensions essential to democracy.

Pressure groups have their functions in a democracy but of late they have transgressed all reason. Hugh Sidey has said that they take advantage of the intricate interdependency of our society and single-mindedly threaten to wound the entire society unless they get their own way. We have long been accustomed to strikes by laborers, and usually they can be borne. What is new is that there are now no income or social barriers to the exercise of these threats—they are used by policemen, firemen, operators of essential public utilities, teachers, and doctors. As Carl Becker pointed out long ago, when democracy loses its tensions it can fall prey to exploiters as vicious as those in a communist society.

During the last generation we have seen a salutary movement in the direction of greater civil rights and more widespread prosperity for minorities (though the canker of racism persists), but liberal zealots have at times failed to look before they leaped—as, notoriously, in promoting the Great Society. Unwise promises have led to unreasonable expectations on the part of the beneficiaries, to huge deficits in budgets—*vide* the federal budget and New York City's budget—and to unparalleled waste and extravagance. Conservatives have failed in their duty to temper and rationalize reform, to rectify the balances, not expunge the reforms. Neither liberals nor conservatives have lived up to the most essential function of public men—that is, to educate the people in an objective view of problems.

There has been such a barrage of pros and cons about the waste and pollution of our national resources that there are signs the public has become weary of the subject. Corporations can and should plan for the future, but it seems evident that they oppose national planning because it would hamper their own plans to gobble up resources. They have taken advantage of the inbred American aversion to national planning and made it appear to be undemocratic. Corporations have (along with others) contributed to the alarming deterioration of our streams and lakes and the rape of our minerals and timber.

Alvin Toffler, author of *Future Shock*, in testimony before a Senate subcommittee, pointed to the disaster that confronts us in the near future, not only on the domestic scene but abroad, and indeed menaces the entire planet. Other nations are reaching for resources—as ocean fisheries and minerals—and conditions are shaping up for what could be a bloody clash.

We must, says Toffler, "invent wholly new forms of planning that involve not merely a handful of technocratic experts, but millions of ordinary citizens. We must become an anticipatory democracy." The same might be said for the world as a whole. Pollution of air, water, and soil cannot be confined to one country, for what happens in one must sooner or later affect all. Ideological victories will be useless if the headlong rush toward world suicide is not stopped in favor of some scheme by which we agree to live and let live on our planet and to husband and use our natural resources efficiently.

Here we might hazard the opinion that our governmental problems rise not so much from big government as from unresponsive, sloppy, inefficient and, sometimes, downright dishonest government. Bureaucracy has become powerful through sheer size and complexity, and reform is well-nigh hopeless not only because of its inertia but because it serves vested interests of all kinds. It has become Byzantine in its mysterious circumlocutions, its amorphous jargon, and its readiness to pass the buck. The fact that the bureaucracy of Byzantium lasted a thousand years is no comfort to us. Of course such a tremendously complex society as ours requires government interference to protect the consumer, the investor, and the environment. On the other hand, there can be no doubt that in many respects government is too much on the back of the citizen by multiplied rules and regulations, many of which are nothing but the whims of bureaucrats, perhaps only busywork. Our bureaucracy is a dismaying proof of Parkinson's Law and the Peter Principle.

Not only does bureaucracy multiply itself, but every new program installed by well-meaning liberals adds to the effect. All too often overpaid managers in Washington and their sub-managers in the field first spend their funds in providing jobs for their friends and for luxurious offices and expense-account entertainment and travel; what remains over is spent on those the program was designed to benefit; even then, what is the use in training a man for a nonexistent job or one that a labor union will refuse to let him fill? The bureaucracies at all levels have become so big, amorphous, and lazy that there is serious doubt they can be managed. Any program or mandate can be buried, deflected, or disobeyed.

As a general, Eisenhower had sought to give an impression of cool, crisp, authority. He had severely criticized his predecessor as ineffective, and Truman took some comfort in a bit of prophetic gloating. "He'll sit here," said Truman, "and he'll say 'Do this!' *and nothing will happen.* Poor Ike—it won't be a bit like the army. He'll find it very frustrating." The situation is even worse today. We are not far from the bureaucracies of the Spanish Philips, where functionaries sometimes went on the motto: the king's decree is to be obeyed but not carried out.

Serious as the above conditions are they pale beside the dangers inherent in the power the various bureaucracies wield, unresponsive to either executive or legislative oversight. A succession of presidents actually stood in fear of J. Edgar Hoover, Director of the Federal Bureau of Investigation. Why? We can only suppose that he threatened them implicitly or directly with public exposure of their peccadilloes. We have already suggested that the CIA in its secret operations had the power to thwart national policy.

The computerization of our society—and of the social sciences—has a frightening resemblance to the model "scientific state" of the Soviets. We readily acknowledge the fallacies in the latter, but fail to recognize the fallacies in our attempt to control human behavior so as to fit the citizen to the subliminal Procrustean bed being constructed to exploit human passions and irrationalities—as by advertisers, politicians, and bureaucrats. Then there are those who wish to implant the psychology of the ant hill, except, of course, for the manipulators. (It is perhaps significant that science fictioneers usually delineate just such a future for the world.) Actually, it would seem impossible in the long run either to anticipate or govern the whimsies of man and nature that have created and are creating history.

Any proposal to remedy these and other flaws in the nature or performance of our democratic system will inevitably be regarded by some as unrealistic and unwise—as they were by most people in 1787. But the neglect of our mounting national problems is creating a vacuum, and nature abhors a vacuum; if we do not fill it ourselves, it will sooner or later be filled by some Orwellian "Big Brother." He may not enter by *coup d'etat*, but we have recently had a chilling demonstration of the more insidious processes available to him, and the present bogging down of government is an open invitation to the Huey Longs and Nixons that are always waiting in the wings of our national stage.

Now this does not mean—despite our failures—that our freedoms are gone. We still have relative freedom of speech, of religion, of the press, of assembly, and of opportunity. The fact that we have these freedoms and the degree of justice rising from them explains why totalitarianism has thus far failed to make serious inroads on our domestic scene and why we are still the hope of all those who believe in human dignity and freedom. Nevertheless, it must be acknowledged that these freedoms are stained and frayed around the edges. True, they always have been, but today the stain is moving rapidly toward the center of our national institutions, encouraged by the failure of national will and by the bogging down of effective government. We have reached the pass where freedom can be chipped away unless it is defended by an aroused public opinion, clear-sighted enough to throw off shibboleths and sweep away self-centered interests.

The remedies fall into two categories: the technical and the psychological, though of course they must affect each other. Among the first, desirable but perhaps at the moment impossible, is the need for a reframing of our creaking Constitution, or at least a considerable amendment, *but without sacrificing its protection of fundamental human rights.* There is a widespread opinion that the Constitution is an "ark of the covenant" and anyone who lays profane hands on it will, like Uzzah, be smitten by the Lord. This mythus is so firmly implanted that the nation has quite failed to recognize the lesson of Watergate.

Two years of national agony followed on the Watergate break-in and the subsequent cover-up and related actions. Finally President Nixon was cornered by inescapable proof of his duplicity and had to resign. Thereupon there went up a chorus of hosannas to the effect that the Constitution had definitively refuted any claims that it was not suited to the twentieth century. *Quite the contrary!* Surely there is some defect in a fundamental law that cannot deal with palpable executive malfeasance—or even nonfeasance—without going through years of trauma.

Today we have a president, or at least an office, that is over-powerful, over-worked, over-exposed, and—perhaps even worse—over-reverenced. Save in sporadic instances the Executive is not responsive or responsible to Congress as the framers of the Constitution intended. The result is that Congress is diminished, and so tends to become pettish and spiteful. It is an interesting observation that commentators on public affairs usually circle all about the above conditions, apparently either too blind to recognize the cure or afraid to voice it: the adoption of some modification of the parliamentary system. This should diminish the presidency without making it powerless, enhance the role of Congress, and stop most of the present endemic bickering—and also clarify national purpose and increase national decisiveness. The Watergate agony would have been by-passed simply by the removal of the President on the ground of lack of confidence.

When the Constitution was drawn up the framers had an exquisite sensitivity to the meaning of freedom, and it has been observed that they were as much concerned with limiting government as with implementing it. They could hardly have envisioned the technological changes that were to complicate the human condition, reduce the ability of the individual to be independent, and make him dependent on government protection. Certainly they distrusted political parties, and had little or no concept of their role in adjusting conditions to the requirements of freedom—to preserving the necessary tensions between liberty and order. As it was, the separation of powers between President and Congress (the vital role of the Supreme Court was apparently not fully envisioned) meant that the two would not work together unless bound by some common discipline—and that meant political parties.

Unfortunately that is not enough, for even when President and Congress belong to the same party they each have their separate constitutional powers, and their jealousies and ambitions; how much worse when they belong to different parties as they do much of the time. In a simpler day when there were relatively few crises the system worked fairly well, especially when there was no enormous bureaucracy and no plethora of laws. Now we live in a complex society, crises are perennial, and though laws are plethoric still many of them if not most are needed. There is not time for President and Congress to bicker and delay while the world goes to hell in a handbasket.

Mark Twain observed that the only native criminal class in this country was Congress. If Congress is no longer criminal, it certainly exudes a distinct aroma of special privilege, and perhaps even worse is reluctant to get down to a dispassionate view of national problems and an honest search for solutions. The citizen can hardly be blamed for believing that it listens first to the lobbyists of special interests, then considers its own perquisites, and only as an afterthought hearkens to the voting public. Thus far it has refused to reform the tax system and wipe out the inequities. It blows hot and cold on vital issues such as energy, inflation, crime, and racism. It is relatively willing to subsidize the jobless, but not to do much to subsidize jobs; for example, rehabilitating railroads—thus creating jobs, increasing the number of taxpayers, and furnishing a national transportation system adequate for passenger service and long-distance hauling. Delay has become a fine art. Congress and also the executive put off decisions by engaging in repetitive investigations that give the illusion of relentlessly moving forward while intransigently standing still. At the end of the investigation a report is rendered and then either quietly shelved or lost in the legislative shuffle. If the issue happens to be resurrected a new investigation is begun and the whole process is repeated. It should be evident that the electorate's faith in government had been undermined long before Watergate.

The parliamentary system should alleviate the neglect of the Congressional functions of oversight and the perpetual thwarting of reasonable national policies by delays and by quarrels between President and Congress. It should more frequently refer policies to the electorate, and this should also do something to remedy the tendency of Congress to devote itself to internal fights (often pointless) when it is not fighting the President. The President, himself, since he would be responsible to Congress and would not necessarily serve out a set term of years, should be more willing to meet the desires of Congress—though he should always be able to appeal to the people in special elections. This does not necessarily mean a complete abandonment of separation of powers, for the Supreme Court or some modification thereof could still exercise checks.

While on the subject of the Constitution we may name other aspects of the problems inherent in its provisions. No doubt under the conditions of 1787 sovereignty had to be divided between the nation and the states. The Civil War and various Supreme Court decisions have ameliorated that condition, but we are still suffering from the schizophrenia of divided sovereignty of which Richard Hooker warned four centuries ago and over which Madison and Hamilton argued in *The Federalist*. As it is, the states, for many complex reasons, including lack of will and an insufficient tax base, are abandoning one power after another to the federal government—one reason for the alarming accretion of power in Washington and in the federal bureaucracy.

No doubt sovereignty must remain divided constitutionally and in daily practice between states and federal government, at least in many aspects. But perhaps an amalgamation of states into regional or megapolitan entities would enable them to resume more functions. Perhaps the problems of bureacracy can never be fully solved, but it should be possible to reduce their Byzantine complexities and duplications by the reassumption of powers by the remodeled states. When Ex-President Hoover undertook in 1947—under Congressional mandate—to recommend guidelines for reorganization of the bureaucracy, he found that Congress itself was under such pressure from bureaucratic and other interests that it refused to approve more than half of them. The situation is probably even worse today than it was then, for in the meantime an executive bureaucracy has mushroomed.[3]

There can be no doubt that the duplication of functions in the many bureaucracies and the multiplication of local governments and districts waste vast sums of the taxpayers' money. Meanwhile there is not enough money for more useful purposes. The problem of crime may not be fully solved by technical adjustments, but there is need for justice to be more prompt and sure. This means more police, more courts, more and better prisons, a considerable reformation of the law, and a greater willingness by society to help in the rehabilitation of former criminals; and, moreover, a recognition that society is not always responsible for crime—that there are men who deliberately choose a life of crime.

The scandalous condition of public education might or might not be alleviated by more money; at least more could be done for the ten million children handicapped by dyslexia. Certainly educational techniques have gone far astray when the average college freshman has difficulty in grasping an idea from his reading and cannot write an intelligible paragraph. At least there should be some way of teaching these basic skills so essential to an understanding of modern complexities. If there is not, our doom as a democracy is sealed regardless of all other facts and factors.

Technical changes would no doubt be useful, but then can mean little without a reformation of the spirit, without a rebirth of intellectual and moral integrity. Daniel Bell in *The Cultural Contradictions of Capitalism* (1976) has pointed out that the current craze for "modernism" has laid the axe to the cultural and institutional roots of society by rejecting out-

---

[3]For more extended thoughts on constitutional reform, see Leland D. Baldwin, *Reframing the Constitution: An Imperative for Modern America* (Santa Barbara, Calif.: ABC-Clio Press, 1972).

of-hand the old traditions and conventions which fostered "civility." The result is a perpetual, unwholesome rage for the new which destroys our essential links with the past and affects the Establishments in numerous walks of life—education, art, literature, home life, business enterprise, etc. It has bred a state of mind that is shown variously as tendencies ranging from ennui through sickness to suicide, both of individuals and of enterprise. What is needful—nay, imperative, says Bell is a restoration of "the spontaneous willingness to obey the law, to respect the rights of others, to forego the temptations of private enrichment at the expense of the public weal—in short, to honor the 'city' of which one is a member."

Since our failures can be attributed in large part to failures in education, and our failures in education to failures in family responsibility, our spiritual renaissance must begin with the young and with a new sense of responsibility in the family. At any rate, we could stop teaching the starry-eyed version of American perfection—which breeds cynicism in the young when they learn the truth—and seek to inculcate a more realistic view of democratic rights and duties and of the tensions between order and liberty.

Furthermore, education has failed of one basic purpose unless it has taught youth to look beneath the surface of things and to distinguish among facts, desires, and sentimentalities, and to realize that choices are not always between good and evil, but are often between the greater and the lesser evils. Abraham Maslow warned us: "If you demand a perfect leadership or a perfect society, you thereby give up choosing between better and worse. If the imperfect is defined as evil, then everything becomes evil, since everything is imperfect." These are the realms in which we as a nation have most often fallen short. We must enlarge our comprehension that no man, and no nation, is an island; that we can no longer live to ourselves. We must temper our historic impatience and fecklessness. We must pay more for our material blessings because the world will not long endure our hogging of resources. Above all we must be reconciled to the truth that problems will never be permanently solved but will appear in new forms generation after generation.

The Bitterness of Dreams Realized

America has come through a bitter experience of realized dreams and found it the prescription for unhappiness. It is no longer in the mood for dreams about the future. It has achieved affluence only to find it a mixed blessing, plagued by problems of poverty and race whose solutions are hampered by "sociological lag." It has come into international power undreamed of by nineteenth-century flag-wavers only to find it a heavy and unrelenting burden. It thought it had finally realized democracy, only to become aware that it operates unevenly, even at times unjustly, and that it can become the cat's-paw for power-hungry presidents and bureaucrats. Bewildered by modern complexities and pulled and hauled among bitterly competing doctrines, many people are retreating into a simulated indifference, avoiding decisions by refusing to "become involved." Americans had built a system based on service to the masses only to find themselves puzzling over deep questions of values and purposes.

America became great not merely because of its tremendous resources, but because those resources had been dedicated to the fulfillment of the dream of the City of God. Now American society seems no longer to be impelled by a clear vision of a goal. What, is the plaintive refrain voiced by many, has become of the America we knew? What has happened to the dream of America as the pure and perfect example to the world? The nation's central dream, the belief in continuous progress, has been drastically altered even though not altogether lost. No longer can people answer the question: progress toward what? Nor are they any longer sure that what they have long taken for progress is anything more than change. If what they have experienced is really progress, why has every decade thrust them deeper into a morass of problems which seem insoluble?

Perhaps in this very disillusionment there is hope for the maturity that comes when a people learns through experience the meaning of tragedy. Tragedy in the epic sense occurs when a person is overtaken by sorrows either as the result of his defects or limitations or of the wrath of the gods. The tragic hero is best seen in Western history and literature, for it is only in the West that the individual dares on behalf of a great cause to do evil—that is, to defy the gods or the dictates of his fellows and venture on forbidden paths.

The tragedy follows when the hero falls from his euphoric height. Thus Prometheus brought fire from heaven and paid the penalty by being chained to a rock and being forever torn by an eagle. Moses was forbidden to enter the Promised Land because in his hubris he had dared to chide God. Lincoln defied the slave power and led the Union through its darkest hours, then fell in the moment of victory to a bullet launched by erratic fate. Most tragic of all was the death of Christ, crucified because he came to bring the new law of love to an unbelieving and resentful world. There was purgation in their ends, if not for them at least for those who came after, for they appeal to "our sense of pity, beauty, and pain; to the latent feeling of fellowship with all creation" (Joseph Conrad). Mussolini hanging head downward and Hitler frying in his bunker are neither heroic nor tragic.

Closely allied to the above is tragic irony, seen when trying to put an ideal into practice the results are the opposite of those intended. As a nation we have had considerable experience with irony, though we have not always been sophisticated enough to recognize it as such. Indeed, the results of our imperial ventures have often been ironical, for too frequently they have resulted in evil even when good was intended. The culminating example was our well-intentioned venture in Vietnam, undertaken to block communist expansion and plant the seeds of democracy and prosperity, but which resulted not merely in frustration and defeat but in the encouragement of the very expansion we sought to thwart.[4]

It is said that a person or a nation draws dignity if not actually grandeur from tragedy fully as much as from success—that indeed tragedy is the great chastener and teacher without which maturity cannot be attained. Tragedy for a nation must have magnitude, must show the consequences of the failure of an ideal or the violation of a standard, and must purge the victim through the emotions.

Europeans have pointed out that Americans have historically had little experience with tragedy, and they may be right. Youth, optimism, and abundant resources have served to stave off tragedy or at least ameliorate its effects. The most notable exception that comes to mind is the South during and after the Civil War. But the United States has had no experience comparable, to use a classic instance, with that of the Athenians when Alcibiades persuaded them to send their fleet and army on the disastrous expedition against Syracuse, and whose loss began the chain of debacles that exhausted Athens and enabled victorious Sparta to raze its protecting Long Walls. There are those who say that we are showing the same hubris as Athens—that is, a violent disregard of moral restraints, a wanton pride so offensive to the gods that it must bring

---

[4]Definitions of tragedy and irony are legion, and the above conform to none. Those interested should pursue the subject in Reinhold Neibuhr, *The Irony of American History* (1952), and Herbert J. Muller, *The Spirit of Tragedy* (1956).

punishment and downfall in its train—that the Vietnam War was our Syracusan expedition, that Lyndon Johnson was our Alcibiades, and that hubris has brought us to the brink of national tragedy.

Well, there is no real reason to believe that downfall or decadence is our immediate lot, no real reason to think that we cannot emerge from the slough of disillusionment and cynicism in which we presently wallow. We still have enormous potential power, not only resources and technology but experts on every problem under the sun if we will only listen to them. The pall of cynicism obscures but it cannot conceal the fact that there is still tremendous faith in our ideal of government by the people—that we can and must shape our own destiny; and most of us believe that the shaping must be done with due regard to the welfare of the rest of the world. We are still a nation of seekers and sometimes finders. We still struggle against disease and poverty, and refuse to accept them as inexorable mandates of fate. We are learning that it is the quality of life that counts, not the quantity of goods. Americans today are better informed—or can be—than ever before and are well fitted for participating in the political process.

On the other hand we must look at certain disturbing conditions. Perhaps the basic trouble lies in the long series of wounds we have suffered during the last decades—the stalemate in Korea, the Vietnam debacle, Watergate, the long national ordeal while our fellow citizens were imprisoned in Iran, the flouting of established morals by the counter-cultures, the decay of integrity. The result, it would seem, is something very like an erosion of will, a fear of greatness. There is a creeping distrust of our institutions, justified only in part, but nevertheless dangerous because if institutions fail or are jettisoned civilization cannot survive.

It may be suggested, that neither liberals nor conservatives have much to offer that will stand rational examination. Both look to the past, the liberals to Roosevelt and the conservatives to McKinley. There is a paucity of real debate; declamation has taken the place of reasoned argument. Our leaders are often more interested in alleviating the symptoms than in solving our problems—which admittedly are legion in number and legendary in their complexity—so inevitably we must lack a national purpose. Long ago the wise Solomon warned that "Where there is no vision the people perish." Today one looks in vain for credible leaders, men with vision and constructive ideas. Is this because of a failure in society itself? Must we have another catastrophic crisis to give rise to a new vision and the willingness to put it into effect?

By the 1980's the march toward a new world—or no world—has plainly begun. And yet, such aims as are expressed by the most articulate revolutionaries are no longer Stalinist, but are basically revivals of those sought a century before—liberalism, socialism, anarchism, and nihilism. Both the communist and the democratic spheres are plagued and weakened by internal contradictions and out-moded rhetoric. The Red monolith built by Lenin, Stalin, and Mao has begun to crack and its parts to develop antagonisms. One cause is the resurgence of nationalism, a force that has by no means run its historic course. Another is the evident fact that socialism does not automatically solve economic problems; indeed, its centralized planning is often wasteful and inefficient and has to be modified by paying attention to the demands of the market. But most significant of all is the weakening of the sense of mission among the communist peoples and a revitalization of liberalism as scientific and cultural leaders, industrial managers, and especially the young—as yet ineffectually—demand the freedoms that seem so elementary to those reared in the democratic tradition.

On the democratic side, also, internal contradictions have cracked the monolith of Containment. Nationalism plays a part, of course, but most significant is a demand that the values of democracy be put into practice. One form this takes is the rejection by peoples and governments alike of the old forms of economic enterprise, both classical economic liberalism with its automatic control by the market and American oligopoly with its conscious control of the market. A less glacial movement in the democracies is a parallel to the resurgence of liberalism in the communist countries. Though extremists still seek ideological polarization, there is a widespread belief (whether or not valid) that the Cold War is over, or at least has moderated, and it is time to return to the tasks of wiping out those old hindrances to freedom—national rivalries, economic oppression, race prejudice, social hierarchy, and maleducation of the young.

It is a hopeful sign that youth has in large part refused to adopt the emotional preoccupations of their elders, in fact some of them reject ideological wrappings of all kinds. It may be this refusal that lies behind youth's rebellion all over the world against whatever Establishments there are. Whether or not they realize it, youth has hit upon a fundamental teaching of history: that the strategies and rhetoric of yesterday do not necessarily fit the facts of today.

But do they recognize one further teaching of history? When forced to choose between the polarizations of chaos and tyranny, the overwhelming majority of people will take the latter. This is nothing but an extreme version of the old dilemma over which Jefferson and Hamilton quarreled: which is most precious, liberty or order? The United States has maintained a tension between the two except for those tragic years of the Civil War, but this is no assurance that it can be continued. In the danger that this tension might be destroyed by a violent polarization lies the chief threat to progress in the world and the great hope of revolutionists. The institutionalization of terrorism and its probable nuclearization may yet confront us with this choice.

Our hoped-for City of God is subject to temporal forces, unlike St. Augustine's City of God which was expressed in spiritual terms and could not be overthrown by worldly means. For a little while our quest has been like a wheel rolling down hill, gathering speed and seeming to have a life of its own. But the wheel must keep its speed to maintain its balance; else when it reaches the bottom it must collapse. It is high time for a reinterpretation of the meaning of our quest. To find that city not only of peace and plenty but of ordered freedom it is essential that we rethink our social, economic, political, and psychological processes.

This is the task that faces the bicentennial generation. We must evolve new techniques and inculcate a new devotion to duty and to public service, and these must be confirmed in our souls and our national habits. Only thus can we learn to preserve the tensions and equilibrate the uncertainties essential to our democracy. Our method of experimental pragmatism means that politicians and people must have iron endurance, steady nerves, and a superb sense of balance as we walk the tight rope over the gulf that separates us from the City of God.

Index

DATE DUE

GAYLORD			PRINTED IN U.S.A.